READ and W

*A Guide to Effective
Composition*

READ and WRITE
A Guide to Effective Composition

James F. Dorrill / Charles W. Harwell

University of South Alabama

HARCOURT BRACE JOVANOVICH, PUBLISHERS

San Diego   New York   Chicago   Austin   Washington, D.C.
London   Sydney   Tokyo   Toronto

ISBN: 0-15-575510-2

Library of Congress Catalog Card Number: 86-81625

Printed in the United States of America

Copyrights and Acknowledgments appear on pages 387–90, which constitute a continuation of the copyright page.

PREFACE

Read and Write unites the composing process with traditional methods of developing the essay. Consequently, it offers greater versatility and flexibility than do most rhetoric/readers. During the composing process, students will discover topics for potential essays and generate details that support those topics. They will determine their audience and establish their purpose. Eventually, they will opt for one of the usual modes of development, the one that will best achieve their purpose. They can also study essays that exemplify their chosen mode, and they can find strong organizational strategies for their materials. *Read and Write* provides for continuous interaction between process and mode.

Four features enrich the section entitled "The Composing Process," which moves from picturing an audience through proofreading the final draft. First, both informal and formal techniques of composition are included. For example, freewriting, using a circular chart, creating a narrowing chart, brainstorming, and employing the journalistic formula are discussed and illustrated. Second, actual examples of student writing follow the steps in the composing process from initial notes through the proofread draft. Third, exercises provide practice for the various steps, such as identifying the grammatical structure of a thesis statement in order to determine the emphasis of the essay. Finally, all the exercises and examples used in "The Composing Process" are drawn from the essays in the second part of the textbook. This cross-referencing enables the student to see the examples in their complete context.

The second section of *Read and Write* consists of introductions and essays arranged by the usual modes of development—narration, description, example, and so on. The arrangement moves from the easiest form of composition (narration) to the most difficult (persuasion). Each rhetorical mode is introduced with specific strategies for organizing an essay in that mode. Three criteria govern the selection of the essays that exemplify a particular method of development. First, these essays are contemporary without being faddish. Some of them are often anthologized; many have never been. They reflect a variety of subject matters and attitudes. Second, these essays are relatively short without being abridged. They range in length from about 300 words to about 2000. Third, the essays provide topics for student writing in each mode. For six of the seven modes, a student essay on one of the "Suggestions for Writing" is included.

Preceding each essay are a couple of questions about its content to guide the student's thoughtful reading of it. Following each essay is a series of questions designed to help the student analyze the essay as a whole, its paragraphs, its sentences, and its diction. Furthermore, the "Suggestions for Writing," which follow the questions, are based on both the essay and the student's experience. Some of the writing assignments specify an audience whose characteristics the student must consider before completing the assignment.

The third section of *Read and Write*, "Grammar and Mechanics," offers basic information and guidance for clarity and accuracy. It includes a section on common sentence problems and a section on errors in subject-verb agreement.

We wish to thank Joe Bennett, field representative for Harcourt Brace Jovanovich, for suggesting that we pursue this project; and Bill McLane, senior editor at HBJ, for wise counsel and warm encouragement.

A number of our colleagues who are concerned about student writing offered suggestions and advice. Our thanks go to Mary Blackburn, Tom Brennan, Lloyd Dendinger, Gene Hamner, Pat Harkins, Tim Lally, Ann Leatherwood, Dan McDonald, Tom Rountree, and Pat Stephens.

For aid in manuscript preparation, our thanks go to June Williams, Elizabeth Barnes, and especially Debbie Hopkins. Many thanks go to Giles Townsend, HBJ manuscript editor, for his welcome contributions. And thanks too, to Parma Yarkin, production editor, for shepherding the manuscript through the production stages.

Finally, our thanks to Professor Barbara Haxby of Triton College, Professor Juliet Kincaid of Johnson County Community College, and Professor David Roberts of the University of Southern Mississippi for their careful reviews of the manuscript of this book.

James F. Dorrill
Charles W. Harwell

CONTENTS

9   DEFINITION   254

10   PERSUASION   283

11   OTHER ESSAYS   322

PART THREE
Grammar and Mechanics

THEMATIC
TABLE OF CONTENTS

EDUCATION

LANGUAGE

LIFE-STYLES

MALE-FEMALE

MORAL VALUES

RELIGION

SCIENCE

PART ONE

The Composing Process: Prewriting, Writing, Rewriting

WRITING: THE SEQUENCE

Would you take a collegiate writing course if it were not required? If you are like most students, your answer is probably "No!" In fact, your answer may be *"Bleep,* no!" After all, you're already a somewhat experienced writer. You've written about your summer vacation; you've described your favorite teacher. Perhaps you've kept a journal or a diary. You've written book reports and term papers, letters and essay exams. You are already a writer.

But are you completely confident about your writing skills? If you are like most of your classmates, and if you answer honestly, your answer is probably "No," again. In other words, you are about to begin a course that you would prefer not to take, to strengthen skills that you know are weak. Two honest "No" answers reveal the tension inherent in a writing class: writing is important, yet writing is sometimes frustrating.

Writing *is* important. It's one way you communicate your emotions and relay your knowledge. You write to influence and inform others. In addition to the writing you have done in the past, you'll have new writing challenges in the future. During your collegiate career you'll write lab reports, research projects, and persuasive essays. More and more colleges and universities are emphasizing "writing across the curriculum," a program that includes a writing component in every discipline, from accounting to zoology.

Your future career will also have its share of writing opportunities. You will probably have to prepare a résumé and write a letter of application to get your initial position. Once you secure that job, your writing ability will help you fulfill its demands and achieve your goals. You may have to write reports or memos, or articles for a newsletter. You may have to write proposals for new ways of increasing productivity, or advertising copy to increase sales. You may have to write and deliver speeches. You'll surely have to write letters—to government officials, to potential clients, to irate customers, to negligent suppliers, and to job applicants. You may even have to write evaluations of your employees or of yourself.

You have already experienced the frustration that sometimes accompanies a writing challenge. If you are like most college students confronted with a writing assignment, you immediately think about the finished product, the essay or report your instructor will evaluate. You become tense because you don't know what to write; you're afraid your writing skills are inadequate; you worry about a poor grade. Your concerns are legitimate. After all, a writing assignment may be an important part of your collegiate courses, and this course is *primarily* writing. However, some of your anxieties can be lessened if you think about the process of composition rather than the finished product. If you follow the sequence of *prewriting, writing, and rewriting,* your progress will be steady, and your final draft will represent your best effort. Furthermore, if you master the various techniques in the composing process, you'll be prepared to fulfill any writing challenge, whether collegiate or professional.

Prewriting

If approached with a curious rather than a grim attitude, prewriting can be fun. For example, think about your potential readers. Do they eat pizza? Are they in love? Do they worry about being successful in college? What are they majoring in? Do they get up early in the morning? Let your imagination soar. Later you can bridle your imagination and picture your audience in detail.

Since the initial steps in prewriting are tentative, you are free to be playful. Rather than sitting and staring at a blank sheet of paper and worrying about an essay, you are free to write anything you wish—curse words, love phrases, algebraic formulas, or even nonsense rhymes. This freewriting may lead to an essay, maybe not. As you think about a possible topic for your assignment, continue your playful approach. Look at your potential topic as if you were a Martian who had never heard of such a thing. What questions would you ask? Write them down. Pretend your tentative topic is disgusting; jot down why it disgusts you. Consider your possible topic as material for a segment on "Sixty Minutes." What kinds of details would you need to produce the segment? Soon you'll have a topic with which you feel comfortable.

As you continue your prewriting, maintain your playful attitude. You have a topic; now, what are you going to say? Making notes permits you to be outrageous even as you generate ideas that will find their way into your essay. What is the most outlandish thing you can imagine about your topic? Write it down.

What is the least interesting thing about your topic? Write it down. Now write down all the ideas that fall between these two extremes. You should have some amusing notes. As you review them, you'll begin to see connections between and among ideas. Become an artist and link related ideas with circles or hearts and lines. Your note sheet may reflect your whimsy, but you're working toward an idea that will develop into an essay.

Writing

When you move on to the writing stage in the composing process, you have to be a bit more serious, not grim or anxious, just serious. In this stage you actually write the essay you've been preparing to write. This essay isn't the one you're going to submit to your instructor. It is the one you're going to review. It's at this stage that you check your essay's unity and coherence, its beginning and ending. This initial draft gets refined into a working draft.

Rewriting

In the final stage in the composing process, you revise your working draft. You have an essay that is beginning to represent your best efforts. Now you can enrich your paragraphs, fine-tune your sentences, and sharpen your diction. Soon you'll have a final draft of your essay. When you finish proofreading that final draft, your initial anxiety about the assignment should be replaced by a feeling of confidence. Instead of laboriously fulfilling a writing assignment, you have composed an essay.

You can affirm: "Yes, I'm confident of my writing skills."

1
PREWRITING

PICTURING YOUR AUDIENCE

1. Picture Your Audience in as Much Detail as Possible.

The topic you choose, the words you use to develop that topic, and the attitude you convey in your essay are all governed, to a degree, by the audience you are addressing. Consequently, you should imagine your audience with as much precision as possible. You know, of course, that any description of your audience is risky. But you also know that without a definite feeling for your audience, your effort may be dulled.

For example, suppose you are engaged and wish to write a letter describing your future spouse to your grandparents, your older sister, and your former boyfriend or girlfriend. To complicate matters, suppose that your future spouse is a twenty-eight-year-old college dropout who plays lead guitar in a rock group and is actively involved in a Unitarian church. You will approach your description differently in each letter because the character of the audience is different. Specifically, your description will be very selective if your grandparents are college-educated, retired former bankers, staunch members of a conservative political party, devout Roman Catholics, and exceedingly fond of you.

Of course, you may never face a writing assignment as far-fetched as this example. However, some of the Suggestions for Writing that follow the essays in Part Two specify an audience. These particular audiences range from the executives of your local power company to the employees of a fast-food restaurant, from junior high school pupils to senior citizens. Each audience has its own characteristics, and you should, before you address it, note its pe-

culiar features. The more you know about your audience, the better prepared you are not only to choose an appropriate topic, but
also to compose an effective essay.

2. Examine Your Own and Your Audience's Experiences, Interests, and Knowledge for Possible Topics

Unless you are assigned a particular audience to write for, you
should plan to address your classmates. Look around your composition class. Who do you think, other than yourself, is the
smartest student? You are probably wrong, but that is all right.
Who do you think, other than yourself, is going to have the most
difficulty with this course? You are probably wrong again. Nevertheless, you are looking at individuals, individuals who make up
your audience. You are writing for the smartest and the weakest,
and all your classmates in between.

You and your classmates have at least one thing in common:
you are all enrolled in this composition course. But certainly you
have other shared characteristics. All of you have had experiences
that lend themselves to retelling. Perhaps none of you has been
to Micronesia, but each of you has been someplace (a new shopping mall, a nearby historical site, a favorite ski resort, an impressive church or sports arena). None of you has been kidnapped,
probably, but each of you has had a frightening experience (having
a vivid nightmare, being involved in an accident, getting lost, being
stopped by the police). Not all of you have been awarded a presi-
dential citation, but each of you has had a thrilling experience
(getting that first job, receiving an unexpected gift, attending a
special concert, winning a crucial game). These shared experiences help you picture your audience.

Furthermore, your audience—your classmates—has a broad range
of interests. Some of your classmates may be interested in horror
movies; some in action films; others in science fiction flicks. Some
of your classmates may share a hobby (collecting stamps or coins
or beer cans, playing cards or a musical instrument or billiards, or
writing poetry). Some of your classmates are interested in sports,
others in politics. Some may be interested in everything. There
may even be one or two of your classmates who are interested in
nothing. Why do you suppose nothing interests them? Learning
about your classmates' interests helps you picture your audience.

Perhaps you are passionately interested in French cooking, but only one of your classmates shares that interest. You and the other gourmet chef could write for one another. But your essays on *coq au vin* or *boeuf bourguignon* will have little or no appeal to the majority of your audience. In such a case, you need to look at shared interests for potential topics. Private interests, such as body building or sky diving or herpetology, may not be appropriate topics for your audience.

In addition, you and your classmates know a great deal. You know more than you may realize. You may have practical knowledge acquired through direct experience (how to prepare an omelet or adjust a carburetor, or scuba dive or eat with chopsticks). Or your knowledge may have been gained through reading and research (the goals of the National Organization of Women, the ecological effects of acid rain, General Lee's tactics at Gettysburg). Sharing your knowledge with, and learning from, your classmates make you appreciate that audience.

EXERCISE

To gain experience in picturing an audience, read the following essays carefully and try to describe in some detail the audiences' characteristics. Base your description on the specific words, phrases, allusions, and references, as well as on an educated guess based on the original place of publication.

1. Anne Fadiman, "The Egress of B.J. Whiting," *Harvard Magazine*. (p. 90)
2. Mimi Sheraton, "A Matter of Taste: Chocolate," *New York Magazine*. (p. 104)
3. Sue Hubbell, "The Cicada's Song," *Time* Magazine. (p. 117)
4. Lewis Thomas, "Death in the Open," *New England Journal of Medicine*. (p. 142)
5. Arnold Benson, "The Taming of the Old Wild West," the *New York Times*. (p. 327)
6. James E. Sefton, "Good Résumés—A Lost Art," *Signet*, the national magazine of Phi Sigma Kappa (a social fraternity). (p. 198)
7. Dave Barry, "Do-It-Yourself Pig Rendering," the *Miami Herald*. (p. 244)

CHOOSING AND LIMITING YOUR TOPIC

Most of the time your writing assignments will include some directions, e.g., "Define happiness" or "Analyze the goals of a liberal arts education" or "Give examples of how men attempt to attract women." In each of these examples, you are not only assigned a topic but also a method of developing that topic. In this text there are suggestions for writing following each of the essays, and these suggestions include both a topic and a method of development.

But suppose you are just told, "Write an essay."

1. Try Freewriting

If you are told, "Write an essay" and you are given no further guidance, you should try freewriting. As its name suggests, freewriting has no immediate goals and no restrictions. Its function is to encourage you to think on paper.

Take a blank sheet of paper and write whatever comes to mind. Pretend your pen is part of your brain and record your thoughts as they come. Don't stop writing until you have filled that page up or until fifteen minutes have passed. Let your pen record every idea as it comes. Your mind will probably jump from idea to idea; that's natural. Record those jumps; don't stop writing. Don't worry about any of the conventions of grammar, spelling, or punctuation, just write.

When Jill Bruley was told to write for fifteen minutes, here's what she wrote:

Martini please ... it certainly would help out in a situation that appears to have no beginning — end or purpose. Very strange indeed to be asked to write and that's it — write. How many times have I wished that I could write about anything I wanted to ... Anything and everything that was in my head ... all the little thought squiggles that passed by on the brain screen in my head. But given the opportunity to do so can only draw a blank slide. It's actually

9

kind of scary; a fear of stupidity almost. Am I stupid (or even worse — ~~is~~ unimaginative) because nothing wonderful and exciting pops on the big ~~z~~ screen? [I think being unimaginative would be a fate worse than death — or to be labeled as such.] It almost reeks as a word — stagnant, ~~sum~~ unmoving & thoughtless. I suppose if one had never written with fervor or excitement being labeled unimaginative would not seem extremely ~~terrible~~ terrible. But if ~~you~~ one's hand had not been ~~abl~~ able to write all the thoughts, phrases and catchy little words that the brain ∧had produced — because it was too slow with a BIC pen and you lost some of the best word & sentence ~~senten~~ ~~centen~~ combinations ~~uue~~ in history (in your own opinion), THEN ~~you~~ ~~yuuu~~ being called stagnant or uncreative would seem horrifying!!! Had all the neat thoughts & words been used up? Thought out? created?

After you've written for fifteen minutes, read what you've written. Is there anything on your page that you think could be a topic for an informal essay? If so, put it in brackets or circle it. In Jill's case she found a topic in her sentence *I think that being unimaginative would be a fate worse than death—or to be labeled as such.* It may be, however, that your page of freewriting does not produce a topic at all. Maybe you've only doodled or written profanities or the weather report. Nevertheless, you were writing, and that is the purpose of freewriting.

2. Remember Your Audience

Another way to discover a topic if you are told, "Write an essay" is to think about your audience. From what you already know about your audience, you can come up with a topic. You know that each member of your audience has had a thrilling experience. Why not tell them about a thrilling experience of yours? You know that your audience is interested in current films, and so are you. "Films" then becomes your topic. Or you know your audience is curious about a variety of things. Why not share your knowledge? Tell them how an internal-combustion engine works, or why you are planning a career in personnel management.

These examples of topics drawn from your experience, interests, and knowledge would be appropriate for your classmates. Of course, "My Thrilling Experience," "Films," and "Career Choices" are topics that need considerable refining before you begin to write, but you have discovered a viable starting point. As you continue the composing process, you may come to feel that "Career Choices" would have no interest for your audience. If so, ask two or three of your classmates if they would like to read your essay on that topic. If they confirm your suspicion, then you should begin searching for another topic.

3. Narrow Your Topic

Most of the time, your topic will be assigned, and you won't have topic selection to worry about. Instead, you can direct your attention to limiting the assigned topic. Your immediate question will probably be, "How long does the essay have to be?" Your instructor may answer, "Long enough to develop the topic." Both your question and the instructor's answer need explanation. Every writer works within limits. Your limits may be included in the assignment ("Write a 500-word essay on women's rights") or they may be defined by the situation ("You have the class period in which to write your essay" or "Your 2,500 word research project is due in six weeks"). Within the limits of both space and time, you must strive for completeness. Completeness is assured when you look at your finished essay and can honestly state, "I've said all I meant to say as well as I can."

Recognizing the given limits of an essay helps you choose a topic that can be reduced or expanded to meet those limitations. Some topics cannot be completed in 500 words; others do not require that many. In other words, *the shorter the essay, the narrower the topic.*

4. Think Small

Because relatively short essays (500 to 1,000 words) are the standard in composition courses, you must learn to "think small." When you think small, you are not thinking superficially. In fact, short essays often require greater intellectual effort than long ones: saying much in few words is not easy (nor is it common). Rather, thinking small means limiting your topic to one that is specific, sharply focused, and manageable. It means developing the ability to see in the midst of a forest a single tree, or even a single leaf, and in the midst of a city, a single window.

a. Create a Circular Subject Chart   An imaginative and relatively unstructured way to narrow a broad topic is to use brainstorming in a circle. For another assignment, Bruley was given the general topic "My Ideal Place," and instructed to write that topic in the center of a blank sheet of paper. As you can see from her work sheet, there were five narrower topics that she thought of. (See opposite page.)

b. Create a Narrowing Subject Chart   The following chart illustrates the range of broad topics covered by some of the essays in Part Two. (A thematic index appears on p. 387.) The topics are arranged, somewhat arbitrarily, under the headings of Knowledge, Experiences, and Interests.

Knowledge	Experiences	Interests
People	Male-female Relationships	Sports
Drugs	Education	The Arts
TV	Alcohol	Life on Other Planets
Language	Memorable Events	Death
Ecology	Dwelling Places	Moral Values

None of the above topics is restricted enough to serve as the focal point of a short essay. Consider "Dwelling Places," for example. In order to treat this topic adequately, you would need to discuss most of the places where people live—farms, cities, trailer parks, residence halls, fraternity houses, high-rise apartments, and on, and on, and on. You could neither cover "Dwelling Places" in 500 words, nor would you try. You would, of course, narrow it.

5. Limit Your Topic to a Specific, Manageable Part of a Larger Whole

Breaking "Dwelling Places" down into two main types, "urban" and "rural," helps—but not much. Each type still covers too much ground for adequate treatment in relatively few words.

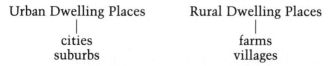

Urban Dwelling Places	Rural Dwelling Places
cities	farms
suburbs	villages

Even "cities" or "villages" alone would prove too extensive for brief coverage. But if you were to narrow the focus still more to a *specific* city or a *specific* village, you at last bring the topic close to manageable limits:

13

Cities   Villages
|
New York, New York   Sololá, Guatemala

PREPARING TO WRITE

At this stage in the composing process, you have identified your audience, and chosen and limited your topic. Now you are ready to prepare to write a specific essay. Your preparation should include four additional activities: making notes, reviewing those notes, formulating a thesis, and selecting a method of development if one has not been assigned.

Making Notes

1. Brainstorm

Write your topic at the top of a blank sheet of large paper. Then jot down every idea that occurs to you. Don't bother with spelling or grammar. Just write ideas. You'll discover that these ideas may stimulate additional ideas through free association. Whatever you do, don't let the page remain blank. Fill it up.

2. Use Freewriting Again

You now have a topic, so fill up a sheet with whatever comes to mind as you write about your topic. When Bruley wrote freely about the beach as her ideal place, here's what she produced:

The beach. What a joke? I am from Vermont and we do not have such things as beaches. Sure people visit them - as a matter of fact every February my family packed up and left for Virginia Beach, Daytona Beach, Myrtle Beach, St. Petersburg Beach - you name it, we visited it. But still in Vermont there is ~~no such~~ nothing called "THE BEACH". We have lakes, lakefront property, lakeshore etc. (it is very strange to note that we have SEA weed in our lakes.)

In first arriving at "South" I could _smell_ the beach... it was definitely in the air. People exuded beach... Even they way they talked sounded like the surf (up & down & up & down). We have beachwear, beach ~~para~~ paraphenalia, special glasses, and funky cords to keep them on. Bright colored shorts, neon sneakers, cut up beach t-shirts... ~~Shoelaces~~ Shoelaces, watches, haircuts— ~~everything~~ everything accomodates the beach... (There is profit in this beach stuff.) Well, anyway the Beach Syndrome is an easy one to fall in – skimpy bikinis & tanned men are also nonexistant in Vermont. Initially it was just a beach party here, a pool party there, a loua next week, and ~~~~ an afternoon at "Gamma Beach". But inevitably, after my skin became an unrecognizable ~~~~ brown, ~~~~ ~~~~ I was hooked – laughing at the beach with friends At the beach things are more funny, pretty, sexy & fun & wild ... The real world is light years away (tan years?) Life moves at a different pace – slower yet faster – its own orbit... Last time I went home my family nearly disowned me when I asked "Where's the beach?"

> Falling into the beach syndrome
>
> > Description

3. Use the Journalistic Formula

Write the *journalistic formula* down the left side of your page, leaving space between the items. The journalistic formula asks: who? what? when? where? why? and how? Ask these questions of your topic and try to get a variety of answers.

For example, you're writing about your college. Answers to the question *who?* might include vice-presidents, deans, department heads, and, of course, students. Answers to the question *what?* might include a board of trustees, a faculty senate, the student-government association. *When?*—the year your college was founded, the year it became accredited or added a new college or major field. *Why?*—to satisfy specific education needs, e.g., to train teachers or engineers or journalists. As you work with the journalistic formula, one or more of its questions may be irrelevant and one or more may generate a wealth of answers. If a question doesn't stimulate answers, go on to the next question. Once you've answered all or most of them, go back to the unanswered ones and try again to provide answers. Remember, the more details and ideas you have at your disposal, the more selective and definite you can be when you finally begin to write your essay.

Mary Kramer wrote an essay that was published in *Playbill*, a monthly publication given free to New York theatergoers. Her audience is recognized as being sophisticated and literate. She knew she was going to develop her material by telling what happened (narration), so she put that method's question at the top of her note-sheet. Her notes may have looked something like this:

Narration

A collegiate production of Hamlet
what happened?
Everything that could go wrong went wrong

Jack Norton from LA

WHO I was assistant to the director - he was interested in pretty coeds
he was a male chauvinist pig

Disaster: Titanic $17,000
WHAT big production including big budget - opening the cast
Drama Society
too ambitious

June 1972   drunk King
WHEN my senior year - rehersals -   the duel   torn dress
8   scene   something each
performances   night
longest period of my life!

WHERE large university (Ohio State)

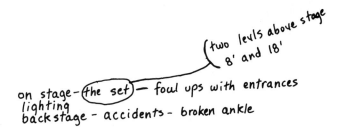

on stage - (the set) - foul ups with entrances
lighting
backstage - accidents - broken ankle

WHY   cast problems - beautiful girls / PE majors —

Ophelia - measles Polonius lines bad breath Hamlet

Horatio hiccups

HOW   God knows!

Paul Pattacini was assigned to write a descriptive essay about his ideal gathering place. (The assignment is given on p. 111.) Below are his actual notes. Notice the prominence he gives to the five senses. Notice also that *why?* is the focusing question for his notes. Thus he asks: why is the beach an ideal gathering place?

Sight - Sound - Taste - Feeling - Smell   ①

ideal gathering place: the beach   (sand) clean NATURE
                                                      air
(appreciate) why: ① sun; tan, looks (improved)[[healthy]] waves natural

        ② relaxation - rest - get away

    ✱ ③ girls - meeting watching

        ④ EXERCISE - jog - freesbe - volleyball - surfing

        ⑤ EXPLORING - HOBBIES - collecting sea shells

———————— ○ ————————

Reviewing Your Notes

Once you have filled a page with notes, you should look over them carefully to clarify your understanding of, and attitude toward, your topic. The notes represent your spontaneous mental and emotional responses to your topic. Now comes a more leisurely opportunity to examine each answer carefully. Not all your ideas will find their way into your essay.

For example, in the notes attributed to Mary Kramer there are specific details that are not incorporated into her essay. (By the way, the writers of this textbook did not have access to her actual notes, so they recreated them imaginatively to illustrate the note-taking step in the composing process.) In her essay, Kramer does not include the name of the director of *Hamlet*, nor where he was from; those details are irrelevant. She also drops her characterization of him as *a male chauvinist pig*; that label would offend most men and some women readers and gain Kramer nothing in return. She also does not name her university, the year of the production, or the exact amount of its budget. Omitting those details frees her essay from a specific time and place and gives it an enduring quality.

Paul's notes are rather skimpy, but he now has some ideas he can use in his essay. He doesn't use them in the order in which they appear in his notes, and he certainly enriches them with specific details as he writes his initial draft.

Formulating Your Thesis

1. Make Sure Your Topic Can Become a Central Idea That Will Govern the Essay

You cannot consider the prewriting process over and the essay ready to be written until you have clearly in mind what you want to say about your topic—what attitude you intend to take toward it. *Thesis* is the formal name given to the central attitude or position that you develop in your essay. In other words, thesis is the judgment or conclusion you have been searching for as you thought about your topic, made notes, reviewed them carefully, eliminated some and kept others. From the standpoint of your audience, only a definite attitude on your part makes your essay worth the time it takes to read it. From your standpoint as a writer, a clearly formulated thesis acts as a built-in censor, deciding which ideas are relevant and which irrelevant. Without such a definite focus to regulate its content, even your essay on a limited topic can ramble.

Think again about New York and Sololá as manageable topics. You and your classmates probably each have a different attitude toward these places. One final step thus remains: to select a *single* aspect of each place that interests you, seems significant, and has potential appeal to your audience:

New York	Sololá
its massive	its inhabitants'
size	dress

You have now gone as far as you need to go in reducing a large and unworkable topic to two smaller topics, each a reasonably limited subject for a short essay, and each controlled by a specific thesis.

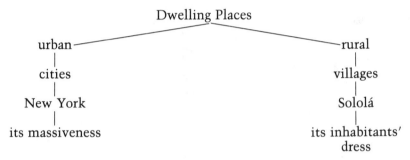

These two topics serve as the subjects of two essays in Part Two: "Sololá" (p. 101) and "New York" (p. 108).

Two additional points: first, making a thesis as specific as possible means making it the central focus of attention to which every idea in the essay is more or less directly related. But it does *not* mean that an essay on New York's huge size cannot include any mention of its inhabitants or their distinctive characteristics. Environment and social attitudes are, after all, closely related, and Thomas Griffith is perfectly justified in devoting attention to the gruff impersonality that he sees as typical of those who live and work in a city the size of New York. The same principle justifies Aldous Huxley's including some comments on the economic situation that may change the Quiché Indians' dress.

The second point is related to the first. A limited thesis may have unlimited applications. "New York" says much about the impersonality of *any* large city. "Sololá" reinforces the idea that *all* native costumes are worth preserving. In short, writers may wish to let topics that are limited to a particular set of circumstances *stand for* other similar circumstances. In that way they can acquire a richness and relevance beyond the scope of their immediate concerns.

EXERCISE

Choose two of the following general topics and, using a chart similar to the one on page 19, reduce each topic to a specific, manageable idea.

Advertising	Plants
Battles	Pollution
Fashions	Resorts
Magazines	Rivers
Museums	Science Fiction
Movies	Sports
Music	Superstitions
The Olympics	TV Programs
Pets	Vacations

Make notes for the two topics. Be sure you have *at least* 15 further ideas on each topic idea.

2. Prepare a Carefully Worded Statement That Establishes a Controlling Idea

A thesis expressed in a sentence or two somewhere in the essay (usually at or near the beginning) is called a *thesis statement*. Not every essay has a thesis statement, but every essay has a thesis. If your thesis statement is precisely worded, it can be a great help, both to your reader in understanding your essay and to you in writing it. The reason is that a good thesis statement contains key words that act as guides to the organization and emphasis of your whole essay.

For example, Mary Kramer's thesis statement is her second sentence (p. 82). *For me, it [Hamlet] represents a trying experience and a Grand Guignol farce.* The key words are *it [Hamlet], trying experience,* and *Grand Guignol farce.* This sentence is a concise and accurate expression of her opinion. Remember, she is writing for a literate audience; she expects them to recognize her allusion to *a Grand Guignol farce.* An allusion is a figure of speech that refers to some famous historical or literary figure or event. *Grand*

Guignol refers to plays of a gruesome character, such as *Punch and Judy*, and *farce* is a dramatic piece intended to amuse the audience through exaggerated, improbable situations. Kramer's essay narrates her *trying experience* during a gruesome, improbable production of *Hamlet.*

Furthermore, the key words in your thesis statement require special emphasis in your essay. In fact, the *degree* of emphasis is suggested by the grammatical construction of the sentence. Consider these thesis statements:

a. The *market* at Sololá was a walking *museum* of fancy dress. (Aldous Huxley, p. 101)
b. The American people were sold *a pig in a poke* when they replaced the *saloon* with the *cocktail lounge.* (Harry Golden, p. 166)

The first example is, in grammatical terms, a "simple" sentence. *Market* is the subject of the copulative (linking) verb, and *museum* is the predicate nominative. Thus, grammatically speaking, there is an extremely close relationship between the two terms, amounting to virtual equality. This near equality is reflected by a nearly equal emphasis given to each idea in the essay. There is, however, a somewhat greater stress on the market as a showplace for costumes, since what is being emphasized is not the market as a *market* but the market as a *museum.*

The second thesis statement is a "complex" sentence made up of an independent clause *(The American people were sold a pig in a poke)* and a dependent clause *(when they replaced the saloon with the cocktail lounge).* The very fact that the second clause is dependent in the sentence means that its ideas should also be dependent in the essay. In other words, the replacing of *saloons* with *cocktail lounges* receives less emphasis than the idea that Americans were duped *(sold a pig in a poke)* into accepting the change.

As you formulate your thesis statement, keep in mind that its grammatical structure will help you distribute emphasis throughout your essay.

Even when a thesis statement comes at the end of an essay, it still reflects the emphasis of the essay. Instead of placing his thesis statement at the beginning of his essay, Paul Pattacini describes his ideal gathering place first. From his descriptive details, his attitude toward the beach emerges, and he states it in his next-to-last sentence (p. 68): *I concluded that enjoying nature, relaxing, exercising, working on hobbies, and, most important, girl-watching, made the beach my ideal meeting place.*

EXERCISE

For each of the following thesis statements, indicate its grammatical type, pick out the key words or phrases, and determine the attitude it establishes.

1. So maybe it's time to give up trying to stamp it [pot] out, and consider legalizing it, thereby controlling it. (p. 299, par. 7)
2. Serendipity, more often than necessity, is the mother of invention, and it was unplanned parenthood of this kind that resulted in the birth of the phonograph. (p. 248, par. 1)
3. What reasonable picture (of intelligent life, roughly man-shaped in form) can we draw on the basis of what we now know of Mars—bearing always in mind that the conclusions we reach are not to be taken seriously, but only as an exercise in fantasy? (p. 120, par. 2)
4. Everything in the world dies, but we only know about it as a kind of abstraction. (p. 142, par. 3)
5. Three passions, simple but overwhelmingly strong, have governed my life: the longing for love, the search for knowledge, and unbearable pity for the suffering of mankind. (p. 196, par. 1)
6. The letter raised a moral issue: does an individual have the obligation to go on living even when the beauty and meaning and power of life are gone? (p. 302, par. 2)

3. Consider the Persona Your Thesis Statement Reveals to Your Audience

In addition to establishing your attitude toward your topic, your thesis statement also reveals your attitude toward your audience. As you develop your thesis, keep in mind that you are creating your writer's persona. *Persona* comes from a Latin word meaning "mask." It originally referred to the facial covering worn by actors to identify a character for an audience. A smiling mask meant a comic character, a frowning mask a tragic one. In this context, a persona clarified rather than disguised. The mask kept the audience from being confused; it let them know who was speaking.

Every writer assumes a persona. Your persona will vary depending on the way you wish your audience to perceive you. For example, suppose you are a talented musician, an excellent athlete, and an honor student. Your description of your abilities will differ depending upon whether you are applying for a music scholarship or an athletic one. In the one case, your persona is that of a musician; in the other, that of an athlete.

When Pattacini writes in his thesis statement . . . *and, most important, girl-watching* . . . he is presenting himself as a healthy male animal whose persona may be insulting to some feminists in his audience. Kramer's thesis statement reveals a persona that is sophisticated and literate without being pretentious. Of course, readers have no way of knowing whether the persona and the writer are identical.

EXERCISE

Analyze these essays and then describe the persona of the writer as it emerges from the essays.

1. "Is Human Imagination Going Down the Tube?" (p. 330)
2. "You're Not What You Think You Are" (p. 171)
3. "The Ugliest Word" (p. 146)
4. "Keep Sports' Priorities in Order" (p. 306)
5. "What's a *Ms.?*" (p. 261)
6. "Of Commas and Teachers" (p. 323)

EXERCISE

Prepare a thesis statement for the two topics you made notes for on p. 20.

Selecting Your Method of Development

Picturing your audience, limiting your topic, and formulating your thesis are preludes to selecting a method of development. If you are assigned a particular method—"Describe your favorite place" or "Analyze the attitude of your campus toward women's lib"—then your choice is already made. A descriptive essay is called for in the first case, an analytical essay in the second. Most of the time your method of development will be included in the assignment. If, however, the method of development is left up to you, you need to consider the various methods and select from them the one best suited to your topic and thesis. Always keep in mind, however, that almost every topic could be developed by any of the methods.

For example, suppose that "My College" is your general topic, and that you are writing for a high school friend who does not attend college. You have generated a page of notes and you have formulated a thesis. To discover an effective means of both limiting and developing your topic, you will need to review your notes, keeping your thesis in mind, and see which of these questions your notes answer:

1. What happens during a typical day at your college or university? (Narration; see pp. 71–73.)
2. Where is your institution located? What do you see, hear, smell, and feel while there? (Description; see pp. 96–101.)
3. What is the chief feature, or features, of collegiate life? (Example; see pp. 128–132.)
4. What is a college education? (Definition; see pp. 254–261.)
5. How is a college education like other education (professional, high school)? (Comparison; see pp. 158–166.) How does a college education differ from other education (vocational training, high school)? (Contrast; see pp. 158–164.)
6. How is your college or university organized? How does it function? (Analysis; see pp. 191–196, 238–241.)
7. Should everyone go to college? Should your best friend join you at your university? (Persuasion; see p. 283.)

Jill Bruley's notes led to description as a method of development. "Sololá," and "New York" are both developed by appeals to the senses. They, too, use description. "Theatre of the Absurd" tells what happened; it uses narration.

2
WRITING

YOUR INITIAL DRAFT

Your investment of time and effort in the prewriting process is now ready to produce dividends—the initial draft of your essay. You have a limited topic, a concise thesis, and specific details to support your thesis. Now you need to write. Don't expect this draft to have the polish of the essays in Part Two; after all, you have no way of knowing how many times those essays were revised and rewritten. However, you can get an idea of what a first draft looks like. Here is Paul Pattacini's:

leave space

~~ANFUNGPOTFAGM~~   As we were walking from class,

My friend Mario had a great idea! He suggested that we [ought to] go to the beach this weekend. The more I thought about it, the more I realized how much I had missed the beach. ~~in~~ It had been [exactly] two and a half months since I ~~last~~ last [enjoyed] ~~much more~~ saw the ~~of~~ crystal-blue waters and the... ~~neighbourhood~~

*experience that great atmosphere   ~~getting~~ Now, once again, I would get to *(all) be in my ideal gathering place. Yeah! The sun, the relaxation, the exercise, the exploring, and the girl-watching are all

great ~~features that make the beach~~ ways which make the beach
~~the perfect location to enjoy oneself~~ to enjoy

Now, once again, I would get to (experience) enjoy
my (utopian) favorite place.

Saturday morning arrived, and I was feeling great!
~~With a great deal of enthusiasm I prepared all~~ I could
not wait to get to ~~s~~ the beach and have some fun.*
~~Twenty~~ minutes after I finished packing ~~the towels~~
the towels ~~and~~, the (suntan) lotion and the rest of
~~the~~ ~~necessities~~, Mario arrived.

* I quickly started packing the towels, the (suntan)
lotion, and the rest of the necessities. As a finished,
Mario arrived with the car. We were finally on our
way.

⌈ When we reached the beach, the first thing we
decided to do was to work on our tans. ~~There was~~
~~nothing~~ While we were (laying) down we could
sense
(sence) the beauty of nature: ⌋

When we reached the beach, the first thing we
decided to do was to exercise. We started jogging
north for about one mile. ~~as we jogged we~~ We saw
several people playing freesbe* one person, however,
was playing freesbe with his dog. That was really
something to watch!* ~~s~~ On our way back we saw
several guys surfing. It was ~~really~~ amazing to
see how they could ~~s~~ stay on top of such huge waves.

towards the end of our run, we met with some
people collecting sea-shells. Together, they had

collected over one-thousand shells. One of these shells was huge. The founder claimed that by putting it near ~~the~~ the ear, ~~one~~ one could hear the ocean. ~~[illegible crossed-out text]~~

~~[illegible crossed-out text]~~

~~[illegible crossed-out text]~~

When we finished jogging, we were fairly tired and we decided to relax. ~~As we layed in the sand, we could feel the hot rays of the sun~~

~~[illegible crossed-out text]~~

~~[illegible crossed-out text]~~ really is. We could see the blue-green waters.

*   We (layed) in the sand and we could feel the hot rays of the sun on our faces. At the same time, the warm breeze would ~~⅗~~ blow sand onto ~~our~~ my feet making them tickle. Despite these <u>enjoyable distractions</u>, I was able to notice the blue-green ~~waters~~ ocean. It's salty and cool waters really looked tempting. ~~[illegible crossed-out]~~ ~~[illegible crossed-out] them~~ That day, the ocean was really rough. The waves, with their white (crests), ~~was~~ seemed angry ~~and~~ They constantly kept crashing against the water causing white bubbles to cover the surface. One could really hear these bubbles disintegrate as the wave retreaved.

Your primary concern in this first draft is to finish it. You want to complete it as quickly as possible. Consequently, you should not worry over whether your sentences are complete or if you've chosen the most precise words and spelled them correctly. As you write, a new idea may come to you. Jot it down in the margin; don't try to incorporate it into the body of your essay at this time. In subsequent drafts, you may use that idea or discard it.

As you write, you may be tempted to pause and consider whether one word is better than another. Instead of pausing, do what Pattacini does: write both words. Pattacini writes, *Now, once again, I would get to* (experience) *enjoy my* (utopian) *favorite place.* If you are unsure about a sentence or word, put an asterisk by it or enclose it in parenthesis. Above all, keep writing.

If, as you write, you get to a point where you experience writer's block (total inability to express your idea), skip that point. Go on to another point that needs expression. It may be that the blocked point needs additional brainstorming. Or perhaps it needs to be omitted entirely.

Furthermore, as you write you may sense that your arrangement of materials is flawed. Don't try to rearrange while you're writing. Put the material in brackets or use some other marker to remind you to take a long look at that paragraph later. For example, in Pattacini's draft on page 26 he has a bracketed paragraph. It's obvious that after he wrote that paragraph he had a change of mind. He decided that *exercise* was a more appropriate first activity at the beach than *tanning.* His idea about working *on our tans* was saved for another place in his essay.

REVIEWING YOUR DRAFT

If you are like most writers, when you finish your initial draft you feel both relief and dismay. You're relieved because you have written a draft; you're dismayed because you think your essay isn't good enough to share with your classmates. You may think your audience will find your essay boring or simple-minded, or too difficult. These are healthy signs; you know your initial draft was not designed for your audience. The initial draft is for your eyes only.

If you have enough time, you should put your draft aside for a day or two, or at least, a few hours. During this waiting period, try not to think about what you've written. What you're trying to do is to clear your mind. You want to return to your draft with a fresh outlook. When you return, approach your draft as if you were the audience rather than the writer. Using this approach may seem strange, but it should help you in the reviewing portion of the composing process.

Check Your Draft for Unity

It's your thesis or thesis statement that helps you check for *unity*. Remember that the thesis statement has announced the main idea of your essay. Read the first sentence of each of your paragraphs. Does each sentence say something that supports the key words in your thesis statement? If you're not sure, draw a line from the first sentence of each paragraph to the key words in your thesis statement that you think that sentence supports. If you discover that one of your paragraphs has no linear connection to the thesis statement, then you know that that paragraph needs to be either rewritten or omitted.

Check Your Draft for Coherence

After you're sure your draft has unity, then check it for *coherence*. Coherence is the quality in effective writing that permits the ideas supporting the thesis to unfold smoothly and continuously. Coherence has to do with the arrangement of your essay. Specifically, the topic thought of each paragraph should logically follow from the topic thought of the preceding paragraph and, in turn, logically introduce the topic thought of the next paragraph. (A topic thought is to a paragraph what a thesis statement is to an essay: the controlling idea.) Like the organs of your body, the paragraphs of your essay are important in themselves, but much more important because of the way they work together for the good of the whole. A body whose organs function cooperatively is said to be *healthy;* an essay whose paragraphs function cooperatively is said to be *coherent*. Both health and coherence are signs of life.

1. Arrange Your Paragraphs in a Logical Order Logical arrangement depends partly on the nature of your topic, partly on your specific audience, and partly on the overall effect you wish to achieve. But primarily, logical arrangement depends on your method of development. Each method, remember, invites or requires certain patterns of paragraph arrangement. Narration, for example, usually presupposes a chronological ordering (see pp. 71–74); description, a spatial arrangement of visual details supported by other sense impressions (see pp. 96–101); example, an

29

ordered presentation of specific illustrations to clarify a generalization (see pp. 128–132). Comparison/contrast and definition usually require an arrangement of concrete details around a single dominant idea or impression (see pp. 156–166 for comparison/contrast and pp. 254–261 for definition). Analysis and persuasion involve other methods of organization more suited to handling a number of ideas (see pp. 191–196, 216–220, 238–241 for analysis and p. 283 for persuasion).

2. Make Sure Your Point of View Is Consistent Logical arrangement of paragraphs is the first test for coherence that you apply to your draft. Logical arrangement is necessary, but alone it will rarely hold your paragraphs together. In addition, you need to make sure you've maintained a consistent *point of view*. In film-making, point of view means the camera angle. How is the action being presented? Does the camera view the landscape as if seen from heaven? Is the action seen through the eyes of one of the participants? In fiction, point of view has a similar meaning. It means the position from which the author presents the actions of the story. In persuasion, point of view means your opinion on the issue in question. Why do you agree or disagree with your classmates? In expository writing, point of view has to do with your attitude toward your topic and audience, and the grammatical choices you make in developing your topic. Your thesis statement commits you not only to a persona (p. 22) but also to a grammatical point of view. In other words, you are proposing to treat your topic in a definite *person, number,* and *tense.*

If your draft is based primarily on your experiences, then you have adopted *I* as your grammatical person. You have chosen first person because the entire essay is presented through your eyes. In William Burroughs' personal story (p. 79), every paragraph uses *I* as the grammatical subject of one or more sentences, except his brief flashback. First person tends to create a bond of intimacy between you and your audience. You're inviting your classmates to see through your eyes, perceive through your senses, and reason along with you as you think about a topic.

If your draft is based on the experiences of others or your thoughtful examination of a topic, then you will adopt *he, she* or *it* as your grammatical person. You have chosen third person because your entire essay is presented in a more objective, less personal point of view. In Bonnie Angelo's "Good Ole Boys" (p. 278), she uses *good ole boys* or *he* or *good ole boy* in every paragraph.

Third person distances you from both your topic and your audience. It carries the suggestion of an impersonal, authoritative handling of the topic. For the most part, the kinds of subjects you will be assigned in college courses are best treated in third person.

Closely related to person is the grammatical *number* you choose. Again, your thesis guides you in maintaining either a singular or plural number. Pattacini introduces his friend Mario in his first sentence. Consequently, when Pattacini is alone he uses first person singular. But when he and Mario are together, first person plural is called for; they are experiencing the same delights of the beach. (Of course, Mario's description might be different because his persona is not exactly the same as Pattacini's.) Sue Hubbell casts her essay, "The Cicada's Song" (p. 117) in third person plural. She maintains that number except for her last two paragraphs when she focuses on a single cicada.

Most errors in person and number come in the middle of your essay or toward the end of a paragraph when you lose your concentration and write *you* instead of *we* or *they*. Reread your draft to see if any *you*'s appear in it. If you discover a *you*, your essay's coherence may be dislocated.

You need to review your draft for one other matter that affects coherence—*tense*. Again, your thesis statement establishes the dominant tense for your essay. If you are looking back on events that have already happened, then your primary tense is past. If you are presenting events or ideas as they occur to you now, you use present tense. If, however, there is a reason to combine tenses, as Stewart Alsop does in his essay on p. 86, be sure the shift in tense does not fracture your essay's coherence.

As you review your draft, be sure you have maintained a consistent person, number, and tense.

EXERCISE

Analyze one of these essays: "The Effects of Alcohol" (p. 229), "Biblical Bloopers" (p. 132), or "Business as Usual Down at the Old Necropolis" (p. 135). What does each paragraph contribute to the development of the thesis statement? Point out uses of transitional words and phrases, repetition of key words, and the use of synonyms and substitutions. Does the writer maintain a consistent point of view? If not, why is there a shift?

Check Your Beginning

After you've checked your draft's unity and coherence, take a reader's-eye view of your beginning and ending. Because of their location—first and last—your initial and final paragraphs are in the strongest positions of emphasis.

Reread your first paragraph as if you were a member of your class. Would you want to continue reading that essay? If not, your opening needs work. Only if your paragraph catches your reader's attention will that reader be likely to continue reading. Furthermore, remember that this paragraph introduces the topic, establishes your attitude toward both the topic and your audience, and often contains your thesis statement. In fact, the success or failure of your essay may well depend on your opening paragraph.

All of the following examples are intended to be attention-getting, but in different ways. All together, they suggest a number of techniques both for getting the essay underway and capturing your readers' interest.

1. Begin Your Essay with a Little Story

The fable goes this way: An African child came home from school one day and told his mother of a story his teacher had read to him. It was about a man in the jungle named Tarzan and he was mightier than even the lion, whom the child had always thought to be the king of the jungle. When his mother heard the child's expression of dismay, she replied: "Always will it be that way, my son, until lions learn to write." (Robert C. Maynard, p. 295)

When I was a child growing up in Brooklyn many years ago, my family moved a great deal. My father worked for the Metropolitan Life Insurance Company, and depending on our financial status—well, we moved a great deal. The first cardboard carton that got packed when we were leaving the old apartment, and the first that got unpacked when we moved into the new apartment, was a box simply labeled "Mama's paintings and records." Before the furniture was in place, she was setting up her thumbtacks for her pictures and Galli-Curci was heard at the top of her lungs throughout the apartment. (Beverly Sills, p. 310)

Maynard uses an African fable to introduce the importance of being able to write. Sills uses a personal anecdote (story) to show how important the arts were to her mother. In both cases, the story fits the topic in both attitude and content.

2. Make a Surprising Statement

> The other day I confessed to my brother, a lawyer, that until last June, one month after I graduated from college, I did not know the difference between "that" and "which." Whenever I had to decide which relative pronoun to use, I simply took my chances: Heads it was "that," tails it was "which"; I didn't take the time to fuss. (Edna Goldsmith, p. 323)

> I was on junk for almost fifteen years. In that time I took ten cures. I have been to Lexington and have taken the reduction treatment. I have taken abrupt withdrawal treatments and prolonged withdrawal treatments; cortisone, tranquilizers, antihistamines and the prolonged sleep cure. In every case I relapsed at the first opportunity. (William Burroughs, p. 79)

This technique can be used with any type of essay, but you must be certain that your content is serious and important enough to justify such a beginning. Otherwise, your readers may think it is merely a trick opening. Goldsmith's confession probably strikes a sympathetic chord for most readers. She introduces a serious topic with a typical dilemma. Burroughs' dramatic confession draws the readers compellingly into his personal experience with drug addiction.

3. Present Necessary Information

> For more than twenty years, *Ms.* has appeared in secretarial handbooks as the suggested form of address when a woman's marital status is unknown; a sort of neutral combination of *Miss* and *Mrs.* Now, *Ms.* is being adopted as a standard form of address by women who want to be recognized as individuals, rather than being identified by their relationship with a man. After all, if *Mr.* is enough to indicate "male," then *Ms.* should be enough to indicate "female." (*Ms. Magazine,* p. 261)

> Four years ago when I moved back home to Mobile after a ten-year odyssey to college and New York and Germany, I found a situation that in my book is very close to heaven: a downtown apartment with a balcony right on the Mardi Gras parade route. (Franklin Daugherty, p. 108)

An editorial writer informs her readers that *Ms.*, as a form of address, is not the creation of the women's movement, a fact most readers would not know. She argues that the term has an unimpeachable background. Providing *necessary* background information does not, however, open the door for you to begin every essay with a history of the world. Daugherty compresses a fourteen-year period into one sentence in order to emphasize his return home. In both cases, the essays have begun successfully.

4. Indicate Why Your Subject is Significant

The world of religion and philosophy was shocked recently when Henry P. Van Dusen and his wife ended their lives by their own hands. Dr. Van Dusen had been president of Union Theological Seminary; for more than a quarter-century he had been one of the luminous names in Protestant theology. He enjoyed world status as a spiritual leader. News of the self-inflicted death of the Van Dusens, therefore, was profoundly disturbing to all those who attach a moral stigma to suicide and regard it as a violation of God's laws. (Norman Cousins, p. 302)

There can be little doubt from Cousins' paragraph that the topic of his essay is both controversial and significant.

5. Begin with a Challenging Question

Is television changing human consciousness? Is it possible that the rapid pace of presentation, the quick shifts of focus, the speeded-up blend of visual, musical, and verbal material that characterize American TV may actually be impeding our capacities for sustained attention, deliberate thought, and private imagery? (Dorothy G. Singer and Jerome L. Singer, p. 330)

Be aware that beginning with a question could be deadening, especially if your question has no bite to it.

6. Repeat or Paraphrase the Title

Yes, your essay should have a title. The title is the first thing a potential reader notices, and if it is eye-catching, you have captured your reader. Of course, titles of scientific papers and reports are usually descriptive; the titles reflect the information that is then developed in the reports. But if your essay is intended for a general audience, create a title that will whet their expectations and arouse their curiosity. "A Matter of Taste: Chocolate," "Grant and Lee: A Study in Contrasts," and "How Edison Stumbled on His Phonograph" are titles of essays in this text. Each suggests the content of the essay; you know what to expect. On the other hand, these titles are designed to arouse your curiosity: "Do-It-Yourself Pig Rendering," "Stud Bulls and the Big Blow," "Legal Marijuana—A Pot of Gold," "The Ugliest Word." Each is imaginatively suggestive of its content.

If you are having difficulty beginning your essay, repeat or paraphrase your title. Even though your readers have presumably just read the essay's title, you still have the responsibility of introducing the topic independently of the title. For example, suppose your essay is entitled "Father Knows Best." Your first sentence should not read, "It took me a long time to learn this lesson." One method of avoiding this error is to repeat the title in the same or, preferably, slightly different words: "It took me a long time to learn that Dad knows what he is talking about."

7. Avoid Irrelevant or Trite Ways of Beginning Your Essay

Don't complain about the assignment. Don't apologize for lack of ability or information. Don't announce boringly, "In this essay I shall do so-and-so." Don't ignore your thesis. Don't try to be too ingenious or your opening paragraph may have little to do with your essay as it unfolds.

Check Your Ending

Take a look at the closing paragraph of your draft. Does it need reworking? It does if it isn't emphatic. You must resist the temptation to restate boringly, "In this essay I have done so-and-so." If restatement is necessary—as it may be when your thesis is unusually complex or important—it should be rephrased. Furthermore, you must beware of summarizing material mentioned only two or three paragraphs earlier. Your readers' attention span probably lasts long enough to recall those points. In addition, do not introduce entirely new material, for you will be unable to develop it adequately in the last paragraph. And finally, avoid being either moralistic or apologetic. If you have written clearly and imaginatively, your readers will get your "message." If you are dissatisfied with your effort, apologizing only compounds the failure.

Your closing paragraph is almost as important to the success of your essay as your opening one; it permits you to round out your essay. You need to exploit this emphatic position to make a last impression on your readers. An effective final paragraph leaves your readers nodding in agreement, shaking their heads in disapproval, or gazing thoughtfully into space. A closing paragraph that elicits no response whatever weakens your total effort and disappoints your readers.

Here are some closing paragraphs; they suggest several techniques for ending your essay.

1. Make a Summarizing Judgment

When the curtain came down, the cast and crew applauded considerably harder than the audience, and in sheer relief. To my knowledge, none of the cast acted together again, and the director has since restricted himself to modern drama. Several of the cast immediately changed their majors and still today the mention of *Hamlet* invokes responses more appropriate to stomach flu or letters from the IRS. (Mary Kramer, p. 86)

The saying of "Oh-oh" should be forbidden by federal statute. It is the most frightening, nerve-shattering locution to come into general usage since Noah Webster quit slopping pigs on his father's farm in Connecticut. It is, in fact, so low-down mean in its usual implications that even the dictionaries won't let it in. I scorn it, and deride it, and let my mind dwell on its opposite—that most beautiful of words . . . (H. Allen Smith, p. 128)

Both Kramer and Smith have firmly stamped their judgments on their materials. For Kramer, the mention of *Hamlet* recalls disaster; for Smith "Oh-oh" is an expression that should be abolished.

2. Build to a Climax

Just before Sever 11 explodes with applause, Professor B. J. Whiting passes through the Emergency Egress. (Anne Fadiman, p. 93)

Inevitably, the alcoholic develops a fatty liver, and his chances of developing cirrhosis, a condition in which liver cells have been replaced by fibrous scar tissue, are at least one in ten. A severely damaged liver cannot adequately manufacture bile, which is necessary for the digestion of fats; as a consequence, the alcoholic often feels weak and suffers from chronic indigestion. This may be made worse by gastritis, which is caused by alcohol irritation of the sensitive linings of the stomach and small intestine. The troubles of a heavy drinker do not end there, and through damage to the central nervous system and hormonal imbalance, alcohol may even cause impotence. (*Time* Magazine, p. 230)

Fadiman's essay has pointed toward this last paragraph from the beginning. The *Time* writer's analysis of the long-term effects of alcohol builds toward what many males would consider to be the worst possible effect.

3. Make Suggestions

Nobody is suggesting that headgear, thicker gloves, computerized records, new federal bureaucrats, or volumes of new rules can ensure that there will never be another death in the ring. Boxers are too powerful and the brain is too fragile to guarantee that. But further changes in regulations are clearly needed to bring professional boxing back a few more steps from the fatal limits of human endurance. (Denise Grady, p. 338)

While recognizing that some of the recommendations for increasing safety in boxing will not assure the boxer's safety, Grady does suggest that changes are needed to protect him.

4. Echo Your Opening Paragraph

After all, think of how our views of the jungle would be enhanced if, as the African mother said in the fable, the lions had learned to write. Besides, if you don't double up in pain before you begin, writing is actually fun. (Robert C. Maynard, p. 295)

Maynard closes his essay by returning to details mentioned in his first paragraph. (His first paragraph was used in discussing opening paragraphs on p. 32.)

5. Ask a Provocative Question

> With that kind of air to breathe, who needs gunsmoke? (Arnold Benson, p. 327)

> But I am afraid the cocktail lounge is here to stay. Where is the politician who would have the courage to stand up like a man and say, "Give us back the old-time saloon"? (Harry Golden, p. 167)

The questions of Benson and Golden are appropriate endings for their essays. Remember that your question, like theirs, must be carefully phrased to match the content and purpose of your essay.

6. Close with an Effective Allusion

> The use of *Ms.* isn't meant to protect either the married or the unmarried woman from social pressure—only to signify a female human being. It's symbolic, and important. There's a lot in a name. (*Ms. Magazine*, p. 261)

> A crypt in this Hilton of Mortality will cost from $2,000–$3,500, which recalls the words of Bumble the beadle to Sowerberry the undertaker as Oliver Twist was being sold by the former to the latter: " 'You'll make your fortune, Mr. Sowerberry,' said the beadle, as he thrust his thumb and forefingers into the proffered snuff-box of the undertaker: which was an ingenious little model of a patent coffin. 'I say you'll make your fortune. . . .' " (Patrick Ryan, p. 136)

An allusion, remember, is a reference to some widely known event, person, or literary work. Closing your essay with an allusion encourages the attentive reader to respect the significance of your thesis. The *Ms. Magazine* editorial writer uses an allusion to Shakespeare to emphasize the importance of *Ms.* as a title:

> What's in a name? that which we call a rose
> By any other name would smell as sweet.
>   (*Romeo and Juliet*, II,ii)

Ryan alludes to the Hilton Hotel chain and lets his final words come from a Charles Dickens character to emphasize the commercial aspects of death.

7. Use a Striking Single-Sentence Paragraph

I came to like even New York. (Thomas Griffith, p. 115)

From the angle of "interfaith," the meeting was a tremendous success. (Harry Golden, p. 75)

Griffith's reluctant confession contrasts with his long paragraphs criticizing New York. Golden's eager affirmation stresses the value of his unusual speaking engagement.

8. Close with a Signaling Word or Phrase

In Isaac Asimov's last paragraph (p. 124) begins *So ends our speculation. . . .* You know he is concluding his essay. Other words or phrases at your disposal include *finally, in conclusion, thus,* and *last.*

Ask yourself these questions after you've reviewed your initial draft.

1. Is my essay unified?
2. Have I achieved coherence?
3. Do I have an effective opening and closing?

If you can answer each question "Yes," then you are ready to prepare a second or working draft.

Here's what Pattacini's working draft looked like:

THE BEACH

My friend, Mario, had a good idea! As we were walking home from class, he suggested that we go to the beach this weekend. The more I thought about it, the more I realized how much I had missed the beach. It had been two and a half months since I last saw the crystal-blue waters and the multitude of people enjoying themselves. Now, once again, I would get to be in my favorite place.

Saturday morning arrived, and I was feeling

great! I could not wait to get to the beach and have some fun. I quickly started packing the towels, the suntan lotion, and the rest of the necessities. As I finished, Mario arrived with the car. We were finally on our way.

~~decided~~ When we reached the beach, the first thing we decided to do was to exercise. We started jogging north for about one mile. We saw several people playing ~~freesbe~~ frisbee. One of these persons was playing ~~freesbe~~ frisbee with his dog. That was really something to watch! On our way back, we saw ~~some~~ other people surfing and others scuba-diving. We also met with some people collecting sea shells. Together, they had collected over one thousand shells. One of these shells was huge. Its founder said that by putting it near the ear, one could hear the ocean.

~~We recollected what~~ From what Mario ~~and I~~ we had seen, ~~and~~ and heard ~~B~~ on our little jogging we real-ized that the beach offered many opportunities to exercise and, at the same time, enjoy a hobby such as shell collecting or scuba diving.

When we finished jogging, we were fairly tired and decided to relax. ~~We layed~~ I lay in the sand and ~~we could feel~~ felt the hot rays of the sun on ~~our~~ my faces. At the same time, the warm, breeze blew fresh-smelling sand onto my feet, making them (tickle). ? <u>ticklish</u> Despite these enjoyable distractions, I ~~was able to~~ noticed the ^infinite^ blue-green ocean. Its salty and cool waters ~~really~~ ^tempted^ me to take a dip. But ~~looked tempting.~~ That day, the ocean was ~~(really)~~ ^a little^ rough. The waves, with their white crests, seemed angry. They ~~constantly~~ kept cresting and rolling ~~crashing against the water~~ causing white bubbles to cover the surface. ^I heard^ A smooth, hissing sound ~~could be heard~~ as the bubbles ~~to~~ quickly disintegrated when they raced on to the beach.

While I had my mind on the white bubbles, ~~something~~ ~~someone really~~ ^I was^ distracted ^by^ ~~the boy that was~~ a gorgeous blonde wearing a red (buy kini) ^bikini^, ~~As I met~~ as she passed by ~~...~~ ~~and I couldn't stop staring~~ we simultaneously greeted each other. ~~As the afternoon went by~~ ^Mario and I^ ~~we~~ saw many beautiful ~~g~~ women that afternoon and Mario and I agreed that these beautiful girls had to be the primary reason we were there.

* ^the beautiful blond was not the only pretty girl there^

C

~~The afternoon flew by like~~

The afternoon flew by and the sun began to set. It was time to head back home. ~~...~~ ~~was feeling a bit tired and would really use a good night's rest~~ On the trip back, I thought about all the things that we had seen and done. ~~...~~

~~Things~~ Finally, I ~~said thought~~ concluded that ~~these things:~~ enjoying nature, relaxing, & exercising, &
working on hobbies, and $\overset{most\ important}{girl-watching}$ ~~were all
the things that~~ made the beach my ideal meeting
place. That's why next week, ~~for~~ Mario and
I ~~would please come~~ $\overset{are\ going}{}$ back.

3
Rewriting

Your working draft should be more unified and coherent than your initial draft, so you'll probably feel somewhat better about it. Probably, but not necessarily. If you have followed all the steps in the writing process, this draft should be a dramatic improvement over your initial one. However, your work is not yet finished. As with your initial draft, you should put your working draft aside for a time. You want to clear your mind, so that when you return to it you'll be able to evaluate your work critically.

Seek some friendly criticism of your working draft. When you return to your working draft, seek the advice of two or three of your friends. Get them to agree to criticize one another's writing. Set up ground rules to govern these reading sessions. One rule might be that the writer is to read the essay aloud twice. During the first reading, the listeners are to make no comments. After the first reading, there should be a couple of minutes of silence before the second reading. During the second reading, the listeners may interrupt at any time to ask what the writer meant, or why he or she used a particular word, or why this point came before that one. After the second reading is completed, discuss the essay's strengths and weaknesses. Focus this discussion on the paragraphs, the sentences, and the diction in the draft.

REVISING YOUR PARAGRAPHS

As you know, a paragraph develops an idea (a topic sentence) while, at the same time, it contributes to the development of a thesis. How long should a paragraph be? A one-sentence paragraph, conceived by a thoughtful writer, may contain enough supporting details to be complete. Such a paragraph, however, should be used sparingly in your essay and must be as specific as possible. The following examples illustrate its use of details.

> Exposed portions of the body, such as the arms, legs, ears, and even portions of the face which are not protected by the outer skin and the airtrap within, could be feathered for warmth in the night. (Isaac Asimov, p. 123)

> I did see one authentic-looking cowboy—lean, weatherbeaten, booted—in a 10-gallon hat, but he was wearing a hearing aid and climbing into a Volkswagen bug in a supermarket parking lot. (Arnold Benson, p. 329)

Of course, if you quote from conversations, you'll probably have some one-sentence paragraphs. Each time the speaker changes, you'll need a new paragraph to differentiate the speakers.

Examine your working draft to see if you have any one-sentence paragraphs. If you do, does each paragraph have adequate supporting details? Or does it differentiate the speakers in a conversation you're reproducing? Or does it provide a transition, or summarize previously developed material? If your answer to the question is "No," then that paragraph needs to be developed.

1. Provide Supporting Details

You develop paragraphs by providing details that support your topic sentence. (A topic sentence, you'll recall, is to a paragraph what the thesis sentence is to an essay.) Making a statement isn't enough; you must develop that statement. Consider these topic sentences:

a. We humans have always been divided about the best way of disposing of ourselves after we have shuffled off this mortal coil. (Patrick Ryan, p. 136)
b. How quickly the alcohol takes effect depends on many factors. (*Time*, p. 229)
c. There is a growing body of evidence that suggests that our brain processes information in at least two major systems. (Dorothy G. Singer and Jerome L. Singer, p. 330)

Certainly these statements seem reasonable. But to "prove," as it were, their validity, their writers went on to produce these adequately developed paragraphs.

a. We humans have always been divided about the best way of disposing of ourselves after we have shuffled off this mortal coil. Egyptians practiced mummification; Romans generally preferred entombment; Vikings launched their late lamented in blazing boats. Hindus burn cast-off bodies on kindling pyres; Muslims bury their departed lying on their right sides facing Mecca; and Parsees expose their dead on 'towers of silence' as provender for vultures. Solomon Islanders have lain those not lost but gone before on coral reefs as food for sharks; other Melanesians have eaten up their time-expired relatives themselves. The Irish hold wakes which threaten to dissolve both mourners and loved ones in alcohol; and the Koryak tribe of northern Siberia make their last farewells by playing cards on the corpse.

Note that the ten specific ways of *disposing of ourselves* move from the familiar to the unfamiliar, from the solemn to the bizarre. There is no doubt that the topic thought controls this paragraph.

b. How quickly the alcohol takes effect depends on many factors. One person may be bombed after a glass, while another stays relatively sober after several. Because alcohol is diluted in the blood, a 200–lb. man can usually tolerate more liquor than a 110–lb. woman. Food also retards absorption of alcohol from the gastrointestinal tract, and a few ounces taken with a meal are less powerful than an equal amount downed an hour before. By the same token, some drinks with food in them—eggnogs made with the eggs, milk and cream, for example—have slightly less wallop than straight drinks. The tomato juice in a Bloody Mary or the orange juice in a screwdriver is not enough to make any appreciable difference.

The second sentence offers little concrete development of the topic thought, but it narrows the topic to a consideration of the factors that hinder drunkenness. The second, third, and fourth sentences give specific details of the effects of alcohol with respect to body weight and food. The final sentence contrasts the use of fruit juices in drinks with the use of more substantial mixes mentioned in the preceding sentence. The rather shapeless topic thought has been given definite form through the use of very specific details—for example, *200–lb. man* and *110–lb. woman*, *eggnogs*, *Bloody Mary*, and *screwdriver*.

c. There is a growing body of evidence that suggests that our brain processes information in at least two major systems.

The image system appears to be associated with the right hemisphere of the brain. This hemisphere seems to be specialized to process visual and auditory imagery, spatial representation, pure melodic thought, fantasy, and the emotional components of consciousness. Imagery allows us to continue to process information when we are not actively looking at or listening to new stimuli. It reproduces the sounds or sights of the past, enriching our thoughts, dreams, or fantasies with a sense of "actuality" or context. As a coding system, imagery operates by what is called "parallel" processing: e.g., we imagine the face of a friend in one instantaneous configuration.

Note that sentence two identifies one of the *two major systems* as the *image system*. The remainder of the paragraph focuses on the kinds of imagery processed in this system.

A final warning concerning paragraph length is appropriate. A handwritten paragraph is deceptive, for it usually looks much longer than it really is. When it is reproduced in type, it will often surprise you by its truncated appearance. To avoid this appearance and to encourage adequate development, remember this general rule: a paragraph usually contains from three to five sentences.

2. *Reinforce the Coherence of Your Paragraph*

No paragraph can hope to be coherent unless its sentences follow logically one after the other according to a definite plan. Even with such order, however, a paragraph can still lack full coherence. There are other devices you can use to reinforce the coherence of your paragraphs. One of them is maintaining a consistent point of view (p. 30). Others include repeating key words; using synonyms, substitutions, and pronouns for key words; and using transitional words and phrases. With regard to transitional words and phrases, consider this paragraph:

In thinking about a course of study at college, it is tempting to suppose that the principal goal is to assimilate as much as you can of the most important writings, the most important theories, the most important bodies of information that humankind has yet produced. This approach typically emphasizes courses that survey the broadest areas of knowledge or the most important list of books. *Now* no one will deny the importance of becoming familiar with the works of great thinkers or broad areas of human knowledge and experience. Such knowledge is not only interesting in itself; it is essential to most forms of intellectual activity, *and* you will absorb a great deal of it while you are here. *But* there are limits to the value of accumulating more and more information. We must all be realistic enough to recognize that you will soon forget many of the facts and theories you have learned—and some of what you do remember will eventually be invalidated by new discoveries. As a result, do not suppose for one moment that being informed about a broad area of human activity and thought is the only goal, *or* even the primary goal, of a liberal education. It is much more important to use your education to help you think more effectively so that you can continue to develop and learn more productively after you graduate. (Derek Bok, p. 334)

Now, and, but, as a result, and *or* are the signposts that, planted in the right places, point your way from one sentence to another and give you the assurance of being guided toward a definite goal.

Following is a list of some of the more familiar transitional words and phrases assembled under logical headings. Make sure the markers you use in your paragraphs express the relationship you intend between and among your sentences.

ADDITION

and
also
again
besides
in addition
moreover
furthermore
beyond that
first (in the first place, second, third. . .)
next
finally

CONTRAST

or
but
yet
nor
however
on the contrary
nevertheless
conversely
instead
rather
in contrast
on the other hand

COMPARISON

by the same token
similarly
likewise
in the same way

ILLUSTRATION

for example
for instance
namely
specifically

REASON

because
for
since

INTENSIFICATION

indeed
in fact
surely

RESTRICTION, QUALIFICA-
TION

if
unless
in case
provided (that)
usually
especially
particularly, in particular
generally, in general
perhaps

CONCESSION

(to opposing viewpoint)
no doubt
doubtless
certainly
of course
to be sure
granted (that)
though, although

TIME

when
occasionally
frequently
meanwhile
in the meantime
then
immediately
at length
eventually
and then

RESULT, SUMMARIZATION

accordingly
as a result
thus
therefore
consequently
in short
in other words
in conclusion
all in all
and so
hence

RETURN

(to writer's viewpoint)
nevertheless
nonetheless
still
even so

PLACE

beyond
next to
nearby
adjacent to
close to
near
opposite
behind

3. *Use Parallel Construction*

Finally, your paragraph may be held together coherently by means of parallel constructions in sentences. When the grammatical structure of consecutive sentences is identical, the paragraph acquires an even greater degree of cohesiveness than it achieves by simply developing a single topic thought.

In the following paragraph, the second, third, fourth, and fifth sentences all share the same pattern (adverb-subject-verb-object) because they are all equally important responses to the initial question, *Is there a solution?* Furthermore, the reiterated *perhaps* emphasizes the tentative nature of each of the responses.

> Is there a solution? *Perhaps* the publishers could get together and jointly run their own "Blackwell's in New York." *Perhaps* a few hundred writers could invest a thousand dollars each . . . but what a nightmare: Imagine a stockholders' meeting at which everyone keeps screaming that his or her book isn't being given adequate display. *Perhaps* a wealthy young man in love with letters would do for bookselling what James Laughlin did for avant-garde publishing some decades ago. *Perhaps* a bookseller both highminded and shrewd could make a go of a first-rate bookshop. (Irving Howe, p. 114)

You're revising the paragraphs of your working draft to make sure that each paragraph is adequately developed and coherent. You're "working" on your draft; that's why its called a *working* draft.

EXERCISE

Identify the topic thought of each of these paragraphs and indicate how it is developed:

1. "Sololá" (p. 102, par. 2)
2. "The Ugliest Word" (p. 147, par. 9)
3. "You're Not What You Think You Are" (p. 172, par. 6)
4. "A Matter of Taste: Chocolate" (p. 106, par. 7)
5. "Grant and Lee: A Study in Contrasts" (p. 181, par. 12)

How many transitional devices are used in each of the following paragraphs? Are they used effectively? What changes, if any, would you make?

1. "A View of the Review" (p. 210, par. 12)
2. "What I Have Lived For" (p. 196, par. 2)
3. "Anatomy of a Martian" (p. 122, par. 8)
4. "Kicking Drugs: A Very Personal Story" (p. 80, par. 3)

Examine the following paragraphs for their effectiveness in using repetition, synonyms and substitutions, or pronouns:

1. "Library of Congress: Many Books, But Not All Books" (p. 201, par. 3)

2. "In Bed" (p. 274, par. 4)
3. "A View of the Review" (p. 210, par. 12)
4. "In Horror Movies, Some Things Are Sacred" (p. 325, par. 4)

REVISING YOUR SENTENCES

Your ideas most commonly come, not as separate concepts (frost—azaleas—death), but as relationships between concepts (The frost killed the azaleas). In other words, a definite connection is established between persons or things, on the one hand, and actions (dying, running, falling, laughing) or states of being (existing, having, containing, sitting), on the other. Grammatically speaking, the persons or things form the *subject* (that about which something is said); the actions or states of being form the *predicate* (that which says something about the subject).

Sometimes subjects or predicates are missing from sentences as written or spoken, but they are nevertheless clearly implied. In such cases true sentences result because the thought is complete:

Listen! = You listen!
Louise? = Is that you, Louise?
Now? = Shall I begin now?

The higher up, the closer to paradise; the nearer the top of the tower, the nearer, my God, to Thee. (Patrick Ryan, p. 136)

is the same as

The higher up *one goes*, the closer to paradise *one gets*; the nearer *one is* to the top of the tower, the nearer *one comes*, my God, to Thee.

You may use such sentences frequently in both conversation and writing. However, practiced writers often go further and use genuine sentence fragments—mere parts of sentences, lacking subject or predicate and, *in themselves*, not even expressing complete thoughts. Usually, however, the context supplies the meaning the fragment lacks:

1. Dancing in the street. A book I read not long ago on architecture and modern cities had a whole chapter on the widespread

absence these days of dancing in the street. (Franklin Daugherty, p. 109)

2. All rather unlikely, all tokens of fantasy? Probably so. (Irving Howe, p. 140)

3. The word is *End.* With a capital "E." (H. Allen Smith, p. 146)

These writers know what they are doing. But the following writer has no such excuse:

> They spent the evening at the movies. Because there was no flight out until midnight.

The words to the right of the period constitute a fragment that has no justifiable reason for standing by itself. In the preceding examples the fragments are reasonably clear by virtue of their contexts. In the last example there is no such connection. Consequently, the error has to be eliminated. The easiest way of doing so is to join the fragment to the sentence and thus make one complete thought:

> They spent the evening at the movies because there was no flight out until midnight.

As you revise the sentences in your working draft, make sure that you have no sentence fragments. Most fragments in your writing are the result of carelessness, not intention, and are therefore inexcusable. (Common sentence errors are illustrated and discussed on pp. 365–71.)

1. Check the Length of Your Sentences

The length of your sentences is determined by your persona and your audience. Harry Golden's chatty and humorous narrative about an accident on the lecture circuit (p. 74) uses relatively short sentences to create its humorous effect, while in Thomas Griffith's "New York" (p. 112) the sentences are as suitably spacious as the vistas they describe.

How long should your sentences be? It is impossible to formulate an exact rule. Some modern stylists say you should limit your sentences to between twelve and eighteen words. Others would make no such limitation. Thus, only one very general rule about sentence length is derivable from the many subjects, purposes, attitudes, and audiences available to you. But there is no more important rule of good writing than this: *in every sentence make every word count.* A long sentence is not too long if it contains no superfluous words or ideas. A short sentence is not too short if it lacks no essential words or ideas.

2. Include a Variety of Sentence Types

Now is the time to raise a warning flag about the monotony and simple-mindedness of the so-called "primer style." Suppose, for instance, that the first paragraph of a narrative began:

> I woke up suddenly. I felt very wide awake. I pulled the light cord. I sat straight up in bed.

Much more of this kind of thing would be intolerable. Yet it is not at all uncommon for adults to write in this childish fashion all the time. Don't be one of them. One way to avoid the stylistic horror of "primer style" is to use compound elements to achieve variety.

a. Use Compound Predicates   A predicate makes a statement about the subject of the sentence. Stewart Alsop's first paragraph actually reads:

> I *woke up* suddenly, *feeling* very wide awake, *pulled* the light cord, and *sat* straight up in bed. (p. 86)

Alsop uses a compound predicate; he gathers the four statements about the subject into one sentence. This practice, too, can become tiresome if overindulged, but, as the Alsop sentence illustrates, four ideas can gain notably in compactness and vigor when they are gathered together in one sentence under one subject. In the following example of compound predicates, Joan Didion links ten predicates to a single subject.

> I fought migraine then, ignored the warnings it sent, went to school and later to work in spite of it, sat through lectures in Middle English and presentations to advertisers with involuntary tears running down the right side of my face, threw up in washrooms, stumbled home by instinct, emptied ice trays onto my bed and tried to freeze the pain in my right temple, wished only for a neurosurgeon who would do a lobotomy on house call, and cursed my imagination. (p. 273)

b. Use Compound Subjects   Variety and strength also result when the compounding is reversed, and several subjects are made to govern a single predicate:

> Children in famine, victims tortured by oppressors, helpless old people a hated burden to their sons, and the whole world of loneliness, poverty, and pain make a mockery of what human life should be. (Bertrand Russell, p. 197)

c. Subordinate Less Important Ideas   Subordination indicates that one idea is less important than another. Consider these two sentences:

> The phonograph provided entertainment in countless homes in the early part of the century. Its feeble and shallow sound offered no more than a faint suggestion of musical reality.

Both ideas are informative, but is each of equal importance? Hans Fantel answers "No." He subordinates the first idea by writing:

> Though the phonograph provided entertainment in countless homes in the early part of the century, its feeble and shallow sound offered no more than a faint suggestion of musical reality. (p. 251)

If you have two or more ideas and you wish to subordinate one of them, think carefully about which idea you wish to stress. That main idea goes in the main clause.

Also, make sure the subordinating conjunction you use expresses the proper relationship between the ideas. Use *while* for time; *where* for place; *although* for concession. Make these subordinating conjunctions a part of your writing vocabulary: *after, although, as, because, before, if, once, rather than, since, that, though, unless, until, when, whenever, where, wherever,* and *while.*

d. Combine Independent Clauses   Bonnie Angelo wanted to show that women have no place in *the good ole boy's world.* She could have written:

> The good ole boy excludes women from his social gatherings. Some social events include men and their wives. The men stay at one end of the room. The wives stay at the other.

Instead, she combines sentences and ends up with two independent clauses and two dependent constructions.

> Women are outsiders; when social events are unavoidably
> mixed, the good ole boys cluster together at one end of the
> room, leaving wives at the other. (p. 278)

As you rewrite, make sure you have a variety of sentence types
and structures in your essay. Variety cannot be sought directly. If
it is, chances are that your resulting essay will be burdened with
an overabundance of "elegant variants," inverted sentences, shifts
in point of view, and other evidence of a relentless effort to be
"different." If, instead, you concentrate on setting down your
thoughts in the most appropriate constructions from the standpoint of logic and emphasis, you will find that you have produced
variety automatically. Some sentences will be long, others short;
some simple, others compound and complex. In a word, your essay will be spared the primer-style blight on the one hand, and
the overblown-rhetoric blight on the other. Your sentences will
be crisp.

3. Eliminate All Deadwood

One way of making sure that every word in a sentence counts
is to eliminate all instances of "deadwood"—words or ideas that
complicate, retard, or smother meaning and exasperate even the
most patient reader. Deadwood appears when you preface your
idea or specific noun or verb with some vague phrase or modifier.
The technique expands a sentence without making it more precise or vivid. Certain set phrases provide ready material for deadwood. Here are some of the more prevalent ones:

the above reasons	it is noted that
am of the opinion that	I want to say that
be that as it may	last but not least
couldn't care less	my intention is
down through the ages	needless to say
due to the fact that	needs no introduction
few and far between	point in time
first and foremost	reference is made to
in a very real sense	slowly but surely
in the final analysis	to make a long story short
in the near future	means different things to different
in view of the fact that	people

Make sure that none of your sentences contains one or more of these deadening phrases. Remember, be economical in your use of words in your sentences. Eliminate all unnecessary verbiage. Be thrifty with words—but not miserly.

4. Check for Indefinite *This's*

Are there any sentences in your draft that begin with the word *this?* If there are, you need to examine them carefully because beginning a sentence with an indefinite *this* usually produces a vague idea.

a. I feel that the main reason for the ban on selling alcohol on Sunday is religion. This is made obvious by the fact that Florida begins selling alcohol at 1:00 p.m. on Sunday afternoon. (From a student essay)

b. Sometimes when a couple are engaged for only a short time, they get married and find that they did not know each other very well when they were engaged. This is what causes the majority of the divorces in this country. (From a student essay)

c. Male web-spinning spiders have a tougher life than any other males in the animal kingdom. This is because the female web-spinning spiders have very poor eyesight. (James Thurber, p. 152)

As a demonstrative pronoun, *this* is supposed to point to something specific. Thurber's sentence that begins with *this* is logically connected to his preceding one. His use of *because* keeps the sentence from being vague. The student writers have not made that logical connection. Neither student writer's *this* points to anything specific. If you have a sentence that begins with *this,* put a definite noun after *this,* or at least be sure that the antecedent reference is clear, as Thurber's is. If you can't put a noun there, rewrite the sentence.

EXERCISE

Analyze the sentences in Ronald Knox's "Pharisee and Publican" (pp. 168–69) on the basis of sentence variety (length, grammatical structure). Are there any fragments? How many words are in the longest sentence? The shortest? Which sentences have compound elements?

STRENGTHENING YOUR DICTION

Experienced writers have learned the power of words; they know that one carelessly chosen word or phrase may weaken their essays and confuse their readers. They know that words convey an essay's meaning and specify its audience. Consequently, they attempt to follow Jonathan Swift's advice to a young clergyman: "Proper words in proper places, make the true definition of a style." As you rewrite your working draft, keep Swift's advice in mind.

Usually, you choose words haphazardly; you rely on your limited conversational vocabulary. These words have served you in the past, but you may not realize that they carry only rather general meanings. You may not yet have learned that the first word that comes to mind may not express your *precise* meaning. You should check your reading vocabulary for more exact words. You recognize far more words when you read than you employ in conversation. Use this larger reservoir when you examine the words you've written. The more words at your command, the greater attention you can pay to the various shades of meaning that words have. Always select a word or phrase that is precise, vivid, and simple.

1. Use Precise Words

Denotation refers to the explicit meaning of a particular word; that is, the relationship between a certain combination of letters and that combination's assigned meaning. Denotative meanings are arbitrarily assigned to combinations of letters and dutifully recorded in dictionaries.

Often you determine a word's denotation by the context in which you use it. Consider the word *spot*. Taken out of context, it communicates virtually nothing. But now consider *spot* in each of these contexts:

a. I'll remove the *spot* when I clean the coat.
b. The *spot* he came from was isolated by mountains.
c. Now, he's on the *spot*.
d. Have you seen the *spot* for Pepsi?
e. She holds that *spot* on the committee.
f. Immediately following a trained dog act is a tough *spot* to be in.
g. My history professor has a *spot* on his left cheek-bone.

h. Among the fish we caught was one *spot.*
i. The *spot* was focused on the actor's head.
j. May I have a *spot* of tea?
k. That was the one *spot* on an otherwise admirable character.

So, contexts help clarify meanings, but a word that has a variety of meanings can usually be replaced by a more precise word or phrase. If you can replace *spot* with another word or words in each of the above sentences, almost every replacement will be more precise. Try it. For example, "I'll remove the *bloodstain* when I clean the coat."

One of the major weaknesses in student writing is the use of general words rather than specific ones. General words are often called *abstractions,* for they tend "to draw away" from the item to which they refer; *specific words* refer to what can be grasped by the senses. General words merely suggest a number of traits or qualities; specific words single out a particular trait or quality. For example, *color* is a general word, whereas *scarlet* is far more specific; *fruit* is general, *kumquat* specific.

Too many general words in your sentences make a vague, rather than vivid, impression on your audience. Consider these sentences:

a. The person was wearing old clothes.
b. He has a pet dog.

Person, clothes, he, and *dog* are fairly general words. Each should be replaced with a more specific one. For example,

a. The bearded secretary was wearing a tattered green jacket, out-of-style baggy pants, and scuffed shoes.
b. Dan McDonald has a lovable but dumb German shepherd named Rex.

Note that the replacements have specific denotations that can be grasped by the senses. You should choose such words whenever possible, for the specific word will almost always be the proper one. Whenever possible, use specific names, dates, addresses, amounts, dimensions, distances, titles, and so on.

You have two invaluable resources to aid in your search for the proper word—a dictionary and a thesaurus. As a careful writer you should use a dictionary to check a word's meaning, and, if your dictionary records them, you will discover examples of how other writers have used the word. Use your thesaurus as well (a collection of synonyms and antonyms) to determine shades of meaning among words having similar denotations.

2. *Be Aware of Connotations*

Many words have, in addition to an explicit meaning, an implied significance—a *connotation*. Connotation refers to the emotional associations accompanying a word. For example, the denotation of "mother-in-law" is obvious, but the word has attracted the connotation of a meddling, possessive intruder.

Sometimes connotations are purely personal. The word *marshmallow*, for instance, may forever be tainted for you by the time when, as a child, you ate too many toasted marshmallows and got sick. But *marshmallow* has no such unpleasant associations for most people; not everyone's stomach, like yours, turns over at the mere mention of the word. Or consider *saloon*. For most patrons of saloons, as for Harry Golden (p. 166), the word evokes images of lively and satisfying fellowship. But for a recovering alcoholic, it conjures up nightmares of wasted hours and money, of lost dignity, of a lack of self-worth.

Obviously, the connotations that will prove useful to you as a writer cannot be of the unique or private kind that *marshallow* has for you or *saloon* has for an alcoholic. However, English has many thousands of words rich in suggestive meanings familiar to every educated reader, and these are the words you should draw on to give your writing life and power. *Horse,* for example, is a perfectly good word, and there are times when this general term is the proper one to use (as in the sentence, "I could see what appeared to be a horse galloping in the distance"). But whenever possible say *steed* or *charger* or *stallion* or *palfrey* or *bronco* or *nag* or *thoroughbred*—whatever the particular context calls for. Each of these words, besides having its specific denotation, releases a particular set of connotations into the subconscious mind of everyone who encounters it in print or hears it spoken. (You are not likely to associate a plumed and armored knight with a *bronco,* nor a lady riding sidesaddle on a *nag*. A knight rides a *steed* or a *charger;* a lady, a *palfrey*.) By incorporating such words, your writing not only gains in precision, but it also takes on the added dimensions of color and suggestiveness.

3. *Strive for Vividness*

If it were possible to discuss two or more elements of effective diction simultaneously, precision and vividness would be considered together. They are closely related, for precise diction usually creates vivid writing. The elements of precision—context, denotation, and distinctness—are also the elements of vividness. To these elements must be added the importance of verbs and figurative language. Most often, vividness is achieved by using *active verbs* and *fresh, figurative language.*

a. Use Active Verbs

Learn to appreciate the energy of verbs; recognize that they move, vibrate, act, explode. In particular, concentrate on using the active voice whenever you can, and avoid the weaker passive voice. The active voice stresses the doer of the action; the passive voice, the receiver.

> *Active:* I *signed* the contract.

> *Passive:* The contract *was signed* by me.

The first sentence emphasizes who signed the contract by making *I* the subject. The second sentence emphasizes the receiver of the action of signing by making *contract* the subject. Both sentences are grammatically correct, but the first is more vigorous and more compact than the second, and thus better able to contribute life to the essay.

If overused, the passive voice can seriously weaken an essay's vitality. It can also make it difficult to keep your point of view consistent:

> As we entered the building, an alarm was heard.

The sudden shift from active voice in the first part of the sentence to passive voice in the second part, and from first person to third, creates considerable confusion. Who heard the alarm—*we,* or someone else? If an explanatory phrase is added:

> As we entered the building, an alarm was heard by us.

the result is an even more clumsy and lifeless sentence than the original. However, by making the second verb active, both clarity and energy are guaranteed:

> As we entered the building, we heard an alarm.

Examine your draft to see if you have any uses of the passive voice. Keep in mind that you should use the active voice whenever possible.

b. Create Fresh, Figurative Language

Figurative language also contributes to your essay's vividness. An unexpected but appropriate comparison, a perceptive analogy, or a striking allusion delights your audience and captures their interest. Furthermore, by using these imaginative techniques, you can clarify an obscure point or emphasize an important one while giving color to the writing.

Simile and Metaphor   The basic element of figurative language is a comparison of two essentially different things. The comparison may be made either directly (using words such as *like, as,* or *so*) or indirectly (using no such words). When Arnold Benson writes (p. 328), *Shining like a star in the finite firmament of my mind was the name Santa Fe,* he is directly comparing the name of the capital of New Mexico to a star. Santa Fe is like a star; this is a simile. On the other hand, when Aldoux Huxley writes (p. 101), *The market at Sololá was a walking museum of fancy dress,* he is indirectly comparing an Indian marketplace and a museum. Sololá's market *is* a museum; this is a metaphor.

As a developing writer, you may be depending on stale figurative language. You need to check your working draft to see if you have used any trite metaphors and similes—clichéd comparisons that were once fresh and vivid but are now ready for retirement. If you discover a worn-out metaphor or simile, drop it and create a fresh one to replace it.

Analogy   Another type of comparison, in addition to metaphor and simile, is *analogy.* Analogy refers to an extended comparison between items that are similar in some respects but different in others. For example, throughout his essay James Thurber (p. 150) keeps calling attention to the similarities that exist between the courting habits of certain animal species and those of *Homo sapiens.* In "I Didn't Stop in Baltimore" (p. 86), Stewart Alsop compares dying to a train ride. If you can discover an effective analogy, it will add vividness to your essay. You may use analogy to explain, persuade, and emphasize, as well as to add color to your writing.

Allusion   Allusion, you recall, is another figure of speech that refers to some person or event, either historical or fictional, that has dramatic and vivid connotations. You remember Mary Kramer's thesis statement when she referred to *a Grand Guignol farce.* Thomas Griffith writes that the streets of New York need *a new Dante to bring hell up to date.* Readers who recognize this allusion immediately think of the poetic power of the *Inferno* section of *The Divine Comedy.* Allusion can be a particularly effective device for securing both vividness and brevity. An appropriate reference not only invites the readers' active involvement but also reduces the number of words you need to make your point.

A word of warning needs to accompany this discussion of allusions. You must know your audience; you must choose allusions that, if not immediately recognizable, are readily accessible. Kramer assumes that her readers will recognize her allusion or that they are curious enough to look it up. Griffith's allusion should be familiar to most educated people. If your audience is composed of farmers, you should be careful when using allusions drawn from sculpture, or if your audience is primarily musicians, you should be careful when using allusions from sports.

EXERCISE

Consider the following examples of trite figurative language. First decide whether the example is a metaphor or simile. Then, identify the items being compared and determine the literal meaning of the statement. Finally, write a new, fresher metaphor or simile that retains the meaning.

Descriptions of Persons

1. Debbie has teeth like pearls.
2. Sam is an ugly duckling.
3. Molly is as pretty as a picture.
4. Becky is as brown as a berry.
5. Nick is a chip off the old block.

Descriptions of Character

1. Dan is a wolf in sheep's clothing.
2. Tom is as mad as a hatter.
3. Jim is as sly as a fox.

4. Sarah is rotten to the core.
5. Sally is as cool as a cucumber.

Life and Its Meaning

1. All the world's a stage.
2. Life is a bed of roses.
3. Money is the root of all evil.
4. Life is a journey from the cradle to the grave.
5. Pat, Sally, and Steve form the eternal triangle.

Here are some items that could be used as allusions. Decide what each means and connotes, and then write a sentence in which an allusion to it replaces a statement of meaning and connotation.

1. Archie Bunker   4. Li'l Abner
2. Charlie Brown   5. Pete Rose
3. Mr. T   6. Gloria Steinem

Simplicity   *Simplicity* is the final test for determining the proper word or phrase. Your diction will be effective if you make use of simple expression—unadorned, uncomplicated, and unpretentious. Complexity, the enemy of simplicity, creeps in when you neglect to check your work for jargon, euphemisms, and redundancy.

Jargon   *Jargon* may refer to three types of language: meaningless language or gibberish (the babbling of an infant); the technical language of a discipline or group (sociology, psychology, music, sports, ballet, and so on); inflated language characterized by scientific-sounding qualifications, multiple words when one word will do; and pretentious substitutions.

An example of jargon as the language of a particular discipline occurs in John Simon's essay about ballet (p. 221). He expects his audience to understand him when he writes *The danseur noble at the height of an entrechat or jeté . . .* and *Even a simple pas de bourrée. . . .* His use of jargon is appropriate for it contributes to, rather than distracts from, his point.

Here is the first sentence of a sociologist's essay: "The contention here is that the conditions of American sport constitute a fundamental obstacle to the achievement of women's equality in American society." Stripped of its jargon, the sentence reads "The conditions of American sport hinder women from achieving social equality." Check your sentences for such pretentiousness.

Euphemisms and Redundancy   *Euphemisms* and *redundancy* are the other nuisances that complicate diction. A euphemism substitutes a genteel, inoffensive word or phrase for what is thought to be a coarse or offensive expression. It is objectionable whenever it replaces candor with prudishness. Euphemisms abound in areas considered embarrassing, such as death, bodily functions, and sex. For example, *died* is replaced by *passed away, been called home, entered into eternal reward,* and so on. Euphemisms also appear whenever a writer attempts to sound learned or dignified. In this case, common words such as *look, drink,* and *garbage collector* are replaced by *peruse, liquid refreshment,* and *sanitation engineer. Redundancy* refers to needless repetition, saying the same thing in different words without achieving either emphasis or clarity. When an essayist writes, "the contemporary modern scene today" or "in my own personal opinion," the point has been made three times in each case.

Always review your draft to discover and eliminate jargon, euphemisms, and redundancy.

Here's what Pattacini's reviewed and revised draft looks like.

PLEASANT SENSATIONS
~~THE BEACH~~   A

My friend, Mario, had a good idea! As we
were walking home from ∧ class, he suggested that
                         biology
we go to the beach this weekend. The more I
thought about it, the more I realized how much
I had missed the beach. It had been two and
a half months since I last saw the crystal-blue
waters and the multitude of people enjoying
themselves. Now, once again, I would get to
be in my favorite place.

Saturday morning arrived, and I was feeling
great ≠ I could not wait to get to the beach and
have some fun. I quickly started packing the
                              the ice-chest
towels, the suntan lotion, ∧ and the rest of the

necessities. As I finished, Mario arrived with ~~his~~ in his Toyota.
~~car.~~ We were ~~finally~~ on our way.

decided When we reached the beach, the first thing we decided to do was to exercise. We ~~started~~ jogged
~~jogging~~ north for about one mile. As we jogged We saw
frisbee well tanned
several people playing ~~freesbe~~. One ~~of these~~
man of about 50 frisbee Labrador retriver
~~persons~~ was playing ~~freesbe~~ with ~~his dog~~.
The frisbee sailed across the beach and the dog leaped up
~~That was really something to watch.~~ On our to catch it.
some If the frisbee
way back, we saw ~~surfing~~ people surfing went into
an elderly the water
and others scuba-diving. We also met ~~with some~~ the Lab
couple who were swam for
~~people~~ collecting sea shells. Together, they had it.

collected over one thousand shells. One of these
finder it was a conch.
shells was huge. Its ~~founder~~ said that ~~by putting~~
She told me to put it up to my ear. I heard what sounded like
~~the ocean~~. the ocean.

From what and heard on our little jogging
~~Having realized what~~ we had seen, ~~we~~ we real- adventure

ized that the beach offered many opportunities
to exercise and, at the same time, one can enjoy a hobby
such as shell collecting or scuba diving.

When we finished jogging, we were fairly
tired and decided to relax. We layed in the
sand and we ~~could feel~~ the hot rays of the
sun on our faces. At the same time, the
warm, breeze blew sand onto my feet, making
them (tickle). ? ticklish Despite these enjoyable
infinite
distractions, I was able to notice the blue-
green ocean. Its salty and cool waters really
looked tempting. That day, the ocean was
a little
(really) rough. The waves, with their white

crests, seemed angry. They constantly kept crashing against the water, causing white bubbles to cover the surface. A smooth, hissing sound could be heard as the bubbles ~~&~~ quickly disintegrated.

While I had my mind on the white bubbles, ~~something~~ someone really distracted me. It was a gorgeous blonde wearing a red (~~buykini~~) bikini. ~~As I look~~ as She passed by ~~&~~ ~~this~~ ~~was totally appropriate~~ we simultaneously gre_ated_ ee each other. ~~As the afternoon wore on~~

* We saw many beautiful ~~&~~ women that afternoon and Mario and I agreed that these beautiful girls had to be the primary reason we were there.

the beautiful blond was not the only pretty girl there

~~The afternoon flew by~~

The afternoon flew by and the sun began to set. It was time to head back home. ~~We were~~ ~~was feeling a bit tired after and would really use a good night's rest~~ On the trip back, I thought about all the things that we had seen and done. ~~I wondered about these things~~ Finally, I ~~said~~ ~~thought~~ concluded that these things: enjoying nature, relaxing, ~~&~~ exercising, ~~&~~ working on hobbies, and girl-watching ~~were all~~ the things that made the beach my ideal meeting place. That's why next week, ~~then~~ Mario and I would ~~rather~~ come back.

most importantly

65

PROOFREADING

After you have written your next draft, you're ready for the final step: proofreading your essay. If you follow two guidelines, you can be fairly confident of your final draft.

1. Read it Aloud

Have a friend or family member read your essay aloud to you or read it aloud yourself to another person, including your essay's title. Do the ideas move smoothly? Is there any point that sounds unclear or awkward? Do you hear any harsh expressions? Sometimes you'll hear something that grates on your ears. If so, the problem can usually be solved by changing a word or two.

2. Read Forward and Backward

Take a ruler or piece of paper and place it under each sentence as you read it both forward and backward. This technique will help you concentrate on your syntax and diction. As you read the sentence from left to right, ask yourself these questions: Is this sentence punctuated accurately? Do I need a semicolon or a comma somewhere? Have I chosen the most effective words? Is there a title in this sentence that should be underscored to indicate italics? Does the sentence communicate my idea? When you read each sentence from right to left, your focus is on spelling because the word order won't make any sense. If you're not sure about spelling, look the words up.

You may think this process—prewriting, writing, rewriting—is too complex. But if you genuinely wish to improve your writing, you will if you follow this process. In fact, you may discover that writing is not as difficult as you had thought. Furthermore, you may come to agree with Robert C. Maynard (p. 297): *Besides, if you don't double up in pain before you begin, writing is actually fun.*

Here's Paul Pattacini's final, proofread and typed draft.

PLEASANT SENSATIONS

Paul Pattacini

Paul Pattacini: student. Pattacini was born in Argentina in 1966. He graduated from Kenwood High School in Chicago, Illinois. He is presently majoring in biology. Pattacini's essay is based on Suggestions for Writing 1 on p. 111.

My friend, Mario, had a great idea! As we were walking home from biology class, he suggested that we go to the beach on the weekend. The more I thought about it, the more I realized how much I had missed the beach. It had been two-and-a-half months since I last saw the crystal-blue waters and the multitude of people enjoying themselves. Now, once again, I would get to be in my favorite place.

Saturday morning arrived, and I was feeling great. I could hardly wait to get to the beach and have some fun. I quickly started packing the towels, the suntan lotion, the ice-chest, and the rest of the necessities. As I finished, Mario arrived in his Toyota. We were on our way.

When we reached the beach, the first thing we decided to do was exercise. We jogged north for about one mile. As we jogged, we saw several people playing frisbee. One well-tanned man of about 50 was playing frisbee with his Labrador retriever. The frisbee sailed across the beach, and the dog leaped to catch it. If the frisbee went into the water, the Lab swam after it.

On our way back, we saw some people surfing and others scuba diving. We also met an elderly couple who were collecting seashells. Together, they had collected over 1,000 shells. One of these shells was huge. Its finder said it was a conch. She told me to put it up to my ear; I heard what sounded like the ocean. From what Mario and I had seen and heard on our little jog, we realized that the beach offered opportunities to exercise and, at the same time, enjoy a hobby such as shell-collecting or scuba diving.

When we finished jogging, we were fairly tired and decided to relax. I lay in the sand and felt the sun's hot rays on my face. At the same time, the warm, fresh-smelling breeze blew sand onto my feet, making them tickle. Despite these enjoyable distractions, I noticed the infinite, blue-green ocean. Its salty and cool waters tempted me to take a dip. But that day, the ocean was a little rough. The waves, with their white crests, seemed angry. They kept cresting and rolling causing white bubbles to cover the surface. I heard a smooth, hissing sound as the bubbles quickly disintegrated when they raced onto the beach.

While I had my mind on the white bubbles, I was distracted by a gorgeous blonde wearing a red bikini. We simultaneously greeted each other as she passed by. The beautiful blonde was not the only pretty girl there. Mario and I saw many more beautiful women that afternoon. And we agreed that those beautiful girls had to be the primary reason we were there.

The afternoon flew by and the sun began to set. It was time to head back home. On the return trip, I thought about all the things we had seen and done. Finally, I concluded that enjoying nature, relaxing, exercising, working on hobbies, and, most important, girl-watching, made the beach my ideal meeting place. That's why next week, Mario and I are going back.

PART TWO

The Modes of Development

4
NARRATION

You may think of narration as being short stories or novels, and you are right. But when you tell your best friend what you did last weekend, you are using narration. When you tell your grandfather what happened during your first term of college, you are using narration. You use narration to answer the question, "What happened?"

When Harry Golden writes, *I do not want to lose any speaking assignments and so I promise that this will never happen again, but I have to tell you of a terrible tragedy on one of my speaking engagements last year in a South Carolina city,* you know he is going to tell you what happened. Furthermore, you know when and where the event happened and why this event was significant.

1. Determine the Significance of Your Narrative

Why are you telling what happened on this particular occasion? As you look over your prewriting notes, you are searching for a thesis that will bind the various events together, a unifying idea that will assure your audience that the narrative is worth reading. Furthermore, your thesis will aid you in deciding which events to include in your narrative and which to omit. You want to be sure what your thesis is before you prepare your initial draft. Harry Golden's thesis statement is the second half of the sentence quoted above. The first half of the sentence hints at why this occasion was significant.

2. Choose an Appropriate Point of View

Decide whether to tell what happened from a first-person point of view or from a third-person point of view. You usually choose first person when the events happen to you; third person when

you assume the role of an observer rather than a direct participant. Harry Golden tells what happened to him—first person; Tom
Perez (p. 76) tells about *The fiercest battle ever waged against
Gulf Coast humidity . . . in 1916*—third person. Mary Kramer
uses both points of view as she relates what happened during a
disastrous collegiate production of *Hamlet* (p. 82). When she relates her experience (1–3), she uses first person. For the most part,
she uses third person as she tells what happened during casting,
rehearsals, and performance.

3. Establish Your Narrative's Beginning Point

You may opt to begin at an indefinite point, e.g., "a few years
ago," or "before I became old enough to know better." You may
choose to begin on a relatively specific date, as Tom Perez does
when he begins in 1916. Or you may elect to be very precise, as
Anne Fadiman does on p. 90 when she writes: *At 12:06 p.m.,
Wednesday, April 30, 1975. . . .* Whether you choose to be somewhat indefinite or very specific, you need to establish a beginning
for your narrative.

4. Present the Events in Chronological Order

Your narrative will flow smoothly when the events you include
are carefully arranged. You observe strict chronological order when
the events are presented in the order in which they happened, as
Tom Perez presents his. Or you may violate precise chronology
by using a flashback telling of an event that occurred earlier. Harry
Golden and William Burroughs (p. 79) use flashbacks for effect; if
you use a flashback, be sure you have a valid reason.

As you organize the events of your narrative, keep in mind that
a story usually has a beginning, a middle, and an end. It is in the
middle of your narrative that you must use transitional markers
to keep the reader aware of where you are in time. Beware of the
juvenile style of "and then he . . . and next he . . . and he. . . ."
Certainly, *then* and *and* are acceptable transitional markers. But
use them only when you wish to present a series of brief events
rapidly. Stewart Alsop uses *then* six times in paragraph 9 (p. 87).
He wants to mention his medical complications and get on with
his narrative. Instead of "and then," use more precise markers.
Tom Perez moves you through the spring and summer of 1916
with these phrases: *In the spring of 1916, All that spring and well*

of 1916 with these phrases: *In the spring of 1916, All that spring and well into the summer, Later that summer, In those final few minutes, Five minutes later,* and *After the hurricane passed.* Notice how these phrases not only mark the passage of time but also give you a chance to experience that movement through time.

In addition to precise markers, consider using dialogue to move your narrative along. Perez uses this technique in paragraphs 5–7. William Burroughs incorporates dialogue into a flashback as drug addicts bemoan their withdrawal symptoms. These uses of dialogue keep the narrative flowing.

5. Include Only Those Events That Contribute to Your Thesis

Harry Golden's speaking engagement lasted only about an hour. The primary event of that hour was the unexpected appearance of the pint of whiskey. That event helped establish the success of the gathering. William Burroughs' narrative covers a general time-span of some fifteen years and a specific time-span of ten days. He is careful to select from the myriad events of those ten days only those that support and clarify his purpose—to tell about his kicking drugs. Remember that every event you include should reinforce your purpose. Ask yourself, "Am I selecting only events that give this narration significance?"

6. Include Specific Details

These details contribute to your essay's overall purpose and must be chosen with care. Harry Golden mentions the name of the book he was reviewing, *The Mature Mind*, because the title of the book contrasts with his and the audience's behavior. That detail is important. William Burroughs' first paragraph is filled with specific details about drug cures. Every detail that you mention helps clarify your purpose. Ask yourself, "Am I omitting any details that would indicate why this event is worth relating?"

7. Limit Your Comments on the Significance of What Happened

The significance of your narrative emerges from the choices you have made. You need not point out the significance of this or that if you have chosen carefully. But because your narrative has importance, you may wish to offer a few brief generalities by way of conclusion. Harry Golden's last paragraph, *From the angle of "interfaith," the meeting was a tremendous success,* catches the spirit of his *terrible tragedy.* Mary Kramer's last paragraph emphasizes the short- and long-term aversion to *Hamlet* felt by those who had anything to do with that production. Stewart Alsop devotes two of his last three paragraphs to *certain conclusions.*

IT'S THE SPIRIT THAT COUNTS

Harry Golden

Harry Golden: author, editor, and publisher. Golden was born in New York City in 1903 and attended City College of New York 1919–1922. In 1942 he founded The Carolina Israelite, *a newspaper distinguished by its advocacy of tolerance among religions and races. Golden's books include* Only in America, Mr. Kennedy and the Negroes, *and* The Greatest Jewish City in the World. *This essay is from* Only in America *(1958). Golden died in 1981.*

Why is the title deliberately ambiguous?

What makes this essay more than just an entertaining little narrative?

1   I do not want to lose any speaking assignments and so I promise that this will never happen again, but I have to tell you of a terrible tragedy on one of my speaking engagements last year in a South Carolina city.

2   It was a small literary group, and I had been asked to review a book. I was introduced, and they provided me with a table and a chair. I carry a zipper brief case for my papers, etc. Since I was reviewing a book, I wanted to take out a copy of the volume, and keep it in front of me as I spoke. Everything was quiet. I sat there, and took my brief case and zipped open the zipper, when lo and behold a pint bottle of whiskey pops out. I had forgotten all about it.

3   Earlier in the week I had developed a very dry throat and someone suggested that I try whiskey, and I had forgotten all about it. The bottle actually bounced on that mahogany table, and you have no idea the noise it made in that schoolroom. I made a dive for it just as it was ready to fall on the concrete floor and luckily I caught it.

4   The audience meanwhile was in hysterics. Men and women were rolling in the aisles laughing and some of the women were running out toward the ladies' room. Meanwhile I had sort of collected myself, put the book out, and the bottle back in the zipper case, and I sat there, trying to be as nonchalant

as possible. I went on with my lecture telling the folks about Professor Harry Overstreet and *The Mature Mind*, but it was no go. Every few minutes someone would burst out laughing; then everybody would laugh; and I had to laugh, too.

As I was getting into my car to leave, I heard folks laughing 5 down the street, and through the night. Oddly enough, this meeting has resulted in more lasting friendships than any other in which I have participated. The folks write me from time to time and they are nearly all regular subscribers.

From the angle of "interfaith," the meeting was a tremen- 6 dous success.

Organization

1. From what point in time is the narrative written? Does it follow a strict chronological development? If not, where does it vary and for what purpose?
2. Identify the thesis statement. Point out its key words or phrases.

Paragraphs

1. What is the topic thought of paragraph 2?
2. What is the topic sentence of paragraph 4? How is it developed?
3. Identify the transitional devices in paragraph 4. What other device gives this paragraph coherence?
4. Harry Golden was a Jew who edited a newspaper called *The Carolina Israelite*. How does this information relate to the closing paragraph?

Sentences

1. Are the first paragraph and the second sentence of paragraph 4 to be taken literally? If not, what do these two sentences reveal about the author's attitude?
2. What specific details contribute to the imagery of the second sentence of paragraph 3?
3. What is the effect of the first sentence of paragraph 5? How is it achieved?

Words

1. What does *nonchalant* (4) mean?
2. Why is *The Mature Mind* (4) italicized?

Suggestions for Writing

1. Relate what happened in one of the following situations:
   a. A particularly embarrassing moment—yours or someone else's.
   b. An occasion when you did something that could have had terrible results, but instead turned out to have a positive effect on you. (See Anne Bradley's essay on p. 94.)
   c. An unusual lecture—one that may have been interrupted by a lapse of memory, a heckler, a blackout. . . .
2. The *small literary group* before which Golden appeared was united by a "spirit" of laughter. Tell what happened when a group of which you are a member experienced a sense of "togetherness" (a club initiation, an athletic contest, a musical or dramatic production, a wedding). Try to select details that clarify the "spirit" of the occasion.

STUD BULLS AND THE BIG BLOW

Tom Perez

Tom Perez: securities salesman, playwright, columnist. Perez is a native of Mobile, Alabama where he was born in 1943. After receiving a degree in history and political science from Auburn University, he attended Lousiana State University, where he earned a Master's degree in English. He taught at East Texas State University and LSU, then he returned to his home town. He is the founder of the South of the Salt Line Regional Theatre. Perez' plays include Cockroach Hall *and* Ambushed by the Holy Majority. *He writes occasionally for* The Azalea City News and Review.

What two or three words would you use to describe Papa?

What details does Perez provide to capture the fury of the hurricane?

1   The fiercest battle ever waged against Gulf Coast humidity was fought by my paternal grandfather in 1916. Papa lived with his wife and seven children in a raised Creole Cottage in the middle of residential Mobile, where he kept a flock of Rhode Island Reds, six goats, and four Jersey cows. Rather, Grandma and two houseservants tended these animals while Papa traveled the Gulf Coast from Pensacola to New Orleans tending his chain of picture shows. Later he sold his theatres when he heard rumor of talkies. Papa agreed with Harry Warner, who said, "Who the hell wants to hear actors talk?"

2   In the spring of 1916 Papa traveled first-class to the Chicago

stockyards and returned in the baggage car with a prized Holstein bull. He had the notion that crossing a Holstein with his Jerseys would double milk production. Grandma asked why he wanted her to milk the cows twice as often when she was already giving milk away, and the picture shows were providing a comfortable living. Papa ignored her logic and led the bull into the backyard—he called it the "pasture"—and tied him to a chinaberry tree. The bull took one deep breath of Gulf Coast humidity, sank to his knees, and never got up again.

All that spring and well into the summer, Papa let the picture shows go to pot, stood over the prized bull and fanned him vigorously with a large palmetto leaf. The houseboy, meanwhile, massaged the bull's neck with crushed ice while Grandma stood on the backporch, clasping her head and moaning "Eight hundred dollars!" That was 1916 when $800 meant something. 3

Later that summer, the Great Hurricane of 1916 hit the Gulf Coast, and the eye passed over Mobile. My grandmother gathered her children and the servants in the middle hall which had no windows. She banked the doors with mattresses and sat down to wait the storm out, hoping Papa would miss the hurricane in New Orleans where he was checking on his picture shows. 4

In those final few minutes, that eerie lull just before the hurricane hits with full force, the kitchen door blew open and Papa hurried in with the prized bull—the $800 bull who had not yet recovered from the humidity to perform his stud service. "I'm not about to leave him out in the middle of a hurricane!" Papa announced, and he led the bull through the hall and let him choose the two softest pallets in the room. Then Papa fled again into the storm. 5

Five minutes later Papa arrived leading a single Jersey cow. "I can understand the bull," Grandma said calmly. "But why the cow? If she gets blown away we can replace her! Jersey cows are a dime a dozen!" 6

Papa pulled her over to the side, hoping the children wouldn't hear him: "She's just started her cycle," he whispered. "The high winds—maybe the storm will excite his passion!" More babies are born in nine months after a Gulf Coast hurricane than were conceived in the New York Blackout of 1968. But during the great hurricane of 1916, neither babe nor beast was conceived in Papa's house. 7

The hurricane hovered off the coast for three full days and three full nights, pounding the city with high winds and torrential rains before it finally decided to come ashore. For three days and nights Grandma and the children hovered at one end 8 of the great hall while at the other end Papa fanned the prized bull, and the houseboy paraded the Jersey cow up and down and around the bull. The bull had thought the backyard was humid—it was nothing compared to the stickiness inside a sealed house while a hurricane rages outside. The cow mooed—she moaned, she even tried serenading the bull, but he just lay on the pallet, his tongue hanging out in heat prostration while the winds battered the house.

9   After the hurricane passed, the bull was returned to the "pasture" where he remained for the rest of his life—coddled, fanned, and massaged daily with crushed ice—where many years later he died a virgin. It was in 1925 when he finally died, to Grandma's great relief, one year before the Great Hurricane of 1926.

Organization

1. This essay seems not to have a thesis statement, but it does have a single unifying idea. Write a thesis statement for this essay.
2. What is the general time-span of the essay? What is the specific time-span?
3. Point out the time-markers for this essay.
4. How does dialogue help make the essay flow smoothly?

Paragraphs

1. What devices give coherence to paragraph 3?

Sentences

1. How many specific details are in the second sentence of paragraph 1?
2. Nine years are compressed into the first sentence of paragraph 9. Is this sentence effective?

Words

1. Who was *Harry Warner* (1)?
2. Be sure you know the meaning of these words:

   eerie (5)   pallets (5)
   heat prostration (8)   torrential (8)

Suggestions for Writing

1. Tell what happened when you or a member of your family did something that the other members of the family thought was outrageous. It could be purchasing something extravagant, acquiring an unusual pet, accepting an off-beat job.
2. Have you ever experienced a severe storm or power outage? If so, tell what happened. What preparations did you make, or were you unprepared? Assume that your audience is a group of power company executives. Make them feel your frustration and anger, but don't be too harsh on them.

KICKING DRUGS: A VERY PERSONAL STORY

William S. Burroughs

William Burroughs: novelist and activist for the decriminalization of drug use. Burroughs was born in St. Louis in 1914. He received an AB from Harvard in 1936. For some 13 years (1944–1957) he was a heroin addict. His novel Naked Lunch *(1959), which included experiences related to his addiction, received some critical acclaim. It circulated, originally, in the literary underground, but it was reissued in 1962. Burroughs' subsequent books have dealt with sensational elements of the grotesque, and science fiction. The following excerpt originally appeared in* Harper's *magazine.*

Does Burroughs make overcoming an addiction seem too easy?

Do you feel that chemical dependence is a matter of *willpower, whatever that is?*

I was on junk for almost fifteen years. In that time I took   1
ten cures. I have been to Lexington and have taken the reduction treatment. I have taken abrupt withdrawal treatments and prolonged withdrawal treatments; cortisone, tranquilizers, antihistamines and the prolonged sleep cure. In every case I relapsed at the first opportunity.

Why do addicts voluntarily take a cure and then relapse? I   2
think on a deep biological level most addicts want to be cured. Junk *is* death and your body knows it. I relapsed because I was never physiologically cured until 1957. Then I took the apomorphine treatment under the care of a British physician, the late Dr. John Yerbury Dent. Apomorphine is the only agent I know that evicts the "addict personality," an old friend who used to inhabit my body. I called him Opium Jones. We were mighty close in Tangier in 1957, shooting 15 grains of methadone every hour, which equals 30 grains of morphine and

that's a lot of junk. I never changed my clothes. Jones likes his clothes to season in stale rooming-house flesh until you can tell by a hat on the table, a coat hung over a chair, that Jones lives there. I never took a bath. Old Jones don't like the feel of water on his skin. I spent whole days looking at the end of my shoe just communing with Jones.

3   Then one day I saw that Jones was not a real friend, that our interests were in fact divergent. So I took a plane to London and found Dr. Dent, with a charcoal fire in the grate, Scottish terrier, cup of tea. He told me about the treatment and I entered the nursing home the following day. It was one of those four-story buildings on Cromwell Road; my room with rose wallpaper was on the third floor. I had a day nurse and a night nurse and received an injection of apomorphine—one twentieth grain—ever two hours.

4   Now every addict has his special symptom, the one that hits him hardest when his junk is cut off. Listen to the old-timers in Lexington talking:

5   "Now with me it's puking is the worst."

6   "I never puke. It's this cold burn on my skin drives me up the wall."

7   "My trouble is sneezing."

8   With me it's feeling the slow painful death of Mr. Jones. I feel myself encased in his old gray corpse. Not another person in this world I want to see. Not a thing I want to do except revive Mr. Jones.

9   The third day with my cup of tea at dawn the calm miracle of apomorphine began. I was learning to live without Jones, reading newspapers, writing letters (usually I can't write a letter for a month), and looking forward to a talk with Dr. Dent who isn't Jones at all.

10   Apomorphine had taken care of my special symptom. After ten days I left the hospital. During the entire cure I had received only two grains of morphine, that is, less than I had been using in one shot. I went back to Tangier, where junk was readily available at that time. I didn't have to use will power, whatever that is. I just didn't want any junk. The apomorphine treatment had given me a long calm look at all the gray junk yesterdays, a long calm look at Mr. Jones standing there in his shabby black suit and gray felt hat with his stale rooming-house flesh and cold undersea eyes.

Organization

1. What is the *general* time span of the essay?
2. What is the *specific* time span?

3. Point out the time markers.
4. What feeling or effect is created by Burroughs' repeated references to *Opium Jones?*

Paragraphs

1. Paragraph 1 is introductory. How many specific details does it contain?
2. What is the purpose of the question that opens paragraph 2? How many answers are given in the paragraph? What is the thesis statement?
3. Why are paragraphs 5, 6, and 7 so short and enclosed in quotation marks?

Sentences

1. To what attitude do the details in the second sentence of paragraph 3 contribute?
2. How do the third and fourth sentences of paragraph 8 differ in construction from the ordinary English sentence? What is the effect of this difference?
3. Identify the parallelism in the second sentence of paragraph 9.
4. What is the emotional effect of the final sentence?

Words

1. To what does *Lexington* (1) refer?
2. Where is *Tangier* (2)?
3. What is meant by *physiologically cured* (2)?
4. Why is *addict personality* (2) enclosed in quotation marks?
5. What does *divergent* (3) mean?

Suggestions for Writing

1. Assume that you have an addiction to some food or drink of which you are particularly fond (pizza, hamburgers, ice-cream, beer, wine, orange juice). Tell how you would go about "kicking" your addiction.
2. Tell how you felt during an illness or injury and how you recovered from it (a cold, the measles, an allergy, a broken bone, a sprained ankle).

THEATRE OF THE ABSURD

Mary Kramer

Mary Kramer: teacher, writer. Kramer was preparing for a career in the theater when she was appointed assistant to the director for a collegiate production of Hamlet. *Several years later, while teaching in college, she submitted this article to* Playbill. Playbill *is a monthly publication given to theatergoers in New York City. Its major emphasis is on current theater topics, but it occasionally publishes humorous pieces if they are offbeat. Kramer's article appeared in 1976.*

What aspects of this theatrical production developed major problems?

How many specific examples of disasters does Kramer provide?

1   Most people think of *Hamlet* as the greatest of plays, an actor's stiffest challenge or something similar in superlatives. For me, it represents a trying experience and a Grand Guignol farce.

2   I went to a large university which had a lavish budget for drama productions. My last year there, the decision was made to produce an uncut *Hamlet,* using a professional director and opening casting to undergraduates, graduate students and faculty. The Drama Society and the university wanted it to be a memorable production, and it was, in the same way the Titanic's maiden voyage, the Chicago Fire and the Johnstown Flood were. After it, I dropped all plans of a career in the theatre and although I have taught in a university for some years now, I still approach *Hamlet* with moist palms, rapid breathing and a sensation that nameless, maniacal shadows are lurking outside the classroom.

3   Almost certainly as retribution for some unspeakable sin in my past, I was appointed assistant to the director, a position which I came to realize had all the allure of being point man on a Viet Nam scouting expedition or demolition expert in Northern Ireland.

4   Problems began immediately with casting. The director wanted female courtiers who looked like Hollywood starlets. He believed girls who looked like that majored in physical education. Accordingly, he called that department's chairman and gave a magnificent performance, inviting all physical education majors to join the production, prove their versatility, contribute to the arts, etc. The first six who appeared were wearing sweat socks and looked like rejects from the L.A. Rams. The director, a shaken man, retired to a corner muttering. "I thought with all that fresh air and exercise they'd really be

built." I retired to the cafeteria, an action that became increasingly frequent as the rehearsals staggered along. The fact that you could buy beer there insured its popularity.

After the fiasco with the physical education amazons, the director dispatched the male cast with instructions to accost any exceptionally endowed female and recruit her. Aside from several encounters with irate boyfriends, this was successful. It was fortunate that the courtiers' roles were non-speaking as the girls needed all their time to find ways of keeping their gowns up. Engineered to show off the girls' most obvious assets, the gowns had a tendency to slip and slither; the girls finally settled on spirit gum, breath holding, and slow movements.

As rehearsals progressed, other cast problems became evident. The queen, a motherly woman who had returned to graduate school when her children were grown, refused to have anything to do with the Oedipus theory, although Hamlet played on it with determination. Hamlet himself had a monumental and continual case of halitosis, which led his fellow actors into much gesturing and strange postures. Polonius, who was an exceptionally good actor, could not memorize his lines. His costume was modified to give him wide, deep sleeves into which he could thrust a script. His appearances were always accompanied by rustling of paper and on some occasions his attempts to retrieve the script made him seem to be chasing fleas. The priest continually mixed up the line about the dead Ophelia's "crants and strewments" and referred to her "screwments." Horatio was revealed to suffer from nervous hiccups. The first gravedigger was flunking calculus and took his textbook into the grave along with his shovel. Ophelia caught the German measles.

The set was massive, with two levels above the stage, one at 8 feet, and the second at 18 feet. The floor was built out over the orchestra pit in an attempt to imitate the Renaissance apron stage. With a multitude of possible entrances, the director kept changing his mind, reassigning doorways to the various actors but usually forgetting to tell the lighting crew. Thus an act would open with a bright spot on one entrance, the rest of the stage dark, while above or off to the side we would hear a rich stream of invective as the actor would walk into blackness and some forgotten bit of lumber or piece of the wings. When the play finally did open, the lighting crew was close to revolt and many of the cast had heavily bandaged shins.

On opening night, the king and queen made a spectacular entrance from the third level to the second level, where they

83

stood regally 8 feet above the stage. We were just beginning to breathe a collective sigh of relief in the wings when we realized that the king, clutching his proclamation, was about to walk right off the platform. We watched in horrified fascination as the queen reacted enough to stamp on the train of his royal robe and grab his arm in what she hoped the audience would believe was a loving embrace rather than a wrestling hold. As the king intoned his edict, the director, offstage, mimed to the queen, asking if his majesty had lost his contact lenses. She returned a look of pure disgust as she mimed back, "drunk."

9 Why I did not take that as a divine warning and hop the first bus out of town I will never know, but for each of the eight performances there was some crisis. Guards tripped over their halberds and each other and fell down stairs. Laertes was accidentally locked in a dressing room and missed a cue. Someone stepped on Ophelia's flowing robes, removing an embarrassing amount. Osric forgot his jock strap and had to do his scenes with a large feathered hat clutched to him in the manner of a shy fan dancer. Finally, on the last night, during the crucial duel between Hamlet and Laertes, when they exchanged poisoned swords, Hamlet dropped his and it rolled gracefully off the stage into the remnants of the orchestra pit. The director, who could express himself as quaintly as an enraged navy quartermaster, merely gave a sign like an expiring balloon and walked out of the theatre, not to be seen by anyone until the next day. Horatio mercifully stepped into the breech and thrust his own sword at Hamlet, unfortunately point first, but it was a minor wound, and the play continued.

10 When the curtain came down, the cast and crew applauded considerably harder than the audience, and in sheer relief. To my knowledge, none of the cast acted together again, and the director has since restricted himself to modern drama. Several of the cast immediately changed their majors and still today the mention of *Hamlet* invokes responses more appropriate to stomach flu or letters from the IRS.

Organization

1. The thesis statement appears in paragraph 1 and establishes an exaggerated attitude. Where are other exaggerations in the essay that maintain and reinforce that attitude?
2. What is the general time-span of the essay? What is its specific time-span?
3. Point out the time-markers for the essay.

Paragraphs

1. What is the topic sentence of paragraph 6? How is it developed?
2. Paragraph 3 is one sentence. How effective is the paragraph?
3. What is the principle of arrangement for the crises in paragraph 9?

Sentences

1. The third sentence in paragraph 2 is effective only if the audience recognizes the allusions. Do you recognize their specific references?
2. Is the fifth sentence of paragraph 4 a simile? Is the comparison effective?

Words

1. What does *Oedipus theory* (6) mean?
2. Be sure you know the meaning of these words:

accost (5)	invective (7)
amazons (5)	maniacal (2)
courtiers (4)	retribution (3)

Suggestions for Writing

1. Have you ever participated in a group activity that did not run smoothly? Perhaps it was a dramatic production, a musical fest, a club field trip, a church outing, a family reunion, a birthday party. Tell what happened to disrupt the activity.
2. Have you ever held a position of responsibility for an activity or event and everything went wrong? Perhaps it was as a club president or program chairman, a camp counselor, a choir director, in a money-raising venture, or in a school political campaign. Tell what happened.
3. Have you ever had an experience that you feel changed your life? That made you reconsider your career plans? That still gives you *moist palms, rapid breathing,* and a sense of impending doom? Tell what happened. Assume that your audience is vocational counselors. How can your experience help them as they guide their clients? Tell them what you wish someone had told you before you had the experience.

I DIDN'T STOP IN BALTIMORE

Stewart Alsop

Stewart Alsop: political columnist, author. Alsop was born in Avon, Connecticut in 1914. He graduated from Yale in 1936. Six years later, he enlisted in the British Army in order to fight in World War II. After the War, he and his brother Joseph wrote a political column for Newsweek *from 1945–1958. Alsop's book, A* Stay of Execution *(1974), is a fuller account of his battle against cancer, a battle he lost in 1974. The following essay originally appeared in* Newsweek *the year of his death.*

How is the title of the essay related to its content?

What changes in procedures and practices would Alsop like to see made in the Solid-Tumor Ward of the cancer clinic of the National Institutes of Health?

1   I woke up suddenly, feeling very wide awake, pulled the light cord, and sat straight up in bed.

2   "We'll be stopping in Baltimore," I announced loudly, in an authoritative voice. I looked around me. A private car, evidently. Good of the railroad people to supply those fruits, and all those flowers. The furniture looked a bit shoddy, but what can one expect these days? My wife was no doubt in the next stateroom. Where was the connecting door? I got up to explore.

3   The car was swaying heavily—the roadbed must be a disgrace. I supported myself on a table, and then a desk. Then there was a space of empty floor. I was halfway across it when the car gave a lurch, and I fell down. I sat on the floor for a bit, getting my bearings, then scrambled to my feet again, and opened a narrow green door. A locker, with my own clothes in it. I opened another door—a small bathroom.

4   Then I came to a much bigger door, and opened it, and leaned against the doorjamb. The swaying had stopped—the train, apparently, had halted. Outside was what I assumed was the Baltimore station—wide platform, dim lights, green tile. A whimpering noise, then silence, and no one to be seen. There was something hellishly grim about the place. Suddenly I was quite sure I didn't want to stop in Baltimore.

5   "We won't stop here," I said, again in a firm, authoritative voice. "Start up the train, and carry on."

6   I turned back toward my bed, and the big door closed behind me. I fell down twice on the way back—the crew must be pouring on the power, I thought—and getting into bed was like mounting a bucking horse. Safe in bed, I turned off the light, and was asleep in an instant.

This small episode did not happen on a private railroad car. 7
(Who the hell did I think I was? Some ancient Belmont or
Vanderbilt?) It happened in my room on Floor 12, the Solid-
Tumor Ward of the cancer clinic of the National Institutes of
Health. My room, a room I'd been in for going on eight weeks,
was the private car, and the corridor of the Solid-Tumor Ward
was the Baltimore platform. But the falling down was real
enough—the next morning I had the bruises to prove it.

I was in the Solid-Tumor Ward because NIH, for mysterious 8
bureaucratic reasons, has ended the adult leukemia program,
and the adult leukemics who are still about are taken care of
in other wards. Leukemia is a sneaky disease—it attacks by
indirection. It weakens the blood cells that fight infection, and
then sends in surrogate diseases to finish off the victim.

In the two months I was in the Solid-Tumor Ward, my leu- 9
kemia (or whatever it is—it is a most atypical disease) tried
hard to finish me off. I had pneumonia; then an infection of
the lower intestines; than a lung clot; then an edema of the
lungs; then a second pneumonia; then two minor operations
and a major operation; then another infection.

The major operation—opening my chest and snipping off a 10
thumbnail-size bit of lung—was necessary because pneumonia can't be treated unless the doctors know what kind it
is, and my second pneumonia stubbornly refused to identify
itself. The bit of lung was given every known test—and the
brilliant doctors at NIH know every known test—but it still
refused to identify itself. Meanwhile the lethal "infiltrate"
continued relentlessly to spread across both lungs, and my wife
was told that the prognosis was "grim."

It was four days after the operation that I decided not to 11
stop in Baltimore. The next day the able young doctor in charge
of my case, Jack Macdonald, told me that he might be imag-
ining things, but the X-rays of my lungs looked a bit better—
certainly no worse. The day after, he said there was no doubt
about it—the infiltrate was receding. Some days later, my battered old lungs were as close to normal as they will ever be.

Why? Jack Macdonald and the other doctors say frankly they 12
don't know, though they all have a favorite guess. I have a
favorite guess, too. My guess is that my decision not to stop
at Baltimore had something to do with it. In a kind of fuzzy,
hallucinated way, I knew when I announced the decision that
it was a decision not to die.

Death is a word rarely mentioned in the NIH cancer clinic. 13
But one is more aware of its presence in the Solid-Tumor Ward
than in the now defunct leukemia ward. Leukemia is a sneak-
ier disease than solid-tumor cancer, but it is also kinder at the

end. Most leukemics drift into a quiet death, while the victims of a solid tumor can (although they by no means always do) suffer agonies before death comes.

14   All the rooms at NIH are double rooms, and almost all the 14 patients (except those thought soon to die, which may be why I was alone on my private car) have roommates. Several of my roommates were terminal solid-tumor patients, who were given opium-based analgesics or painkillers at predetermined intervals, usually four hours. Almost always, the analgesic wore off too soon. To hear grown men, and brave men, whimpering, or howling, or pleading with a helpless nurse for another "shot" is not an experience likely soon to be forgotten.

15   As a result of that experience, I reached certain conclusions. 15 NIH, like most hospitals, goes to great lengths to prevent suicide—patients are forbidden pills of their own, and the windows and even the rooftop solarium are firmly screened. It seems to me that a patient suffering beyond endurance should be given the option of ending his own life, and the means to do so should be supplied on request. An unquestionably terminal patient should be given another option. He should be given as much painkilling drug as he himself feels he needs. The drug probably ought to be heroin, which is estimated to be about four times as effective an analgesic as the synthetic painkillers now mostly in use. If a human being must die, it is surely better that he die in the illusion of painless pleasure—and heroin is very pleasurable—than in lonely agony.

16   Another conclusion is harder to define. Shakespeare, as usual, 16 came closest, in the familiar cliché-quote from Hamlet: "There are more things in heaven and earth, Horatio, than are dreamt of in your philosophy." Perhaps my decision not to stop in Baltimore had nothing to do with my astonishing recovery. But there are mysteries, above all the mystery of the relationship of mind and body, that will never be explained, not by the most brilliant doctors, the wisest of scientists or philosophers.

17   For the rest, I hope to put back some (but not all) of the 43 17 pounds I have lost, to get a bit of rest, to get rid of the tail end of that second infection, and then again to examine in this space the more mundane mysteries of political Washington.

Organization

1. Trace the chronology of paragraphs 1–11. Are events presented in the order in which they occurred? Identify the time markers.

2. How do 12–16 relate to 1–11?
3. What words give coherence to the essay through their repetition?

Paragraphs

1. Identify the topic sentence of paragraph 9. How does the author develop it?
2. Paragraph 12 has a one-word topic sentence. How does the author develop it?
3. Identify the topic sentence of paragraph 15. How does the author develop it?
4. How does the closing paragraph relate to 15 and 16? How does it relate to the rest of the essay?

Sentences

1. What is unusual about the third and fourth sentences of paragraph 2 and the fourth sentence of paragraph 4?
2. Discuss the structure of the second sentence of paragraph 9.

Words

1. Explain the figurative significance of *Baltimore.*
2. To what do *Belmont* and *Vanderbilt* allude (7)?
3. What does each of the following mean?

atypical (9)	mundane (17)
defunct (13)	prognosis (10)
edema (9)	surrogate (8)
hallucinated (12)	terminal (14)
lethal "infiltrate" (10)	

Suggestions for Writing

Tell what happened in one of the following instances:

1. A particularly vivid dream.
2. Your own or someone else's stay in a hospital.
3. Your own or someone else's brush with death from an illness or accident.

THE EGRESS OF B. J. WHITING

Anne Fadiman

Anne Fadiman: freelance writer, journalist. Fadiman was born in New York City in 1953. She graduated from Harvard with honors in history and literature. While in college, she was the undergraduate columnist for The Harvard Bulletin. *She worked as a freelance writer from 1976–1978 and had articles published in* Esquire, Saturday Review, *and* The New York Times. *She has been a staff writer at* Life *since 1981. The following essay was written in 1975 while Fadiman was an undergraduate.*

Describe B. J. Whiting's teaching method.

Do you feel Whiting's embarrassment is genuine?

1   At 12:06 p.m., Wednesday, April 30, 1975, Bartlett Jere Whiting, Gurney Professor of English Literature, ambles into Sever 11 to deliver the final lecture of English 116, "Chaucer." It will also be the final lecture of his 49-year career at Harvard.

2   His entrance is unceremonious. As he descends the creaky wooden steps toward the podium, he directs his attention first at his feet and then at some cryptic graphs in two colors of chalk left on the blackboard for the benefit of a previous class. He does not appear to notice the several luminaries of the Harvard English department who have congregated in the last row.

3   Whiting is wearing a rumpled greenish-gray tweed suit. It strikes us as exactly the sort of suit one ought to wear when reading Chaucer aloud. It would have been equally suitable in 1926, when Whiting gave his first class on Chaucer to a few Harvard undergraduates. Whiting's hair is also a little rumpled, as if just before the class he had been running his hand through it while pondering the etymology of some difficult Middle English word. We know, however, that this did not happen. For Whiting, there are no difficult Middle English words.

4   Whiting asks the class to turn to line 1335 of *The Canterbury Tales*. "Thus seyde oure Hoost, 'and lat hym telle his tale.' " This is the opening of the Friar's Tale, which is about a thoroughly nasty summoner who meets a thoroughly nasty devil. Naturally, both parties end up in Hell, where they belong. It is a short but satisfying story. Whiting reads it with relish.

5   Whiting's method of teaching has budged not an inch from

its original conception half a century ago. It is based on the assumption that Chaucer teaches himself. Therefore, although works of criticism crop up every year on the reading list, there has rarely been a lecture that has not revolved around a goodly chunk of Chaucer, read aloud with feeling, explicated, glossed, and cheerfully digressed from.

Whiting does not subscribe to the theory, widely held at 6 Harvard, that poetry should be read aloud in such a manner as to make the professor sound as erudite as possible while leaving the student as confused as possible. He pronounces Middle English as if it were a dialect spoken somewhere in Maine. (Whiting hails from Penobscot Bay. After Commencement he and his wife will leave Cambridge and return to the house in which he was born.) It sounds just fine like that, and everyone can understand it.

As Whiting meanders through his three hundred-odd cho- 7 sen lines today, he seems not unlike one of Chaucer's pilgrims, making a pleasant journey through interesting country in good company. Every once in a while he stops to nod to an old friend. Sometimes it's a favorite word, such as "avowtie" (line 1372), which means adulterer, or "waryangle" (line 1408), a species of ferocious little bird. Sometimes it's a point of grammar. "Thee thar" (line 1365), he reminds us affectionately, is "that old preterite present"; "divers art" (line 1486) is, of course, a splendid example of the collective singular. Most often it's a piece of trivia, one of the thousands he has stored up in his brain, from which they burst forth at intervals to delight his students. Today we learn that the word "wench" has three separate meanings in Chaucer; that in the Middle Ages Hell was supposed to be in the far north; that green is the color of fiends; that in line 1467 occurs the first instance in written English in which the word "lousy" (here, the more picturesque "lowsy") is used "in the derogatory as well as the infestive sense"; that St. Dunstan (924–988), mentioned in line 1502, was an amateur blacksmith before whom, while he was working at his forge, the Devil once appeared. St. Dunstan was so peeved at being thus interrupted that he seized the Devil's nose with a pair of red-hot tongs. Whiting really likes this one. He does a little dance on the podium to illustrate the saint blowing into his bellows, pounding his anvil, and finally giving the Devil what-for.

When Whiting finishes line 1664, he removes his glasses 8 and blinks at the audience. The glasses are gold wire-rims, apparently of 1926 vintage. They have unsteady-looking temples that stick out at an oblique angle from the rest of the frame. Whiting's own temples, thus exposed, reveal two ancient dents left by his glasses. He puts the glasses back on, having some difficulty with his left ear.

9   He clears his throat.

10   "Of course, this little tale has a moral. Actually, several morals. One. Don't become a summoner. Two. Whatever you do, remember the words of a later poet: 'Oh, what a tangled web we weave/When first we practice to deceive.' Three. Do not enter into unduly intimate relationships with strangers. Four. When you find yourself in a tight fix and there's a way out—take it. Five. Some people seem bound to be damned.

11   "And now—" Whiting glances around with a cornered expression. It is 12:55. "There are, hmm, in every Harvard course, two embarrassing moments. One occurs at the first meeting, when the teacher and the students see each other for the first time and wonder with wild surmise how the grab bag of fate could possibly have brought them together. And the other embarrassing moment occurs, er, right now.

12   "The embarrassment is caused by the well-meant convention that at the end of any course the students must applaud the teacher. Now this is *doubly* embarrassing. It is embarrassing for many of the students, who would rather sit on their hands, or *hold* hands, or assume the lotus position. Many, perhaps, would prefer curses." (At this point more than one of the students is in tears.)

13   "It is also embarrassing for the teacher. In the first place, he's well aware of the convention, especially if he's, well, been about for half a century. In the second place, he's supposed to remove himself somehow from the classroom, feigning complete obliviousness of the applause . . . *wafted out*, as it were.

14   "Well." Whiting smiles brightly at his students. "In order to relieve these tensions, I'm going to conclude with an anecdote from Harvard history."

15   He takes a mysterious step backwards.

16   "At the beginning of this century, at a time when the custom of exchanging professors between Harvard and the Sorbonne was in full flower"—another mysterious step—"Harvard was graced by the presence of an eminent *professeur* and *savant* whose time"—another step—"was largely absorbed by entertainment and parties"—another step—"and who had so *good* a time that he failed to familiarize himself with the local prejudices, such as examinations and grades." Another step, this time gracefully off the podium.

17   It is becoming clear where Whiting is headed. Sever 11 possesses, in addition to the rather grand double door at the top through which both teacher and students customarily enter and exit, a less assuming side door at the front right corner of

the room. On this door, to the delight of all freshmen (at least, it delighted us when we were freshmen, and still does), is emblazoned in bright red letters, EMERGENCY EGRESS.

"After his last lecture, our friend took a train to New York,   18
and from there a ship home to *la patrie*." Another step. "But alas for Harvard. No *professeur*, no exam. No exam, no grades." Another step. "What to do?" Another step. "Deans shivered. Secretaries in University Hall trembled at the knee." Another step. "Finally, a cable was sent to Paris. All of Harvard was waiting for the reply . . ." Another step. Without looking backwards, Whiting places his hand unerringly on the doorknob.

"A cable came back." Whiting turns the knob. *"Give them*   19
all A's." The door opens. *"I enjoyed the course very much."*

Just before Sever 11 explodes with applause, Professor B. J.   20
Whiting passes through the Emergency Egress.

Organization

1. What is the general time-span of the essay? The specific time-span?
2. How does the essay manage to unite 1926 and 1975?
3. While primarily narrative, the essay relies on description and example for its sub-structure. Point out uses of these other methods of development.

Paragraphs

1. What devices give coherence to paragraph 7? How is it developed?
2. Paragraphs 9 and 15 both contain only one sentence. What is the function of each?
3. What makes 16 an effective paragraph?

Sentences

1. The seventh sentence of paragraph 7 may seem excessively long. What do you think?
2. How effective are the sentence fragments in paragraph 18?

Words

1. Do you think the use of French words *professeur* and *savant* (16) and *la patrie* (18) adds to or detracts from Whiting's anecdote?

2. Be sure you know the meaning of these words:

cryptic (2)	glossed (5)	summoner (4)
erudite (6)	luminaries (2)	unceremonious (2)
etymology (3)	oblique (8)	*wafted out* (13)
explicated (5)	obliviousness (13)	
feigning (13)	podium (2)	

Suggestions for Writing

1. Have you ever attended a ceremony at which someone was honored (retirement, promotion, an academic or athletic achievement, some extraordinary service)? Tell what happened. Focus on what both the recipient and the audience did.
2. Tell what happened when you attended a particularly memorable lecture (a first class meeting, a presentation by an outstanding scholar or preacher, a graduation, an orientation to college). Include in your narrative the actions of both the speaker and the audience. Assume that your audience is junior high school pupils. Use narrative detail that will convince them of the importance of the occasion and its benefits to you.

GOOD GIRLS DON'T, BUT I DID, AND I PAID

Anne Bradley

Anne Bradley: student. Bradley was born in Mobile, Alabama in 1965, but now lives in Robertsdale, Alabama, where she graduated from high school. She is studying physical therapy to prepare for a career in the health professions. Her essay is based on Suggestions for Writing 1b on p. 76.

1   "Hey, Anne. Why don't we skip the rest of school and hit Gulf Shores?"

2   "Sure, Connie. That sounds like fun."

3   "All right, let's go."

4   Cutting classes was not a usual practice for Connie and me. We were seniors and good friends with most of the teachers. We knew they wouldn't turn us in if we weren't in class. Also, because we were in the National Honor Society and consistently made good grades, no one would ever suspect us of cutting classes. However, this decision harbored severe consequences and almost ruined my reputation.

5   While Connie and I were in Gulf Shores, we met our friends

Tommy and Wade. They had been drinking Coors all day and were rowdy. Connie and I didn't want to get into any trouble, so we left them in a hurry. Unfortunately, they followed us to a Tastee Freez where we had stopped to use the restroom. They broke into the restroom, and in the process, Wade stumbled and knocked a small hole in the wall. We didn't think anything serious had happened, so we left.

I went to Gina's house to study. About fifteen minutes after 6 I got there, my mom called to inform me that a warrant had been issued for my arrest for vandalism. I promptly went to the police station to declare my innocence. The policeman told me that I was not going to be arrested and that my name was cleared of any wrong-doing. Boy, was I relieved.

That feeling of relief lasted only until the next morning. 7 The next morning at school, Mr. Farris, the principal, called me to his office and immediately confronted me. He told me the police were still investigating the incident; an officer had come by the school to find out if I had been in class yesterday. The warrant had been re-issued because a worker at Tastee Freez had told a different story, and the police believed her. Mr. Farris immediately suspended me for three days off campus and threatened to forfeit my membership in the National Honor Society.

I was crushed. How could anything done so innocently re- 8 sult in such a tragedy? Before this episode, I was considered an outstanding student; now, I was considered trash. My parents treated me like a diseased juvenile delinquent. My friends laughed at me and called me "Jailbird Annie." I was humiliated and degraded. I wanted to drop out of school and life.

However, I did not break under these pressures. If anything, 9 my suspension strengthened my character. After getting over those feelings of humiliation, I became determined to prove that I was not a loser. I resolved to overcome this degrading blow and bounce back twice as high.

Eventually, my determination paid off. I did not get kicked 10 out of the National Honor Society. In fact, I pulled my grades up so much that I placed fifth academically in my class of two hundred. Consequently, by concentrating on my grades, I won back the respect of my teachers, family, and friends.

I am almost glad that this incident happened. It strength- 11 ened my character to the point where I feel almost infallible. I have regained much more respect than I commanded before. Even though the initial results were tragic, this incident made me a much better person.

5

DESCRIPTION

Every time you tell someone what happened to you or to another person, you are employing narration; every time you translate your sense perceptions into words, you are using description. Description answers the basic question: what did you see, hear, feel, smell, and taste? Anything that engages your senses is a potential topic for description. Furthermore, you also use references to your senses to describe emotions. For example, *love* is a warmness in the heart or a racing of the blood through the veins; *anxiety* is sweating palms or a dry mouth. Description puts sense perceptions into words. And unless your description is purely technical—a lab report or a marketing analysis—it encourages you to offer a personal evaluation or comment on those perceptions. In other words, description is both objective and subjective.

OBJECTIVE DESCRIPTION

Objective description records perceptions that are independent of your private apprehensions and feelings. It is the data of scientific research. Outside of the laboratory, description may begin with objectivity, but rarely will you find an essay devoid of the writer's subjective response. On the other hand, no matter how subjective a description ends up, it begins with objective data.

1. Begin with Visual Details

Objective description usually begins with visual details—size, shape, color—because for most people sight is the dominant sense. Next time you are in your composition classroom, try this exercise. Look around the room. Concentrate on the place, not your classmates. What is the dominant color? What are the other colors? What is the most common geometric shape? Is it a square or a rectangle? Are there any circles? What are the dimensions of the room? How many students will it hold? These are all questions that are answered by your sense of sight.

2. Include Appeals to Other Senses

In addition to supplying visual details, your classroom engages other of your senses. What do you hear in the room? Does the heating/cooling system hum or sputter? Does the chalk scrape or tap as your instructor writes on the chalk board? Do the occupied chairs squeak as your classmates squirm? Can you hear your immediate neighbor sigh or a classmate across the room cough? What do you feel? Is the room too hot or too cold? Is your chair comfortable? Can you feel grit on the floor? What do you smell? Is there an odor in the room? Does the student in front of you wear cologne? Is there tobacco on the breath of the student behind you? There probably isn't an appeal to your sense of taste, but there may be.

This exercise is similar to what you would do as a part of your prewriting for a descriptive essay. As you make notes for your descriptive assignment, you need to keep all five senses in mind. To remind you of that fact and to guide you in prewriting, write the five senses on your note sheet. Jot down what you feel, smell, hear, and taste, as well as what you see. Remember that the more specific the sense perceptions you generate during your prewriting, the greater your options when you begin to write.

SUBJECTIVE DESCRIPTION

Subjective description filters the data through your private apprehensions and feelings. It is your evaluation or comment on those perceptions. Assuming that you and your classmates have senses that are unimpaired, you will see the same colors, hear the same sounds, feel the same temperature, and smell the same odors. These are objective perceptions. Suppose the temperature in your classroom is 72 degrees Fahrenheit. This is an objective fact. For some, the room may be too cold, for others it may be too hot. These are subjective differences. For some, the chairs may be uncomfortable; for others they are comfortable. This is another sub-jective difference. Objectively, however, the chairs are of the same design.

1. Include Your Response to Your Sense Perceptions

Now you should have a sense of the difference between subjec-tive and objective description. But subjective description includes another dimension. How do you *feel* about this classroom? What is your emotional response to being in this place? What is your evaluation of the cumulative effect of these sense impressions? In answering these questions your individuality emerges. You are looking for an attitude that will govern your presentation of the perceptions.

Of course, your subjective description of the classroom is influ-enced by your attitude toward this composition class and its in-structor. Objectively, you are all enrolled in a class designed to strengthen your writing skills, and your instructor is here to en-courage you. Subjectively, you may resent having to take a course in composition. Or you may welcome the opportunity to develop your skills. You may consider your instructor to be aloof or, per-haps, ingratiating. Your response to the course and its instructor filters your objective sense descriptions and contributes to your subjective description.

2. Select Your Descriptive Words Carefully

Subjective description is conveyed by the words you choose. If you choose positive ones, your opinion of what you're describing emerges as pleasant. If you choose negative ones, obviously your subjective response is unpleasant.

Consider paragraph 3 in Sue Hubbell's essay (p. 117):

These periodic cicadas are not so big as the common annual variety, but they are large as bugs go, broad, sturdy and nearly two inches in length. They have black bodies and huge showy wings that look like they are made of isinglass, *delicately* veined and edged in brilliant orange. Their legs are orange too. Their big, bulging eyes are a deep red, and each is cen-tered with a *meaningful-looking* dark brown dot. They are *beautiful, spectacular* bugs, and their appearance is *exuber-ant* and *exciting*, a *marvel*, a *celebration*. Their presence is a reminder that there are other life cycles than ours, other rhythms of living than the human one.

Hubbell has skillfully combined objective and subjective description. Her attitude toward the cicada is positive. Suppose the cicada has been described by one of the people down at the cafe who considers the cicada as *hostile aliens from a grade-B science fiction movie*. That Missourian's description might replace *delicately* with *grotesquely*, and *meaningful-looking* with *ominous*. Instead of being *beautiful* and *spectacular*, the cicada would be *monstrous*, *ghastly* bugs, and their appearance would be *unwanted*, *unnerving*, a *nuisance*, a *blight*.

Arrangement of Materials

1. Begin with Visual Details

Description usually begins with visual details arranged in some sort of spatial order. Using your classroom as an example, you might arrange your visual details by starting at the door and moving counter-clockwise around the room. Or you could start in the front of the class and move clockwise around the room. Thomas Griffith (p. 112) uses a high-to-low and near-to-far order to let you "see" the full extent of New York's massiveness. Neither method alone would have done New York justice. For most places, however, a single method of arrangement—horizontal or vertical—is sufficient.

Spatial arrangement may be the most common way of ordering sense perceptions, but it is not the only way. Your topic will often present you with options for arranging your details. For example, Sue Hubbell uses the life-cycle of the cicada as her organizing principle—a chronological arrangement. Isaac Asimov (p. 120) uses cause-effect as his organizing principle to describe a Martian.

2. Use Other Methods of Development to Support Your Description

Usually, within the dominant method of arrangement, other methods of development are employed. The methods most frequently combined are probably description and narration, but the emphasis is on the description, not the narrative substructure. In

"New York" notice the extent to which the description is laid out in *contrasting* patterns of various kinds. First of all, the high-to-low spatial order of the opening paragraph contrasts with the near-to-far order of the next paragraph. A second contrast occurs when Griffith turns his attention from the housing-project residents of paragraph 2 to the monied *successes* of paragraph 3. Finally, within the four-paragraph section of subjective description (3–6), there is the contrast between the negative and positive aspects of the New York character. In addition, since these negative and positive qualities are portrayed as the direct outgrowth of the city's physical make-up, they may be viewed as the *effect* of which the city's size is the *cause*.

Rather than let the thought of a combination of methods frighten you, you should see combining as a way of expanding and enriching your original thesis. In the case of "New York," description (objective and subjective), contrast, and cause and effect all work together smoothly to produce an interesting short study of New York City. The same methods, or some other combination of methods, can yield equally good results even if your topic is the local playground.

3. Engage as Many Senses as Possible

If your description is to be complete, visual details alone are not sufficient. Whatever you're describing probably engages the other senses as well. Griffith's first paragraph is based on visual details arranged in a high-to-low spatial pattern. But his last two sentences engage other senses:

> It is a city whose towers house businessmen who hire psychologists to study human fears which can be exploited to sell deodorants [smell] or tooth paste [taste], and where glamor is set by synthetic personalities trained to appear relaxed and natural before hot lights [touch] and stop watches, so that they can create the right air of conviction about products they themselves never use. It is a city where people do not do, but *watch*: crowd [touch] stadiums *to see* others play baseball or football, go to galleries *to see* what others paint or concerts *to hear* others play, and pay comedians *to bring them laughter.*

These non-visual sensations draw the reader even more compellingly into the New York atmosphere. The additional sense-peals let the reader capture the sensations of the city besides merely "seeing" it.

Specific details assure your descriptive essay's effectiveness. If you engage your readers' senses, you will have succeeded. If you offer unsupported subjective conclusions, your description will fail. For instance, if you write, "It was the most beautiful sunset I had ever seen," and provide no details that engage the senses, you've offered a conclusion but no description. What specific sense perceptions led you to that conclusion? It may have been a *most beautiful* sunset, but what were the colors? What were the shapes of the clouds? Was there a breeze? What was the temperature? Could you hear anything? Were there trees or mountains or bridges between you and the sunset? As in all writing, a careful choice of precise nouns and active verbs conveys your perceptions better than a string of adjectives. It's the note-taking step in the pre-writing process that enables you to avoid the unsupported conclusion.

SOLOLÁ

Aldous Huxley

Aldous Huxley: novelist and essayist. Huxley was born in Surrey, England in 1894. While a student at Oxford, he read philosophy and English literature. Brave New World *(1932) is probably his best known novel. He received the Award of Merit for the Novel and the Gold Medal from the American Academy of Arts and Letters. He died in 1963. "Sololá" comes from Huxley's* Collected Essays.

How many different costumes does Huxley describe?

How do economic forces affect the way the Quiché Indians dress?

The market at Sololá was a walking museum of fancy dress.　1 Unlike the Indians of Mexico, who have mostly gone into white cotton pajamas, with a blanket slung over the shoulder in lieu of great-coat, the Guatemaltecos of the highlands have kept their old costumes. This conservatism has been to some extent affected by the slump and the persuasive salesmanship of shopkeepers and commercial travelers. Nobody starves in this self-supporting agricultural community; but money is a great deal scarcer than it was a few years ago, when the coffee *fincas* were in full production and called, during the picking season, for whole armies of workers from the hills. Those were the glorious times when a man could earn as much as twenty-five or thirty cents a day. The Quiché villages were rich: their *fiestas* were grand events and the more elaborate of their old dances were staged on a lavish scale; *aguardiente* flowed like water, and when a man needed a new suit of the traditional clothes he could afford to buy the hand-woven cloth, the richly patterned sashes and kerchiefs, the hat bands and tassels. Today he has to think twice and three times before he renews his wardrobe. A new outfit will cost him the equivalent of four or five pounds, and at the present moment this is, for a Quiché Indian, an enormous sum. At the local store the price of a suit of blue dungarees is only a few shillings, and when it is worn out, which it will be very soon, he will be able to afford to buy another. It looks, I am afraid, as though the traditional dress of the Indians were doomed. All the forces of industrialism are arrayed against it. Conservative prejudice cannot long resist the assaults of economics.

2   Meanwhile a majority of highlanders still wear the old costumes—a different one in every village. The most curious feature, for example, of the Sololá costume is the black varnished hat, which is a strangely flattened version of John Bull's topper. From another village (I never discovered which; but it cannot have been far from Sololá, for I saw several of its representatives at the market) came men in large mushroom-shaped hats, exactly like those worn by very distinguished old English ladies when they go gardening. I had a slight shock each time I saw one of them. It was as though Miss Jekyll had suddenly gone mad and taken to staining her face with walnut juice and wearing, with her old hat, a gray monkey-jacket and white cotton pants.

The most remarkable thing about these Indian costumes is that they are not Indian at all, but old European. Little scraps of seventeenth- and eighteenth-century Spain have been caught here and miraculously preserved, like flies in the hard amber of primitive conservatism. The Chichicastenango Indians, for example, wear a short-waisted embroidered jacket and knee-breeches of brown cloth, a gay woven sash and an embroidered kerchief tied round the head. It is, almost without modification, the costume of Sancho Panza. Elsewhere one finds a number of small variations of the Spanish theme. Thus, long kilts will sometime be worn below a neatly tailored bullfighter's jacket—a reminiscence, perhaps, of the loin-cloths of an earlier dispensation.

3   The women's dress has been much less profoundly affected by Spanish fashion than the men's. There is no sign here of the long trailing skirts and Lancashire-lassie shawls of the

Mexicans. The Filipino lady's low-cut corsage and puffed sleeves, her white petticoat and coquettishly looped-up skirt are unheard of. True, the Quiché women's embroidered bodices may have borrowed something from European peasant costume; but their short skirts, reaching in many cases only to the knee—these are unquestionably Indian. Perhaps their color has changed since the conquest; for they are now dyed with indigo which was introduced by the Spaniards. But the cut is surely the same as it was when Alvarado passed this way.

Organization

1. Identify the key word in the thesis statement (first sentence of paragraph 1). How does it provide coherence for the essay?
2. Is the description used to support the thesis statement objective, subjective, or both?

Paragraphs

1. Point out uses of contrast in the development of paragraph 1.
2. Discuss the transitional devices used in paragraph 1.
3. What is the topic sentence in paragraph 3? How is it developed?

Sentences

1. Discuss the effectiveness of the sixth sentence of paragraph 1. How many specific details does it contain?
2. What kinds of figures of speech are used in paragraph 3?

Words

1. How many uses of figurative language appear in the essay? Do they convey their meaning especially well?
2. To what do the following allude? *Alvarado* (4). *John Bull* (2), *Sancho Panza* (3).
3. Be sure you know what each of the following means:

aguardiente (1)	*fincas* (1)
arrayed (1)	indigo (4)
coquettishly (4)	in lieu of (1)
dispensation (3)	monkey-jacket (2)
fiestas (1)	reminiscence (3)

Suggestions for Writing

1. Describe the types of clothing you would see at a shopping mall, a rock concert, or some other public gathering. Assume that your audience is senior citizens. Justify people's wish to dress differently from how they did 60 years ago.
2. Describe the native costumes of a foreign country either from firsthand observation, or from photographs taken by friends or seen in encyclopedias, travel magazines, and other sources.

A MATTER OF TASTE: CHOCOLATE

Mimi Sheraton

Mimi Sheraton: food critic, Time. " 'Getting paid to do what you like is almost always fun. And what I like to do most is eat. I'm especially crazy about restaurants because there is always an element of excitement about a meal: What will happen, how is it going to be?' . . . To be sure she is not recognized by maitre d's and waiters, Sheraton never makes reservations in her own name. She also declines to be photographed fullface. 'So I don't fight back, except of course in my reviews.' But critics, Sheraton believes, whether of food or fashions, movies or books, 'are willing to put up with the bad for the privilege of doing what they relish for a living.' " (Time, August 26, 1985) The following article appeared in New York magazine in 1975.

What details support Sheraton's assertion that *L. Russell Cook combines the objectivity of a scientist with the passion of a devotee?*

What techniques does Cook use to judge chocolates?

1   Anyone who thinks that ignorance is bliss need read no further; the subject is expertise. As an antidote to the reams of purple prose we are subjected to in the name of gourmandise, it seemed a good idea to explore some hard facts about foods-of-all-sorts, as they are known to bona-fide connoisseurs, with the relevant experts. Just as a wine connoisseur can tell a Bordeaux from a Burgundy, and name the château and vintage, so an herb expert differentiates between the best bay leaves from Turkey and their paltry imitator, California laurel, and knows whether the true sage, grown only in Yugoslavia, comes from the sunny or shady side of the hill. A trained coffee connoisseur sniffs and tastes and knows if the brew is based on fresh or stale beans from Columbia or Indonesia, if they were properly roasted and ground, and if they were brewed in a percolator (wrong) or a drip pot (right).

If the prospects of achieving such expertise seem hopeless, 2
take heart. Experts are made, not born, and as a rule are self-
taught. Depending on the food that interests you, the price of
such knowledge may or may not be high. Sampling beluga
malossol caviar will set you back more than developing dis-
cernment in chocolate, but interest in the particular food is
vital if you are to stick with it long enough.

A man who wears any color suit as long as it's brown, L. 3
Russell Cook combines the objectivity of a scientist with the
passion of a devotee. The subject of his expertise and his de-
votion (and the inspiration for his monochromatic wardrobe)
is chocolate. Since earning degrees in biochemistry and dairy
husbandry some 43 years ago, he has served as chief chemist,
technical director, and president to such large chocolate-man-
ufacturing firms as Wilbur, Ambrosia, and W. R. Grace's
Chocolate and Confectionery Division, and was president of
the Chocolate Manufacturers Association of the U.S.A. Although he describes chocolate in chemical formulas and has
developed a completely synthetic product, his personal taste
runs to the homemade chocolate in mom-and-pop confectionery shops.

He prefers dark, bittersweet chocolate to milk chocolate, 4
and feels the Swiss and Germans are best at producing it; Lindt
is his all-around favorite. Dutch chocolate he regards as somewhat second rate, and he doesn't think the Belgians are any
good at it at all. Godiva chocolates produced in this country,
he says, are made of a mediocre base product and sell for far-
above-average prices.

After spending a day in his study learning of all the things 5
that happen to chocolate between the bean and eating stages,
I decided the layman barely stands a chance. Yet Mr. Cook,
by looking, feeling, and tasting, can tell where the beans in a
blend came from, whether or not they were properly cleaned,
crushed, roasted, fermented, if they were "dutched" (treated
with an alkalizer to neutralize acids and darken color), or
"conched" (a cooking process that develops a nutlike flavor).
He can determine what other substances the chocolate contains (cocoa butter, soy lecithin, vanilla, vanillin, sugar),
whether or not it was properly tempered (a heating and cool-
ing process that develops finish and durability), and if it was
packed and handled well or poorly. What he knows could fill
a 500-page book, and, in fact, it has. *Chocolate Production
and Use* (Books for Industry, $29.95) is a trade bible.

Still, Cook was able to come up with a few general guide- 6
lines that might help would-be connoisseurs.

7   The first test is visual. Dark chocolate should have a reasonable gloss—a sort of satiny, but not high, oily finish, indicating it was properly tempered. The color can vary from yellow-brown to red-brown—that choice is personal. Mr. Cook prefers the yellow cast, indicating that the chocolate contains a fair amount of the mildest, most expensive beans, but others prefer the red, either for appearance or for its stronger taste. What it should *not* be is gray-brown. If chocolate has turned white, it is said to have a "bloom" which affects its look but does not mean it is inedible. The bloom may be from fat—i.e., the cocoa butter in the chocolate may have risen to the surface and stayed there (because it had been softened or not correctly tempered). If the bloom feels gritty, sugar has crystallized, which is harmless but creates an unpleasant texture. Chocolate should have a rich, mouth-wateringly aromatic "chocolate" smell—but don't test it when it is cold.

8   To taste properly, Cook takes what he considers a comfortable bite, holds it in his closed mouth, chews lightly, and lets it melt so the aroma will rise. He then makes sure it covers the surface of his tongue and looks for a smooth, creamy mass, a "well-rounded" flavor with "no jarring overtones or flat spots on the wheel." Then the chocolate must be swallowed to judge its aftertaste.

9   One of the most important telltale reactions is the chocolate's "melt-down" qualitites. If it remains solid too long or leaves a skinlike film on the tongue, it could be synthetic. On the other hand, it might be real chocolate tempered to withstand high temperatures for added shelf life, and so not meltable on the tongue. Chocolate should soften and melt slowly at 90 to 92 degrees Fahrenheit.

10   Milk chocolate shows less gloss, and shows bloom less readily, but both can be ascertained if you look carefully in good light. Well-tempered dark chocolate will snap sharply when broken, but milk chocolate, which is naturally softer, will not.

Organization

1. Is there a thesis statement for this essay? If not, write one.
2. Much of this essay appeals to the sense of taste. Point out places where Sheraton engages the other four senses.
3. What other methods of development are used to support description?

Paragraphs

1. What method of development is used to develop paragraph 1?
2. What specific details support the topic sentence of paragraph 7?
3. Paragraph 6 is one sentence. What is its function?

Sentences

1. What method of development, other than description, is used in the second sentence of paragraph 5? In the third sentence of 5?
2. How many specific details are there in the third sentence of paragraph 3?
3. Why are *well-rounded* and *no jarring overtones or flat spots on the wheel* enclosed in quotation marks in the second sentence of paragraph 8?

Words

1. What does *trade bible* mean in the last sentence of paragraph 5?
2. What does *beluga malossol caviar* mean in the last sentence of paragraph 2?
3. Be sure you know the meaning of these words:

antidote (1)	devotee (3)
chateau (1)	gourmandise (1)
confectionery (3)	monochromatic (3)
connoisseurs (1)	vintage (1)

Suggestions for Writing

1. Do you consider yourself an expert on some food (pizza, hamburgers, fried chicken, bread) or beverage (soda, beer, wine)? Describe the food or beverage so that your audience can appreciate your expertise.
2. Do you know an expert who *combines the objectivity of a scientist with the passion of a devotee?* Describe that person's field of expertise and the person.

LIFE ON A PARADE ROUTE

Franklin Daugherty

Franklin Daugherty: linguist, teacher, fiction writer. Daugherty was born in Birmingham, Alabama in 1950, but was raised in Mobile, Alabama, where he graduated from high school and now makes his home when he isn't out of the country. He holds degrees from Duke University, Tulane University, and Yale University. His speciality is languages, and he is certified to teach English as a Second Language. Daugherty has published in Mississippi *magazine, the* Azalea City News, *and* Southern Living. *At present he is under contract to teach English in Saudi Arabia.*

According to Daugherty, why are the festivities associated with Mardi Gras *the natural state of things*?

How do the Mardi Gras parades fit into a broader social context?

1   Four years ago when I moved back home to Mobile after a ten-year odyssey to college and New York and Germany, I found a situation that in my book is very close to heaven: a downtown apartment with a balcony right on the Mardi Gras parade route.

2   It is a roof, really, with a railing around it. Guests must clamber through a window, but there is room for almost thirty people, and plenty of landing space for the manna of bean bags, taffy kisses, Cracker Jacks, beads, and doubloons that shower nightly soon after dusk during that happy two weeks.

3   I love Mardi Gras. Save me from lukewarm revelers and practical people who say it costs too much money, for there is nothing, nothing like it. I love big crowds and excitement. I love costumes, masking, and pretending. Every year now I can have my fill. The parades pass twice by the old mansion, once in front on Government Street, then looping back around down Washington Avenue underneath my balcony so that we are right on top of several thousand screaming people and passing palaces and sea monsters and eye-to-eye with the maskers on the floats in their eerie, statue-faced "neutral masks."

4   There should come a moment in the perfect Mardi Gras when you feel that it will last forever. I first experienced it one year during the Crewe of Columbus parade ("Children's Favorite Stories") the Friday night before Fat Tuesday. I was standing at the kitchen stove hurriedly checking on a big pot of chicken and sausage gumbo. Inside, the apartment was still. Through the window I was watching my friends on the balcony jumping for Moon Pies, and big floats passing in an up-

roar of drums and shouting, when all at once the feeling came over me that this was the natural state of things, and the rest of the year, the days with no parades or parties, the exception. What could be more self-evident than that night after night high school bands were stopping right below to break-dance in the street, the tuba, and drum players balancing back on one hand and kicking up their legs while teenage girls shrieked.

Dancing in the street. A book I read not long ago on architecture and modern cities had a whole chapter on the widespread absence these days of dancing in the street. It was a necessity of life, they said. In medieval cities during carnival holidays it was a way the community recognized publicly and for all to see that beyond the careworn and workaday world there could be a keener life of undiluted merriment, perhaps joy. Luxurious excess. Transformation.   5

During the rest of the year, Washington Avenue is not a parade route but only a rather empty downtown street, full of vacant lots where Victorian city houses once stood jampacked. In the early morning, black maids in white uniforms walk in twos and threes to Government Street, where they will catch the bus to affluent Spring Hill. At night hobos en route to Florida or Louisiana go through the garbage looking for aluminum beer and soft drink cans they can cash in. Firetrucks use the street on their way back to the central fire station.   6

But by the time of the Crew of Columbus parade, the carnival juggernaut has been winding up to a fever pitch. Since the Camellia Ball on Thanksgiving night there have been unremitting debutante parties, suppers, and mystic society balls— the "winter social season" of the 19th-century cotton port is still very much alive. Harbingers have been appearing for weeks on ball nights: women in long gowns in the grocery store checkout lines, and men in white ties and tails pumping gas at self-service filling stations. There have been five night parades.   7

In the daytime children walk along Washington Avenue searching for doubloons and candy hidden in the weeds and bushes. Beads dangle from the branches of the old live oaks. Country youths ride down the street in pickup trucks, acid rock blaring and Confederate flags flying, yelling, "Yee-hi!"   8

When night falls, the tide of parade-goers begins to flow downtown. The dead vacant lots, holes torn out of the city, are filled again. Cars are parked on every inch of space, abandoned corners repeopled. Transformation.   9

The neophytes at the Greek mysteries saw their apparitions only when they stepped into the caves suitably prepared and worked up. Last year I watched every single parade. I taped   10 purple, green, and gold tragedy and comedy masks imported from New Orleans to the front door (a compromise: every purist in the Mother of Mystics knows that the colors of Mobile Mardi Gras are *only* purple and gold). I hung a Mardi Gras flag and strewed serpentine around the living room, wore my very own tuxedo to several balls, rented tails for others, marched as a Roman in the Joe Cain people's parade on Shrove Sunday, went party-hopping in a gaudy second-hand Knights of Revelry satin suit through the downtown historic districts on Mardi Gras Day.

11   Certain scenes, evanescent as fireworks, pass the balcony again and again as though the year between were only an instant. The marching cats and elephants of the Infant Mystics. Quivering papier-mâché, with bits of goldleaf glued all over that flutter in the light of the flares. Huge heads that wink and turn jerkily as if just on the point of rolling off into the street. And on the last night, with Ash Wednesday fast approaching, the sublime emblem float of the Order of Myths, the oldest parading mystic society (1868). It is *the* symbol of Mobile Mardi Gras: the jester Folly chasing Death around the broken column of Time, beating the skeleton specter with gilded pig bladders and always winning.

12   Certain situations never end. Somebody knows a masker on float No. 7, right-hand side, fourth person, and we're all counting and getting ready to yell. "Hey, Ron!" Or cutting across back streets to see the parade a second or third time. It is as though I am fourteen again and running with my friend Ed down Dauphin, across Lawrence toward Government, and in the distance we can hear muted band music and catch, yet again, glimpses of the very first costumed parade marshals on horseback.

13   As I write this, Washington Avenue is only Washington Avenue. Or is it more correct to say, we are merely in between parades?

Organization

1.   What is the spatial pattern used to present the visual details?
2.   Indicate where senses other than sight are engaged.

Paragraphs

1.   What method of development is used in paragraph 4?
2.   Paragraph 5 begins and ends with sentence fragments. Justify the construction. How does paragraph 5 relate to paragraphs 4 and 6?
3.   How is the topic sentence of paragraph 10 developed?

Sentences

1. How many details are there in the second sentence of paragraph 2?
2. Are the sentence fragments of paragraph 11 effective?

Words

1. Why is *neutral masks* enclosed in quotation marks in the last sentence of paragraph 3?
2. What is meant by *unremitting debutante parties* and *mystic society balls* in the second sentence of paragraph 7? Why is *winter social season* in quotation marks?
3. What are *Moon Pies* (4)?
4. Make sure you know the meaning of the following:

affluent (6)	manna (2)
apparitions (10)	masker (12)
doubloons (2)	neophytes (10)
evanescent (11)	odyssey (1)
gaudy (10)	serpentine (10)
harbingers (7)	specter (11)
juggernaut (7)	sublime (11)

Suggestions for Writing

1. Daugherty's apartment is an ideal place from which to experience Mobile's Mardi Gras. Write a description of your ideal gathering place or a particularly memorable place. Be sure that your description includes specific details that appeal to all five senses. (See Marcia E. Gainey's essay on p. 125 or Paul Pattacini's essay on p. 67.)
2. Describe an annual parade that occurs in your hometown or in a nearby city. What is the occasion? What do you feel, taste, hear, and smell as well as see? From what vantage point do you experience the festivities?

NEW YORK

Thomas Griffith

Thomas Griffith: reporter, editor, author. Griffith was born in Tacoma, Washington in 1915. After graduating from the University of Washington, he studied at Harvard. He spent six years as a reporter for the Seattle Times *(1936–1942) and then joined the staff of* Time, *where he rose from contributing editor to senior staff editor. Griffith is now a contributor to* Time. *The following is excerpted from "Go East, Young Man," an essay in his book* The Waist-High Culture *(1959).*

———————

How does Griffith's use of movement through space contribute to his description of New York?

Do New Yorkers, as Griffith describes them, have what you would call "good manners"? Why or why not?

1   After Boston, almost unwillingly I settled down in what called itself the greatest city in the world. Not the city, but the work to be found there, drew me. The jagged towers forming an asymmetrical harmony out of a thousand individual decisions had their celebrated postcard beauty, but the streets below needed a new Dante to bring hell up to date. New York is a city where millions are forced to work in the center, piled high in skyscrapers, borne up and down in crowded elevators in close body contact ("Make room for one more"). They must be taken there and removed each night through underground tunnels of lurching subway cars, where they stand packed, dull-eyed with fatigue and noise, self-concentrated and hostile, hurrying home to steel shelves where on unpaid furniture they spent their evenings watching the gray glare of the television screen. It is a city whose towers house businessmen who hire psychologists to study human fears which can be exploited to sell deodorants or tooth paste, and where glamor is set by synthetic personalities trained to appear relaxed and natural before hot lights and stop watches, so that they can create the right air of conviction about products they themselves never use. It is a city where people do not do, but watch: crowd stadiums to see others play baseball or football, go to galleries, to see what others paint or concerts to hear others play, and pay comedians to bring them laughter.

2   Wipe the soot from your eyes and examine the city about you. Travel the trains, out to the shining suburbs which are neither city nor country, where rows of empty automobiles beside the railroad platform reproachfully, wastefully await

their owners, away in the city until dark making a living. Those who live in these bedroom towns—people with sufficient salaries to command a place with clean air and a plot of green, along with the patience to make a long journey to enjoy it— realize the artificiality of any community where people do not work among those they live with, but what else can they do? As the commuter train makes its slow, dull, interrupted passage, peer out at the platforms where people lean resignedly against pillars as they wait for their trains: their eyes buried in newspapers or staring out and seeing nothing, their numbness apparent not only in their faces but in their elbows, their slouching hips, the way their feet are flatly planted in the concrete, and in the way they barely hear, and seem not to resent, the racket and roar of the express train hurtling by on the center tracks. Or come back to the city itself, past the abandoned brick buildings with windows empty, across the industrial river hedged by oil stations and warehouses and gravel pits—the only life stirring in the river below the slow shunting of barges. Now come the large housing projects all alike, geometrically sterile, with apartment buildings scientifically placed to catch the light yet somehow designed to keep out the life that agitated the slums they replaced. And beyond are the older places: fire escapes with laundry hanging out; grimy brick facades with upper windows open and fat women, leaning elbows on dirty pillows, looking torpidly out, or calling petulantly down to their children in the street below— black, Puerto Rican or white—who play among ash cans and parked cars, or sometimes flee to a concrete playground beside the river. Where is the equality of opportunity here?

Not from them, but from among the ambitious all over the 3 country must the big city draw constantly to replenish its talent and vitality, for the big city is not, as those who dream of it imagine it to be, a creator, but only an assembly point and consumer of talent. Ignore the multitudes about you, those Italians and Puerto Ricans with the look in their eyes of expecting a hurt; ignore too the well-to-do ladies for whom the city is the place where everything can be done for those who can pay; look instead at the city's most virile people—the successes. And what do you see? Too often it is marriage without communication; insatiable search for what, if found, will not satisfy; people who read detective stories or lending-library romances to pass the time; who otherwise read reviews, not books; who do not express thoughts but repeat remarks; who read magazines, hear music and tour museums not so much in pleasure as out of a felt need to keep up; who judge by dress and not by character; who shun the unexpected encounters of living for fear of other human beings will make demands on them; who even spend vacations in places where they know the other guests will have been screened to be like them—polite, decent and facile in talk that says nothing and will not disturb. These are the kind that fill the apartment buildings on the desirable streets, who crowd the proper cafés and fill the bars. Those who come from outside the city have to learn to draw on their accumulated capital of tolerance, for something in the city dries one up, killing instinctive sympathy, and substituting a conscious and detached politeness which is not at all the same.

4   But as the seasons turn, as the static heat of summer, lodged oppressively between the tall buildings, turns to wind-swept autumn days when people walk head down against the wind, each with his mind only on his own purposes, self-centered and melancholy, oblivious of the gutter sight of collapsed ribs of abandoned umbrellas blown inside out by the storm, indifferent to the frail city trees shivering and shedding their gold leaves—on these days, one discovers a community of shared frustrations with his fellow New Yorkers, a common pride in resistance to the harassments about one: noise, dirt, crowds, hurry, rain, the slam of brakes, fume of buses and chatter of riveting. It must be easy to be well-behaved in heaven, we think to ourselves; but we have learned adaptability and even a mutual forbearance on the cliffsides of hell. Civility breaks but rarely through the prevailing rudeness of New York. When it does, it makes no profession of sympathy, fears to be identified as softness, and does its good deed gruffly as if half-expecting to be rebuffed. And then one comes to contrast his own lot—his advantage in having been brought up in the confident open spaces; having a job that stimulates, and the opportunity to get away from it; having the price of good restaurants and theaters to escape the turmoil of the city streets—and marvels at any good nature at all in people whose whole lives have been spent here, condemned to work at tedious jobs and live in squalid quarters.

5   Out of the congested streets of New York comes a toughness and resilience of character that knows what it wants and is unsentimental in demanding it. Its most familiar product is that pushing, fast-talking, ruthless fellow who will step on faces to get where he wants. The quality manifests itself also in that mordant, unsparing wit that is the style of those big-time comedians who honed themselves on hecklers on the borscht circuit in the Catskills; it is also to be heard among thousands of New Yorkers, cab drivers and delivery boys, who pass off their daily complaints in the same rhythm of caustic

wisecrack and deadpan response, as if wit would be spoiled if given too good a reception. Economy of words, and those slurred, is the New York speech; courtesy, consideration and sympathy are carefully rationed: "So what? We all got problems."

The unsentimental, demanding metropolitan quality that is   6
New York's gift to the rest of the country has its origins in harsh circumstances and European beginnings. Here there is none of the West's sunny benevolence conferred on all but on none deeply: Old World families, a unit to themselves, are capable of strong feeling within it, but against everyone else are armored like armadillos. Among these people—the Italians, the Poles, the Russians, but above all the Jews—humor is never far from melancholy. They seem to have been born generations ago, and never to have passed through naïveté. They know the price of things, and think you a fool if you do not. They demand value. They know that they must work to get ahead, and are not indulgent of those who plead their charm to escape being judged on their merit. It is not only the poor who have this severity of judgment; among Jewish intellectuals, among wealthy Jews, among other European groups in New York are inherited standards in music, in art, in medicine, in science: if you would claim a special distinction, then deserve it. I do not mean that all Jews, all Europeans, have good taste (any more than all Negroes have rhythm) and if it is tawdriness they want, they can be just as demanding of value. But there is in New York City a sophisticated nucleus centering around them that makes for exacting critics and appreciative audiences. This is not the world of the Western United States, pleased to have heard an evening of chamber music at all: New Yorkers insist that the performance must measure up, and from their ruthlessness come the big city's standards of quality, the seeming heartlessness that sets it off from the rest of the country.

I came to like even New York.   7

Organization

1. The key phrase in the thesis statement is *the greatest city in the world*. That phrase is tempered, however, by the preceding phrase, *in what called itself*. In other words, New York may or may not be the greatest city in the world. Which paragraphs suggest that New York does not deserve its reputation? Which suggest that it does?

2. At what point does a transitional device indicate a shift in time?

Paragraphs

1. Is there a topic sentence in paragraph 2? If not, write one.
2. What is the topic sentence of paragraph 3? How is the paragraph developed?
3. Is the one-sentence closing paragraph effective?

Sentences

1. What senses are appealed to in the last two sentences of paragraph 1?
2. What senses are appealed to through the details in the first sentence of paragraph 4?
3. Two questions appear in the essay (the third sentence of paragraph 3 and the eighth sentence of paragraph 2.) What is the function of each?
4. Discuss the figure of speech in the second sentence of paragraph 6.

Words

1. To what do the following refer?
    a new Dante to bring hell up to date (third sentence of paragraph 1)
    borscht circuit in the Catskills (third sentence of paragraph 5)
2. What is the meaning of each of the following?

asymmetrical harmony (1)	oblivious (4)
facades (2)	petulantly (2)
facile (3)	squalid (4)
geometrically sterile (2)	tawdriness (6)
insatiable (3)	torpidly (2)
mordant (5)	virile (3)

Suggestions for Writing

1. Describe a city or town, emphasizing only its attractions or only its negative qualities. Assume that your audience is its governing body. Include suggestions that would improve the city or town.
2. Describe the individual human beings you see waiting in line (at the supermarket checkout counter, at the movies, at college registration, at a bus stop, at a sporting event). Let your description reveal the individuals' attitudes.

THE CICADA'S SONG

Sue Hubbell

*Sue Hubbell: "a sometime trucker who, for the past seven years, has been using a three-quarter-ton pickup to deliver honey around the country. She sleeps in truck stops because they are safe and coffee is always available." (*Time, *June 3, 1985). Hubbell is an occasional contributor to "American Scene," a feature of* Time. *This article appeared there in 1985.*

What positive benefits does Hubbell find in the invasion of the periodic cicadas?

How do the periodic cicadas manage to survive?

To hear people talk down at the café, you'd think we were being invaded by hostile aliens from a grade-B science fiction movie. A new brood of 13-year cicadas, estimated to be in the millions, has crawled up out of the ground in a big part of the country's midsection. Its members are trying their wings, singing like crazy and mating in a very public way. In a few weeks they will die off and be gone, but for now they are quite the topic of conversation. 1

There are annual cicadas all over the U.S. Most people call them dog-day cicadas, and their buzzy song is a part of the sound of late summer, like those of katydids and whippoor-wills. But in the Eastern half of the country at long intervals early in the summer, periodic cicadas emerge from the ground where, in their juvenile form, they have been feeding on the sap of tree roots. All cicadas in a particular region are presumed to be of the same origin and appear in synchrony in early summer. In Northern states and along the eastern edge of the Great Plains, they appear every 17 years: in the Southern and Mississippi valley states, it takes 13 years for a new brood to emerge. 2

These periodic cicadas are not so big as the common annual variety, but they are large as bugs go, broad, sturdy and nearly two inches in length. They have black bodies and huge showy wings that look like they are made of isinglass, delicately veined and edged in brilliant orange. Their legs are orange too. Their big, bulging eyes are deep red, and each is centered with a meaningful-looking dark brown dot. They are beautiful, spectacular bugs, and their appearance is exuberant and exciting, a marvel, a celebration. Their presence is a reminder that there are other life cycles than ours, other rhythms of living than the human one. 3

4   When they first come out of the ground, they are still wearing their golden-brown nymphal skins, which they shed. After
crawling out of that wingless skin, which splits neatly down
the back, the handsome adults sit quietly and visibly on tree
trunks tentatively trying their new wings. Then they set out
for a few weeks of courtship and mating. During those weeks
the males sing, the paired couple reproduce and then they die.

5   Scientists speculate that the periodic cicadas's infrequent
but abundant above-ground appearance is a survival strategy.
Predators cannot thrive on a dinner that shows up so seldom,
and the cicadas' sheer numbers guarantee that even though
individuals are easy to catch, many will survive.

6   Some also claim that the cicada's peculiar, burning, raspy
song, produced by a pair of ribbed membranes at the sides of
the male's abdomen, is irritating to predators. That seems fan-
ciful, but perhaps it is true because people are uncommonly
cross about cicadas and complain that their song is nerve-
racking. In Missouri, these days, it is constant and pervasive.
The cicadas have three things to say. One is a steady, insistent, buzzy trill: *zs-zs-zs-zs-zs*. It is a background to a more
varied *kee-o-keeeee-o-kee-o* that punctuates the steady drone.
When picked up and held, the cicadas emit a sharp *bzz-t-byzzt*
that sounds troubled and probably is.

7   Once the insects have paired, they mate openly on tree trunks
and branches, without regard for the fact that they can easily
be picked off and eaten by predators or squashed and dusted
with poison by humans. But most survive, and the female is
able to lay upwards of 500 eggs in slits that she makes in
twigs. The lives of the adults are soon over, and they die. But
in eight weeks the cicada nymphs hatch and burrow down
into the ground to reach the tree roots, on which they will
feed and grow slowly for the next 13 years.

8   The periodic cicadas do not kill trees in their feeding, and
at no point in their lives do they hurt garden vegetables or
flowering plants, although their egg laying can damage young
trees. They are bugs of such innocence and beauty and specialness that their appearance, one would think, would be regarded with interest and appreciation, like that of a comet or
a rare bird. But it is not.

9   Down at the post office the talk among people waiting for
their mail is of how bad the cicadas are and how much worse
they will get as they become more numerous. Over at the café
the morning crowd is discussing how to do them in. Squish-
ing them between thumb and forefinger was held to be effective but unaesthetic. A stick was recommended for bashing
them. Since the adult cicadas do not chew leaves, only con-

tact poisons will kill them, and the effectiveness of various kinds was being hotly debated. Some of the official types have been recommending dusting them with serious insecticides, but one of the coffee drinkers remembered the local state forester had said that that could cause increased levels of pesticide in the groundwater supply. The coffee cups were drained without reaching an agreement on methods, but the general opinion was that these bugs are annoying, lascivious, untidy, unruly—in short, a nuisance.

Back in my woods where I am cutting the winter's fire- 10 wood, the cicada's song fills my head, seems to reverberate inside it. Cicadas, the sun catching their wings and reflecting rainbows, line every tree trunk, every branch. One lights on my shoulder. His broad face with its big red eyes is inches from mine.

Kee-o-keeeee-o-kee-o, he says zestfully right into my ear. 11 He sounds pleased with himself; I know I am mightily pleased with him.

Organization

1. How does the organization of paragraph 1 guide the organization of the essay as a whole?
2. Point out examples of objective and subjective description.
3. How many senses are engaged by the essay? Where are these appeals?

Paragraphs

1. What is the method of development in paragraph 4?
2. What method of development supports description in paragraph 6?

Sentences

1. The last sentence of paragraph 8 is only four words. How effective is it?
2. Is the second sentence of paragraph 8 objective or subjective description?

Words

Be sure you know the meaning of these words:

dog-day (2)	predators (5)
exuberant (3)	reverberate (10)

isinglass (3)	synchrony (2)
lascivious (9)	tentatively (4)
membranes (6)	unaesthetic (9)
nymphal (4)	unruly (9)
nymphs (7)	zestfully (11)
pervasive (6)	

Suggestions for Writing

1. Pets (dogs, cats, goldfish, hamsters, parakeets, snakes) are considered by their owners to be pleasant additions to a household; others consider them to be nuisances. Describe a pet that you or someone else has had. Why would a non-pet owner consider your pet an inconvenience? Be sure your description engages as many senses as possible.
2. Describe the life-cycle of something you have studied in biology or with which you are familiar (a chicken, a butterfly, a hamster, a pet bird). Be sure your description includes as many senses as are engaged by each stage of the cycle.

ANATOMY OF A MARTIAN

Isaac Asimov

Isaac Asimov: biochemist, writer of science fiction. Asimov emigrated to the United States from Russia in 1932 at the age of twelve. He received his B.A., M.A., and Ph.D. in biology from Columbia. His science fiction won a Hugo Award, the highest honor in the field. In addition to biochemistry texts and science fiction, he has written numerous books that explain scientific concepts to laymen. This essay comes from Is Anyone Out There? *(1965).*

What are some of the conditions on Mars that might affect a Martian's anatomy?

Why does the Martian need two sets of eyes?

1   Conditions are so different on Mars and—to our earth-centered feelings—so inferior from those on earth that scientists are confident no intelligent life exists there. If life on Mars exists at all (the probability of which is small, but not zero) it probably resembles only the simplest and most primitive terrestrial plant life.

2   Still, even granted that the likelihood of complex life is virtually nonexistent, we can still play games and let our fancy roam. Let us suppose that we are told flatly: "There is intelligent life on Mars, roughly man-shaped in form." What reasonable picture can we draw on the basis of what we now

know of Mars—bearing always in mind that the conclusions we reach are not to be taken seriously, but only as an exercise in fantasy?

In the first place, Mars is a small world with a gravitational force only two-fifths that of earth. If the Martian is a boned creature, those bones can be considerably slenderer than ours and still support a similar mass of material (an inevitable mechanical consequence of decreased weight). Therefore, even if the torso itself were of human bulk, the legs and arms of the Martian would seem grotesquely thin to us.   3

Objects fall more slowly in a weak gravitational field and thus the Martians could afford to have slower reflexes. Therefore, they would seem rather slow and sleepy to us (and they might be longer-lived because of their less intense fight with gravitation). Since things are less top-heavy in a low-gravity world, the Martian would probably be taller than earth people. The Martian backbone need not be so rigid as ours and might have two or three elbowlike joints, making stooping from his (possible) eight-foot height more convenient.   4

The Martian surface has been revealed by the Mars-probe, Mariner IV, to be heavily pockmarked with craters, but the irregularities they introduce are probably not marked to a creature on the surface. Between and within the craters, much of the surface is probably sandy desert. Yellow clouds obscuring the surface are occasionally detected and, in the 1920s, the astronomer E. M. Antoniadi interpreted these as dust storms. To travel over shifting sands, the Martian foot (like that of the earthly camel) would have to be flat and broad. That type of foot, plus the weak gravity, would keep him from sinking into the sand.   5

As a guess, the feet might be essentially triangular, with three toes set at 120° separation, with webbing between. (No earthly species has any such arrangement, but it is not an impossible one. Extinct flying reptiles, such as the pterodactyl, possessed wings formed out of webbing extending from a *single* line of bones.) The hands would have the same tripod development, each consisting of three long fingers, equally spaced. If the slender finger bones were numerous, the Martian finger would be the equivalent of a short tentacle. Each might end in a blunt swelling (like that of the earthly lizard called the gecko), where a rich network of nerve endings, as in human fingertips, would make it an excellent organ for touching.   6

The Martian day and night are about as long as our own, but Mars is half again as far from the sun as we are, and it lacks oceans and a thick atmosphere to serve as heat reservoirs. The Martian surface temperature therefore varies from   7 an occasional 90° Fahrenheit, at the equatorial noon, down to a couple of hundred degrees below zero, by the end of the frigid night. The Martian would require an insulating coating. Such insulation might be possible with a double skin; the outer one, tough, horny, and water impervious, like that of an earthly reptile; the inner one, soft, pliable, and richly set with blood vessels, like that of an earthly man. Between the two skins would be an air space which the Martian could inflate or deflate.

8   At night the air space would be full and the Martian would appear balloonlike. The trapped air would serve as an insulator, protecting the warmth of the body proper. In the warm daytime, the Martian would deflate, making it easier for his body to lose heat. During deflation, the outer skin would come together in neat, vertical accordian pleats.

9   The Martian atmosphere, according to Mariner IV data, is extremely thin, perhaps a hundredth the density of our own and consisting almost entirely of carbon dioxide. Thus, the Martian will not breathe and will not have a nose, though he will have a strongly muscled slit—in his neck, perhaps—through which he can pump up or deflate the air space.

10   What oxygen he requires for building his tissue structure must be obtained from the food he eats. It will take energy to obtain that oxygen, and the energy supply for this and other purposes may come directly from the sun. We can picture each Martian equipped with a capelike extension of tissue attached, perhaps to the backbone. Ordinarily, this would be folded close to the body and so would be inconspicuous.

11   During the day, however, the Martian may spend some hours in sunlight (clouds are infrequent in the thin, dry Martian air) with his cape fully expanded, and resembling a pair of thin, membranous wings reaching several feet to either side. Its rich supply of blood vessels will be exposed to the ultraviolet rays of the sun, and these will be absorbed through the thin, translucent skin. The energy so gained can then be used during the night to enable the necessary chemical reactions to proceed in his body.

12   Although the sun is at a great distance from Mars, the Martian atmosphere is too thin to absorb much of its ultraviolet, so that the Martian will receive more of these rays than we do. His eyes will be adapted to this, and his chief pair, centered in his face, will be small and slitlike to prevent too much radiation from entering. We can guess at two eyes in front, as in the human being, since two are necessary for stereoscopic vision—a very handy thing to have for estimating distance.

It is very likely that the Martian will also be adapted to 13
underground existence, for conditions are much more equable
underground. One might expect therefore that the Martian
would also have two large eyes set on either side of his head,
for seeing by feeble illumination. Their function would be
chiefly to detect light, not to estimate distance, so they can
be set at opposite sides of the head, like those of an earthly
dolphin (also an intelligent creature) and stereoscopic vision
in feeble light can be sacrificed. These eyes might even be
sensitive to the infrared so that Martians can see each other
by the heat they radiate. These dim-vision eyes would be
enormous enough to make the Martian face wider than it is
long. In daytime, of course, they would be tightly closed behind tough-skinned lids and would appear as rounded bulges.

The thin atmosphere carries sound poorly, and if the Mar- 14
tian is to take advantage of the sense of hearing, he will have
to have large, flaring, trumpetlike ears, rather like those of a
jackrabbit, but capable of independent motion, of flaring open
and furling shut (during sandstorms, for instance).

Exposed portions of the body, such as the arms, legs, ears, 15
and even portions of the face which are not protected by the
outer skin and the airtrap within, could be feathered for warmth
in the night.

The food of the Martian would consist chiefly of simple plant 16
life, which would be tough and hardy and which might incorporate silicon compounds in its structure so that it would be
gritty indeed. The earthly horse has teeth with elaborate
grinding surfaces to handle coarse, gritty grass, but the Martian would have to carry this to a further extreme. The Martian mouth, therefore, might contain siliceous plates behind
a rounded opening which could expand and contract like a
diaphragm of a camera. Those plates would work almost like
a ball mill, grinding up the tough plants.

Water is the great need. The entire water supply on Mars is 17
equal only to that contained in Lake Erie, according to an estimate cited by astronomer Robert S. Richardson. Consequently, the Martian would hoard the water he consumes, never
eliminating it as perspiration or wastes, for instance. Wastes
would appear in absolutely dry form and would be delivered
perhaps in the consistency, even something of the chemical
makeup, of earthly bricks.

The Martian blood would not be used to carry oxygen, and 18
would contain no oxygen-absorbing compound, a type of substance which in earthly creatures is almost invariably strongly
colored. Martian blood, therefore, would be colorless. Thus

the Martian skin, adapted to ultraviolet and absorbing it as an energy source, would not have to contain pigment to ward it off. The Martian therefore would be creamy in color.

19   The extensible light-absorbing cape, particularly designed for ultraviolet absorption, might reflect longwave visible light as useless. This reflected light could by yellowish in color. This would cause our Martian to seem to be (when he was busily absorbing energy from solar radiation) a dazzling white creature with golden wings and occasional feathers.

20   So ends our speculation—in a vision of Martian forms not so far removed from the earthman's fantasies of the look of angels.

Organization

1. The thesis statement (the second sentence of paragraph 2) announces that the conditions on Mars will determine the picture of a Martian. Is there any observable order to the way these conditions are arranged in the essay?

Paragraphs

1. What is the topic thought of paragraph 8? How is it developed?
2. Identify the topic sentence of paragraph 13. How is it developed?
3. In what way is paragraph 17 analytical?
4. Identify and discuss the transitions in paragraph 18.
5. The closing paragraph is a one-sentence summary. Is it significant enough? Why or why not?

Sentences

1. Identify the transitional devices in the first sentence of paragraph 7. Discuss their functions.
2. Discuss the appropriateness and effectiveness of the figurative language in the third and fourth sentences of paragraph 16.
3. The first sentence of paragraph 17 contains only five words. Justify its brevity.

Words

1. Be sure you know the meaning of each of the following:

anatomy (title)   membranous (11)
equable (13)   pliable (7)

fantasy (2)	terrestrial (1)
grotesquely (3)	torso (3)
impervious (7)	translucent (11)

Suggestions for Writing

1. Choose a sport (swimming, skiing, tennis, basketball . . .). Considering its demands, describe the anatomy of the ideal participant.
2. Imagine and describe a sports or recreational activity ideally suited to the Martian anatomy as described in Asimov's essay. It may be a variation of a human activity or something altogether new.

REFLECTIONS OF THE PAST

Marcia E. Gainey

Marcia E. Gainey: student. Gainey was born in Jackson, Mississippi in 1948 and graduated from Pascagoula High School in Pascagoula, Mississippi. Her undergraduate major is sociology. This essay is based on Suggestions for Writing 1 on p. 111.

It has been fifteen years or more since I was in my grandparents' home. Granny Bessie died in 1965 and Grandpa passed away in 1968. The house was sold, and few of the family members have gone back. 1

I know that the neighborhood has changed. I'm sure the familiar people have moved away or died. I suspect the landscape is different. For all I know, the house itself may be gone. But in my mind, nothing has changed. Time has stopped. It's as though I expect to go back to Memphis and find it the way it was in 1959. 2

Granny's house was built in the early 1900s. All of the houses around it were a simplified version of the southern colonial style. Her house was distinctive because it sat back from the street. A short, iron fence separated the sidewalk from the yard. 3

Grandpa had made a unique walkway to the house. He used small wooden blocks to pave a sidewalk through the middle of the yard. The wood was treated with creosote, and the scent lingered in the air. The walkway was rough and a little bit wobbly, something like cobblestone. I have never seen another sidewalk like it. It served the purpose, however, and was never changed or replaced. 4

5   A wide porch was built across the front of the house. Grandpa had painted it battleship gray. The paint was worn and chipped in spots where two metal rocking chairs sat. He repainted the porch every spring, and it was always starting to chip by July.

6   A large green swing hung on one side of the porch. It was attached to the ceiling with heavy duty chains. Five or six people could easily sit on this swing. A four o'clock bush grew directly behind the swing. The fragrance of those red, sweet smelling flowers filled the air. My sister and I would swing for hours and make up silly songs. Those happy times made a lasting impression on my young mind.

7   Just beyond the glass front door was the living room. There was an Early American couch, several chairs and an ottoman. Another couch and chair of no particular period filled out the room. One side of the room had a fireplace, but it was never used. The inside bricks had crumbled and the firebox was closed off. A space heater sat in front of it.

8   On the mantel sat a clock, several antique vases and assorted nick nacks. The clock was from Germany and had a little boy and girl who moved in and out of two doors in rhythm with the mainspring.

9   On the far left sat Granny's piano. It was a huge upright monster. The keys were yellowed and chipped with age. It never seemed completely in tune, either. That never bothered Granny. She was always eager to pound out a tune. Although there was plenty of sheet music on the music stand, she seldom needed it. She played by note and by ear, so her tattered sheet music was mostly a decoration.

10   Inside the house, the distinct odor of pine oil wafted through the air. Granny always kept a coffee can filled with water and Pine Sol on the main space heater. In the winter, the scent of heated pine oil was especially heavy.

11   The floor of the house was covered by several layers of linoleum. The top layer was worn down to make a path from the front of the house to the back. Looking at the edges, it was easy to see that the pattern had been printed to resemble a floral carpet.

12   The main bedrooms were in the middle of the house. To get to the back of the house, it was necessary to walk through these rooms. Consequently, when the family gathered, all parts of the house were in use. If the living room was crowded, family and friends sat on the beds. In the first bedroom was a vanity with a huge, round mirror. Granny kept dominoes and other toys there. All of the grandchildren considered this their toy box and sat there to play.

13   In the back of the house was a bathroom, kitchen and enclosed porch. The floor of this part of the house had a definite

slant toward the back door. Visitors were always warned to watch their step.

The kitchen was usually full of good things to eat. Granny 14 prepared for our visit for days ahead of time. She baked custard pies, coconut cake and other treats. She was sure to serve turkey and dressing. If a big crowd was expected for dinner, she made a gigantic pot of spaghetti. If we were lucky, she made her famous ravioli. Her pasta was entirely home made and most of the filling and sauce were Granny's secret. It took two days to make and no one *ever* turned down Granny's ravioli.

This may sound odd, but one of Granny's best treats was 15 grits. She used the old fashioned kind that had to be cooked for an hour or so. She got up before everyone else so she could cook the grits. They were smooth and had lots of butter. I guess she took the recipe to her grave, because I've never tasted any other grits like hers.

As a child, I always thought Granny would be a perfect Mrs. 16 Santa Claus. She was short and round with curly, gray hair. Her glasses were gold wire rims. She wore sturdy, sensible shoes and seldom was without an apron. Granny was a jolly person and laughed easily. She was devoted to her family, friends and church. It was rare to hear her complain.

Grandpa was a funny little elf of a man. He was about five 17 feet tall and barely weighed one hundred pounds. His fingers were yellowed from years of smoking unfiltered Pall Malls. The smell of his cigarette smoke could be detected day or night. He didn't care much for progress. We could never convince him that man would some day walk on the moon. He was very skeptical and died about six months before Neil Armstrong did walk on the moon.

Grandpa was a private man, and he often sat on the back 18 porch when company came. Sometimes the grandchildren would go back there and sit with him. If a train whistle blew, he could tell us the train number and where it was headed. Good-byes were difficult for Grandpa, and he frequently disappeared when we got ready to leave. Many people didn't understand him and were baffled by his peculiar habits.

Our ability to remember is a wonderful mystery. Things that 19 we thought were too dim to recall can come tumbling back with just a little prodding. It seems strange that my memories are so sharp, even after all of these years. I know that a few faded photographs and some wispy childhood memories are all that remain. The people are gone and probably the building is, too. Somehow, it is comforting to know that those memories are stored away and can be called up on a moment's notice.

6
Example

Probably the most common method of developing a thesis is by the use of examples. For instance, in ordinary conversation you do not talk about television programs or baseball teams in general—at least, not for long. You talk about TV talk shows or the Atlanta Braves or, even more specifically, about Phil Donahue or Dale Murphy. In other words, you feel the need of "getting down to cases," of illustrating your general remarks with specific examples for the sake of clarity and vividness. This need is even greater for the essay, dealing as it does with topics generally more complex and abstract than those encountered in daily conversation.

Many of the essays you write in college will be expository ones. Expository writing explains what something is, and often the clearest explanation presents an illustration or example. Sometimes a single extended illustration, buttressed by description and narration, provides sufficient explanation. At other times, several brief examples may be more effective. In either case, illustration makes writing more interesting by offering concrete examples of a general statement. This method of development answers the basic question: what is the chief feature or features of *X?*

1. Distinguish Example from Description

Here is a thesis statement that should be developed by description:

> Four years ago when I moved back home to Mobile after a ten-year odyssey to college and New York and Germany, I found a situation that in my book is very close to heaven: a downtown apartment with a balcony right on the Mardi Gras parade route. (Franklin Daugherty, p. 108)

Note that the key words and phrases are relatively specific. They refer to a *downtown apartment with a balcony* on the *Mardi Gras parade route*. The details that follow should (and do in the essay) supply additional information about these items and no others.

The following thesis statement should be developed by example:

In this volume you can learn all about cricket, cotton, costume designing, crocodiles, crown jewels, and Coleridge, but none of these subjects is so interesting as the Courtship of Animals, which recounts the sorrowful lengths to which all males must go to arouse the interest of a lady. (James Thurber, p. 150)

Note that the latter part of this thesis statement is more abstract than the earlier one. Its key words and phrases are indefinite. *Courtship of Animals* is unspecified; *sorrowful lengths* is a general attitude, covering a wide range of negative reactions; *arouse the interest of a lady* is vague. The details that follow this thesis statement, then, should (and do) clarify it by citing specific courtship patterns that males of various species employ in an attempt to attract females. In other words, the essay furnishes *examples* of what the thesis statement says in general terms.

2. Include Enough Examples to Support Your Thesis

Thurber sets out, with tongue in cheek, to show what a difficult time males of the species, including *Homo sapiens*, have in winning the fancy of the females. To make his case, he could hardly be expected to mention *every* species in the animal kingdom, but neither could he rest his case on only one or two examples. His thesis is, after all, a statement about species in general; therefore, he makes a large enough selection—five major examples and six minor ones—to convince the reader that his generalization is sound. Furthermore, his examples include fowls, insects, crabs, spiders, snails, and *Homo sapiens*—six species. When you finish reading Thurber's essay, you know the chief features associated with the courtship of animals.

3. Use Specific Details in Your Examples

Like the descriptive essay, the essay developed by examples uses details. In the descriptive essay, all the details more or less directly develop the key ideas of the original thesis statement. But in the illustrative essay, the *example* develops the thesis while the details develop the example. For instance, Thurber's paragraph 4 has this topic sentence: *The bowerbird is another creature that spends so much time courting the female that he never gets any work done.* This example is directly related to the thesis. The details of the paragraph relate all the effort the bowerbird expends in *courting the female.* So in writing example, keep in mind the function of both the example and the details that support the example.

4. Arrange Your Examples Carefully

As you look over your prewriting notes for your essay to be developed by example, a primary concern is the order in which you will present your materials. Your arrangement is determined, for the most part, by the nature of the examples you choose. What do your examples have in common, other than supporting your thesis statement? Can you arrange them in an ascending order of importance? For example, George W. Hunt in his "Biblical Bloopers" (p. 132–33) uses public outrage as his principle of organization. In paragraph 6 he writes, *But the champion of biblical bloopers . . . ;* and in paragraph 7, *Still, the greatest brouhaha. . . .* Patrick Ryan (p. 135) arranges his examples in "Business as Usual Down at the Old Necropolis," for the most part, geographically. In paragraph 1 he mentions *European morticians.* Paragraph 2 begins, *From Italy . . .* paragraph 3, *In France . . .* and paragraph 4, *In Russia . . .* Thurber's organizing principle is, basically, the elaborate displays males engage in to attract the attention of females. Beginning with *a certain little trick* of the peacock, he describes a series of increasingly intricate male gyrations, culminating in the *web-twitching* of spiders who have *a tougher life than any other males in the animal kingdom.* In paragraph 7, Thurber's list of briefer examples is likewise arranged in an order of increasing ostentation.

A careful examination of your examples will suggest a method of arrangement. Would some of your examples be more familiar to your classmates than others? If so, a familiar-to-unfamiliar order is appropriate. Are some of your examples more dramatic than others? If so, a climactic arrangement would work for you.

Sometimes a single extended illustration may be sufficient for your purpose. For example, Irving Howe (pp. 138–40) uses the closing of one bookshop—that of Colombia University—to illustrate his contention that it's important for students to *learn what a first-rate bookshop looks like.* His supporting details all spring from a single example.

5. *Fit Your Examples to Your Audience*

All of the following writers support their theses with examples that are easily recognizable by a general audience. Some readers of H. Allen Smith's essay (p. 146) may never have thought about whether a particular word is aesthetically pleasing or not, but the concept is easily understood. Readers of Thurber's essay need no special knowledge of zoology to understand the courting habits of peacocks, butterflies, and fiddler crabs—all of them familiar inhabitants of nature, and all of them made even more recognizable here by being characterized in human terms. The point is, the examples fit the audience. When you write an illustrative essay, be sure your examples are relevant, convincing, and closely related to your thesis statement.

6. *Choose an Appropriate Place for Your Thesis Statement*

Your thesis statement may precede or follow your examples. Either position is acceptable; the choice of one over the other depends on the particular effect you are trying to achieve. You could begin with your examples and allow your thesis statement to be a conclusion drawn from them. (Of course, you must know what the thesis is *before* you begin writing.) In thus letting your readers feel that they have been following your reasoning process, you will lead them to accept your thesis. The essays that follow take a different approach. Hunt and Thurber place their thesis statements in their first paragraphs. Lewis Thomas puts his thesis statement in paragraph 3; Howe, in paragraph 4; and H. Allen Smith, in paragraph 5. These three writers delay presenting their thesis statements in order to prepare their readers for them. Ryan's thesis is implied, not stated.

7. *Combine Methods of Development*

Example often relies on other methods of development to achieve its purpose. For instance, Howe uses a narrative as the substructure for his illustration; Smith employs contrast; Thomas enlists both description and analysis. You, too, may combine methods of development, but remember that your primary goal is to give an example or examples.

BIBLICAL BLOOPERS

George W. Hunt

George W. Hunt: Jesuit, editor, author. Hunt was born in New York City in 1937. He holds degrees from Fordham, Yale, and Syracuse. He entered The Society of Jesus in 1954. Hunt has taught at LeMoyne College and Georgetown University. His critical studies include John Updike and the Three Great Secret Things *and* John Cheever: The Hobgoblin Company of Love. *In 1984 he became editor-in-chief of* America, *a weekly magazine intended for an adult, educated, largely Roman Catholic audience.* America *publishes poetry as well as articles on literature and current political and social events. The following essay appeared in* America *in 1985.*

How many examples of biblical bloopers does Hunt include?

Which of Hunt's examples of bloopers are mistranslations and which are misprints?

1   G. K. Chesterton said: "The Bible tells us to love our neighbors, and also to love our enemies; probably because they are generally the same people." Chesterton, as usual, is correct, but I keep wondering what text of the Bible he himself used. Recent research of mine suggests where he might have gotten the idea of linking neighbors with enemies—not by ironic design but by accident.

2   The history of English texts of the Bible is fraught with howlers that must chill the soul of any fundamentalist who emphasizes the verbal inerrancy and literalist interpretation of Scripture. In 1631, the King's printers, for example, omitted the word "not" from a key commandment in Exodus and so enjoined "Thou shalt commit adultery." Thereafter, this edition was known as the "Wicked" or "Adulterous" Bible.

3   This edition is not to be confused with the "Unrighteous" Bible printed in 1653 that rendered 1 Cor. 5:9 as "know ye not that the unrighteous shall inherit the Kingdom of God?" It also translated Rom. 6:13: "Neither yield ye your members as instruments of righteousness unto sin," in another charming reversal.

4   Inevitably it was the printer who bore the wrathful burden for such gaffes. So perhaps it was subconscious guilt that prompted the editors in 1702 to rephrase David's complaint in Psalm 119:161: "printers (instead of princes) have perse-

cuted me without cause." Not long before in the reign of Charles I (1625–49), Psalm 14:1 had read: "The fool hath said in his heart there is a God." The printers were fined 3,000 pounds and all the copies were suppressed, but the edition actually came to a better end than Charles himself.

Over the centuries these choice editions have taken on their 5 own distinctive nomenclature. Coverdale's Bible of 1535 is more affectionately known as the Bug Bible, for it translated Psalm 91:5: "Thou shalt not need to be afraid for any bugs by night" (instead of "terrors"). The Judas Bible of 1611 had Judas and not Jesus in the Garden of Gethsemane. The name Breeches Bible has a more sartorial and modest ring than does the actual Geneva Bible because it rendered Gen. 3:7, where Adam and Eve realize their nakedness, this way: "and they sowed fig-leaves together, and made themselves breeches." The second edition of the same Geneva Bible was known as the Whig Bible, a jibe at the British party of landed gentry and merchants, who opposed the Tories and upheld the power of Parliament against the King, because it rendered one of the beatitudes: "Blessed are the placemakers (not peacemakers): for they shall be called children of God."

But the champion of biblical bloopers is the Lions Bible is- 6 sued in 1804, which contains a countless number. In his address to the people, Solomon recalls Yahweh's promise to his father David this way: "thou are not the man to build the temple, but thy son shall come forth out of thy lions (instead of loins)." In Paul's letter to the Galatians 5:17, we hear this: "For the flesh lusteth after the Spirit (and not against the Spirit)."

Still, the greatest brouhaha was caused by the "Leda Bible." 7 This 1572 edition was so called, because its decorations for some incongruous reason were inspired by scenes from the pagan Ovid's *Metamorphoses*. Readers were startled, for instance, upon opening the Epistle to the Hebrews to see an explicitly artistic woodcut depicting the scene where Jupiter, in the guise of a swan, has his way with the lovely mortal Leda. Needless to say, the protests were vigorous.

Yet God's word manages to transcend all human goofs. After 8 all, as Huckleberry Finn observed, "It ain't those parts of the Bible that I can't understand that bother me, it is the parts that I do understand."

Organization

1. What is the thesis statement? How many specific examples support this thesis?

2. How effective is the use of quotations in the opening and closing paragraphs? How do the quotations relate to the thesis statement?

Paragraphs

1. How many details support the example in paragraph 5? Are there enough?
2. How many details support the example in paragraph 6? Are there enough?

Sentences

1. The last sentence of paragraph 4 refers to the death of Charles I. What happened to him?
2. What method of development supports example in the last sentence of paragraph 5?

Words

1. What is "Ovid's *Metamorphoses*" in the second sentence of paragraph 7?
2. Who was *G. K. Chesterton* (opening words)?
3. Be sure you know the meaning of these words:

explicitly (7)	inevitably (4)
fundamentalist (2)	nomenclature (5)
gaffes (4)	sartorial (5)
incongruous (7)	verbal inerrancy (2)

Suggestions for Writing

1. Chesterton said our neighbors and our enemies "are generally the same people." If you agree that the statement is true, write an essay that provides examples to support your agreement. If you disagree, write an essay that provides examples that support your disagreement.
2. Choose some activity that is usually taken seriously. Use multiple "bloopers" to illustrate how the activity's serious feature can be transformed into a humorous one. Consider these activities as possible topics: dating, athletic contests, classroom activities, travel, a church service, a home improvement project.

BUSINESS AS USUAL DOWN AT THE OLD NECROPOLIS

Patrick Ryan

Patrick Ryan: essayist. Ryan is a Britisher who lives in Surrey. He occasionally contributes to Smithsonian, *a monthly published by the Smithsonian Institute. Articles on folk and fine arts, history, natural sciences, and hard sciences are included in the magazine. The publication has a circulation of 2,000,000, 85 percent of whom are college-educated. The following essay appeared in 1974.*

Does Ryan have an implied serious purpose in his essay?

Do all of Ryan's examples *lampoon the commercial accent* of funerals?

Thanks largely to Evelyn Waugh and Jessica Mitford, it has 1 long been a literary fad to lampoon the commercial accent of American funeral rites. Now reports from across the Atlantic indicate that European morticians are coming up fast.

From Italy comes news of the opening of the first undertak- 2 er's supermarket in Milan where customers may pick up at discount everything from a coffin to a black-edged card. Competition among the city's 80 funeral firms is so cutthroat that doctors, nurses and parish priests receive payola from their retaining morticians for dropping first word of a visit from the Grim Reaper. As for the general public, the first to the telephone after a loved one breathes his last can choose from such prizes as a suit, dress, 100 pairs of stockings, two spring mattresses or—perhaps on the chance that a replacement spouse is in the wings—a baby carriage.

In France, the sepulchral industry is currently racked by 3 conflict between the monopolistic Pompes Funèbres, Europe's largest layers-to-rest, and a network of small funeral parlors. Allegations have been made that in some towns political corruption has helped give the "PF" the lion's share of France's 550,000 burials a year. One firm has been caught tapping the PF telephone to find out their price of an interment, and then dashing round to the relicts with a cut-rate offer.

In Russia, complaints have been made about officials of the 4 state funeral bureau exploiting the bereaved for a fast ruble. From Moscow it has been reported that bribery is essential if the dear departed is to get a coffin, a grave dug and headstone mounted before the Archangel Gabriel announces the end of the world and renders the whole process superfluous. Cemetery officials illegally and unfeelingly charge money for the grave site, digging of the grave and for giving it a finished appearance. The available hearses in the state funeral car pool operate on a tight time schedule, speeding to and from the cemeteries so rapidly that, according to a Soviet paper, "one cannot easily tell whether the dead man is going to his eternal rest or to put out a fire."

5   We humans have always been divided about the best way of disposing of ourselves after we have shuffled off this mortal coil. Egyptians practiced mummification; Romans generally preferred entombment; Vikings launched their late lamented in blazing boats. Hindus burn cast-off bodies on kindling pyres; Muslims bury their departed lying on their right sides facing Mecca; and Parsees expose their dead on "towers of silence" as provender for vultures. Solomon Islanders have lain those not lost but gone before on coral reefs as food for sharks; other Melanesians have eaten up their time-expired relatives themselves. The Irish hold wakes which threaten to dissolve both mourners and loved one in alcohol; and the Koryak tribe of northern Siberia make their last farewells by playing cards on the corpse.

6   Now, a new dimension in disposal has been reported from Nashville, Tennessee, where the first part of a three-winged skyscraper mausoleum is under construction. The Cross Mausoleum, a 20-story building, will accommodate about 100,000 defunct customers and is forecast to release a whole lot of Tennessee acreage for jollier purposes. "The land for 100,000 cemetery lots would require 192 acres," calculated an official of the controlling Woodlawn Mortuary Incorporated. "With the mausoleum, including parking facilities, it will require 14 acres."

7   That's quite a point when you recall that Père-Lachaise cemetery in Paris covers more than 100 acres. In Britain, advertisements have recently appeared urging newspaper readers to opt now for final cremation and thus, "Be a land-saver. . . . Join the Cremation Society."

8   Apart from land-saving, the Woodlawn "High-Rise Necropolis" will make it possible for the remains of Nashville's wealthy to be borne heavenwards, as though by angels, in a flower-decked elevator. The higher up, the closer to paradise; the nearer the top of the tower, the nearer, my God, to Thee.

9   A crypt in this Hilton of Mortality will cost from $2,000–$3,500, which recalls the words of Bumble the beadle to Sowerberry the undertaker as Oliver Twist was being sold by the former to the latter: " 'You'll make your fortune, Mr. Sowerberry,' said the beadle, as he thrust his thumb and forefingers into the proffered snuff-box of the undertaker: which was an ingenious little model of a patent coffin. 'I say you'll make your fortune. . . .' "

Organization

1. The thesis is implied in paragraph 1. From information in the essay and guidance given in the first paragraph, formulate a thesis statement.
2. Is there a consistent attitude throughout this essay? If so, identify it and indicate how it is maintained. If not, give examples of where it shifts and indicate whether the shifts are proper.
3. How does paragraph 5 relate to paragraphs 4 and 6? Could this paragraph appear at another place in the essay? Could it be omitted entirely?

Paragraphs

1. Write a topic sentence for paragraph 2.
2. Identify the topic sentence of paragraph 4. How is it developed?
3. How is the quotation in the final paragraph related to the thesis of the essay? Is the quotation appropriate as a concluding device?

Sentences

1. What is unusual about the last sentence of paragraph 8?
2. How do you react to the sudden use of a quotation in the last sentence of paragraph 4?
3. How many substitutes for *dead person* (or *people*) are used in paragraph 5?

Words

1. To what do the following allude? *Evelyn Waugh* and *Jessica Mitford* (1) and *Hilton of Mortality* (9).
2. *Bumble, Sowerberry,* and *Oliver Twist* (9) are all references to what?
3. Be sure you know the meaning of each of the following:

allegations (3)	payola (2)
bereaved (4)	proffered (9)
defunct (6)	provender (5)
interment (3)	pyres (5)
lampoon (1)	relicts (3)
mausoleum (6)	sepulchral (3)
necropolis (title)	superfluous (4)

Suggestions for Writing

1. Striving for the same attitude as that of this essay, discuss and illustrate the amusing, extravagant, or peculiar aspects of some "serious" activity with which you are familiar (church services, formal lectures, symphony concerts).
2. Defend or attack the notion that Ryan has a serious purpose in this essay—the correction of abuses in funeral customs. Use illustrations drawn from the essay itself. Address your essay to funeral directors who see no abuses in American funeral customs.

DEATH OF A BOOKSTORE

Irving Howe

Irving Howe: historian, author, critic. Howe was born in New York City in 1920 and attended City College of New York. After teaching at Brandeis and Stanford, he returned to Hunter College of CCNY in 1963 where, in 1970, he was honored as Hunter's Distinguished Professor. Among his numerous prizes are an award from the National Institute of Arts and Letters and a Guggenheim Fellowship. His critical works include studies of Sherwood Anderson, William Faulkner, and Thomas Hardy. This article originally appeared in the New York Times *in 1973.*

What does Howe say are the minimum requirements for a first-rate bookshop?

What reasons does Howe give for maintaining a comprehensive bookstore?

1 Once every five or six weeks, on a day when my work has gone very well or very badly, I take the 104 bus up to Columbia University, where I lunch on ghastly food in those Broadway joints the students seem to like, glance through the little magazines in the nearby stores, and spend half an hour at the Columbia University bookshop. I've been doing this for eight or nine years now, as a way of passing some time in contented aloneness. Usually I buy book or two at the Columbia store, telling myself that I "need" them, and sometimes that's even true.

2 A few weeks ago I again undertook this ritual journey, went to the Columbia bookshop—and suffered mild shock. It was no longer there. It had been replaced by a "new bookstore," sublet to Barnes & Noble, featuring paperback texts used in classes. (Also, about 30 hardcover new books, half of them written by Columbia professors—distinguished volumes, no doubt, but comprising a somewhat narrow selection.)

Those tempting shelves of solid, hardcover history, philos- 3
ophy and sociology, those generous selections of poetry, fiction, literary criticism and classics—some of them published
as far back as four or five years ago!—all gone. In their place,
a dispirited, mediocre paperback store, better, to be sure, than
the one at the college where I teach, but not, by the most
generous description, a serious bookshop.

It seems a pity, a real loss for those few thousand people in 4
New York who care about books, and a loss too for Columbia,
probably the most distinguished university in the city. For if
it's important to provide students with first-rate physics labs,
gyms and professors, then it's also important that they learn
what a first-rate bookshop looks like. They might try it; they
might like it. At Columbia they no longer can.

A little while after this piece appears in print there will 5
probably arrive at the Book Review a letter from a Columbia
vice president saying that the university, caught in a budget
squeeze, had to abandon its once-distinguished bookshop because it was losing a sizable number of dollars each year. Perhaps, by way of reply, I'll say that Columbia should feel obliged
to subsidize a bookshop for the same reasons that it subsi-
dizes other educational facilities, or perhaps I'll get irritable
and snap something about cutting the number of academic
bureaucrats in order to have enough money for the things that
really matter. But whatever answer I give won't be easy or
entirely persuasive, since it's foolish to look down one's nose
at the financial problems of universities like Columbia. Those
problems are all too real.

But there is another reality: that in the whole of New York, 6
with its many universities, we don't have a bookshop that
could match in range and depth of holdings a store like Blackwell's in Oxford or the stores one sees in Rome and Paris and
even a provincial town like Palermo. We have the Gotham
Book Mart, fine for literary people, and the Eighth Street
Bookstore, fine for recent and topical books; but we don't have
a store that will stock, as the one at Columbia used to, both
recent and not-so-recent books of intellectual substance, a store
that will also carry, say, the Everyman series and perhaps even
a few Loeb Classics.

It's a scandal. Not one of the major scandals in this sad and 7
beaten city, nothing to arouse the indignation that a score of
our injustices can or should still arouse; but a scandal nevertheless. And in saying this I'm aware of the problems that
publishers and booksellers will cite: the high rents, the excessive number of books published each year, the small sales of

serious books, the sheer cost of keeping a book on the shelves for more than a few months.

8   All true enough, but not reason enough. For we should not accept in regard to a small matter like a comprehensive bookshop the argument that we ought also to reject in regard to large matters like poverty, schools and employment—the argument, I mean, that circumstances must overwhelm intentions, that policy creates its own defeats, and that in an admittedly complex world the best we can do is to reflect upon our sense of complexity.

9   Is there a solution? Perhaps the publishers could get together and jointly run their own "Blackwell's in New York." Perhaps a few hundred writers could invest a thousand dollars each . . . but what a nightmare: Imagine a stockholders meeting at which everyone keeps screaming that his or her book isn't being given adequate display. Perhaps a wealthy young man in love with letters would do for bookselling what James Laughlin did for avant-garde publishing some decades ago. Perhaps a bookseller both high-minded and shrewd could make a go of a first-rate bookshop.

10   All rather unlikely, all tokens of fantasy? Probably so. Yet the fact remains that serious books, never to be best sellers, do get published, there are people who might buy them if they could so much as get a look at them—and that gets harder and harder.

Organization

1. Write a thesis statement for this essay.
2. Howe's attitude toward his material is established in paragraph 2. Identify it and indicate how it is maintained throughout the essay.

Paragraphs

1. How is paragraph 1 developed?
2. How is paragraph 6 developed?
3. What devices give coherence to paragraph 9?

Sentences

1. Identify the parallelism in the first sentence.
2. Discuss the unusual features of the last sentence of paragraph 2.

3. Compare and contrast the two sentences of paragraph 8. Is the imbalance in sentence length a flaw?
4. How do the first and second sentences of the closing paragraph fit in with the attitude expressed in the essay?

Words

1. Why are *need* (1) and *new bookstore* (2) enclosed in quotation marks? Account for the italics in paragraph 3.
2. Do the allusions in paragraphs 6 and 9 mean anything to you? Does the context provide enough information?
3. Be sure you know the meaning of the following:

avant-garde (9)	mediocre (3)
dispirited (3)	ritual (2)
ghastly (1)	shrewd (9)
indignation (7)	subsidize (5)

Suggestions for Writing

1. Formulate a thesis about the bookstore from which you secured this textbook; develop your thesis by example.
2. Choose something meaningful to you that has been abandoned, destroyed, or changed (a park, a tree, a house, a store, a vacant lot). Adopt Howe's attitude and illustrate why your chosen object should and could have been left intact. Assume that your audience made the decision to alter your chosen object.

DEATH IN THE OPEN

Lewis Thomas

Lewis Thomas: physician, medical researcher, teacher, author. Thomas was born in Flushing, New York in 1913. He attended Princeton University and the Harvard Medical School, where he chose pathology as his medical specialty. His institutional affiliations include stints at the University of Minnesota Medical School, the New York University-Bellevue Medical Center, and the Yale University Medical School. In 1971 Thomas started writing a column for the New England Journal of Medicine. *A number of these essays were collected and published in* The Lives of a Cell: Notes of a Biology Watcher, *which won a National Book Award in 1974. Thomas is currently president of the Memorial Sloan-Kettering Cancer Center in New York. The following essay is from* The Lives of a Cell.

It is the nature of animals to die alone, Thomas writes. How many examples does he provide to support his assertion?

According to Thomas, how should we view death?

1   Most of the dead animals you see on highways near the cities are dogs, a few cats. Out in the countryside, the forms and coloring of the dead are strange; these are the wild creatures. Seen from a car window they appear as fragments, evoking memories of woodchucks, badgers, skunks, voles, snakes, sometimes the mysterious wreckage of a deer.

2   It is always a queer shock, part a sudden upwelling of grief, part unaccountable amazement. It is simply astounding to see an animal dead on a highway. The outrage is more than just the location; it is the impropriety of such visible death, anywhere. You do not expect to see dead animals in the open. It is the nature of animals to die alone, off somewhere, hidden. It is wrong to see them lying out on the highway; it is wrong to see them anywhere.

3   Everything in the world dies, but we only know about it as a kind of abstraction. If you stand in a meadow, at the end of a hillside, and look around carefully, almost everything you can catch sight of is in the process of dying, and most things will be dead long before you are. If it were not for the constant renewal and replacement going on before your eyes, the whole place would turn to stone and sand under your feet.

4   There are some creatures that do not seem to die at all, they simply vanish totally into their own progeny. Single cells do this. The cell becomes two, then four, and so on, and after a while the last trace is gone. It cannot be seen as death; barring mutation, the descendants are simply the first cell, living all

over again. The cycles of the slime mold have episodes that seem as conclusive as death, but the withered slug, with its stalk and fruiting body, is plainly the transient tissue of a developing animal; the free-swimming amebocytes use this organ collectively in order to produce more of themselves.

There are said to be a billion billion insects on the earth at 5 any moment, most of them with very short life expectancies by our standards. Someone has estimated that there are 25 million assorted insects hanging in the air over every temperate square mile, in a column extending upward for thousands of feet, drifting through the layers of the atmosphere like plankton. They are dying steadily, some by being eaten, some just dropping in their tracks, tons of them around the earth, disintegrating as they die, invisibly.

Who ever sees dead birds, in anything like the huge num- 6 bers stipulated by the certainty of the death of all birds? A dead bird is an incongruity, more startling than an unexpected live bird, sure evidence to the human mind that something has gone wrong. Birds do their dying off somewhere, behind things, under things, never on the wing.

Animals seem to have an instinct for performing death alone, 7 hidden. Even the largest, most conspicuous ones find ways to conceal themselves in time. If an elephant missteps and dies in an open place, the herd will not leave him there; the others will pick him up and carry the body from place to place, finally putting it down in some inexplicably suitable location. When elephants encounter the skeleton of an elephant out in the open, they methodically take up each of the bones and distribute them, in a ponderous ceremony, over neighboring acres.

It is a natural marvel. All of the life of the earth dies, all of 8 the time, in the same volume as the new life that dazzles us each morning, each spring. All we see of this is the odd stump, the fly struggling on the porch floor of the summer house in October, the fragment on the highway. I have lived all my life with an embarrassment of squirrels in my backyard, they are all over the place, all year long, and I have never seen, anywhere, a dead squirrel.

I suppose it is just as well. If the earth were otherwise, and 9 all the dying were done in the open, with the dead there to be looked at, we would never have it out of our minds. We can forget about it much of the time, or think of it as an accident to be avoided, somehow. But it does make the process of dying seem more exceptional than it really is, and harder to engage in at the times when we must ourselves engage.

In our way, we conform as best we can to the rest of nature. 10

The obituary pages tell us of the news that we are dying away, while the birth announcements in finer print, off at the side of the page, inform us of our replacements, but we get no grasp from this of the enormity of scale. There are 3 billion of us on the earth, and all 3 billion must be dead, on a schedule, within this lifetime. The vast mortality, involving something over 50 million of us each year, takes place in relative secrecy. We can only really know of the deaths in our households, or among our friends. These, detached in our minds from all the rest, we take to be unnatural events, anomalies, outrages. We speak of our own dead in low voices; struck down, we say, as though visible death can only occur for cause, by disease or violence, avoidably. We send off for flowers, grieve, make ceremonies, scatter bones, unaware of the rest of the 3 billion on the same schedule. All of that immense mass of flesh and bone and consciousness will disappear by absorption into the earth, without recognition by the transient survivors.

Less than a half century from now, our replacements will 11 have more than doubled the numbers. It is hard to see how we can continue to keep the secret, with such multitudes doing the dying. We will have to give up the notion that death is catastrophe, or detestable, or avoidable, or even strange. We will need to learn more about the cycling of life in the rest of the system, and about our connection to the process. Everything that comes alive seems to be in trade for something that dies, cell for cell. There might be some comfort in the recognition of synchrony, in the information that we all go down together, in the best of company.

Organization

1. What is the principle used in presenting the examples?
2. What is the persona revealed in the essay?
3. How is analysis as a method of development used in support of example?

Paragraphs

1. What devices give coherence to paragraph 10?
2. What details support the topic sentence of paragraph 7? Are the details adequate?
3. What is the function of paragraph 8? How does paragraph 8 relate to paragraphs 4–7 and to 9?

Sentences

1. Is there a simile in the second sentence of paragraph 5? If so, is it effective? If not, is the comparison effective?
2. In the introductory phrase to the third sentence of paragraph 8 is there an indefinite *this?* What noun would be appropriate after *this?*
3. The second sentence of paragraph 4 contains only four words. What do you make of this sentence?

Words

1. Can the title have more than one meaning? Explain.
2. Are the phrases *mysterious wreckage of a deer* (last sentence of paragraph 1) and *an embarrassment of squirrels* (last sentence of paragraph 8) effective or ineffective? Discuss.
3. Be sure you know the meaning of each of the following:

amebocytes (4)	plankton (5)
anomalies (10)	progeny (4)
impropriety (2)	stipulated (6)
incongruity (6)	synchrony (11)
inexplicably (7)	transient (4)
mutation (4)	voles (1)
obituary (10)	

Suggestions for Writing

1. Have you ever attended a funeral or memorial service? What was the essential feature of the ceremony? Write an essay in which you use examples to make that feature clear. Remember, your primary emphasis is not on what happened.
2. Thomas says that if you stand out in the open *almost everything you can catch sight of is in the process of dying. . . .* Write an essay giving examples of what you see dying when you stand in an open field or park.

THE UGLIEST WORD

H. Allen Smith

H. Allen Smith: journalist, humorist, author. Smith was born in McLeansboro, Illinois in 1907. After he completed the eighth grade, he dropped out of school. At fifteen he got a job on a newspaper and wrote for papers in Louisville, Tulsa, Denver, and New York. His 1941 book Low Man on the Totem Pole *established him as a humorist of best-selling proportions. That book inspired a syndicated column, "The Totem Pole." Other books include* Robert Gair *and* Mr. Klein's Kampf. *Smith described his work this way: "I prefer to think of myself as a reporter, a reporter with a humorous slant. I am funny only in the sense that the world is funny." He died in 1976.*

What are the criteria for determining *beautiful* and *ugly* words?

What examples does Smith give to support his choice for the ugliest word?

1   *Lullaby. Golden. Damask. Moonlight.* Do these words seem aesthetically attractive to you? They have appeared with some regularity on lists of "the ten most beautiful words in our language." Along with *luminous, hush, anemone, mother,* and various others. These lists appear from time to time in public prints, and there is almost always disagreement among the scholarly people who mine the dictionaries looking for lovely words. Sometimes these disagreements reach a point where ugly words are used. I can't recall ever having seen a list of the ten ugliest words in the language but I do remember that the late Ring Lardner, coming upon one of the beautiful word lists in a newspaper, remarked with chagrin and bitterness: "Why did they leave out *gangrene?*"

2   The people who assemble these lists actually can't make up their minds what they are after. Is a beautiful word beautiful because of its musical sound or because of the thing it describes? If *moonlight* was the name of the diamond-back rattlesnake, would *moonlight* be considered a romantic-sounding and pretty word? If there were no such word as *mother,* and your mother was your *sludge,* would *sludge* be poetically beautiful? You ask my opinion and I'll tell you that *gangrene* is a downright lovely word, provided you keep your mind off gangrene. You want to hear a *real* ugly word? *Ugly.*

3   My own choice for the most beautiful word of them all would not appeal to the generality of people; it is a word of glowing, glimmering loveliness and arouses intense feelings of well-being and even sensuality within me. The word is *End.* With a capital "E." As a professional writer of books and magazine arti-

cles, I almost swoon with gladness when, on the last page of the third draft of a long manuscript, I write: *The End.* I sit and stare at it, and the longer I do so, the more excruciatingly beautiful it becomes. *Lullaby* my ass! I have left instructions that *The End* be chiseled on my gravestone.

As for ugly words, almost every literate person has in his 4 head an agglomeration of them—words that can cause him to wince, and even shudder, such as *agglomeration.* I lay claim to several hundred of the uglies. *Mulcted* almost nauseates me. I cringe in the face of *albeit, and/or, yclept, obsequies, whilom,* and *tinsmith.*

My own nomination for the meanest and low-downdest and 5 ugliest word of them all is *Oh.* Said twice, with maybe a hyphen, this way: *Oh-oh.* In its maximal ugliness, it is customarily spoken softly with inflections that would curl the toes of a South Georgia mule.

Something is wrong, let us say, with the engine of your car. 6 You take it to the garage. The mechanic lifts the hood and pokes around a bit and then you hear him murmur: "Oh-oh." The wretched creature says it in such a restrained dramatic manner that you know instantly that your whole motor has to be derricked out and thrown away and a new one put in.

Oh-oh almost always suggests tragedy, or impending trag- 7 edy. I remember standing with another man at a cocktail party when he, glancing across the crowded room, said, "Oh-oh." I followed his gaze. A prominent actor and an equally prominent newspaperman were squaring off, and blows began raining, and a nose was bloodied, and it took some doing to pry the two gentlemen apart.

Consider again our friends the dentists. Most of them have 8 enough gumption to conceal their opinions and judgments, but sometimes you'll run across one who forgets his chairside manner. He'll be inspecting a big molar in the back and suddenly he'll say, "Oh-oh." Or he'll come out of his darkroom carrying an X-ray taken a few minutes earlier, and he'll put it up against the light, and he'll look at it briefly, and then his head will give a jerk and he'll say, "Oh-oh." You know at once, without ESP, precisely what is meant. Out: All of them. From now on, plates. And you know what Aunt Gert says about plates. No apples. No corn on the cob. No a lot of things. You are a captive in the dentist's chair but you feel like busting out of the place and hiding in the woods.

Physicians as a general thing have schooled themselves 9 carefully to conceal any sinister condition they may find during an examination. Yet I have run across one offender in my checkered medical career. He was giving me the annual checkup. He took my blood pressure and tapped me for knee jerks and scratched me on the bottoms of my feet for God knows what and stethoscoped me front and back and had me blow into a machine to test my "vital capacity" and then he turned the electrocardiograph loose on me. As he studied the saw-toothed dossier on my heart, his brow crinkled and I heard him say quite softly but with an undercurrent of alarm, "Oh-oh." Everything inside me suddenly bunched together in one large knot.

10   "What is it?" I gulped. "Whad you find there?"

11   "Nothing really," he said. "Nothing important."

12   Nothing! Cancer of the heart is *nothing?* It had to be that at the very least.

13   "I heard you say 'Oh-oh,' " I told him. "Come on. Give it to me. I'm a man. I can take it. Let me have it straight."

14   "Okay," he said, and I steeled myself manfully for seven seconds and then began to turn chicken. He resumed: "I said 'Oh-oh' because I just happened to think that I haven't made out my tax return yet, and the deadline is tomorrow."

15   I quit him the next day. Took my aches and agues elsewhere. I can't use a doctor who is mooning over his income tax problems while he is looking at the record of my frightful heart disorders. I don't want a doctor *ever* to say "Oh-oh" in my presence, unless perhaps he has dropped his sphygmomanometer on the floor and busted it all to hell. Even in that contingency I think he should employ a more masculine and earthy expression. I surely would.

16   The saying of "Oh-oh" should be forbidden by federal statute. It is the most frightening, nerve-shattering locution to come into general usage since Noah Webster quit slopping pigs on his father's farm in Connecticut. It is, in fact, so low-down mean in its usual implications that even the dictionaries won't let it in. I scorn it, and deride it, and let my mind dwell on its opposite—that most beautiful of words . . .

Organization

1. What is the thesis statement?
2. What other methods of development are used to support example?

Paragraphs

1. What devices give coherence to paragraph 8?
2. What methods of development are used in paragraph 1?
3. Is the last paragraph effective? Explain.

Sentences

1. Identify the sentence fragments in paragraph 3. What is the function of each?
2. What principle governs the arrangement of the details in the fourth sentence of paragraph 9? Could these details be arranged in another order? Explain.

Words

1. Why are *Lullaby, Golden, Damask, Moonlight, luminous, hush, anemone, mother,* and *gangrene* italicized in paragraph 1?
2. Who were *Ring Lardner* (1) and *Noah Webster* (16)?
3. Be sure you know the meaning of each of the following:

aesthetically (1)	gumption (8)
agglomeration (4)	locution (16)
agues (15)	luminous (1)
anemone (1)	*mulcted* (4)
chagrin (1)	*obsequies* (4)
checkered (9)	sensuality (3)
contingency (15)	sinister (9)
Damask (1)	sphygmomanometer (15)
derricked (6)	steeled (14)
dossier (9)	stethoscoped (9)
electrocardiograph (9)	*tinsmith* (4)
excruciatingly (3)	*whilom* (4)
ESP (8)	*yclept* (4)
gangrene (1)	

Suggestions for Writing

1. Choose one of the *beautiful* words from the essay or a word of your choice (yes, graduation, marriage, kiss) and illustrate why it is beautiful because of its connotations.
2. Choose one of the *ugly* words from the essay or a word of your choice (no, failed, closed, expensive) and illustrate why it is ugly because of its connotations.

COURTSHIP THROUGH THE AGES

James Thurber

James Thurber: cartoonist, humorist, author. Thurber was born in Columbus, Ohio in 1894, graduated from Ohio State University, and began his career writing for the Columbus Dispatch. *After working for the* Chicago Tribune *in Paris, he returned to New York and began his long career with the* New Yorker *in 1926. His fame dates from his association with that weekly magazine, where his whimsical cartoons and humorous pieces soon brought him national recognition. He co-authored* Is Sex Necessary? *with E. B. White, and wrote* My Life and Hard Times *and* Fables for Our Times. *Thurber's most famous story is probably "The Secret Life of Walter Mitty." He died in 1961. The following essay originally appeared in the* New Yorker.

How does Thurber remind you that his primary concern isn't fowls, insects, crabs, spiders, and so forth?

How many examples does Thurber provide to support his thesis that males go to sorrowful lengths to arouse the interest of females?

1   Surely nothing in the astonishing scheme of life can have nonplussed Nature so much as the fact that none of the females of any of the species she created really cared very much for the male, as such. For the past ten million years Nature has been busily inventing ways to make the male attractive to the female, but the whole business of courtship, from the marine annelids up to man, still lumbers heavily along, like a complicated musical comedy. I have been reading the sad and absorbing story in Volume 6 (Cole to Dama) of the *Encyclopaedia Britannica*. In this volume you can learn all about cricket, cotton, costume designing, crocodiles, crown jewels, and Coleridge, but none of these subjects is so interesting as the Courtship of Animals, which recounts the sorrowful lengths to which all males must go to arouse the interest of a lady.

2   We all know, I think, that Nature gave man whiskers and a mustache with the quaint idea in mind that these would prove attractive to the female. We all know that, far from attracting her, whiskers and mustaches only made her nervous and gloomy, so that man had to go in for somersaults, tilting with lances, and performing feats of parlor magic to win her attention; he also had to bring her candy, flowers, and the furs of animals. It is common knowledge that in spite of all these "love displays" the male is constantly being turned down, insulted, or thrown out of the house. It is rather comforting, then, to discover that the peacock, for all his gorgeous plumage, does not have a particularly easy time in courtship; none

of the males in the world do. The first peahen, it turned out, was only faintly stirred by her suitor's beautiful train. She would often go quietly to sleep while he was whisking it around. The Britannica tells us that the peacock actually had to learn a certain little trick to wake her up and revive her interest: he had to learn to vibrate his quills so as to make a rustling sound. In ancient times man himself, observing the ways of the peacock, probably tried vibrating his whiskers to make a rustling sound; if so, it didn't get him anywhere. He had to go in for something else; so, among other things, he went in for gifts. It is not unlikely that he got this idea from certain flies and birds who were making no headway at all with rustling sounds.

One of the flies of the family Empidae, who had tried everything, finally hit on something pretty special. He contrived to make a glistening transparent balloon which was even larger than himself. Into this he would put sweetmeats and tidbits and he would carry the whole elaborate envelope through the air to the lady of his choice. This amused her for a time, but she finally got bored with it. She demanded silly little colorful presents, something that you couldn't eat but that would look nice around the house. So the male Empis had to go around gathering flower petals and pieces of bright paper to put into his balloon. On a courtship flight a male Empis cuts quite a figure now, but he can hardly be said to be happy. He never knows how soon the female will demand heavier presents, such as Roman coins and gold collar buttons. It seems probable that one day the courtship of the Empidae will fall down, as man's occasionally does, of its own weight.

The bowerbird is another creature that spends so much time courting the female that he never gets any work done. If all the male bowerbirds became nervous wrecks within the next ten or fifteen years, it would not surprise me. The female bowerbird insists that a playground be built for her with a specially constructed bower at the entrance. This bower is much more elaborate than an ordinary nest and is harder to build; it costs a lot more, too. The female will not come to the playground until the male has filled it up with a great many gifts: silvery leaves, red leaves, rose petals, shells, beads, berries, bones, dice, buttons, cigar bands, Christmas seals, and the Lord knows what else. When the female finally condescends to visit the playground, she is in a coy and silly mood and has to be chased in and out of the bower and up and down the playground before she will quite giggling and stand still long enough even to shake hands. The male bird is, of course, pretty well done in before the chase starts, because he has

151

worn himself out hunting for eyeglass lenses and begonia blossoms. I imagine that many a bowerbird, after chasing a female for two or three hours, says the hell with it and goes home to bed. Next day, of course, he telephones someone else and the same trying ritual is gone through with again. A male bowerbird is as exhausted as a night-club habitué before he is out of his twenties.

5   The male fiddler crab has a somewhat easier time, but it can hardly be said that he is sitting pretty. He has one enormously large and powerful claw, usually brilliantly colored, and you might suppose that all he had to do was reach out and grab some passing cutie. The very earliest fiddler crabs may have tried this, but, if so, they got slapped for their pains. A female fiddler crab will not tolerate any caveman stuff; she never has and she doesn't intend to start now. To attract a female, a fiddler crab has to stand on tiptoe and brandish his claw in the air. If any female in the neighborhood is interested—and you'd be surprised how many are not—she comes over and engages him in light badinage, for which he is not in the mood. As many as a hundred females may pass the time of day with him and go on about their business. By nightfall of an average courting day, a fiddler crab who has been standing on tiptoe for eight or ten hours waving a heavy claw in the air is in pretty sad shape. As in the case of the males of all species, however, he gets out of bed next morning, dashes some water on his face, and tries again.

6   The next time you encounter a male web-spinning spider, stop and reflect that he is too busy worrying about his love life to have any desire to bite you. Male web-spinning spiders have a tougher life than any other males in the animal kingdom. This is because the female web-spinning spiders have very poor eyesight. If a male lands on a female's web, she kills him before he has time to lay down his cane and gloves, mistaking him for a fly or a bumblebee who has stumbled into her trap. Before the species figured out what to do about this, millions of males were murdered by ladies they called on. It is the nature of spiders to perform a little dance in front of the female, but before a male spinner could get near enough the the female to see who he was and what he was up to, she would lash out at him with a flat-iron or a pair of garden shears. One night, nobody knows when, a very bright male spinner lay awake worrying about calling on a lady who had been killing suitors right and left. It came to him that this business of dancing as a love display wasn't getting anybody anywhere except the grave. He decided to go in for web-twitching, or strand-vibrating. The next day he tried it on one of the near-

sighted girls. Instead of dropping in on her suddenly, he stayed outside the web and began monkeying with one of its strands. He twitched it up and down and in and out with such a lilting rhythm that the female was charmed. The serenade worked beautifully; the female let him live. The Britannica's spider-watchers, however, report that this system is not always successful. Once in a while, even now, a female will fire three bullets into a suitor or run him through with a kitchen knife. She keeps threatening him from the moment he strikes the first low notes on the outside strings, but usually by the time he has got up to the high notes played around the center of the web, he is going to town and she spares his life.

Even the butterfly, as handsome a fellow as he is, can't always win a mate merely by fluttering around and showing off. Many butterflies have to have scent scales on their wings. Hepialus carries a powder puff in a perfumed pouch. He throws perfume at the ladies when they pass. The male tree cricket, Oecanthus, goes Hepialus one better by carrying a tiny bottle of wine with him and giving drinks to such doxies as he has designs on. One of the male snails throws darts to entertain the girls. So it goes, through the long list of animals, from the bristle worm and his rudimentary dance steps to man and his gift of diamonds and sapphires. The golden-eye drake raises a jet of water with his feet as he flies over a lake; Hepialus has his powder puff, Oecanthus his wine bottle, man his etchings. It is a bright and melancholy story, the age-old desire of the male for the female, the age-old desire of the female to be amused and entertained. Of all the creatures on earth, the only males who could be figured as putting any irony into their courtship are the grebes and certain other diving birds. Every now and then a courting grebe slips quietly down to the bottom of a lake and then, with a mighty "Whoosh!," pops out suddenly a few feet from his girl friend, splashing water all over her. She seems to be persuaded that this is a purely loving display, but I like to think that the grebe always has a faint hope of drowning her or scaring her to death.

I will close this investigation into the mournful burdens of the male with the *Britannica*'s story about a certain Argus pheasant. It appears that the Argus displays himself in front of a female who stands perfectly still without moving a feather. (If you saw "June Moon" some years ago and remember the scene in which the Songwriter sang "Montana Moon" to his grim and motionless wife, you have some idea what the female Argus probably thinks of her mate's display.) The male Argus the Britannica tells about was confined in a cage with a female of another species, a female who kept moving around,

7

8

emptying ashtrays and fussing with lampshades all the time the male was showing off his talents. Finally, in disgust, he stalked away and began displaying in front of his water trough. He reminds me of a certain male (Homo sapiens) of my acquaintance who one night after dinner asked his wife to put down her detective magazine so that he could read her a poem of which he was very fond. She sat quietly enough until he was well into the middle of the thing, intoning with great ardor and intensity. Then suddenly there came a sharp, disconcerting *slap!* It turned out that all during the male's display, the female had been intent on a circling mosquito and had finally trapped it between the palms of her hands. The male in this case did not stalk away and display in front of a water trough; he went over to Tim's and had a flock of drinks and recited the poem to the fellas. I am sure they all told bitter stories of their own about how their displays had been interrupted by females. I am also sure that they all ended up singing "Honey, Honey, Bless Your Heart."

Organization

1. Show how human activities attributed to animals give coherence to the essay.
2. Discuss the techniques for attracting females employed by each male in paragraphs 2–6 and in paragraph 7. Can you discover a reason for the order in which the techniques are presented?

Paragraphs

1. What provides the transition between paragraphs 2 and 3? What provides the transition between paragraphs 3 and 4?
2. Write a topic sentence for paragraph 7.
3. How does the closing paragraph relate to the thesis statement?

Sentences

1. Discuss the figurative language in the second sentence of paragraph 1. Is the last sentence of paragraph 4 a simile?
2. How suggestive is the use of multiple details in the fifth sentence of paragraph 4?

Words

1. Be sure you know the meaning of each of the following:

badinage (5)	habitué ((4)
brandish (5)	intoning (8)

condescends (4)	lilting (6)
disconcerting (8)	nonplussed (1)
doxies (7)	rudimentary (7)
etchings (7)	

Suggestions for Writing

1. Discuss and illustrate how men (or women) today attempt to attract women's (or men's) attention.
2. In a sense, this essay stereotypes the female as being totally indifferent to the male. Choose a stereotype that exists today (athletes are dumb, professors are absent-minded, women are careless drivers, men never cry, father knows best) and write an illustrative essay in which you refute the stereotype by using specific examples. (See Debbie Rice's essay below.)

BOLDFACE TYPE (CAST)

Debbie Rice

Debbie Rice: student. Rice is a native of Mobile, Alabama, where she was born in 1966. She graduated from McGill-Toolen High School and is presently enrolled in a curriculum for future teachers. Her essay is based on Suggestions for Writing 2 above.

When I was young, I would burst with pride as I sang the 1 National Anthem or saluted the American flag. I was proud to be a member of a country that promoted freedom and promised Americans life, liberty, and the pursuit of happiness. I learned the traditional values of the American way of life. I remember the Christmas and thanksgiving dinners with their fabulous spread of food. I recall the Butterball turkey, ham, fresh green peas, Ocean Spray cranberry sauce, mashed potatoes with gravy, potato salad, Mom's homemade stuffing, and a good old American apple pie for dessert. Along with the traditional meals, I also remember who cleaned up the dishes.

The women always huddled in the kitchen with the bottle 2 of Ivory Liquid while the men enjoyed the bottle of Bacardi rum. I thought it was unfair that the women had to do all of the cooking and the cleaning. I concluded that women were stereotyped into the role of cook or maid. Later in life as I observed men and women more, I discovered that there were at least three stereotypes of women.

The first stereotype that I discovered was the "dumb blonde" 3

155

one. For years men have associated blondes with being dumb. For example, blondes have been portrayed in film as air-brained sex objects. From the time of Marilyn Monroe to the time of Suzanne Somers, blondes have been stereotyped as being "dumb." This stereotype may have affected some blondes, but there are women who contradict this stereotype. For example, Dr. Joyce Brothers is a world famous psychologist who gives her views on marriage, sex, and family problems. Another example that refutes the stereotype is Diane Sawyer who is an anchorwoman for CBS. Also, Farrah Fawcett has come a long way from being the brainless female in *Charlie's Angels.* Recently she received critical acclaim as a brilliant actress for her portrayal of Francine Hughes, the abused wife who burned her husband to death, in the movie *The Burning Bed.*

4   While blondes suffer through the stereotype of being dumb, there is another stereotype for women that still exists today. This stereotype says that women are incapable of being strong decisive leaders. I think that just the opposite is true. I remember three women who have made their mark on society. Golda Meir is one of these women. She was the leader of Israel until her recent death. Also, Indira Ghandi was a great leader who unified her people as Prime Minister of India. Finally, Margaret Thatcher holds together the country of Great Britain as the Prime Minister. I think that these three women have made men and the rest of society sit up and take notice that women are capable of strong leadership. I think that the stereotype of not being a strong leader has made more women aware that they can be strong leaders.

5   Along with the stereotype of women being incapable of strong leadership, there is the stereotype that a woman's place is in the home and not in business. Women are stereotyped as fragile persons who stay at home because they lack the intelligence and self-confidence necessary for the business world. Some women are affected by this stereotyping, and they might prefer to stay at home and believe that home is where they belong. But I think that women have an innovative business sense and should work in business or have a business of their own. For example, there are two women in business today who show extreme intelligence and a keen business sense. Gloria Steinem is the founder and one of the editors of *Ms. Magazine.* Also, Mary Cunningham is the vice-president of strategic planning at Seagram and Sons. I think that women can succeed in the business world in spite of hearing that their place is in the home.

6   Thus, I still believe that America is the land of opportunity and freedom. But I just do not believe that people, especially

women, should be trapped by a stereotype. I will always sing the National Anthem with pride, and a tear may fall while I sing it. I just hope no one stereotypes me as being one of those weeping females. I have more pride than that.

7

COMPARISON AND CONTRAST

Many times each day observant people compare one person, place, object, or experience with another, and from that comparison make evaluations. You do it yourself without realizing you're doing it. Your roommate last year and your roommate this year, your grandparents' home and your home, your car and your best friend's car, last week's football game and this week's—these or numerous similar comparisons are part of your daily conversation or, at least, your daily thoughts. And the comparisons inevitably lead to conclusions or judgments: this year's roommate is neater than last year's but moodier; your grandparents' home is smaller and cosier than yours; your car is usually dirtier than your friend's; last week's game was more exciting than this week's. You make these comparative evaluations casually, but the method you use can be the basis for comparisons and contrasts of a more formal type. You're no doubt already familiar with the more formal kind from having taken essay tests in which you were asked to compare and contrast two historical figures or two events, two books or two poems, two philosophical systems or two cultures, or any of the other X-and-Y couplings that your instructors seem to take a devilish delight in thinking up and tossing your way. Here are some pointers that should help you in answering such questions, and more immediately, in writing compositions with comparison and contrast as the principal method of development.

1. Limit Yourself to Two Items

For the purposes of a short paper, you'll have enough to handle in evaluating two items well without adding a third, a fourth, or more. Besides, concentration on two makes for easier reading (though not always easier writing) than shifting back and forth among three or more.

2. Deal with *Either* Comparison *or* Contrast

The term *comparison* is often used to denote any kind of evaluation of two or more items. Strictly speaking, however, *comparison* refers to the identification of *similarities, contrast* to the identification of *differences.* Given that distinction, a short composition ordinarily leaves little room for adequate treatment of both, unless they are few or easily explained.

However, this guideline is a matter of emphasis, not of either-or exclusion. An essay in which you stress the differences between two items that are or appear alike will almost certainly begin by at least mentioning the likenesses. And an essay in which you stress the similarities between two items that are or appear different will undoubtedly begin by at least mentioning the differences. In other words, whichever method you emphasize, you'll at least take both the similarities and the differences into account. In that way you'll save yourself from the charge of falsifying the issue, or exaggerating for the sake of a cheap or easy effect.

3. Be Observant

Comparison and contrast begin with careful observation. This is true of other methods of development as well, especially, of course, description. But unlike these other methods, comparison and contrast involve a close examination of *two* items and also the identification of similarities and differences between them. For instance, Liane Ellison Norman's "Pedestrian Students and High-Flying Squirrels" (p. 174) indicates that Norman has carefully observed both the students and the squirrels referred to in her title. She has heard some students complain and whine. She has watched squirrels as they bury nuts, dart among tree branches, and flee from dogs. Above all, she has had insight enough to draw clever comparisons between the behavior of the inhabitants of these two worlds.

You, too, should be as alert as possible to see similarities and differences in the objects around you. A reconsideration of the suggestions for description (p. 96) should help stimulate the careful observation that comparison and contrast are built on.

4. Establish a Solid Basis for the Comparison or the Contrast

For two items to be worthy of being compared or contrasted at all, they have to be similar and at the same time different. They have to be similar because two totally unlike things—a man's top hat and a tractor, for instance, or the Houston Astrodome and the Declaration of Independence—offer no possible basis for comparison, while the contrasts between them are so obvious as to need no pointing out. On the other hand, the two items have to be different because if they are so similar as to be identical, or nearly so—such as two plastic spoons made from the same mold—it would be pointless to compare them, and all but impossible to contrast them. In short, the items have to be *different members* of the *same class or category:* two hats (a top hat and a derby), two farm haulers (a tractor and a mule), two indoor stadiums (the Astrodome and the New Orleans Superdome), two political documents (the Declaration of Independence and the Magna Carta). The comparison called an *analogy*—the identification of similarities between two *essentially unlike* things—is a special case and will be treated below.

Each essay in this section reflects this similar-but-different pairing of items. For example, "The Saloon and the Cocktail Lounge" (p. 166) looks at two drinking establishments (the similarity) that are markedly unlike in atmosphere and patronage (the differences). "Pharisee and Publican" (p. 168) scrutinizes two men supposedly at prayer (the similarity), but only one is really praying (the difference). Thus, each essay examines significant dissimilarities in two items superficially alike. That's the whole purpose of the comparison-contrast method—to probe beneath the appearances of things and uncover their essential nature by seeing each in relation to at least one other.

5. Avoid a Colorless Thesis

An attention-getting thesis doesn't guarantee a fascinating essay, but it's a good start toward one. Harry Golden could have written, "There are several significant differences between a saloon and a cocktail lounge." It would have been a true statement in itself, and an accurate reflection of his attitude. It would also have been routine and unimaginative. Instead, Golden wrote, *The American people were sold a pig in a poke when they replaced the saloon with the cocktail lounge.* (p. 166) This sentence does all that the previous sentence did in pointing toward contrast as the logical method of development, and does so more subtly. But it does more than that. In the figurative term *sold a pig in a poke* it reflects Golden's emotional reaction to the contrast—his resentment over the substitution of the cocktail lounge for the saloon. Thus, a bland thesis statement is replaced by a vivid one that encourages the reader to go on following the writer's reasoning as it unfolds. Even a more sober and less personal essay can be given a thesis that is more arresting than the standard "There-are-many-differences-between-*X*-and-*Y*" type. Bruce Catton's "Grant and Lee: A Study in Contrasts" is proof of that. Who wouldn't continue reading after coming upon this thesis statement in the third paragraph? *They were two strong men, these oddly different generals, and they represented the strengths of two conflicting currents that, through them, had come into final collision.* (p. 178)

6. Choose the Most Suitable Method of Arrangement

There are two basic methods of arranging comparative and contrasting materials. To illustrate these methods, let X and Y represent the two items being compared or contrasted, and X^1, X^2, X^3 (and so on) and Y^1, Y^2, Y^3 (and so on), the various characteristics of each.

The Block Method   The block method devotes one paragraph or section to characteristics of X, and the next paragraph or section to the corresponding characteristics of Y. The paragraph after that is devoted to other characteristics of X, and the following paragraph to the corresponding characteristics of Y, and so on. In other words, each block of X material is followed by a matching block of Y material, as shown below.

$$
\boxed{\begin{array}{c} X^1 \\ X^2 \\ X^3 \end{array}} \qquad \boxed{\begin{array}{c} Y^1 \\ Y^2 \\ Y^3 \end{array}}
$$

$$
\boxed{\begin{array}{c} X^4 \\ X^5 \\ X^6 \end{array}} \qquad \boxed{\begin{array}{c} Y^4 \\ Y^5 \\ Y^6 \end{array}}
$$

This is the method Ronald Knox employs (though in a shorter and slightly different version) in "Pharisee and Publican" (p. 168):

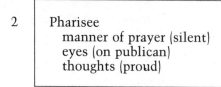

2 | Pharisee
       manner of prayer (silent)
       eyes (on publican)
       thoughts (proud)

3 | Publican
       eyes (downcast)
       manner of prayer (breast-beating)
       thoughts (humble)

The Alternating Method   The alternating method arranges materials so that comparable characteristics are discussed point by point. It differs from the block method in that single characteristics are presented alternately. In other words, instead of a block of X material followed by a block of Y material, the writer discusses the first characteristic of X and then, in the same or a separate paragraph, the corresponding characteristic of Y. In the next paragraph, the second characteristic of X would be discussed, and in that or the following paragraph, the corresponding characteristic of Y, as shown below.

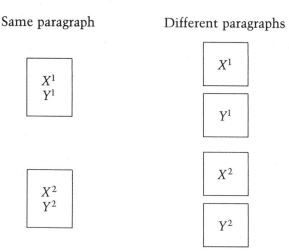

Same paragraph   Different paragraphs

X^1 X^1
Y^1
                            Y^1

X^2 X^2
Y^2
                            Y^2

John Finlay follows this arrangement in a general way in "The American Nature of Football" (p. 183). Here is the breakdown of a few sample paragraphs:

3 | European football: time-calculations (imprecise)
American football: time-calculations (precise)

European football: time-divisions (halves)
American football: time-divisions (quarters)

4 | European football: playing area (loosely prescribed)

5 | American football: playing area (rigidly prescribed)

10 | American football: players (specialized)
European football: players (nonspecialized)

Both methods of arrangement have their advantages and their disadvantages. A few precautions should assist you in choosing the one best suited to your purposes and in using it effectively:

a. As a general rule, use the block method for short papers and less complex topics, the alternating method for longer papers and more complex topics. In following the block method, the reader must keep each block of X material in mind while reading the block of Y material that follows and complements it. This is difficult to do unless the points pertaining to X and Y are few and relatively uncomplicated (as they are, for example, in "Pharisee and Publican"). Thus, the block method usually calls for a short paper. For complex comparisons or contrasts requiring lengthier development, the alternating arrangement—the similarities or differences occurring in paired succession—is preferable.

b. In using the block method, take care to see that each Y block is closely related to the preceding X block. You must do all you can to prevent your reader, when concentrating on block Y, from forgetting what you wrote in block X. The obvious way to maintain continuity is to treat the same points in Y as you did in X. (Notice that "Pharisee and Publican" does just that.) You may *vary the order* of the points ("Pharisee and Publican" does that too) to prevent mechanical presentation and monotonous reading. But you have to keep firm hold on the basic comparative focus.

Another way of maintaining that focus is through parallel sentence structure—that is, putting each Y point in the same general form as the corresponding X point. But since this might only compound the danger of monotonous presentation, you should use parallelism with caution, and only when unusual emphasis is called for.

c. In using the alternating method, vary the X-Y order occasionally. The danger of mechanical presentation is greater in the alternating method than in the block method, since here $X^1 Y^1$, $X^2 Y^2$, $X^3 Y^3$, and usually other characteristics, follow one another in close and rapid succession. One way of varying this pattern is by inverting the X-Y order now and again. Finlay does so in "The American Nature of Football," in which the prevailing order of discussion—European football first, American football second—becomes, in paragraph 10 (and several other paragraphs as well), American football first, European football second.

In either the block or the alternating method, re-arrangement of the X-Y order is usually sufficient to obtain variety in a short composition. In a longer essay, however, variety comes about best through use of the two methods together. Bruce Catton's "Grant and Lee" (p. 178) shows how both methods can be combined smoothly and effectively in a single essay.

ANALOGY

An *analogy* is a special kind of comparison—one that sees similarities between two (or more) *essentially dissimilar* things. Up to now, the comparisons we've been dealing with have been of different but essentially *similar* items: two kinds of drinking places ("The Saloon and the Cocktail Lounge"), two kinds of praying men ("Pharisee and Publican"), two Civil War generals ("General and Lee"), two kinds of football ("The American Nature of Football"). Analogy, however, begins with items that are even more different than these—for example, a city and a beehive, a religious ritual and a bullfight, a snowfall and a mass parachute-jump. And yet it sees some legitimate basis for drawing a comparison between them. A city is vastly different from a beehive, but from the standpoint of complex activity within a limited area, the two are sufficiently alike for a valid comparison to be made. Two essays in this book are extended analogies: James Thurber's "Courtship Through the Ages" (in the Example section), comparing human beings and various species; and Liane Ellison Norman's "Pedestrian Students and High-Flying Squirrels" (p. 174), comparing students and squirrels.

An ordinary comparison plays off each item in the pair against the other for purposes of elucidating both, and thus gives nearly equal emphasis to each one *(X ↔ Y)*. An analogy, however, places greater stress on one item than the other; the less-emphasized one serves simply to throw light on its companion *(X ↔ Y)*. The purpose of Thurber's and Norman's essays, for example, is not to discuss animals and humans equally, but rather to emphasize certain aspects of human behavior by comparing it, in each case, with that of animals. "Emphasis" here doesn't mean simply the amount of space or the number of paragraphs devoted to one or the other item; considered in those terms only, the animals in each essay get more emphasis than the humans (the direct opposite of what the writers intend). The emphasis we mean is that which comes from the writer signalling, partly through space and paragraph allotment but mainly through the thoughtful choices made during the Rewriting step in the process (pp. 43–63), which of the two items is the more important.

A real likeness between two apparently totally dissimilar items can be satisfying to uncover and fun to write about, as well as rewarding for others to read. But avoid the false analogy or forced comparison that tells the reader more about your efforts to be ingenious than about any true similarity in the items themselves. However different the two parts of an analogy may appear on the surface, they must have—and must be *shown* to have—some genuine bond between them, as in an ordinary comparison. You may never have thought that your fellow students could be compared to squirrels, but after having read Norman's essay you may agree that some of them, indeed, can.

THE SALOON AND THE COCKTAIL LOUNGE

Harry Golden

Harry Golden: author, editor, and publisher. Golden was born in New York City in 1903 and attended City College of New York 1919–1922. In 1942 he founded The Carolina Israelite, *a newspaper distinguished by its advocacy of tolerance among religions and races. Golden's books include* Only in America, Mr. Kennedy and the Negroes, *and* The Greatest Jewish City in the World. *This essay is from* Only in America *(1958). He died in 1981.*

What are the specific characteristics of the saloon that make it Golden's preference?

How does Golden exaggerate the glamour of the saloon?

1   The American people were sold a pig in a poke when they replaced the saloon with the cocktail lounge. To appease their sense of guilt after the repeal of Prohibition, they said, "Outlaw the saloon," and everybody was happy, and thus one of the great tragedies of our times. The saloon was a place of *fellowship.* No women were allowed, and the place was as light as day. In the center there was always a brilliantly illuminated chandelier. And what have we today in its place? The cocktail lounge! Dark! Candlelight business! Booths stuck away in a corner where you can plot, nay, accomplish all your illicit stratagems, and the cocktail lounges are loaded with women sitting on those upholstered stools; embarrassing the men, and embarrassing themselves. No more poetry to listen to at the saloon bar, or those fine political and philosophical disputations, and that magnificent lettering on the glass mirrors which announced the picnic or the Tammany outing, or the Christmas fund for the children of the neighborhood. I have no doubt that it was this fellowship, more than the evil of drink, that made the women rise up "against the saloon."

2   They wanted to go, too, but the saloons were too strict. And so the women replaced the saloon with the cocktail lounge so they could tag along. The women outsmarted themselves. They did not leave well enough alone. When their man was in the corner saloon, he was as safe as in his mother's arms. Now look at the situation—in dark corners where the man could

be sitting with his wife's best friend and no one would know it, or he could be taking a shot of heroin and not attract the least attention. These things were impossible in the saloon.

But I am afraid the cocktail lounge is here to stay. Where is 3 the politician who would have the courage to stand up like a man and say, "Give us back the old-time saloon"?

Organization

1. Identify the thesis statement. What key words or phrases in it reveal Golden's attitude toward his topic? How is this attitude maintained?
2. How is the transition between paragraphs 1 and 2 accomplished?

Paragraphs

1. Paragraph 1 is twice as long as paragraph 2 and far longer than paragraph 3. Can its length be justified?

Sentences

1. What is the effect of the seventh, eighth, and ninth sentences of paragraph 1?
2. Discuss the significance of the eleventh sentence of paragraph 1. Is it meant to be taken seriously within the present context?

Words

1. To what do *Prohibition* (1) and *Tammany* (1) refer?
2. Why is *fellowship* italicized (1)?
3. Be sure you know what each of the following means:

   appease (1)   illicit (1)
   disputation (1)   stratagems (1)

Suggestions for Writing

1. Contrast the saloon and the cocktail lounge by emphasizing the advantages of the cocktail lounge. Assume that your audience consists of saloon owners. You'll have to choose your language with care.
2. Choose a place that can be called by more than one name and compare the two names on the basis of the connotations of

each (asylum and sanatorium, hotel and inn, nightclub and tavern, cafe and restaurant, fraternity and guild).

3. Select a common activity (dating, attending classes, going on a vacation, visiting relatives, attending a concert) and contrast the best time you ever had with the worst one. (See Dowling Bowman's essay on p. 189.)

PHARISEE AND PUBLICAN

Ronald Knox

Ronald Knox: clergyman, translator, author. Knox was born in Leicestershire, England in 1888. He entered Balliol College, Oxford in 1906 and graduated with honors in classics in 1910. In 1912 he was ordained a priest in the Church of England, but in 1917 he converted to Roman Catholicism and became a Catholic priest. In 1937 he was commissioned to translate the Vulgate, the Latin translation of the Bible, into "timeless English," a project he finished in 1950. He is the author of some twenty books that include satire, apologetics, commentaries, essays, and detective novels. This essay is from his book Stimuli, *a collection of essays. Knox died in 1957.*

What two or three words characterize the Pharisee? What two or three words characterize the publican?

According to Knox, do both the Pharisee and the publican belong in the Church?

1   Two men went up into the temple to pray; two men, each, in God's sight, just an immortal soul, although their circumstances, their training, were so different. One a Pharisee, highly respected, scrupulous, fastidious, a man of rank; and the other a publican, nobody's friend, nobody's hero, all his thoughts wrapped up in his business, and that business certainly a sordid, perhaps a dishonest one. Both sent up into the temple to pray; religion has that great gift of levelling us; it takes all sorts to make a Church. Went up, separated themselves from the busy din of the streets, isolated themselves for our inspection. We can watch them easily; deep in their devotions, they will not suspect that they are being watched.

2   And the Pharisee prayed thus *within himself*—he was too well-bred to pray out loud; but our Lord has told us the thoughts that passed through his mind. "O God, I give thee thanks"—come, that is a good beginning; he acknowledges his dependence, he recognises that he is highly privileged. "That I am not as the rest of men"—quite true; he has had a good education, a high family tradition; he has much to be thank-

ful for. Extortioners, unjust, adulterers"—was it really necessary to underline his own negative virtues? "Or even as this
publican"—yes, that gives the whole thing away. He looked
so absorbed in his prayers, didn't he? But that was only part
of the performance: all the time he was looking out of the
corner of his eye at the shabby figure over yonder, and despis-
ing him. "I fast twice in the week, I give tithes of all I possess"—what is the use of saying all that? He went up to the
temple to pray, but he forgot his errand; he was too busy contemplating his own good qualities to find time for petition.
Two men went up to the temple, but only one prayed.

And the publican? He stood far off, so as not to disturb the   3
quality at their devotions. He did not dare to lift up his eyes
to heaven; he was too full of shame to challenge scrutiny. He
smote upon his breast, for all to see what manner of prayer
was his. He may have been a kind father and a good friend,
but it does not occur to him to mention all that. He sees himself in God's sight only as God sees him; God be merciful,
though man be unmerciful, to me, a sinner.

We can put a name to the Pharisee: he was called Simon,   4
and he comes in the seventh chapter of St. Luke. We can put
a name to the publican; he was called Zacheus, and he comes
in the nineteenth chapter of St. Luke. Zacheus in his tree, the
Magdalen kneeling on the floor, the publican beating his breast
in the temple court, all give us the same clue; the door of
heaven is low, and we must stoop to enter it.

Organization

1. What is the thesis statement of the essay?
2. Identify Knox's attitude toward his materials. What are the
   main elements contributing to it?
3. Discuss the method of arrangement of the materials in the
   essay.
4. Identify the subject of each of the four paragraphs. Do the
   four, taken together, form a logical pattern?

Paragraphs

1. Discuss the method of arrangement of the materials in paragraph 1.
2. Comment on the coherence of paragraph 2 in light of the biblical account of this event in Luke 18:9–14.

Sentences

1. What is unusual about the second and fourth sentences of paragraph 1? Are they similar in their purpose?
2. What is the function of the first sentence of paragraph 3?
3. How do the sentences of paragraph 3 differ from those of paragraph 2? Is the difference intentional?

Words

1. To what do the following refer? *Magdalen* (4), *Simon* (4), *Zacheus* (4). Do the allusions enrich the essay?
2. Be sure you know the meaning of each of the following:

   extortioners (2)   scrupulous (1)
   fastidious (1)   scrutiny (3)
   Pharisee (1)   smote (3)
   publican (1)   sordid (1)
   quality (3)

Suggestions for Writing

1. Using the biblical reference (Luke 7) given in paragraph 4 as a basis, apply Knox's method of imaginative reconstruction to the story of the Pharisee (Simon) and the woman with the alabaster jar (Magdalen). Compare or contrast these two figures in some way (attitude toward material goods, toward Jesus, toward humility).
2. Compare or contrast two of your relatives, friends, or acquaintances, concentrating on some desirable or undesirable character trait.

YOU'RE NOT WHAT YOU THINK YOU ARE

Willard Gaylin

Willard Gaylin: psychiatrist, author. Gaylin was born in Cleveland in 1925. He attended Harvard, Western Reserve University, and Columbia University, from which he was certified in psychoanalytic medicine. He has taught psychiatry and law at Columbia. Among Gaylin's books are The Meaning of Despair, In the Service of Their Country: War Resisters in Prison, *and* Feelings: Our Vital Signs. *The following essay appeared in* McCall's *magazine in 1980.*

According to Gaylin, what provides the most reliable data about a person?

How is the title of the essay related to and supported by the essay's content?

1   It was, I believe, the distinguished Nebraska financier Father Edward J. Flanagan who professed to having "never met a bad boy." Having myself met a number of bad boys, it might seem that either our experiences were drastically different or we were using the word "bad" differently. I suspect neither is true, but rather that the Father was praising the "inner person," while I, in fact, do not acknowledge the existence of inner people.

2   Since we psychoanalysts have unwittingly contributed to this confusion, let one, at least, attempt a small rectifying effort. Psychoanalytic data—which should be viewed as supplementary information about a person's behavior—are, unfortunately, often viewed as alternative (and *superior*) information. This has led to the prevalent tendency to think of the "inner" person as the real one and the outer person as an illusion or pretender. While psychoanalysis supplies us with an incredibly useful tool for explaining why people behave as they do, most of this has little bearing on the moral nature of that behavior. Psychoanalysis is a fascinating but relatively new means of illuminating the person. But few of us are prepared to substitute an X-ray of Grandfather's head for the portrait that hangs in the parlor. The inside of the man represents another view, not a truer one. People may not always be what they appear to be, but what they appear to be is always a significant part of what they are. A person is the sum total of *all* his behavior. To probe for unconscious determinants of behavior and then define an individual in those terms exclusively, ignoring his overt behavior altogether, is a greater distortion than ignoring the unconscious.

3   Kurt Vonnegut has said, "You are what you pretend to be," which is, after all, simply another way of saying, you are what

we (all of us) perceive you to be, not what you think you are.

4   Consider for a moment the case of the 90-year-old man on his deathbed, joyous and relieved over the success of his deception. For 90 years he has affected courtesy, kindness and generosity—suppressing all the malice he knew was within him. All his life he had been fooling the world into believing he was a good man. This "evil" man will, I predict, be welcomed into the Kingdom of Heaven.

5   Similarly, I will not be told that the young man who earns his pocket money by mugging old ladies is "really" a good boy. Even my generous and expansive definition of goodness will not accommodate that particular form of self-advancement. (That he may be potentially a good boy is another matter.) It does not count that beneath the rough exterior he has a heart of purest gold, locked away from human perception. You are for the most part what you seem to be, not what you would wish to be, nor, indeed, what you believe yourself to be.

6   Spare me, therefore, your good intentions, your inner sensitivities, your unarticulated and unexpressed love. And spare me also those tedious psychohistories that—by exposing the goodness inside the bad man and the evil inside the good—invariably establish a vulgar and perverse egalitarianism, as if the arrangement of what is outside and what is inside makes no moral difference. I do not care to learn that Hitler's heart was in the right place. A knowledge of your unconscious life may be an adjunct to understanding your behavior. It is *not* a substitute for your behavior in describing you. Those character traits, those attitudes, that behavior—that strange and alien stuff sticking out all over you—*that's the real you!*

Organization

1. Identify the thesis sentence, if any.
2. Which method of arrangement—block or alternating—does the essay follow?
3. List the different transitional words or phrases linking the paragraphs.

Paragraphs

1. Are the examples in paragraphs 4 and 5 effective? Explain.
2. Does paragraph 3 serve any useful purpose, or could it be ommitted?
3. Is the topic thought of paragraph 5 implicit or explicit? If implicit, state it in your own words. If explicit, which sentence embodies it?

Sentences

1. Three parenthetical phrases or sentences occur in the essay: in paragraphs 2, in 3, and in 5. Are all three in parentheses for the same reason?
2. What is the meaning of the figurative expression in the last sentence of the essay?

Words

1. To what do the following refer? *Father Edward J. Flanagan* (1), *Kurt Vonnegut* (3), *Hitler* (6).
2. Does *evil* (4) appear in quotation marks for the same reason *bad* (1) and *really* (5) do?
3. Be sure you know the meaning of each of the following:

adjunct (6)
affected (4)
determinants (2)
egalitarianism (6)
expansive (5)
financier (1)
overt (2)

perverse (6)
prevalent (2)
psychoanalysis (2), psychoanalysts (2),
psychoanalytic (2), psychohistories (6)
rectifying (2)
unarticulated (6)

Suggestions for Writing

1. Write a character-sketch (similar to, but longer than, the very brief one in paragraphs 4 and 5) in which you portray a person whose "inner" self is different from his or her "outer" self, with resulting moral ambiguity.
2. Would the author of "Pharisee and Publican" (p. 168) agree with the author of "You're Not What You Think You Are" that *You are what we (all of us) perceive you to be, not what you think you are?* (3) Concentrate on the example of the Pharisee in particular.

PEDESTRIAN STUDENTS AND HIGH-FLYING SQUIRRELS

Liane Ellison Norman

Liane Ellison Norman: teacher, writer, peace activist. Norman was born in Missoula, Montana in 1937. She attended Grinnell College and Brandeis University. Among the places she has taught are Kalamazoo College, Chatham College, and the University of Pittsburgh. Her articles have appeared in, among other publications, the Christian Science Monitor, *the* Bulletin of Concerned Asian Scholars, *and the* Center Magazine, *which is the publication of the Robert Maynard Hutchins Center for the Study of Democratic Institutions. She has completed a book on the Viet Nam war. In 1984 she founded, and is today the director of, the Pittsburgh Peace Institute. The following essay appeared in the* Center Magazine.

What are the characteristics of pedestrian students and high-flying squirrels?

What does Norman want her students to get out of their college experience?

1   The squirrel is curious. He darts and edges, profile first, one bright black eye on me, the other alert for enemies on the other side. Like a fencer, he faces both ways, for every impulse toward me, an impulse away. His tail is airy. He flicks and flourishes it, taking readings of some subtle kind.

2   I am enjoying a reprieve of warm sun in a season of rain and impending frost. Around me today is the wine of the garden's final ripening. On the zucchini, planted late, the flagrant blossoms flare and decline in a day's time. I am sitting on the front porch thinking about my students. Many of them earnestly and ardently want me to teach them to be hacks. Give us ten tricks, they plead, ten nifty fail-safe ways to write a news story. Don't make us think our way through these problems, they storm (and when I am insistent that thinking *is* the trick, "You never listen to us," they complain). Who cares about the First Amendment? they sneer. What are John Peter Zenger and Hugo Black to us? Teach us how to earn a living. They will be content, they explain, with know-how and jobs, satisfied to do no more than cover the tedium of school board and weather.

3   Under the rebellion, there is a plaintive panic. What if, on the job—assuming there is a job to be on—they fearlessly defend the free press against government, grand jury, and media monopoly, but don't know how to write an obituary. Shouldn't obituaries come first? I hope not, but even obituaries need good information and firm prose, and both, I say, require clear thought.

4   The squirrel does not share my meditation. He grows tired

of inquiring into me. His dismissive tail floats out behind as he takes a running leap into the tree. Up the bark he goes and onto a branch, where he crashes through the leaves. He soars from slender perch to slender perch, shaking up the tree as if he were the west wind. What a madcap he is, to go racing from one twig that dips under him to another at those heights! His acrobatic clamor loosens buckeyes in their prickly armor. They drop, break open, and he is down the tree in a twinkling, picking, choosing. He finds what he wants and carries it, an outsize nut which is burnished like a fine cello, across the lawn, up a pole, and across the tightrope telephone line to the other side, where he disappears in maple foliage.

Some inner clock or calendar tells him to stock his larder   5 against the deep snows and hard times that are coming. I have heard that squirrels are fuzzy-minded, that they collect their winter groceries and store them, and then forget where they are cached. But this squirrel is purposeful: he appears to know he'd better look ahead. Faced with necessity, he is prudent, but not fearful. He prances and flies as he goes about his task of preparation, and he never fails to look into whatever startles his attention.

Though he is not an ordinary pedestrian, crossing the street   6 far above, I sometimes see the mangled fur of a squirrel on the street, with no flirtation left. Even a high-flying squirrel may zap himself on an aerial live wire. His days are dangerous and his winters are lean, but still he lays in provisions the way a trapeze artist goes about his work, with daring and dash.

For the squirrel, there is no work but living. He gathers food,   7 reproduces, tends the children for a while, and stays out of danger. Doing these things with style is what distinguishes him. But for my students, unemployment looms as large as the horizon itself. Their anxiety has cause. And yet, what good is it? Ten tricks or no ten tricks, there are not enough jobs. The well-trained, well-educated stand in line for unemployment checks with the unfortunates and the drifters. Neither skill nor virtue holds certain promise. This being so, I wonder, why should these students not demand, for the well-being of their souls, the liberation of their minds?

It grieves me that they want to be pedestrians, earthbound   8 and always careful. You ask too much, they say. What you want is painful and unfair. There are a multitude of pressures that instruct them to train, not free, themselves. Many of them are the first generation to go to college; family aspirations are in their trust. Advisers and models tell them to be doctors, lawyers, engineers, cops, and public-relations people; no one ever tells them they can be poets, philosophers, farmers, in-

175

ventors, or wizards. Their elders are anxious too; they reject the eccentric and the novel. And, realism notwithstanding, they cling to talismanic determination; play it safe and do things right and I, each one thinks, will get a job even though others won't.

9   I tell them fondly of my college days, which were a dizzy time (as I think the squirrel's time must be), as I let loose and pitched from fairly firm stands into the space of intellect and imagination, never quite sure what solid branch I would light on. That was the most useful thing I learned, the practical advantage (not to mention the exhilaration) of launching out to find where my propellant mind could take me.

10   A luxury? one student ponders, a little wistfully.

11   Yes, luxury, and yet necessity, and it aroused that flight, a fierce unappeasable appetite to know and to essay. The luxury I speak of is not like other privileges of wealth and power that must be hoarded to be had. If jobs are scarce, the heady regions of treetop adventure are not. Flight and gaiety cost nothing, though of course they may cost everything.

12   The squirrel, my frisky analogue, is not perfectly free. He must go on all fours, however nimbly he does it. Dogs are always after him, and when he barely escapes, they rant up the tree as he dodges among the branches that give under his small weight. He feeds on summer's plenty and pays the price of strontium in his bones. He is no freer of industrial ordure than I am. He lives, mates, and dies (no obituary, first or last, for him), but still he plunges and balances, risking his neck because it is his nature.

13   I like the little squirrel for his simplicity and bravery. He will never get ahead in life, never find a good job, never settle down, never be safe. There are no sure-fire tricks to make it as a squirrel.

Organization

1. At what point in the essay did you begin to see, or at least suspect, that the squirrel mentioned in paragraph 1 was more than just part of the introductory setting?
2. What is the basis of the comparison between students and squirrels?
3. Who else besides students and squirrels are compared or contrasted in the essay?

Paragraphs

1. Could Norman be accused of having a boastful attitude on the basis of paragraphs 9–11?

Sentences

1. In what way does the movement of the eighth and ninth sentences of paragraph 4 mirror what is said in these sentences? Point to other such examples in the essay.
2. Why does Norman use quotation marks for only one of the complaints she attributes to her students in paragraph 2?

Words

1. Name the figure of speech involved in each of the following sentences, and indicate why each one is or is not effective:

   The second sentence of paragraph 2
   The first sentence of paragraph 5
   The third sentence of paragraph 6
   The first sentence of paragraph 9

2. Indicate why Norman's word or phrase given in italics below is better in each case than the suggested alternative in parenthesis. (Be sure to re-read the sentence before deciding.)

   edges (hovers): second sentence of paragraph 1
   airy (raised in the air): fourth sentence of paragraph 1
   flicks and flourishes (darts and shakes): fifth sentence of paragraph 1
   flare (bloom): third sentence of paragraph 2
   prances and flies (leaps and soars): fifth sentence of paragraph 5

3. Are the terms *pedestrian* and *high-flying* as used in the title and in the essay itself to be taken literally, figuratively, or both? Explain.
4. To what do the following refer? *John Peter Zenger* (2), *Hugo Black* (2).
5. Be sure you know the meaning of each of the following:

analogue (12)	propellant (9)
buckeyes (4)	rant (12)
burnished (4)	reprieve (2)
larder (5)	strontium (12)
madcap (4)	talismanic (8)
ordure (12)	tedium (2)
obituary (3)	unappeasable (11)
plaintive (3)	wistfully (10)
prances (5)	zucchini (2)

Suggestions for Writing

1. Compare and contrast "Pedestrian Students and High-Flying Squirrels" and "Courtship Through the Ages" (p. 150) as analogies. Take into consideration the X's and Y's being compared; the basis, the extent, and the purpose of the comparisons; the method of arranging the comparisons; and any other significant similarities and differences.

2. Defend your fellow-students against the author's criticisms by assuming the role of their spokesperson and comparing teachers with some form of animal life (as the author compares students with squirrels). Be sure to choose an animal whose behavior reflects, analogously, the similarities or differences you see between it and teachers. Or take the role of a squirrel and comment on the author's remarks about you and other squirrels.

3. Compare and contrast "pedestrian" students and "high-flying" students, or one representative of each type.

GRANT AND LEE: A STUDY IN CONTRASTS

Bruce Catton

Bruce Catton: journalist, historian, author. Catton was born in Petoskey, Michigan in 1899. After attending Oberlin College, he worked for several newspapers including the Cleveland Plain Dealer. *Because of his interest in American history, he became an expert on the War Between the States and wrote thirteen books on the subject.* A Stillness at Appomattox *won both the Pulitzer Prize and the National Book Award in 1954. The following essay appeared in* The American Story, *a collection of historical essays. Catton died in 1978.*

What are the characteristics of *the conflicting currents* represented by Grant and Lee?

What is the most striking contrast between Grant and Lee?

1 When Ulysses S. Grant and Robert E. Lee met in the parlor of a modest house at Appomattox Court House, Virginia, on April 9, 1865, to work out the terms for the surrender of Lee's Army of Northern Virginia, a great chapter in American life came to a close, and a great new chapter began.

2 These men were bringing the Civil War to its virtual finish. To be sure, other armies had yet to surrender, and for a few days the fugitive Confederate government would struggle desperately and vainly, trying to find some way to go on living now that its chief support was gone. But in effect it was all

over when Grant and Lee signed the papers. And the little room where they wrote out the terms was the scene of one of the poignant, dramatic contrasts in American history.

They were two strong men, these oddly different generals, 3 and they represented the strengths of two conflicting currents that, through them, had come into final collision.

Back of Robert E. Lee was the notion that the old aristo- 4 cratic concept might somehow survive and be dominant in American life.

Lee was tidewater Virginia, and in his background were 5 family, culture, and tradition . . . the age of chivalry trans- planted to a New World which was making its own legends and its own myths. He embodied a way of life that had come down through the age of knighthood and the English country squire. America was a land that was beginning all over again, dedicated to nothing much more complicated than the rather hazy belief that all men had equal rights and should have an equal chance in the world. In such a land Lee stood for the feeling that it was somehow of advantage to human society to have a pronounced inequality in the social structure. There should be a leisure class, backed by ownership of land; in turn, society itself should be keyed to the land as the chief source of wealth and influence. It would bring forth (according to this ideal) a class of men with a strong sense of obligation to the community; men who lived not to gain advantage for them- selves, but to meet the solemn obligations which had been laid on them by the very fact that they were privileged. From them the country would get its leadership; to them it could look for the higher values—of thought, of conduct, of personal deportment—to give it strength and virtue.

Lee embodied the noblest elements of this aristocratic ideal. 6 Through him, the landed nobility justified itself. For four years, the Southern states had fought a desperate war to uphold the ideals for which Lee stood. In the end, it almost seemed as if the Confederacy fought for Lee; as if he himself was the Con- federacy . . . the best thing that the way of life for which the Confederacy stood could ever have to offer. He had passed into legend before Appomattox. Thousands of tired, underfed, poorly clothed Confederate soldiers, long since past the simple en- thusiasm of the early days of the struggle, somehow con- sidered Lee the symbol of everything for which they had been willing to die. But they could not quite put this feeling into words. If the Lost Cause, sanctified by so much heroism and so many deaths, had a living justification, its justification was General Lee.

Grant, the son of a tanner on the Western frontier, was 7

everything Lee was not. He had come up the hard way and embodied nothing in particular except the eternal toughness and sinewy fiber of the men who grew up beyond the mountains. He was one of a body of men who owed a reverence and obeisance to no one, who were self-reliant to a fault, who cared hardly anything for the past but who had a sharp eye for the future.

8   These frontier men were the precise opposite of the tidewater aristocrats. Back of them, in the great surge that had taken people over the Alleghenies and into the opening Western country, there was a deep, implicit dissatisfaction with a past that had settled into grooves. They stood for democracy, not from any reasoned conclusion about the proper ordering of human society, but simply because they had grown up in the middle of democracy and knew how it worked. Their society might have privileges, but they would be privileges each man had won for himself. Forms and patterns meant nothing. No man was born to anything, except perhaps to a chance to show how far he could rise. Life was competition.

9   Yet along with this feeling had come a deep sense of belonging to a national community. The Westerner who developed a farm, opened a shop, or set up in business as a trader, could hope to prosper only as his own community prospered—and his community ran from the Atlantic to the Pacific and from Canada down to Mexico. If the land was settled, with towns and highways and accessible markets, he could better himself. He saw his fate in terms of the nation's own destiny. As its horizons expanded, so did his. He had, in other words, an acute dollars-and-cents stake in the continued growth and development of his country.

10   And that, perhaps, is where the contrast between Grant and Lee becomes most striking. The Virginia aristocrat, inevitably, saw himself in relation to his own region. He lived in a static society which could endure almost anything except change. Instinctively, his first loyalty would go to the locality in which that society existed. He would fight to the limit of endurance to defend it, because in defending it he was defending everything that gave his own life its deepest meaning.

11   The Westerner, on the other hand, would fight with an equal tenacity for the broader concept of society. He fought so because everything he lived by was tied to growth, expansion, and a constantly widening horizon. What he lived by would survive or fall with the nation itself. He could not possibly stand by unmoved in the face of an attempt to destroy the Union. He would combat it with everything he had, because he could only see it as an effort to cut the ground out from under his feet.

So Grant and Lee were in complete contrast, representing 12
two diametrically opposed elements in American life. Grant
was the modern man emerging; beyond him, ready to come
on the stage, was the great age of steel and machinery, of
crowded cities and a restless burgeoning vitality. Lee might
have ridden down from the old age of chivalry, lance in hand,
silken banner fluttering over his head. Each man was the perfect champion of his cause, drawing both his strengths and
his weaknesses from the people he led.

Yet it was not all contrast, after all. Different as they were— 13
in background, in personality, in underlying aspiration—these
two great soldiers had much in common. Under everything
else, they were marvelous fighters. Furthermore, their fighting qualities were really very much alike.

Each man had, to begin with, the great virtue of utter te- 14
nacity and fidelity. Grant fought his way down the Mississippi Valley in spite of acute personal discouragement and
profound military handicaps. Lee hung on in the trenches at
Petersburg after hope itself had died. In each man there was
an indomitable quality . . . the born fighter's refusal to give
up as long as he can still remain on his feet and lift his two
fists.

Daring and resourcefulness they had, too; the ability to think 15
faster and move faster than the enemy. These were the qualities which gave Lee the dazzling campaigns of Second Man-
assas and Chancellorsville and won Vicksburg for Grant.

Lastly, and perhaps greatest of all, there was the ability, at 16
the end, to turn quickly from war to peace once the fighting
was over. Out of the way these two men behaved at Appomattox came the possibility of a peace of reconciliation. It
was a possibility not wholly realized, in the years to come,
but which did, in the end, help the two sections to become
one nation again . . . after a war whose bitterness might have
seemed to make such a reunion wholly impossible. No part
of either man's life became him more than the part he played
in their brief meeting in the McLean house at Appomattox.
Their behavior there put all succeeding generations of Americans in their debt. Two great Americans, Grant and Lee—
very different, yet under everything very much alike. Their
encounter at Appomattox was one of the great moments of
American history.

Organization

1. With which paragraph does the body begin?
2. Does Catton reveal, either directly or indirectly, any partial-
   ity toward either Grant or Lee?

3. Does Catton succeed in preventing monotony from developing in his presentation, despite frequently alternating between Grant and Lee? If so, how?
4. Since the final paragraph deals with the last in a series of comparisons, can it also stand as a genuine concluding paragraph, or should another paragraph have been added?
5. Why does Catton discuss the differences between Grant and Lee before discussing the similarities?
6. What transitional methods does Catton use to bridge paragraphs 5 and 6? What methods does he use to bridge paragraphs 15 and 16?

Paragraphs

1. Which method of arrangement—block or alternating—do paragraphs 4 onwards follow?
2. Does any paragraph have a topic sentence that is not the first sentence of the paragraph?
3. Can the one-sentence length of paragraphs 3 and 4 be justified?

Sentences

1. Comment on the effectiveness of the sentence variety in paragraph 8.
2. The topic sentences are shorter than most of the rest of the sentences in their respective paragraphs. What effect does this create?
3. Why does Catton invert the word order in the first sentence of paragraph 15?
4. Figurative language occurs in paragraphs 1, 3, and 5. Name the figure of speech in each case. What does such language contribute to the essay?

Words

1. Be sure you know the meaning of each of the following:

aspiration (13)	obeisance (7)
burgeoning (12)	poignant (1)
chivalry (5)	sinewy (7)
diametrically (12)	tenacity (11, 14)
indomitable (14)	tidewater (8)

Suggestions for Writing

1. Select two figures from past or present with whom you are already familiar, or about whom you can do limited research. Compare or contrast them in significant ways. (If you can show them meeting at a dramatic moment in their lives, so much the better.)

2. Have you ever had a personal confrontation with an opponent, or been witness to such a confrontation between two others? If so, describe the scene and indicate the contrasting viewpoints represented by the two individuals involved.

THE AMERICAN NATURE OF FOOTBALL

John Finlay

John L. Finlay: historian, educator, administrator. Finlay was born near Nottingham, England in 1939. At Cambridge University he read history. He concluded his education at the University of Manitoba in Winnipeg, Canada. He began his teaching career in the History Department at Manitoba. Among his books are Social Credit: The English Origins, Canada in the North Atlantic Triangle, *and coauthored with Sprague,* Survey of Canadian History. *He is presently Dean of the Faculty of Arts at Manitoba. The following essay was originally entitled "Homo Ludens (Americanus)" and appeared in* Queen's Quarterly.

According to Finlay, what are the limitations American football has imposed on itself?

What evidence does Finlay provide to contradict McLuhan's quotation in paragraph 1?

In the last two decades North America has witnessed a startling rise in the popularity of football, so that this game and not baseball is now *the* American game. An explanation has been offered by Marshall McLuhan, who writes that "the TV image . . . spells for a while, at least, the doom of baseball. For baseball is a game of one-thing-at-a-time, fixed positions and visibly delegated specialist jobs such as belonged to the now passing mechanical age. . . . In contrast, American football is nonpositional, and any or all of the players can switch to any role during play. . . . It agrees very well with the new needs of decentralized team play in the electric age."

In order to isolate the elements of American football that are prized, it is not sufficient to compare it with baseball. Rather, it is necessary to examine not merely the American game, but other brands of football, too. These games are not

1

2

independent; until about the middle of the nineteenth century there was but an ill-defined "ur-football." It was from this that the individual varieties crystallized, and in doing so they seized upon and developed aspects of the game that appealed to the host society.

3   Ur-football was weakly structured, but any game that is to become a professional mass spectacle must impose limits upon itself. Time is an aspect of limitation. In soccer and rugby the referee is the sole judge of time. Given his other duties, his timing must be rather hit-and-miss. The division of the games is similarly rudimentary; in order to equalize the advantage of sun, slope and so on, the game is simply divided into halves. In North America, not only is the measurement of time taken out of the hands of the referee and lodged in those of a specialist, but the element of "guessing" is removed. The game and the clock are stopped between actions, and time begins to elapse only when the referee whistles for play to resume. There is also a more sophisticated ordering of the game. Each half is divided into two, which helps to equalize opportunity more successfully. In soccer and rugby it is very easy to waste time, but in North America time is not only precise, it is precious.

4   The penalty for time wasting is the loss of territory. Here is another limitation, the way in which space is conceived and handled. European games are most cavalier when it comes to fixing the playing area; in both soccer and rugby, maximum/minimum dimensions are given. These boundary lines serve to mark off a neutral, equal space. The only serious irruption into the emptiness of a soccer field is the penalty area around the goal, a magical exception designed to protect the goalkeeper, the one player permitted to handle the ball. Rugby is somewhat more space conscious. Although overall dimension is equally fluid, the dividing up of the field is more apparent.

5   Such thinking is foreign to the North American pattern. To begin with, the dimensions of the playing area are rigidly prescribed. The game's characteristic—making ten yards' progress in a given number of attempts—calls for marking each yard on the field. No point of the field is of more value than any other. While soccer players know that the relatively small goal is all-important (an infraction inside the magic territory guarding it results in a penalty that is an almost automatic goal), the North American player refuses to acknowledge that any point is more important than another—forward movement at any point of the field is what counts.

6   At this point the deeper significance of space and its han-

dling begins to emerge, a significance that goes to the root of the various codes. Soccer sees its field, other than the goal area, as a neutral space within which the action is allowed to build up. The objective is the goal, and the field exists merely to allow the team to group itself, mount an attack, and move in on that goal. Rugby, while not so pure in this respect, is essentially very similar. On the other hand, for the North American player each piece of the field is, in a sense, the goal line. Whereas the soccer player scores explosively, the North American must score on the installment plan.

The basic divergence may be illustrated by a comparison of 7 penalties. In European games the method of compensating for infraction is a kick or "scrum" taken at the point of infraction, the ball being handed over to the team offended against. This amounts to little more than giving this team a chance of better position. In North America an infraction usually means the loss of a certain number of yards, so that the team offended against creeps another installment nearer.

The North American game is much more precise, standard- 8 ized, indeed efficient than the European. In short, it approaches the scientific criteria of control and replication as closely as any sport can without forfeiting that element of unpredictability that must always be there. The clinching point is the use of statistics. The American sports fan is avid for figures that will make possible "true" comparisons and facilitate that favorite pastime, the composition of "dream teams." While not totally unknown in Europe, such attitudes are exceptional. Nor is it enough to say that North American sports lend themselves to this approach whereas European ones do not; the development of North American games was governed precisely by this urge to quantify.

The next dimension is the way in which the participant is 9 perceived. Until recently European games have restricted a team to the actual number allowed by the rules to be in play at any one time. Should one player have to withdraw, no substitute was allowed. This situation has been modified of late, and limited substituting is now permitted. In North America, however, the practice of substitution has had a long history. Alongside this distinction is another akin to it. The North American coach never relinquishes control of his team, and he and his rooftop spotter are constantly analyzing the game and adjusting the team strategy accordingly: the captain on the field has but limited power of shaping the game.

These two points taken together lead to the conclusion that 10 in North America the player is devalued—the players are not so much playing as being played. When unsatisfactory, the player is removed. The team, in a way, overshadows the individuals who compose it. This impression is confirmed by the American practice of specialization, and here McLuhan is quite wrong in his characterization. Rather than the game being one of interchanging players able "to switch to any role during play," football is a most restricted form. For a long time the game has been played by two squads, one for offense and one for defense, and a total changeover accompanies a change in ball possession. But specialization goes further than this: even on the offense, there are players who are held to be ineligible receivers, and clubs keep players on the roster whose sole function is to kick the ball. In European games the trend has been the other way. In older forms of soccer a distinction was made between the heavier backs and the lighter forwards. But the logic of the game, especially as developed by the Latins, destroyed this nascent specialization, and now all must be potential attackers, all possible defenders.

11   One must conclude that McLuhan was wrong in claiming that football was not "a game of one thing at a time, fixed positions and visibly delegated specialist jobs." Far from football's belonging to the electronic age, it belongs to a way of life now superseded. If any sport is suited to the electronic age, that sport is soccer.

12   But if football belongs to the mechanical age, the problem still remains of why it is rising and baseball declining. In fact, there is one ground on which the two sports diverge radically.

13   Baseball has about it elements that have to be described as unfair. Whereas in football each yard gained is identical, in baseball one hit is not the same as another. For example, a team may load three bases by successively having its hitters gain a base at a time, which, since the game's glory is the home run, may be looked upon as relative failures. At this point the big hitter may unleash a home run and count four for his side. Had the same hit been made at the start of an inning, only one run would have resulted. It is true that the way would be open for the bases to be loaded and for the big hitter to make another appearance; indeed this process could go on indefinitely. The point is that this possibility is not real to the spectators. Another way of illustrating this point is to contrast the episodic nature of baseball with the continuous narrative of football. In baseball, the end of the inning ends any advantage; for instance, three loaded bases count for nothing. But consider the analogous situation in football when there are two evenly matched teams unable to make first downs and obliged to kick. Eventually the superior team will ap-

proach the opponent's goal line, if only by the difference between the two punts, and in this way it is possible for any
interim advantage to be transformed into a score.

Then again, there is the very meaning of the home run. There 14
is something apocalyptic about such an explosion of power
which, once it has connected with the ball, makes a formality
of the hitter's tour of the bases. There is nothing comparable
in football. The nearest is the long pass, but there is nothing
so clear-cut about this—either in definition or in execution—
and there is nothing in the statistics to set beside the home
run. The favorite football statistics are averages, and these are
decidedly nonapocalyptic.

The implication is that if both baseball and football are 15
similarly attuned to a rational capitalist environment, baseball is the game of an early, football of a mature capitalism.
The early capitalist period, above all in the United States, was
a time when the rational, calculating approach was yet shot
through with a gambling, piratical residue—the robber baron
era, in fact. Baseball is a robber baron game. But when capitalism matures and moves into the stage of staid corporate-
ness that prefers safety to spectacle, certain small gains to risky
windfalls, its sports style must similarly shift.

Japan, still in the early, heroic stages of capitalism, has av- 16
idly taken to baseball but not to football. It is not a question
of Japanese physique serving as a determinant, for rugby has
long had a following in Asia. It may be predicted, then, that
when their capitalism moves into a higher stage, the Japanese
will move on to football.

Organization

1. Does this essay show a lack of balance in not taking into account the *similarities* between American and other types of
   football?
2. Into how many sections would you divide the essay, and which
   paragraphs would you include in each? Are the sections joined
   together smoothly?
3. Is there any apparent reason for the order of paragraphs
   2–10?

Paragraphs

1. What function does paragraph 11 serve? What function does
   paragraph 12 serve?
2. Are paragraphs 3 and 13 unified, or should they have been
   divided into two separate paragraphs?

Sentences

1. This essay was originally entitled "Homo Ludens (Ameri-canus)" and first appeared in *Queen's Quarterly,* a Canadian college-based journal with a largely scholarly authorship. In what ways does its style differ from the style which an article on the same subject in *Sports Illustrated* or *Football Digest* would have?
2. What effect do short sentences such as the second sentence of paragraph 3 and the third sentence of paragraph 8 produce, particularly amid the generally longer sentences of this essay?

Words

1. Why are *guessing* (3), *true* (8), and *dream teams* (8) in quota-tion marks?
2. Comment on the italicization of *the* (1) and the construction *maximum/minimum* (4).
3. To what do the following refer? *Marshall McLuhan* (1, 10, 11), *robber baron era* (15), *"scrum"* (7).
4. Be sure you know the meaning of each of the following:

analogous (1)	piratical (15)
apocalyptic (14)	quantify (8)
cavalier (4)	replication (8)
divergence (7)	rudimentary (3)
infraction (5, 7)	staid (15)
irruption (4)	superseded (11)
nascent (10)	ur-football (2, 3)

Suggestions for Writing

1. Discuss two similar-but-different sports (soccer and rugby, tennis and badminton, track and cross country, handball and racquet ball) or male-female differences in playing the same sport.
2. The author sees baseball as in some ways "unfair," as lacking in the continuous action and interest of football, and as being the product of an early, now-outmoded form of the capitalist outlook (13–16). Defend baseball against one or more of these arguments or against other arguments often used by those who prefer football. Address your essay to fanatical football fans.

THE FIRST TEST OF DATING

Dowling Bowman

Dowling Bowman: student. Bowman's home is Pensacola, Florida, where he was born in 1966. He graduated from Pensacola's W. J. Woodham High School. He is presently studying mechanical engineering at Auburn University. This essay is based on Suggestions for Writing 3 on p. 168.

First dates are always the worst. First dates are so emotionally turbulent that midnight is awaited expectantly as an end to the torment. On the other hand, twenty-first dates end too soon; midnight becomes a cage that restricts the freedom of the young. The first dates are a testing period for compatibility. This is an uneasy time for both participants because both are unsure how to act. In later dates though, the two become more comfortable with each other, and each becomes adept at initiating conversations of mutual interest.   1

My worst date was a first (and only) date with a girl named Lauri. The evening was a total flop. We went out with another couple, and the other couple was late to pick us up. Then, I had to meet Lauri's parents showing up late. That was embarrassing! Later at dinner I gracefully spilled my entire glass of tea all over the table and my suit. To make matters worse, I realized I had forgotten the tickets to the dance. So, we drove back home for the tickets and arrived an hour late for the dance. Then followed a time of uneasy and strained conversation. This awkwardness was only relieved by an occasional jaunt around the dance floor. Then came the crowning event that makes the night so memorable; my date got violently ill. Yes, she threw up all over the table where we were sitting. After that main event, the group decided Lauri needed some bed rest. Thus ended one of the worst nights of my life.   2

My best date, on the other hand, was equally memorable, but it was notable for a totally different set of reasons. My date's name was Linda, and we had been dating for about eight months. The evening started out well; I was on time; she was ready; I did not have to meet her parents or worry about other friends. Dinner was exquisite. Not only was the food good but also no egregious social error was committed. Everything went as smooth as clockwork. Dancing was fun, and the gaps between the dances were filled with humorous and lively conversation. After the dance, a stroll along the beach was in order. The clear night was lit by the soft light of the moon and the   3

Milky Way. The faint glow of phosphorescence lit our footprints as we passed. After the dance and stroll along the beach, curfew was fast approaching. So we went to her house and spent another two hours just talking. She is very easy to talk to because she cares about people, and it shows. We didn't want the evening to end; we recognized the specialness of the moment and wanted to keep it as long as we could.

4   First dates are anxious and insecure because of the nervousness of both people. As the conversation wanes and the sounds of silence fill the room, the agitation only increases. If this nervousness is allowed to control the behavior of the dating couple, it can lead only to disaster. By the time the twenty-first date is reached, the couple should have overcome this initial testing period. Yet this period must be experienced to achieve a close and intimate relationship. My only consolation is that first dates only happen once.

Martini please... it certainly would help out in a situation that appears to have no beginning - end or purpose. Very strange indeed to be asked to write and that's it - write. How many times have I wished that I could write about anything I wanted to. anything and everything that was in my head... all the little thought squiggles that passed by on the brain screen ~~in my head.~~ But given the opportunity to do so can only draw a blank slide. Its actually kind of scary; a fear of stupidity almost. am I stupid (or even worse - ~~unimaginative~~ unimaginative) because nothing wonderful and exciting pops on the big ~~s~~ screen? [I think being unimaginative would be a fate worse than death - or to be labeled as such] It almost reeks as a word - stagnant, ~~unmov~~ unmoving & thoughtless. I suppose if one had never written with fervor or excitement being labeled as unimaginative would not seem extremely terrible.

8
ANALYSIS

Analysis comes from the Greek word meaning "to dissolve, to break up." Thus, to analyze something is to divide it into its component parts, each of which may then be studied separately, as well as in relation to the whole. When you disassemble your vacuum cleaner for repair, when you make a report to your English class on the various types of poetry, when you try to determine why you have pride in your school, when you tell your parents how fall term registration operates, you are engaging, in each case, in analysis. That is to say, you are taking a complete entity and reducing it to its individual elements: the vacuum cleaner to its *parts* (motor, brush, belt, and so forth), poetry to its *classifications* (epic, dramatic, lyric), school pride to its *causes* or *reasons* (academic excellence, athletic accomplishment, campus attractiveness, and so forth), and registration to its *steps* (check-in, course enrollment, fee payment, and so forth). Obviously, both the objects you start with and the ways you analyze them differ in these cases. For example, the vacuum cleaner is a physical thing, a mechanism, that you divide physically into its equally physical parts, perhaps to the extent that they actually lie scattered about you on the living room floor. School pride, however, is an abstract concept that you divide into logical categories (causes or reasons). Nonetheless, in both cases you are analyzing.

Considered as a method of development for essays, analysis is thus a general term that covers several different ways of dissecting a whole on paper. The four principal ways are illustrated by the examples above: *division,* also called *partition,* or *structural analysis* (the vacuum cleaner); *classification* (poetry); *cause-and-effect analysis* (school pride); and *process* (or *operational*) *analysis* (registration). Because division and classification are similar, they will be treated together. Cause-and-effect and process analysis will be treated in a separate section for each.

DIVISION AND CLASSIFICATION

Division begins with a single item and reduces it to the parts that make it up. To take two of the examples cited earlier, a *vacuum cleaner* is divided into motor, brush, belt, and other parts. A *poem* is commonly divided into two basic elements: content (what the poem says) and form (how the poem says it).

Classification begins with a multiple item—that is, a number of single items taken in a collective sense—and breaks it down into categories or groups. *Vacuum cleaners,* a multiple item equivalent to *all individual vacuum cleaners taken collectively,* are classified in several different ways, for instance, by brand (Hoover, Eureka, General Electric, Westinghouse), by model (upright, canister), or by price (expensive, less expensive, inexpensive). *Poetry* (= *all poems*) is classified as epic, dramatic, or lyric.

A *university* is *divided* into colleges (Arts and Sciences, Engineering, Business, Medicine, and so forth); *universities* are *classified* according to such categories as age, size, type of ownership (public or private), endowment, and academic strengths and weaknesses. A *state* is divided into counties, but *states* are *classified* as northern, southern, midwestern, western, and so forth. An *essay* is *divided* into introduction, body, and conclusion; *essays* are *classified* as narrative, descriptive, analytical, and so on.

When you write division and classification papers, you will avoid some serious logical and rhetorical dangers if you carefully observe the following suggestions:

1. Use a Single Principle of Division or Classification, and Hold to It

In a paper classifying four major types of fiction, don't discuss the detective story, the spy story, the love story, and the short story. True enough, the short story is a type of fiction, but it doesn't belong in the same category with the other three types. The detective story, the spy story, and the love story are organized according to *content;* the short story is from another category altogether, that of *length.* (To put it another way, the short story overlaps the other three categories instead of being distinct from them, as the fourth category should be. Many short stories contain detective, spy, and love elements.) If your subject is fast-food restaurants in New York, don't divide the city into Manhattan,

Brooklyn, the Bronx, Queens, Staten Island, and Greenwich Village. Greenwich Village doesn't belong in that list on an equal footing with the others. The first five are all boroughs; Greenwich Village is part of the borough of Manhattan. If for some reason you wish to give Greenwich Village special attention, by all means do so. But treat it as what it is: a division of Manhattan.

In other words, when dividing or classifying, don't mix categories. Make sure that all your items are on the same level and are separate from one another. Bertrand Russell observes this rule when he divides "What I Have Lived For" into three items (p. 196): knowledge, love, and pity for suffering mankind. All three are what he calls *passions*, all occupy the same level of abstraction, and all are separate from each other. (Love and pity are certainly closely related, but they have different objects, at least as Russell uses them. Love takes in everyone; pity, only those who suffer.)

2. Make Your Categories Reasonably Complete

In a short paper, you can't treat a subject exhaustively; you have to be selective in what you say. But you do have to be sufficiently thorough to convince your reader not only that you know what you're talking about, but also that you aren't overlooking anything—or worse, concealing anything. Bertrand Russell faced no great problem with thoroughness because he had only three *passions* to talk about. Linda Charlton, however, had a more difficult task. She had to be as complete as possible in discussing the facilities of the Library of Congress without being able (because of space limitations) to give much attention to any one of them (pp. 201–03). She solved the problem in a way you might adopt when confronted with a similar situation—by collecting individual items under several main headings:

> Introduction, paragraphs 1–2
> Body (the divisions), paragraphs 3–14
>   *a.* Holdings, paragraphs 3–6
>   books
>   government publications
>   gifts
>   others
>   *b.* Services, paragraphs 7–10
>   reading rooms
>   programs for the handicapped
>   Congressional services

c. Problems, paragraphs 11–13
  inefficiency
  space
  time
Conclusion, paragraphs 14–15

Grouping related items, as Charlton does here, obviously strengthens the coherence of your presentation. More to the point, it permits you to treat single items only briefly because each gains from its association with the other items in the group. When even grouped items would be too numerous for you to treat, you might try listing *all* the groups first (to show your overall knowledge), and then single out one or two for discussion. Or, as Russell Baker does in classifying handshakes (p. 205), you could limit your presentation from the start to a few representative examples; your reader will understand that you are forced to be selective. (See Example, p. 128.)

How many divisions or classifications should you have? It's impossible to give an exact figure; it depends, as always, on the nature of your topic and your purpose in writing, as well as on practical considerations of time and paper length. Of the essays in this section, for example, none has less than three or more than five. But you must begin with at least two. For instance, you can hardly classify "dwelling places" as "urban" and let it go at that. (But you can *treat* only the urban kind as long as you mention the existence of the rural kind too.) Nor would you be likely to escape challenge if you were to categorize all rock instrumentalists as excellent musicians; some surely are not. But if your challenger, in attempting to correct you, insists that rock instrumentalists be classified as either excellent or poor musicians, he wouldn't be making much of an improvement—any more than someone who said that all car salesmen are either honest or dishonest, or all teachers either easy graders or hard graders. In each instance the required two categories are present, but they don't cover all the possibilities. A third, middle category is needed—one that takes in the musicians who are merely competent, the salesmen who are dishonest sometimes, the teachers who maintain a balance between hard and easy grading.

3. Whenever Possible, Give Your Thesis a Personal Twist

The basic purpose of division and classification is to clarify. Therefore, it is legitimate, especially in the case of complex subjects, for the thesis to be no more than a straightforward, objective statement of the categories that the rest of the essay goes on to explain. "Poems are classified as epic, dramatic, or lyric" may not have the personal touch we've been urging you to bring to your compositions, but it can be very helpful to a student coming to the study of poetry for the first time. This impersonal approach is the one Linda Charlton takes when she introduces the Library of Congress in her thesis sentence (par. 2, p. 201), and then proceeds to discuss the library's principal holdings. Her purpose is simply to convey information more or less objectively, and that is a worthy purpose indeed. If it weren't, textbooks, encyclopedias, histories, scientific reports, and many other kinds of valuable instructional writing would be looked down upon undeservedly.

But division and classification can also be put to less formal uses. For example, James E. Sefton isn't interested simply in exploring the various parts of a résumé. He also wants to impress on you how important good résumés are and how rarely they get written. Therefore, his thesis isn't the bland and uninviting "There are five main parts to a résumé," but rather *The result of the process* [of reducing the essentials of one's personal history to a sheet or two of paper] *is a resume, and the ability to write a good one seems to be an art as lost as the method of building Stonehenge* (par. 1, p. 198). In developing this thesis Sefton gives you as much accurate information as a writer using the other thesis would presumably give, but he does so in a way that is more lively and personal. Scarvia B. Anderson, too, generates unusual interest in what could have been a dull discussion of educational testing by fashioning a thesis sentence that combines a strong viewpoint with a sense of urgency: . . . *it's time school boards, parents, deans, instructors, and students took a careful look at the real* [i.e., teacher-made] *educational tests* (par. 4, p. 213). Russell Baker goes even further in the direction of a personal outlook by informally classifying handshakes as what might be called the "Clinging," the "Grasping," the "Partial," and the "Limp" kinds (pp. 205–207). Baker's essay shows clearly that analysis can be lighthearted and imaginative, as well as serious and factual.

Even when your use of division and classification is as straightforward and objective as Linda Charlton's in "Library of Congress," your composition can be as readable as hers if you draw on the same resources she used—a wide range of support, vivid detail, and lively tone. Above all, avoid the "bare bones" kind of division or classification paper that ends up being little more than an outline. True, your basic job is to get your categories arranged in emphatic order. Once you've done that, however, you have the equally important job of filling them out—putting flesh on the bones.

WHAT I HAVE LIVED FOR

Bertrand Russell

Bertrand Russell: philosopher, mathematician, educator, author. Russell was born in Ravenscroft, England in 1872 and graduated from Cambridge with honors in both mathematics and moral science. He co-authored, with Alfred North Whitehead, the Principia Mathematica *(1910–13). In 1916 Russell lost his teaching position at Cambridge because of his status as a conscientious objector. Throughout his life he championed pacificism, women's suffrage, and civil liberties. Most of his three dozen books deal with philosophy. In 1950 he was awarded the Nobel Prize for literature. Lord Russell was a severe critic of the United States' involvement in the Viet Nam conflict. He died in 1970. The following is his preface to his autobiography.*

What academic subjects would Russell have to study to obtain the kinds of knowledge he mentions in paragraph 3?

According to Russell, what constitutes evil in the world?

1   Three passions, simple but overwhelmingly strong, have governed my life: the longing for love, the search for knowledge, and unbearable pity for the suffering of mankind. These passions, like great winds, have blown me hither and thither, in a wayward course, over a deep ocean of anguish, reaching to the very verge of despair.

2   I have sought love, first, because it brings ecstasy—ecstasy so great that I would often have sacrificed all the rest of life for a few hours of this joy. I have sought it, next, because it relieves loneliness—that terrible loneliness in which one shivering consciousness looks over the rim of the world into the cold unfathomable lifeless abyss. I have sought it, finally, because in the union of love I have seen, in a mystic miniature, the prefiguring vision of the heaven that saints and poets have imagined. This is what I sought, and though it might seem too good for human life, this is what—at last—I have found.

3   With equal passion I have sought knowledge. I have wished to understand the hearts of men. I have wished to know why the stars shine. And I have tried to apprehend the Pythagorean power by which number holds sway above the flux. A little of this, but not much, I have achieved.

Love and knowledge, so far as they were possible, led up- 4
ward toward the heavens. But always pity brought me back to
earth. Echoes of cries of pain reverberate in my heart. Children in famine, victims tortured by oppressors, helpless old
people a hated burden to their sons, and the whole world of
loneliness, poverty, and pain make a mockery of what human
life should be. I long to alleviate the evil, but I cannot, and I
too suffer.

This has been my life. I have found it worth living, and 5
would gladly live it again if the chance were offered me.

Organization

1. The essay follows a very simple outline. Is there a justifiable
   principle for the order of paragraphs 2, 3, and 4? Explain.
2. What is Russell's attitude toward his material? Give specific
   examples to support your answer.

Paragraphs

1. Discuss the use of contrast in paragraph 4.
2. Are the supporting sentences of paragraph 2 presented in the
   most obvious order? Explain.

Sentences

1. Discuss the figurative language in the second sentence of
   paragraph 1 and in the second sentence of paragraph 2.
2. What is the antecedent of *this* in the last sentence of paragraph 2 and in the first sentence of paragraph 5? Would you
   consider these to be indefinite *this*'s?

Words

1. To what does *Pythagorean* allude (3)?
2. Be sure you know what each of the following means:

abyss (2)	ecstasy (2)
alleviate (4)	prefiguring (2)
apprehend (3)	reverberate (4)

Suggestions for Writing

1. Try to be as candid as Russell and write an analytical essay
   entitled "What I Live For."
2. Russell wrote "What I Have Lived For" in his old age. Analyze

the importance of the three *passions* mentioned in paragraph 1 as motivating factors in the lives of your contemporaries. (You may wish to use your circle of friends and acquaintances as representative examples.)

GOOD RÉSUMÉS—A LOST ART

James E. Sefton

James E. Sefton: historian, author. Sefton was born in San Francisco in 1939. Both his undergraduate and graduate training were at the University of California, Los Angeles, where he studied history. His areas of historical expertise include military and naval history, the Civil War and Reconstruction, and United States constitutional history. Sefton's entire teaching career has been at California State University, Northridge, which honored him with the Distinguished Teaching Award in 1970. His books include The United States Army and Reconstruction, 1865–77 *and* Andrew Johnson and the Uses of Constitutional Power. *One of his avocations is folk music, specifically, Scottish, Irish, and American. He is also the faculty adviser for Phi Sigma Kappa. The following appeared in* Signet, *the magazine of Phi Sigma Kappa, in 1976.*

What are the minimal requirements for a well-constructed résumé?

Why should you prepare and, every now and then, update a résumé?

1   It seems odd, perhaps, and rather depressing, to think of reducing the essentials of one's personal history to a sheet or two of paper. The result of the process is a resume, and the ability to write a good one seems to be an art as lost as the method of building Stonehenge. Résumés are important for job applications, financial aid, academic awards, and a number of other things; a poor one may close the door before it gets halfway open.

2   First of all, a résumé should give evidence of care, both in content and appearance. It must not have a slap-dash quality suggestive of haste and inadequate thought. It should be intelligently organized. Personal data comes first: name (James Mark Henderson; not Jim Henderson); place and date of birth; marital status and number of children, if any. Date, branch, and rank of military service or ROTC status also goes in here. Height and weight are informative though not always necessary, but a general indication of health quality is usually expected. The best address and phone number for responses to the resume should be accompanied by a permanent home address.

3   The second large category is education. Begin with high

school: name and location, date of graduation, and an approximation of a grade point average if it can be calculated. As for the college profile, since transcripts will often be requested later, the resume should be a lead-in to the transcripts without duplicating them. List all colleges and junior colleges with dates of attendance and degrees granted. Academic major should be clearly stated along with cumulative grade point average and expected date of graduation.

Employment history includes two things: salaried positions, and significant volunteer work on a regular basis, for example, summer camp counselor. The two should be clearly separated, dates should be given, and salaried positions which are part-time should be so indicated. In view of our modern trend towards vague job titles, a brief statement of duties may be helpful if the position is not an obvious one.

Activities, the next logical heading, requires special care to avoid an uninformative clutter. The fraternity record goes in here, but distinguish clearly among elected chapter offices, voluntary or assigned posts of lesser responsibility, and general participation in social and other events. All sports interests are important, as are hobbies; given specific mention to varsity athletic competition in high school and college. List membership in groups and societies of all kinds, with clear indication in doubtful cases whether the basis of the group is academic, honorary, hobby oriented, service, religious, political, or whatever. Depending on the individual profile, honors and awards can go in separately, or at appropriate points in the activities section along with the organizations that gave them.

Next should come a brief statement of personal and professional goals, both short- and long-range. It is easy enough to express this simply in terms of a job title or functional description; it is more valuable, and more difficult, to add a few comments about one's interests and outlook without subjecting the reader to a chapter from a philosophy text. Finally, indicate personal sources of reference. The best method is to establish a file with the college's placement office and then indicate the address from which the file may be obtained. Alternatively one may list the names and addresses of several people who have consented to be references.

The foregoing is a basic outline, stressing maximum information and clarity in a short space. Solicitors of résumés do not want the first chapter of an autobiography, but they do want clear preliminary evidence of the person's background, abilities, intelligence, and interesting qualities.

There are, of course, many different things that can be added

4

5

6

7

8

in specific cases, and it may sometimes be desirable to modify parts of a basic resume when it is used for particular purposes. In a well constructed résumé, however, the need for changes of this sort will be minimal.

9   Prepare and date a basic résumé early in your college career and review it each semester for possible updating; periodic reviews after graduation are also desirable, even if steady employment begins immediately. In this way a current résumé will always be at hand for any necessity, and it will distinguish itself from those done in the half hour between volleyball and dinner.

Organization

1. Each of paragraphs 2–6 discusses a different section of the résumé. List the topics of each section. Are they given in any particular order?
2. Devoting each paragraph to a separate section of the résumé could make for jerky, stop-and-go reading. Does Sefton avoid this danger? If so, how?
3. Sefton's subject demands specific details. Does he supply them to an adequate degree?

Paragraphs

1. Could the essay have ended with paragraph 7? If so, what function, if any, do paragraphs 8 and 9 serve?
2. Why are paragraphs 7–9 shorter than paragraphs 1–6?

Sentences

1. Point out the sentences which indicate that Sefton is addressing the reader directly. Does this help or hinder his discussion of résumés?
2. Is there sufficient sentence variety to maintain reader interest in this topic?

Words

1. Why is *among* used in the second sentence of paragraph 5, and not *between*?
2. To what does the following refer? *Stonehenge* (1).
3. Be sure you know the meaning of each of the following words:

   cumulative (3)
   slap-dash (2)
   solicitors (7)

Suggestions for Writing

1. Select any object (a written document, a mechanical device, an article of furniture, a building) that, like a résumé, is made up of distinct parts, each part having its own characteristics. Analyze the object by discussing each separate part. Be sure, however, to join the sections of your essay together (just as the object itself is joined) into a coherent whole.
2. Choose any one of the sections of a résumé listed in paragraphs 3–6 of Sefton's essay. Assume that one of the employers, financial aid officers, or academic award-givers referred to in paragraph 1 has asked you for a fuller account of that section than you have provided in your résumé. Expand that résumé section into an analytical essay in which you discuss its meaning or significance in your life.

LIBRARY OF CONGRESS: MANY BOOKS, NOT ALL BOOKS

Linda Charlton

Linda Charlton: journalist. Charlton prepared this piece while she was reporting for the New York Times *out of Washington, D.C. It appeared in that newspaper in 1975.*

What is the most serious problem facing the Library of Congress?

What is the relationship between this essay's title and its content?

1   What Washington institution's assets include the blueprints of a 19th-century Russian Orthodox church in Alaska, President Harding's love letters, a Gutenberg Bible, Sigmund Freud's papers, but not, repeat not, a copy of every book published?

2   The answer, of course, is the Library of Congress. Though it has 17 million books in its collection and adds 7,000 a day, it is a perpetual disappointment to true believers, who come to it convinced that every book ever published can be found somewhere on the library's 325 miles of shelves. Still, with more than 75 million items in its collection, it is—probably—the world's largest library, bigger than the Library of the British Museum and the Bibliothêque Nationale, and, possibly, the Lenin State Library in Moscow (the Russians aren't telling).

3   The library, 175 years old last April, figures that it acquires a new item every three seconds of every working day, far too many to think of housing. Two copies of every book, and of

other materials whose producers are seeking copyright protection, from labels to movies to plastic flowers to record jackets, arrive at the Copyright Office, which is run by the library. The library keeps about half of the copyrighted items, but not all the books it accepts go on the shelves: Some are used for barter with other libraries, here and abroad, for material the Library of Congress does want.

4   The library also receives 150 copies of all Government publications. The 148 extra copies of these, too, are trading cards, used to exchange with foreign governments. One result is that the library has the equivalent of the "Congressional Record" of every other country in the world. Britain's is called Hansard.

5   More glamorous are the gifts. They range from W. C. Fields's collection of vaudeville sketches to the photographic archives of Look magazine, about nine million photographs. They arrived two years ago, and are still being sorted.

6   For books alone, the library employs more than 150 catalogers. But the books are almost the least of it. There are maps, more than four million of them; manuscripts and papers; a superb collection of music scores; motion pictures; files of more than 1,500 American and foreign newspapers; perhaps 30 million letters; magazines and other periodicals, to 20,000 of which the library subscribes.

7   There are 15 reading rooms, including the 160-foot-high domed and pillared main room, which handles between 800 and 1,000 requests daily for books from the general collection, and is open seven days a week to anyone over 16 who is out of high school.

8   The library also runs the only national program that provides books or their equivalent for the blind and physically handicapped. Through a network of regional libraries, it makes the written word available in braille, on discs (the long-playing record was first developed for the blind) and, increasingly, on tape cassettes.

9   It is, then, the closest thing the United States has to a national library—but by default. It is called the Library of Congress. That is what, in 1800, it was set up to be, with an initial grant of $5,000 that was used to purchase 900 books and maps from London. Its budget for the fiscal year that ended last week was $96-million, and serving Congress is still its first priority—though Congress, with what some see as remarkable ingratitude, tried very hard to appropriate the library's newest and desperately needed annex building for its own purposes.

10   So about 700 of the library's 4,500 employees work in the Congressional Research Service, answering 200,000 questions

a year from members of Congress and their staffs. The questions may be simple and require no more than a single reference book; they often are complex and require days or weeks of research. The staff includes lawyers, scientists, experts in any field that Congress may want to know about.

Though its atmosphere is appropriately and soothingly serene, the library is no more problem-free than any other institution. Its hiring practices have been attacked as discriminatory; its functioning as inefficient. (Officially, it takes 35 to 55 minutes to have a request for a book filled in the main reading room; but the library concedes it can take up to two hours, and those familiar with the library's workings say that low staff morale is a major and chronic problem.) 11

It is also fighting an endless, no-win war for space. Thirty people do nothing but shift books to make room for others; there is one man who does nothing but figure out just how books should be moved. 12

Another, perhaps even more serious, battle is that being fought against time, and against ink and paper. Ironically, a 17th-century book is likely to be in far better condition than one printed 50 years ago: since the middle of the 19th century, the chemicals used in those two basic ingredients of books self-destroy. The library has a "brittle books" research program working on ways to preserve the crumbling books it is charged with safeguarding. 13

This year, a new administrator has been nominated, Daniel Boorstin, a historian. It is difficult to tell what impact the man, if confirmed, would have on the institution, and on its problems. Already the Congressional Black Caucus has asked that Mr. Boorstin's nomination be withdrawn because of his alleged "misunderstanding" of minorities' goals. 14

Next year, at any rate, if construction goes on schedule, the library will open its new annex, the James Madison Memorial Building. By then, there will be six million more items to find space for, to catalog, to have rebound in sturdy buckram, to place in manuscript boxes or, for those deemed worthy, in the rare books' temperature-and-humidity-controlled vault. 15

Organization

1. Paragraphs 3–13 may be divided into three sections: 3–6, 7–10, and 11–13. What are the topics of each section? What are the separate topics treated within each section?
2. Are the three sections presented in any particular order?
3. There are more transitional devices between paragraphs in a

section than there are between sections. Is that appropriate or inappropriate?

4. On the basis of where this essay was first printed, what do you suppose was the source of the author's information? Should she have stated her source explicitly?

Paragraphs

1. By what method is paragraph 3 developed? Are most of the paragraphs developed by this same method?
2. What features make the first paragraph a good (or a bad) introductory one?

Sentences

1. Why is figurative language not a feature of this essay?
2. What is unusual about the first sentence of paragraph 5?
3. What is the difference between a remark set off by dashes, as in the last sentence of paragraph 2, and a remark placed in parentheses, as in the same sentence and also in paragraphs 8 and 11?

Words

1. Look up *catalog* (15) in your dictionary. Is any other spelling given? If so, which is preferred?
2. Does the use of numbers in this essay conform to the rules suggested on p. 385?
3. To what does each of the following refer? *Russian Orthodox Church* (1), *President Harding* (1), *Gutenberg Bible* (1), *Sigmund Freud* (1), *Congressional Record* (4), *W. C. Fields* (5), *James Madison* (15).
4. Be sure you know the meaning of each of the following:

braille (8)	deemed (15)
buckram (15)	default (9)
chronic (11)	ironically (13)

Suggestions for Writing

1. Select an institution or an organization you are familiar with that faces a significant problem of some sort (space, money, membership, leadership, morale). Suggest how you would go about solving the problem. Address your solution to the organization's officers.
2. Analyze your campus or city library by discussing its various

holdings and services. (Talking briefly with one of the librarians or consulting a printed library guide, if there is one, should add to what you already know about the library.)

THE HANDSHAKE

Russell Baker

Russell Baker: journalist, author. Baker was born in Virginia in 1925 and graduated from Johns Hopkins University with a degree in English. He began his journalism career with the Baltimore Sun *and then moved to the* New York Times. *In 1962 he started writing his thrice-weekly "Observer" column in the* Times. *Baker was awarded a Pulitzer Prize for commentary in 1979, thus becoming the first humorist to win a Pulitzer. He offered this view of journalism: "I've always felt that journalism ought to be a little spontaneous, and I want my stuff, which is a very personal kind of journalism, to reflect how I feel at the moment." His books include* An American in Washington, No Cause for Panic, *and* Poor Russell's Almanac.

What elements give this essay its predominantly humorous tone?

Do you detect a serious undertone in it?

One of the worst handshakes I have ever been involved in 1 occurred a few weeks ago in the Middle West. This hand placed itself in my hand, as hands commonly do when their proprietors are being introduced, and immediately made itself at home.

Usually hands are satisfied to drop in for a second or two 2 and then go on about their business, but I could tell from the feel of this hand that it was of a mind to settle in for a long stay. Being a social coward, I didn't want to eject it forcibly, so I attempted a subtle withdrawal by moving my torso out of the area occupied by its proprietor.

The hand was not to be evicted that easily. It nestled in 3 snugly between my palm and finger tips and dragged its proprietor right along behind it as I crossed the floor. The proprietor didn't seem to notice. Maybe he didn't like that particular hand anymore and hoped it would run off with somebody else so he could find happiness with another hand he was keeping in an apartment downtown.

In any case, it was obvious that if it stayed much longer I'd 4 never be able to get rid of it without becoming vulnerable to prosecution for abandonment and nonsupport. At that point, one of those hearty men who prowl crowded rooms in search of hands to maul spotted mine, tossed out the long-term tenant and moved his own hand in for a display of pure brute strength.

5   I was so grateful for relief that I barely screamed as his ferocious hand ravaged my knuckles and reduced my finger tips to pulp. This is a kind of handshake I used to dread before discovering that the faster you surrender, the quicker the agony stops. Hands like this are out to embarrass the man they belong to, and usually succeed. You can always recognize him. His smile is wide, but his teeth are gritted as the hand moves in on the host hand.

6   His smile is wide because he wants to be thought a good fellow, and his teeth are gritted because he knows what his despicable hand is about to do. It is about to plunge into your hand with the fury of a berserk Viking and engage in trials of muscularity aimed at forcing the loser to burn his hut, slaughter the cattle and surrender the women.

7   Give that hand the satisfaction of combat in your palm and the pain will be prolonged. But go limp from wrist to finger tip the instant it arrives and it will be content with a quick devastation. When hands like this call, their purpose is to make your hand look contemptible before the world. Give them satisfaction right away and they'll save the worst for the next victim.

8   My own hand is not very comfortable in the intimate society of other hands and cannot understand the necessity for these constant visitations by strange fists, fingers, knuckles, palms, nails, lifelines, love lines, cuticle, small bones, short bristles. I understand, of course. It is peculiarly American, as forming queues is peculiarly English and 10 o'clock dining is peculiarly Spanish.

9   I have tried to persuade my hand that it is a small duty it must pay for our national character, and the hand has agreed to do its best, but sometimes it is still astonished by the hands that come to call. It has never decided, for example, how to entertain the hand that leaves everything but four fingers outside the door.

10   In these cases the hand reaches out to welcome the caller into the parlor and finds itself clutching only a handful of finger tips, which feel like a few spears of overcooked asparagus. Hands like this seem to feel adequately entertained after a light squeeze, but it is very hard to tell whether they might not be secretly yearning to have their fingernails pulled.

11   Not long ago, a man extended his arm in my direction and my hand felt itself entertaining a cold, limp, gelatinous object weighing less than half a pound by the feel of it. A hand's natural instinct at such a visitation is to place the material

under refrigeration until autopsy, and mine would certainly have done so had I not happened to glance down and note that the object was another hand.

It obviously did not want to be shaken, squeezed, kneaded, pummeled or massaged. It just wanted to lie there and be left alone. I was surprised that this man would let a hand in that condition go out, much less let it try to hobnob with other hands, for all the spirit had long since been drained out of it. 12

My own hand, which is merciful, would doubtless have tried to lend it a cup of warmth, but I intervened. It can be dangerous interfering in relationships between a man and his hand, and after all, there is no law saying a man can't treat his hand any way he wants to. 13

So I gave the order and my hand handed the hand back to the man, and then another hand came along and ruined my knuckles while smiling around gritted teeth. 14

Organization

1. Does the essay have an introduction?
2. Look up the word *personify* in your dictionary, or in a handbook of literary terms. To what extent does Baker personify the handshakes he discusses? What effect does this contribute to the essay as a whole?

Paragraphs

1. How many different types of handshake does Baker treat? What paragraph treats each type?
2. What is the function of paragraph 8?
3. Does the last paragraph cause the essay to end too abruptly?

Sentences

1. What effect does the use of contractions contribute to this essay? (Ex.: *didn't* for *did not*, in paragraph 2; *I'd* for *I would*, in paragraph 4; *they'll* for *they will*, in paragraph 7; *can't* for *cannot*, in paragraph 13)
2. Is sentence parallelism a significant feature of this essay?

Words

1. To what does *Viking* (6) refer?
2. Be sure you know the meaning of each of the following:

autopsy (11)	kneaded (12)
berserk (6)	massaged (12)

contemptible (7)   maul (4)
cuticle (8)   proprietors (1)
despicable (6)   pummeled (12)
evicted (3)   queues (8)
ferocious (5)   torso (2)
gelatinous (11)   vulnerable (4)
hobnob (12)

Suggestions for Writing

1. Select some aspect of human behavior (facial expressions, vocal types or inflections, walks, postures) and classify them in ways that reveal something serious or humorous about those who embody them.
2. Select a form of entertainment (movies, TV, music, books, sports) and classify it by breaking it down into its main categories, or into the categories that interest you for some reason.

A VIEW OF THE REVIEW

James Goodfriend

James Goodfriend: reviewer, editor. Goodfriend was record review editor of Stereo Review *when he wrote this essay in 1970.* Stereo Review *was a monthly that published articles on general aspects of component systems, music compositions, and composers.*

How many basic questions must a review answer? What are they?

How many of the four reviews presented here answer all those questions?

1   Reviewing is distinguished from criticism in the same way that apples are distinguished from fruit. There may be one or two specific characteristics that turn up in the smaller category and are not to be found elsewhere in the larger one, but basically the difference is one of proportion. Musical criticism comes in a full range of sizes, from Joseph Haydn's pithy two-line critique of a violin recital heard in London ("On 21st May, Giardini's concert took place in Ranelagh Gardens. He played like a pig.") to Sir Donald Francis Tovey's equally pithy 136-page essay on Beethoven's musical style and accomplishments. But the review, as a form of criticism, ideally comes in only one size: short.

2   The purpose of a review is basically to answer three ques-

tions: (1) What happened?; (2) Who did it?; and (3) How did it come out? Now, of course, both the Haydn and the Tovey examples cited above deal with these three points, but only the Haydn is short, and therefore only the Haydn could be considered a review. It may not be the best possible review (for reasons that will come later), and perhaps it is *too* short, but in establishing brevity as the salient characteristic of a review, we do not mean "short in relation to the extent of the subject"; we mean short, period.

In addition to answering the three basic questions, a review 3 may go on to answer a fourth: Why?, or What about it? This is where the reviewer gets a chance to demonstrate his profundity. However, if something has to be cut in the review, that is what goes first, profundity or no.

If half of Western society has, at one time or another, at- 4 tempted to create a work of art, most of the other half has tried to write a review of one. I come by this admittedly biased view of the world because of the impressive number of unsolicited record reviews I receive. I don't want to appear ungrateful for this correspondence—and, indeed, I'm not—but I would like to offer a few pointers to those who have sent me such reviews and those who are about to on just how and why such things are written.

Rather than bring up any more principles at the moment, 5 suppose we start out with a practical example. A Miss Mastromanovitch, let us say, has just given a piano recital which included Beethoven's "Moonlight" Sonata. Four reviewers were there and all (believe it or not) had basically the same opinion of what they heard. However, that mutual opinion comes out in very different ways.

Case 1: "Miss Mastromanovitch either does not understand 6 Beethoven at all or she has no conception of the seemingly willful distortion her fingers are capable of producing. This was terrible, terrible playing, not at all on a professional level."

Case 2: "On the evidence of my score, Miss Mastromano- 7 vitch played eleven wrong notes in the opening twelve measures of the first movement, at least an equal number in the *Allegretto,* and something over a hundred in the *Presto agitato* (I stopped counting). In addition, she separated the slurred notes in the middle movement and slurred the separated ones, eliminated the *sforzandos* in the trio, and took the final movement at a metronome marking that was anything but *Presto.*"

Case 3: "Miss Mastromanovitch has a keyboard technique 8 insufficiently developed for this music, as was made evident in the excessive number of wrong notes she played and her obvious inability to take the final movement quickly enough to represent Beethoven's intentions accurately. She also, on the evidence of the absent *sforzandos* in the second movement trio (among other things), has no very clear idea of what the music is about."

9   Case 4: "Mastromanovitch played Beethoven last night; Beethoven lost."

10   Now, of these four reports (considering each of them to be, with the addition of full names, program, place, time, *etc.*, a complete review), only one is *generally* sound (I hope you picked the third). I emphasize the "generally" because under certain special circumstances any one of them *might* do, though in the majority of cases the method of the third review alone is correct.

11   Why? The first reviewer has drawn some conclusions but has failed to report the evidence. This is the sort of review that most amateur reviewers, and some professional ones, fall into. It is fast, to the point, and deadly (as Haydn's review of Giardini is), but it is a bit unfair because neither the reader nor the performer is given any idea what the reviewer's standards of measurement are, whether he has based his judgment on a balanced appraisal of what he has heard or simply reacted quickly and emotionally, or even whether he was actually at the concert.

12   The second reviewer, on the contrary, has presented the evidence (all too much of it), but has not drawn the conclusions. Some would-be reviewers spend their whole listening time searching for wrong notes and passages played in ways different from what the score indicates. But wrong notes, in themselves, are not what reviewing is all about. That there are too many of them is a fact worth commenting on, but simply counting them has no value. Similarly, departures from the score are not wrong *per se* (the marking in the score may not even be the composer's but an editor's, and may be different in other editions). The reviewer must say what the departure is, but he also has to say whether he endorses it or not.

13   The fourth reviewer has sacrificed everything for the sake of a wisecrack. Such reviews are colorful, witty (this one was— the first time it was used), and quotable, and they are the *bête noire* of many a professional who cannot resist the impulse to twist the truth for the sake of an effect. You have to be a very big man musically to get away with this sort of thing even on occasion, or the occasion itself has to be so startlingly awful that no other kind of comment can take its measure.

14   Only the third reviewer has given both the marrow and the sense of the matter. He has reported what he heard in sufficient detail, but not at great length. He has given his opinion

of the reason for it (it was not simply initial nervousness). He has implied where he stands on the matter of interpretation (with Beethoven), given an example of where he and the pianist differ, and concluded that she was wrong out of ignorance. In short, he has done the job and the others haven't. Unfortunately, he has also written the least entertaining review of the lot.

Anyone who wants to write reviews had better face this   15
problem right from the start. He has an obligation to the subject of the review to be fair, an obligation to the reader to be informative, an obligation to himself to be truthful, and an obligation to the editor to be short. And, diametrically opposed to all of these, he has the obligation (to everybody, it would seem) to be entertaining. It is no wonder that some who start by writing musical reviews become authors of musicological tomes, while others (who may have covered the same concerts) end up writing witty dialogue for the stage.

Organization

1. Could this essay be considered a *definition* of a review, as well as an *analysis*? Explain.
2. How is coherence maintained in the section setting forth the separate review excerpts (paragraphs 6–9)?

Paragraphs

1. What method of development is followed in paragraph 1?
2. Analyze the transitions between sentences in paragraph 14.
3. Why does Goodfriend discuss the third review (14) *after* the fourth review (13)?

Sentences

1. Explain the meaning of the first sentence in the essay.
2. This essay is noteworthy for the unusually high number of parenthetical remarks it contains. Are there too many?

Words

Be sure you know the meaning of each of the following:

bête noire (13)	pithy (1)
brevity (2)	salient (2)
metronome (7)	slurred (7)
musicological (15)	tomes (15)
per se (12)	

Suggestions for Writing

1. Following the principles for good reviewing outlined in this essay, write a review of a ceremony (an awards presentation, a graduation, a religious or civic celebration) or of a performance (a concert, a play, a lecture, an athletic event).
2. Analyze two reviews of the same book, concert, movie, TV show, or play, and indicate which comes closer to fulfilling the requirements for a good review as set down in this essay.

TESTS THAT STAND THE TEST OF TIME

Scarvia B. Anderson

Scarvia B. Anderson: teacher, research psychologist. Anderson was born in Baltimore, Maryland in 1926. She attended Mississippi State University, George Peabody College for Teachers, and the University of Maryland. She taught in the public schools of Nashville, worked at the Naval Research Laboratory in Washington, D. C., and then joined the Educational Testing Service of Princeton, New Jersey. Among Anderson's books are Meeting the Test *(1963) and* The Profession and Practice of Program Evaluation *(1978). The following essay appeared in the* New York Times *in 1985.*

Into what two categories does Anderson classify tests?

In her view, how do they compare in overall value?

1   The Test has come into its own in recent years. It was selected by the editors of Science 84 as one of the "20 Discoveries That Shaped Our Lives" in this century. It has made it from no space in small-town papers and minimum space in city papers to front-page news. But *what kinds* of tests?

2   The Scholastic Aptitude Test and American College Test for college admissions, the California Achievement Tests in grades 1–6, I.Q. tests—in other words, published or "standardized" tests, as the test makers call them, tests made up in Princeton, Iowa City, or Cleveland. Not the English tests Miss Omie Parker gave Willie Morris and me at Yazoo City High School, not the tests Dr. Peter Sherry gives his chemistry classes at Georgia Tech, not the tests that students at every level take by the millions every year to tell whether they get an A or a C, are promoted, or deserve an instructor's recommendation.

3   Yet these teacher-made tests are the ones that really have something to do with the educational *process.* The others make money for their companies, provide college admissions offi-

cers with semi-objective reasons for turning down candidates, and, with a boost from the media, can get the public exercised about the state of education in the United States.

If S.A.T. scores go down, blue-ribbon panels are appointed to comment at length—and usually at great expense—about what's wrong. (In all fairness, the S.A.T. was never intended to measure the quality of schools.) However, it's time school boards, parents, deans, instructors, and students took a careful look at the *real* educational tests.

Teacher-made tests, more than any other educational device, tell students what the purpose of the instruction is and what is expected of them. As a consultant to schools, I frequently ask to see two things first—the budget and some recent tests given in courses. The first tells me what the administration values—how much, say, for the music department vs. the athletic department, for the library, for prizes for academic achievement. The second thing I ask about is the nature of the instruction. If the teacher asks only one question about "Moby Dick" and it is "What different kinds of whales did they encounter on their voyage?" my initial impression of the senior English course is not very favorable. On the other hand, it's a positive sign if the mathematics teacher in the middle school asks children to tell her what *pi* is, not just use it in calculating the circumference of a circle.

Elaborate course outlines and lists of instructional objectives do not provide nearly as much information about what's being taught as a few examination questions. What students study is what they think they're going to be asked on the instructor's tests. Check with any student. It's a rare one below the graduate level who pursues Shakespeare or thermodynamics in depth because of its intrinsic interest, and some professors complain that even many graduate students are not self-motivated. A colleague noted that his twin sons were preparing for their six-week test in junior English by reading only the introductory material in the literature anthology, not the selections themselves. They explained quite practically that "Mr. Jones only asks about what's in the introductions—when the authors lived, things like that."

The preparation of good tests helps instructors gain a perspective on their courses and sometimes even understand better what they are teaching. Paul Diederich, a distinguished English teacher and scholar, was once asked if he understood Eliot's "Four Quartets." He scratched his head and said, "I don't know. I've never tried to write an exercise on it."

I said "good" tests above. Many of the tests that teachers

make up on their way to class, that are kept in fraternity-house files, or that are stored in the new computers academics are so proud of are *not* good tests. They don't focus on what's most important, don't inspire students to study what's worth studying, and don't present an intellectual challenge to the examinees (or the examiner). Even if the ideas for the test are sound, the translation of those ideas into questions may be weak.

9   The questions may be vague or ambiguous and reward the more verbal students rather than the students who know more about the subject matter:

Discuss the causes of the Civil War.

What is the greatest social achievement of the 20th century?

10   Or questions may be worded so that students get the right answer for the wrong reason. I have seen questions almost as bad as this one:

Which of the following is NOT a Southern woman writer?
A. Margaret Mitchell
B. Katherine Anne Porter
C. Robert Penn Warren
D. Eudora Welty

11   There are basically two functions that educational tests should assess: knowledge and skills. Knowledge, which includes understanding as well as sheer information, can be measured variously through good essay, multiple-choice and short-answer questions—and even the much maligned true-false questions if the task is in fact to identify the truth or falsity of propositions.

12   To measure skills, you usually need to ask students to *do* something—write a paper or computer program, play a piano selection, survey a tract of land, make a scale drawing, or type a letter. It is seldom sufficient to ask them *about* writing, programming, or drawing, though there is usually some basic knowledge important to developing such skills that can be tested separately.

13   Standardized tests, the ones that get all the publicity, may have something to do with *who* gets certain educational opportunities (although the extent to which they serve as gatekeepers is often exaggerated). Teacher-made tests, the silent majority you don't hear much about, are the ones that determine *what* education is, and they deserve much more of our attention.

Organization

1. This essay uses both classification and division. Point out the paragraphs devoted to each.
2. What purpose is served by the author's identifying herself as *a consultant to schools* in paragraph 5?

Paragraphs

1. What is the relation of paragraph 12 to paragraph 11? Could the two paragraphs be combined into one?

Sentences

1. Are the sentences sufficiently varied in form and length to prevent monotonous reading?
2. What is the function of the first sentence of paragraph 8?
3. Point out the allusion in the last sentence.

Words

1. To what does each of the following refer? *Willie Morris* (2), *pi* (5), *Moby Dick* (5), *Eliot's Four Quartets* (7), *Margaret Mitchell* (10), *Katherine Anne Porter* (10), *Robert Penn Warren* (10), *Eudora Welty* (10).
2. Locate the italicized words. Is this kind of emphasis overdone in this essay?
3. Why is *Test* capitalized in the first sentence?
4. Does the author define *real* as used in the last sentence of paragraph 4? *knowledge* as used in paragraph 11? *skills* as used in paragraphs 11 and 12?
5. Be sure you know the meaning of each of the following:

ambiguous (9)	exercised (3)
assess (11)	intrinsic (6)
blue-ribbon panels (4)	maligned (11)
examinees, examiner (8)	

Suggestions for Writing

1. Classify the tests you have taken in high school or college, or both, on some kind of logical basis, e.g., type (essay, multiple choice, and so on), difficulty, the degree to which they were learning experiences, your success or failure. Assume that you are writing for those teachers who designed the tests. Help them prepare better tests.

2. *What students study is what they think they're going to be asked on the instructor's tests* (6). Is this statement true for you with regard to the courses you are currently taking? Explain by classifying what you perceive to be your instructors' emphases on tests.

CAUSE AND EFFECT

Sometimes the parts into which a subject is apportioned are not the elements (divisions or classifications) that make it up, but rather the factors that brought it about (causes or reasons) or the results stemming from it (effects). As the following group of essays indicates, the subjects that lend themselves to this kind of analysis are usually either occurrences (a murder, p. 232; the increased popularity of dance, p. 221) or physical phenomena (tickling, p. 224; drinking alcohol, p. 229). A number of practical guidelines should help you write effective compositions when cause-and-effect analysis is your basic method of develoment.

1. More Often Than Not, Treat Either Causes or Effects

Unless your subject is unusually simple, you'll find it difficult to cover both causes and effects adequately in a short composition. Obviously, causes and effects are closely related, and in an essay concentrating on the one you'll almost certainly begin by at least mentioning the other. But trying to allot equal attention to both, given the limited space available to you, would mean running the risk of superficiality. Stick to either causes, as John Simon (p. 221) and Boyce Rensberger (p. 224) do, or effects, as Ben Fong-Torres (p. 232) and the author of "The Effects of Alcohol" (p. 229) do. Simon doesn't explore the effects of ballet's popularity on such agencies as schools, dance companies, or theaters; he looks for causes only. Similarly, "The Effects of Alcohol," as the title indicates, makes no attempt to determine why people drink; it limits itself to telling what happens to them when they do.

2. Allow for Multiple Causes and Effects

Only rarely does a given cause produce only one effect; only rarely is a given effect the result of only one cause. With but a single exception, the writers of the next group of essays discuss several causes or several effects for each subject they analyze. (The exception is Boyce Rensberger, who is hard pressed to find even one cause for the inability of human beings to tickle themselves.) Don't fear that observing this guideline will give you too much material for a short essay. If you observe guideline 1 and treat *only* causes or effects, you shouldn't be overburdened, even though your causes or your effects are multiple. One way of preventing your paper from being too long is to emphasize the important causes and effects and give less attention to the minor ones (see guideline 3). Nevertheless, an intelligent reader expects your cause-and-effect analysis to avoid oversimple explanations.

3. Separate Major from Minor, Direct from Indirect, and Immediate from Remote Causes and Effects

Besides treating several causes or effects, you should also indicate how they compare with one another in certain significant ways. For example, some causes and effects are more important than others, some are more directly connected to the subject than others, some are closer to it in time than others. These categories are not, of course, mutually exclusive. For example, the most important effect that his brother's murder had on Ben Fong-Torres (p. 232) was also the last (most remote) effect. "The Effects of Alcohol," too, shows that the immediate physiological results of drinking are the least important results (p. 229). John Simon distinguishes one indirect cause of the increased popularity of ballet (par. 1, p. 221) from three direct causes (pars. 2, 4, p. 221–22). But that indirect cause is at the same time more immediate and less important than the direct ones. Plan to make distinctions such as these when sorting out causes and effects. They will contribute to your appearance as a thoughtful writer—and actually help make you one, or at least, a better one than you are already.

4. Be Sure That Your Causes Are Really Causes, and Your Effects Are Really Effects

If you fail a test while suffering from a cold and attribute your failure to the cold, you could be guilty of all the following errors at once:

a. Confusing a Circumstance with a Cause Your cold may not have been causally related to your failure at all, but may only have been an accidental circumstance associated with it. The real cause may lie elsewhere—in your refusal to study all term, or your frequent absences from class, or your overconfidence. Your cold undoubtedly caused your sniffles, your sore throat, and your chest congestion, but it's unlikely that it caused your failure.

b. Rationalization   It eases your conscience, and may even succeed in softening your teacher's heart somewhat, if you excuse your failure on the ground of not having felt well when you took the test. But if the genuine cause is one of those mentioned above, you are only rationalizing—trying to divert attention (your own as well as others') from the unpleasant truth.

c. The post hoc, ergo propter hoc *fallacy*   (See p. 291.) Your failing the test may have happened after you caught cold, but that doesn't make your cold the cause of your failure. Those other factors mentioned above also preceded your failure, and it's likely that one or more of them had a greater bearing on your failure than the cold did.

Boyce Rensberger's investigation of the impossibility of self-tickling (p. 224) conscientiously avoids the foregoing pitfalls. In fact, it goes to unusual lengths to come up with a genuine cause—one that not only *could* produce the effect, but in all likelihood *does*. The cause Rensberger suggests may not be the correct one—he himself calls it *a tentative solution* (par. 11, p. 226)—but it does seem to be more than circumstantially related to the effect.

5. Be Aware That Every Cause Is Itself the Effect of One or More Antecedent Causes

Remember the jingle used to call attention to the significance of seemingly trivial things? "For want of a nail the shoe was lost; for want of the shoe the horse was lost; for want of the horse the rider was lost; for want of the rider the message was lost; for want of the message the battle was lost; for want of the battle the war was lost—all for the want of a nail." The saying is a series of effects stemming from an initial cause, the lack ("want") of a nail. The point is that each effect is itself the cause of the next effect in the series. Even the first cause, the "want of a nail," is the effect of some unnamed antecedent cause; and the last effect, "war," could be assumed to be the cause of some even greater catastrophe that followed. Diagrammed, the pattern of causes and effects might take this form:

NAIL = cause
    ↓
  effect
  SHOE = cause
      ↓
    effect
    HORSE = cause
        ↓
      effect
      RIDER = cause
          ↓
        effect
        MESSAGE = cause
            ↓
          effect
          BATTLE = cause
              ↓
            effect
            WAR

The diagram indicates the importance of not omitting any links in the chain of causation, even though you may be tempted to do so when trying to compress your material into the limited space available to you. Obviously, you can't be expected to trace an interlocking system of causes and effects back to Adam and Eve. But the more complex the problem you're dealing with, the less satisfied your reader will be with a discussion that identifies immediate causes only.

After citing a fatty liver and possible cirrhosis as effects of heavy drinking (par. 7, p. 230), "The Effects of Alcohol" doesn't stop there but goes on to indicate what *they* cause: inadequate bile-production. And it ventures one step further to tell what *that* results in: physical weakness and chronic indigestion. Having arrived at that point, however, the essay has no need to pursue the matter; everyone knows what bad effects weakness and indigestion can cause in everyday living. Instead, it turns to two other effects of heavy drinking—irritation of stomach and intestinal lining and damage to the central nervous system—and develops each of them as it did the first effect. The result is an overall cause-and-effect pattern that looks like this:

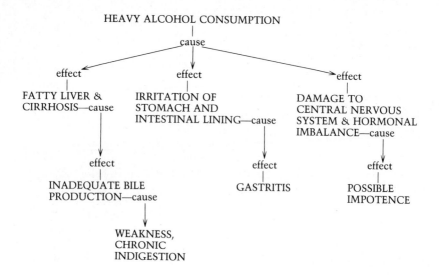

TRIUMPH OVER DEATH

John Simon

John Simon: critic, author. Simon's drama and film criticism has appeared in such diverse publications as New York magazine, a weekly that publishes nonfiction articles that emphasize the New York metropolitan area, and National Review, a fortnightly journal that uses nonfiction articles on current events and the arts, "which would appeal to a politically conservative audience." Simon's books include Ingmar Bergman Directs, Movies into Film, Uneasy Stages, and Paradigms Lost. The following appeared in New York in 1976.

What does the title have to do with the essay?

If you have never seen a classical ballet, does this essay arouse your interest in seeing one? Why or why not?

Why is dance enjoying such all-but-unprecedented popular-   1
ity in our time? At least partly, I think, because of the withdrawal of the word from our culture—or, more precisely, our
withdrawal from the word. Whether in or out of school, Dick
and Jane write, read, and express themselves orally with increasing difficulty. One of the consequences is that, among
the arts, the wholly or largely nonverbal ones become favored—especially dance, where the body has it all over the
mind. In the fine arts and in serious music, the mind seems
to make greater demands than in dance, whose only appreciable competition comes from the movies, where the word appears to be undemanding and the visuals are seemingly all
that matters. Highly kinetic, then, is what dance and film are:
forms, as it were, of body language, which may yet become
our lingua franca.

In the domain of dance, ballet is unquestioned king, be-   2
cause it is the least earthbound, the most death-defying, form
of dance: it appears to defeat the laws of gravity, defy death
itself. The danseur noble at the height of an entrechat or jeté,
the ballerina carried aloft but looking more airborne than
handheld, are no longer a little lower than the angels, but fully
of their company. Even a simple pas de bourrée, perfectly ex-
ecuted, conveys a skimming along the surface of the earth
rather than a walk or run upon it; it is perhaps a water bird
skittering along the mirror of a lake. And dancers are always
young and beautiful. Just as at a university only the sedentary
faculty ages, watching students who are always twentyish come
and go, at the ballet only the audience grows old. The faces
and bodies may not belong to the same dancers—although, in
another way, they do, for the perfectly stylized steps, highly

dramatic makeup, and formalized costumes bestow their own uniformity and continuity—but those privileged beings up there are forever beautiful and young.

3   So our two greatest limitations are overcome before our eyes: we become like unto the angels who need not touch ground, and do not have to die. I think it is no accident that three of the greatest, ever-popular story ballets deal with the triumph over death. In *Swan Lake,* the wicked enchanter and the demanding parent are both bested as the lovers float off into shared immortality. In *Giselle,* the beloved remains faithful to her deceitful lover beyond death, rises from her tomb to save his life, and thus binds him to herself forever. In *The Sleeping Beauty,* Prince Charming awakens the heroine from a sleep perilously resembling death. Even the fourth hardy perennial, *The Nutcracker,* takes us back to the ageless world of childhood, whose animated toys, benign fairies, and transfigured children mortality cannot touch.

4   It is easier to project ourselves into dancers than into actors. Dancers, especially in ballet, are abstract: they symbolize rather than express, they are mythic rather than specific. The particular words of Shakespeare's Ophelia may leave some audiences cold, but an Ophelia balletically transmuted into a symbol of unfulfilled yearning is an image for everybody. Louis MacNeice's poem, "Les Sylphides," begins, significantly, "Life in a day: he took his girl to the ballet"; stanza three runs: "Now, he thought, we are floating—ageless, oarless— /Now there is no separation, from now on/You will be wearing white/Satin and a red sash/Under the waltzing trees." It seems noteworthy how many extremely obese people there are among balletomanes; they, more than anyone, want to think themselves disembodied sylphs. But all of us, regardless of weight, size, and age, would like to soar, be lighter than air, than care.

Organization

1. How many different causes does Simon cite for the recent popularity of dance? Are they listed in any apparent order? Are they classified in any of the ways suggested in guideline 3 on p. 217?
2. Is the ending too abrupt?

Paragraphs

1. What function does paragraph 3 serve?
2. Is the topic thought of paragraphs 2, 3, and 4 the first sentence of each paragraph?
3. By what method is paragraph 3 developed?

Sentences

1. What, if anything, does the allusion in paragraph 4 add to the essay?
2. What is unusual about the construction of the last sentence of paragraph 1?

Words

1. Is the use of foreign terms in paragraph 2 justified? What is the meaning of each?
2. What is the meaning of *lighter . . . than care* (last sentence of paragraph 4)? Does *lighter than air, than care* create an undesirable clash in sound?
3. To what do the following refer? *Swan Lake* (3), *Giselle* (3), *The Sleeping Beauty* (3), *The Nutcracker* (3), *Shakespeare's Ophelia* (4), *Louis MacNeice* (4).
4. Be sure you know the meaning of each of the following:

animated (3)	mythic (4)
ballerina (2)	obese (4)
balletically (3)	perilously (3)
balletomanes (4)	sedentary (2)
benign (3)	skittering (2)
bested (3)	stylized (2)
disembodied (4)	sylphs (4)
enchanter (3)	transfigured (3)
hardy perennial (3)	transmuted (4)
kinetic (1)	unprecedented (1)

Suggestions for Writing

1. Select a specific type of entertainment or recreation (rock music, science fiction movies, tennis), or an individual or a group connected with such entertainment or recreation (Sting, Leonard Nimoy, John McEnroe). Discuss the reasons why your choice has achieved popularity.
2. Discuss either the causes or the effects of one of the following statements:
   (a) *Whether in or out of school, Dick and Jane write, read, and express themselves orally with increasing difficulty* (1).
   (b) *But all of us, regardless of weight, size, and age, would like to soar, be lighter than air, than care* (4).

AN UNCOMMON INQUIRY
INTO THE NATURE OF A COMMON PHENOMENON

Boyce Rensberger

Boyce Rensberger: science writer. Rensberger was born in Indianapolis in 1942. After receiving degrees from the University of Miami and Syracuse, he joined the staff of the Detroit Free Press. *In 1971 he became a science writer for the* New York Times. *He has contributed articles to such different periodicals as* Penthouse, Mademoiselle, *and* International Wildlife. *The following essay appeared in the* New York Times *in 1975.*

Rensberger begins with the premise that self-tickling is impossible. Is he correct?

Does his explanation of why it is impossible seem to you to make sense? How strong a case does he make?

1   Modern science, it would appear, has been guilty of a grevious omission. Although this paper may be taken as an equally grievous commission, I offer it anyway. For, despite the immense accumulation of physiological, psychological and behavioral data in recent years, researchers seem to have overlooked one of the most common, yet puzzling, of all the sensory phenomena in human experience.

2   I refer, of course, to tickling. One of the great unanswered questions of science involves the tickling response. To wit: Why can't people tickle themselves?

3   This question—which, I must concede, is seldom posed—has not set science afire nor has it engaged very many of the best minds in psychology or philosophy. But consider for a moment. Normally when the one who tickles and the one who is tickled (the tickler and the ticklee, if you will) are two different people, the slightest poke or stroke in a sensitive area of the body elicits convulsions of laughter—usually an odd kind of unpleasant giggling. Yet it is a fact of the tickling response that when the fingers between the ribs are one's own, or even when the feather is in one's own hand, the response is rarely more than one of mild, local sensation.

4   Where, when one is trying to tickle oneself, are the violent spasms of grimacing laughter, where is the desperate urge to escape? It is curious indeed. Artists are able to admire their own paintings. Cooks love to eat their best dishes. Lots of people can laugh at their own jokes. So why can't we tickle ourselves?

5   Science has no answer. A diligent search of the medical and psychological literature of the last quarter century has led me

to conclude that no respected authority knows why. None of the half-dozen leading texts in internal medicine, neurology or psychiatry has a single indexed reference on tickling. "Index Medicus,"[1] the massive annual compilation of articles from hundreds of medical journals in many languages, has no subject heading for tickling. "Psychological Abstracts,"[2] a similar compendium of specialized scientific articles, not only lacks a heading for tickling but doesn't even have one for laughter.

If any researcher anywhere has investigated the self-tickling   6 phenomenon, he or she must have published the findings in a periodical even more obscure than the Central African Journal of Medicine, which, I did find, printed an article in 1963 entitled "An Epidemic of Laughing in Bukoba District of Tanganyika."[3] The people in question, it turned out, were not being tickled by anyone.

Admittedly, laughter—merely a component of the tickling   7 reaction—has been explored somewhat by researchers. Although the nature of the laugh is not fully understood, it is known to be a complex phenomenon linking rapid contractions of the abdominal muscles (with attendant gasps of air and sound) with the release of psychological tension. There is a fair amount of discussion in the medical journals about the nature of laughter, suggesting that it isn't always a sign of mirth or pleasure. Some authorities say laughter is physiologically similar to having an epileptic fit, and that certain kinds of brain tumors can cause seemingly unexplained laughter.[4]

The lone scientific article which had anything useful to say   8 about tickling was by Joost A. M. Meerloo, a Dutch psychiatrist, and it appeared in the Psychoanalytic Review in 1966 under the title, "The Biology of Laughter."[5] Although it is a long, rambling piece with little hard data, it does contain some fascinating insights.

Dr. Meerloo theorizes that the response of the ticklee to   9 being tickled is a combination of ambivalent or conflicting

[1] "Cumulated Index Medicus," published annually by the American Medical Association, Chicago, Ill.

[2] "Psychological Abstracts," published annually by the American Psychological Association, Washington, D.C.

[3] Rankin, A. M. and Philip, P. J., "An Epidemic of Laughing in Bukoba District of Tanganyika," Cent. Afr. Jnl. Med., 9:167–70, May, 1963.

[4] I even ran across two articles in British journals on what could be an embarrassing side effect of laughing. They carried identical titles: "Micturition Induced by Giggling." (British Medical Journal, 5439: 879–80, April 3, 1965; Guys Hospital Report, 113:250–60, 1964.)

[5] Meerloo, J. A. M., "The Biology of Laughter," Psychoanalytic Review, 53:189–208, Summer, 1966.

reactions. One is never quite sure whether the tickler is engaging in some kind of sexual assault or something less threatening, the article reasons. Dr. Meerloo writes that the goose bumps that often form during the laugh reflex are a vestigial effort to bristle one's fur, a common defense of frightened animals that makes them look more formidable to an attacker. Yet, paradoxically, laughter usually denotes pleasure. Dr. Meerloo suggests that the tickled person's mood vacillates between two competing reactions. Apparently those who can live with the ambivalent emotions can take a tickle in stride, but those who can't handle the dilemma regard tickling as a cruel and violent attack.[6]

10   All right. But why can't you tickle yourself? Meerloo is silent.

11   Where scientists fear to tread, science writers readily speculate. Given the paucity of enlightenment to be derived from respectable sources, and in the worthy attempt to stimulate scientific interest in this area, I would like to offer a tentative solution to the self-tickling problem until such time as the scientific community has chosen to speak definitively on the matter.

12   The recent findings of animal-behavior researchers show the way. They have found, rather consistently, that when an animal is frightened, its facial expression resembles what might be called a grimace, grin or, indeed, laughter. According to George Schaller, who has made a definitive study of the behavior of wild lions, the lion's bared-teeth grin is a defense strategy born of fear. For example, a lion attacking prey does not snarl and flash its teeth. It attacks with a straight face. However, when threatened by another lion or by a human being, lions bare their teeth. The idea, no doubt, is to look as ferocious as possible but the goal is to avoid a fight. Jane Goodall has found much the same facial expressions in chimpanzees under similar circumstances. Studies of wolves, hyenas and other mammals have led to more or less the same conclusion: when threatened they display their teeth and they bris-

---

[6]Dr. Meerloo contributes two other interesting observations that have some relevance to a consideration of tickling:

(1) The ancient Romans, he notes, sometimes punished criminals by dangling them from a scaffold, rubbing salt on the soles of their feet and letting goats lick the salt.

(2) To be tickled, he notes, once meant to be beaten with a cat-o'-nine tails in an effort to instill virtue. "Ritual striking," the psychiatrist says, "originally signified a fertility symbol, to titillate, to beget; later the king used the gesture to confer knighthood on a subject."

tle their fur.[7] So, we can fit these insights together with Dr. Meerloo's observation that the animals' reflex of bristling fur has its counterpart in the human goose bumps that form during the laugh reflex.

It seems easy now to indulge in a kind of pop ethology 13 interpretation and answer the burning question of why you can't tickle yourself. Consider the typical tickling situation in the light of animal behavior. Tickling, as we have seen, is an ambivalent act. For all its comic overtones, it can be interpreted as a threatening attack. When you are being tickled, your reaction is similar to that of the frightened animals, because you are basically unsure of the intentions of your tickler. What appears for all the world to be laughter—a suggestion that, despite your protestations, you really enjoy the ordeal—is actually a primal fear reaction. You are bristling your fur and baring your teeth like mad, hoping to scare away the attacker. But when you tickle yourself, there is no doubt about the motive. There is no outside threat and no instinctive "laughter." It isn't funny at all.

Unless, of course, somebody catches you doing such a ridic- 14 ulous thing. And then, afraid of what he or she will think, you'll probably flash some silly grin.

Organization

1. What is Rensberger's answer to his own question *Why can't people tickle themselves?* (1)? Does his answer avoid the errors described in guideline 4, p. 217–18
2. In which paragraph does Rensberger answer his question? Why does he take so long in getting to the answer? At what point in the essay does he begin to approach the answer?
3. Is Rensberger's presentation written seriously or with tongue in cheek?

Paragraphs

1. What is the relation of paragraph 6 to paragraph 5?
2. What function do paragraphs 3 and 4 have in the essay?

Sentences

1. The first sentence of paragraph 11 contains a buried allusion. What is it?

---

[7] This behavior has its human counterpart, too. It is well known, of course, that human beings in awkward or socially frightening situations indulge in what is called nervous laughter, or absurd grinning spells.

2. Is an answer given to the question asked in the first sentence of paragraph 4? If not, why not?
3. Is *All right* in paragraph 10 a fragment? To what does it refer?

Words

1. Be sure you know the meaning of each of the following:

ambivalent (9)	grimace (12)
attendant (7)	mirth (7)
component (7)	neurology (5)
compendium (5)	paradoxically (9)
compilation (5)	paucity (11)
convulsions (3)	physiological (1)
dilemma (9)	primal (13)
diligent (5)	psychiatry (5)
epileptic (7)	psychological (1)
ethology (13)	tentative (11)
ferocious (12)	theorizes (9)
formidable (9)	vacillates (9)
grievous (1)	

Suggestions for Writing

1. Select a happening in your past life, or in the life of someone you know, the cause of which was unclear to others or even to yourself at the time. (It could be an illness, a change of behavior or attitude, a political or religious conversion, a bizarre action, a surprising confession.) Discuss, one by one, the possible causes of that happening, eliminating each as inadequate until you arrive at the one that seems the most likely.
2. *Artists are able to admire their own paintings. Cooks love to eat their best dishes* (4). Select a specific accomplishment you were primarily responsible for and about which you feel justifiably proud (an athletic victory, a musical or theatrical performance, an academic honor). Discuss the reasons for your pride. As you present your reasons, assume that your audience is someone who considers you to be a person who boasts constantly. Be proud but not arrogant.

THE EFFECTS OF ALCOHOL

Time *Magazine*

Time: *A weekly news magazine.*

––––––––––

What are the immediate effects of a drink of alcohol? What accounts for the different lengths of time that alcohol takes to make its effects felt?

What two factors determine the alcohol level in the bloodstream?

Is there a cure for the hangover?

What are some possible bad effects of social drinking?

What are the effects of heavy drinking?

Almost immediately after it hits the stomach, alcohol is   1
coursing through the bloodstream to the central nervous system, where it starts to slow down, or anaesthetize, brain activity. Though it is a depressant, the initial subjective feeling that it creates is just the opposite, as the barriers of self-control and restraint are lifted and the drinker does or says things that his well-trained, sober self usually forbids. Only later, after a number of drinks, are the motor centers of the brain overtly affected, causing uncertain steps and hand movements.

How quickly the alcohol takes effect depends on many fac-   2
tors. One person may be bombed after a glass, while another stays relatively sober after several. Because alcohol is diluted in the blood, a 200-lb. man can usually tolerate more liquor than a 110-lb. woman. Food also retards absorption of alcohol from the gastrointestinal tract, and a few ounces taken with a meal are less powerful than an equal amount downed an hour before. By the same token, some drinks with food in them—eggnogs made with eggs, milk and cream, for example—have slightly less wallop than straight drinks. The tomato juice in a Bloody Mary or the orange juice in a screwdriver is not enough to make any appreciable difference.

The total quantity of alcohol in a drink and the rate of con-   3
sumption determine the alcohol level in the bloodstream. Thus a Scotch and water would pack the same punch as Scotch on the rocks or a Scotch and soda if all three were drunk at the same speed; drinking more slowly gives the system a chance to eliminate some of the alcohol. The mixing of different types—beer, wine, whisky and brandy, for instance—might make a drinker sick, but it would not make him any more drunk than the same alcoholic measure of just one of these drinks.

4   So far medicine has found no cure for the hangover, although aspirin can alleviate the headache. Despite a plethora
of folk cures (none of them really effective), the best policy is
to avoid drinking in excess the night before. Actually, no one
knows exactly what causes the hangover's unpleasant symptoms of headache, nausea, depression and fatigue, which many
drinkers experience at one time or another.

5   Some recent research indicates that even social drinking can
have both immediate and possibly long-range deleterious effects on the body. According to Dr. Peter Stokes, a psycho-
biologist at Cornell University Medical College, the liver
becomes fatty and therefore less efficient after only a few weeks
of downing three or four drinks a night. But in the early stages,
at least, the condition can be reversed by abstinence. More
moderate imbibing—two drinks a night with meals, say—almost certainly does no harm to most people. New studies link
drinking to heart-muscle damage and deterioration of the brain.
Research by Dr. Ernest Noble of the University of California
at Irvine shows that alcohol inhibits the ability of the brain
cells to manufacture proteins and ribonucleic acid (RNA), which
some researchers believe play a role in learning and memory
storage. After 20 or 30 years, says Dr. Noble, two or three
drinks a night on an empty stomach may impair a person's
learning ability. Both Stokes and Noble cite studies showing
premature and irreversible destruction of brain cells after years
of heavy drinking.

6   Such frightening studies of the results of drinking have not
yet been accepted throughout the medical profession, but the
physical effects on an alcoholic of very heavy drinking are beyond dispute. A pint of whisky a day, enough to make eight
or ten ordinary highballs, provides about 1,200 calories—
roughly half the ordinary energy requirement—without any
food value. As a result, an alcoholic usually has a weak appetite and often suffers from malnutrition and vitamin defi-
ciency. The slack cannot be taken up by popping vitamin pills;
heavy alcohol consumption impairs the body's utilization of
vitamins. At the same time, excessive intake of alcohol also
affects the production and activity of certain disease-fighting
white blood cells, giving the alcoholic a particularly low resistance to bacteria.

7   Inevitably, the alcoholic develops a fatty liver, and his
chances of developing cirrhosis, a condition in which liver cells
have been replaced by fibrous scar tissue, are at least one
in ten. A severely damaged liver cannot adequately manufacture bile, which is necessary for the digestion of fats; as a
consequence, the alcoholic often feels weak and suffers from

chronic indigestion. This may be made worse by gastritis, which is caused by alcohol irritation of the sensitive linings of the stomach and small intestine. The troubles of a heavy drinker do not end there, and through damage to eh central nervous system and hormonal imbalance, alcohol may even cause impotence.

Organization

1. Does paragraph 4 occur in the proper place in the essay? Explain.
2. How do paragraphs 4 and 6 differ in subject matter? Do they differ in method of development?

Paragraphs

1. By what method is paragraph 2 developed?
2. Comment on the first and last paragraphs as opening and closing ones.

Sentences

1. What is unusual about the structure of the first sentence of paragraph 2?
2. Dashes are used to set off inserted remarks in four sentences:
    a. The fifth sentence of paragraph 2
    b. The third sentence of paragraph 3
    c. The fourth sentence of paragraph 5
    d. The second sentence of paragraph 6
    How does the use of the dashes in *d* differ from the use in *a*, *b*, and *c*?

Words

1. Are the following words properly or improperly used in their contexts?

    bombed (2)   punch (3)
    popping (6)   wallop (2)

2. Be sure you know the meaning of each of the following:

    abstinence (5)   imbibing (5)
    alleviate (4)   overtly (1)
    deleterious (5)   plethora (4)
    fibrous (7)   retards (2)

Suggestions for Writing

1. Write an essay on the effects of *X*, in which *X* represents an event or decision having a significant influence on your life.
2. Write an essay on the effects of *X*, in which *X* represents a significant event or decision affecting a group you know of or have been a part of. Trace the different effects of *X* on several members of the group.

WHEN MY BROTHER WAS SLAIN

Ben Fong-Torres

Ben Fong-Torres: broadcaster, editor, feature writer. Fong-Torres was born in Alameda, California in 1945. He graduated from San Francisco State University with a degree in broadcast journalism. For a time, he had a syndicated radio show in the Bay area. From 1969–1980 he was affiliated with Rolling Stone, *ending his career there as senior editor. He is a feature writer for the* San Francisco Chronicle *and contributes a music column to* Gentlemen's Quarterly. *One of his edited anthologies about pop music,* What's That Sound? *was published in 1976. He describes himself as a freelance writer. The following essay appeared in* Parade *magazine in 1985.*

How many of the effects of Fong-Torres' brother's death are such as *any* brother anywhere might feel?

How many of the effects are specifically related to his ethnic background?

1   It was nearly 13 years ago that I last saw Barry, my older brother. He came by my apartment in San Francisco with some food from our parents across the bay in Oakland. We sat around and chatted, and it struck me as ironic. We lived in the same town, but now that we were well established in our careers— he, at 29, was a probation officer and youth worker; I, at 27, was a magazine editor and writer—we saw very little of each other.

2   He had just returned from Lake Tahoe, where he had taken Dad for Father's Day. They had won a couple hundred dollars. He smiled. "That kind of makes up for what happened at my apartment," he said. Someone had broken in a couple of days before, he said, but had taken only a few antique rifles and guns. His fine collector's swords and jade pieces, a TV set, stereo equipment, cameras, skis and a bike—all had been left alone. Barry shrugged, mystified.

3   I asked about Chinatown. These were troubled times, and

that part of San Francisco abounded with gangs and violence. Barry had taken a leave of absence from his probation work to become director of a youth center there. He said he wanted to do something for "his people." And, though frustrated by the conflicts, he told me he wanted to stay just a little longer.

I started complaining about our parents. I was still going   4 through a mildly hippie phase and (how absolutely American) had had a fight with them over the length of my hair. Barry was no stranger to estrangement from our folks. After all, we had both, in our ways, rebelled, against the strict, traditional Chinese upbringing we'd had. Barry was dating girls who weren't Chinese, and he had studied not law or medicine, which most Chinese parents seemed to encourage, but criminology. Still, he had worked hard at the family restaurants; he had gone to the University of California at Berkeley; and he was always available to help our parents, who don't speak or write English, do various chores. In short, he was a good "number one son," so important to the Chinese family structure.

And now he was sounding just like one, as he counseled me   5 with words I hadn't heard from him before. "Just be patient," he said. "Just go along with them. They're the way they are, and the best thing to do is to give in a little." Barry sounded like a young man who had come home not only to Chinatown but also to his identity. He was telling me that I should understand the Chinese way. I remember thinking that he didn't sound like the Barry I had grown up with.

A few days later, the edgy mysteries of our last visit some-   6 how crystallized even as our lives were suddenly shattered. At about 11:30 p.m. on June 26, 1972, Barry was shot down in his apartment. The next morning, the front page story began: "A brilliant and respected youth worker has become the tenth known victim in a series of Chinatown gangland slayings." Barry, it was made clear, was not a member of any gang himself. There were, reportedly, two assailants; the case was never solved. Although I was a journalist, I couldn't investigate: My parents forbade me from getting involved. And I was bound to obey. After all, as Barry had just reminded me, I am, more than anything else, a Chinese-American.

Don't get me wrong. Our family *is* American, and not with-   7 out a bit of struggle. My father, born in a village of dirt-floor hovels in Guangdong Province in southeast China, slept on wooden planks, using bricks for pillows, and dreamed of doing better. As a teenager, his dreams turned to America, and he labored through his teenage years in Manila, saving money and eventually buying official papers bearing a non-Chinese name that made it easier for him to enter the United States.

8   My mother was born in another Guangdong village. She has one dominant memory of her life as a young girl. "What I wanted most was to come to the United States," she once told me. "I heard that life was much, much better than in the village." It was, but it took much hard work. And it resulted in a dual identity for their five children. Growing up and going to school, we knew we were American, but we spoke Cantonese at home as well as English; in the evenings, we went to "Chinese school."

9   Our parents, understandably, clung to the ways of the country they had left behind; their work, they said, did not afford them the time to learn good English, and so we would have to accommodate them. Besides, they said, we should not forget that we were, first and foremost, Chinese. As such, we had different priorities. The understanding—once we were old enough to understand—was that, just as they had sacrificed for us, we would sacrifice for them.

10   The obligation begins with work. If the family has a business, the child automatically is part of that business. Our family business was the restaurant. I was raised in the New Eastern Cafe in Chinatown, Oakland. At age 8, I was shelling prawns and stripping snow peas; as soon as I could take an order and carry a dish, I was a waiter.

11   Through our high school years and into college, Barry and I worked at various restaurants almost every evening, weekend and summer. We missed out on any semblance of social life. We stayed up late to squeeze in our homework. We covered for each other for the very occasional night off. We were often angry and frustrated, but business was such that we couldn't afford any overhead, and there was no use complaining. "Party? What for? Plenty of time to have fun later—when you grow up." Then, having grown up: "When you get married." I didn't escape until I became an editor on my college daily newspaper at San Francisco State and had to move across the bay. And even then, I felt guilty about not being at the restaurant.

12   In the end, there is no real escape from one's heritage. Thinking back, we saw beyond the boredom and frustration and came to appreciate what we got. We learned to be responsible. And, although there are few outward displays of affection in Chinese families, we earned our parents' respect for sticking by them.

13   The stuff of lower-class life—cardboard swords, paper bags as baseball gloves, cardboard boxes on fences for basketball— may have been embarrassing then; now, it serves to remind me that my parents didn't have much while raising five chil-

dren. All they had were our futures. And, in Barry's case, they were robbed even of that. Thirteen years later, all they have of him are bittersweet anniversaries—on May 8, of his birth; on June 26, of his death. And, of course, memories.

But I have something more. For 13 years, there have been 14
few days when I haven't thought of Barry. And though the pain has lessened over those years, there are indelible thoughts and images, not connected as much with my brother as with his death. Whenever I think of him, he is still my older brother; somehow, right now, he is ageless yet perennially two years older than I. He is wiser. He has kept me forever younger.

In the aftermath of his murder, I was numbed. I witnessed 15
the major events of that summer in a warped daze. I remember thinking of Barry missing the high drama of the Watergate hearings; I thought just of him when the terrorists struck at the Munich Olympics. I remember acting irrationally. I collected and devoured newspaper stories about gangs. Reading the articles, I stopped at every name, wondering. I watched crime shows on TV and lived vicariously through the likes of Peter Falk, whose Columbo always managed to nail the killer, and of Charles Bronson, whose various characters made it their personal mission in life to exterminate the scum of the earth. I've never wanted anything more than answers and justice. But, yes, sometimes, lost in the celluloid vigilante heroics of a Bronson or Clint Eastwood, I thought about the sweetness of revenge.

I looked on people as possible surrogate older brothers. I 16
remember the brother of a girlfriend. A roommate. But that was just wistful nonthinking. I came to realize that, by Chinese tradition, I was now the older brother of the family, and I had obligations and responsibilities, among them not to dwell on the past.

Still, I think of Barry almost every day. Anything will trig- 17
ger it: talking with any member of the family, hearing or reading the name "Barry," any trip into or through the neighborhood where he last lived, a glimpse of an antique sword in a store window, a song by Elton John called "Daniel" (". . . my brother, you are older than me, do you still feel the pain?"). I was unable to listen to Bach, especially to pieces that were on one of Barry's favorite albums, *A New Sound From the Japanese Bach Scene.* We played it at his wake. With the turntable unattended, the record played repeatedly, so that "Minuet in G," "Air on a G String" and other melodies got embedded in my mind—a soundtrack of our loss. Since then, whenever I come across those compositions, I have to tune out or walk away.

18   Our family was never religious, but after Barry was gone, I found myself looking into the heavens and talking with him, with his soul. I did—and do—this usually on visits to the Mountain View Cemetery, high over Oakland. The talk is easy, loving, sometimes eloquent, in a balanced, yin-yang way. I tell him the news of the family, the ups and downs, and I think about how he might fit in, might affect those events. Sometimes, standing at Mountain View, I believe he still does.

19   Barry's death ultimately inspired the bridging of a lifelong language barrier between my folks and me. With help from a family friend, I was able to interview them about their lives in China, their courtship by mail, the beginnings of our family in Oakland. I still haven't asked them about Barry. If he enters my mind almost every day, he must enter theirs almost every hour. The family of any victim of senseless, sudden death knows that it isn't easy being a survivor. But all one can do *is* survive and look for what lessons there are.

20   After years of uninterest in my identity as a Chinese, I had occasion to visit China two springs ago, and I immersed myself in that country. I visited my parents' villages and met relatives I never knew I had. On their walls, I saw framed photos of myself and the rest of our family. We are forever connected.

21   And, in China, in a moment of paying respects to deceased family members, I of course thought of Barry. I remember thinking about him on the ferry from Hong Kong to Macao, our gateway into China. I felt as if I'd somehow taken him to China with me, to a home he'd never seen. On the deck, my fellow travelers were dancing joyously to a song by the Doobie Brothers. In my head, another tune fought through the disco beat, a tune I'd been resisting for years. As we spotted the mountains of China in the distance, the tune took hold in my consciousness. It was a quiet little thing by Bach. And it was really quite lovely.

Organization

1. Enumerate the immediate and the remote effects of the death of the author's brother.
2. Is the author at fault for not giving attention to speculation about the possible *causes* of his brother's murder?
3. Is the section leading up to the brother's murder too long and drawn out?

Paragraphs

1. Are the paragraphs about the background of the author's parents (7–8) irrelevant?
2. Why is paragraph 14, dealing with the author's present thoughts about his brother, placed *ahead* of the section describing his initial reaction to his brother's death?

Sentences

1. Point out three sentences whose shortness is especially effective.
2. Is the last sentence of paragraph 13 an appropriate use of a sentence fragment?

Words

1. The author calls the music played at his brother's funeral *a soundtrack of our loss* (17). Explain what he means by the term.
2. "Barry was no *stranger* to *estrangement* from our folks" (4). Would you guess that this repetition is intentional or accidental?
3. To what do the following refer? *Lake Tahoe* (2), *Watergate* (15), *Munich Olympics* (15), *Peter Falk and Columbo* (15), *Charles Bronson* (15), *Clint Eastwood* (15), *Elton John* (17), *Bach* (17).
4. Be sure you know the meaning of each of the following:

abounded (3)	numbed (15)
assailants (6)	perennially (14)
celluloid (15)	prawns (10)
criminology (4)	semblance (11)
dual (8)	surrogate (16)
estrangement (4)	vigilante (15)
hippie (4)	wistful (16)
hovels (7)	yin-yang (18)
indelible (14)	

Suggestions for Writing

1. *After all, we had both, in our ways, rebelled against the strict, traditional Chinese upbringing we'd had.* (4) Did you ever rebel against the upbringing you were given by parents or guardians, school, church, or some other authority? Indicate briefly the causes of your rebellion, but concentrate on the effects it had on you or others.

2. Discuss the effects on you of the loss (through death or other form of separation) of someone important to you. Address your essay to that person's brother or sister.

PROCESS

Process analysis answers the question *how*. Usually the process is mechanical or physical: how A operates (an internal combustion engine, an assembly line, the Civil Defense warning system), or how to make B (an atomic bomb, a pineapple upside-down cake, an effective speech). But the process can also be historical: how C originated (World War I, the Moral Majority movement, the "divine right of kings" idea), or literary: how D developed (Shakespeare's playwriting skills, David Copperfield's character, Ernest Hemingway's style), or personal: how I came to do E (choose this college, pick my major, take up tennis).

Mechanical and physical process analysis is the stuff of cookbooks, operating-instruction manuals, newspaper household hints columns, and other helpful forms of "how to" advice. Though this kind of writing is by no means as easy as it may seem, it doesn't call on the wide variety of skills that this book and your instructor have been trying to draw from you. A recipe for broccoli casserole or a set of instructions on how to hook up stereo components simply isn't a freshman composition as that term is generally understood. Therefore, none of the three essays that follow is an example of mechanical or physical process analysis for its own sake. But the first two, "Chopsticks" and "Do-It-Yourself Pig Rendering," make use of process analysis in the course of doing other things along the lines suggested by the first guideline below. The third discusses the historical process identified in the title, "How Edison Stumbled on His Phonograph."

To tell how something was or should be done requires a series of step-by-step directions. Here are some guidelines for assembling these directions in an effective process analysis essay.

1. Avoid Complex Subjects

Your subject will presumably be one that is unfamiliar or, at least, unclear to your reader; otherwise it wouldn't need explaining by the process analysis method. But don't choose a subject so complicated or technical that you make unnecessary difficulties for yourself or need seven thousand words for an adequate job rather than seven hundred.

2. Be Familiar with the Whole Process

With process analysis even more perhaps than with other methods of development, you must have the complete picture firmly in mind before beginning to write. You can't present the separate steps of the process clearly and in their proper places unless you do.

3. Formulate an Interesting Thesis

Ordinary "how to" instructions need no thesis in the usual sense of the term. A recipe for pineapple upside-down cake, for example, doesn't have one, other than the implied "Here's how to make a pineapple upside-down cake." Its contents are organized by the built-in need for the correct sequence of steps—not, as an essay's are, by a controlling idea (thesis) fashioned by the writer "from outside," so to speak.

Raymond Sokolov, however, goes beyond the basic "how to" format in his essay on chopsticks. Although he does include a three-step lesson in the proper use of these utensils (pars. 5–7, p. 242), he does a good many other things too. He muses on the difficulty of using chopsticks (pars. 1–2, pp. 241–42), describes a tempting but unacceptable deviation from proper usage (par. 3, p. 241), makes additional suggestions regarding chopstick use (pars. 8–10, p. 242), and even gives a brief history lesson (par. 11, p. 243). A routine process analysis is thus expanded to take in a number of interesting and colorful details, the whole essay developed from the thesis "The art of the chopstick is long to learn" (par. 1, p. 241).

Despite Dave Barry's title, "do-it-yourself pig rendering" and the soap-making process it is part of aren't really what his essay is about. It's about the broader topic of historic preservation, toward which Barry takes a gently mocking attitude. Only one section is devoted to an abbreviated account of soap-making as witnessed by visitors to historical sites (pars. 3–8). The rest, except for an introduction (pars. 1–2) and a conclusion (par. 13), pokes fun at those who actually live—until they can't stand it anymore—in authentically restored old houses. Thus, the actual process analysis is only one prong of a two-pronged attack emerging from the thesis: *And that's exactly the point of preserving things: to remind ourselves that no matter how bad we have it, our ancestors had it worse.* (par. 2)

Sokolov's and Barry's essays, then, are good examples of how to employ physical process analysis—which, by itself, can be dull and uninviting—in imaginative ways. "How Edison Stumbled on His Phonograph" represents, not physical, but historical process analysis. Here, the problem for Hans Fantel wasn't, as it was for Sokolov and Barry, how to give a broader perspective to a relatively narrow process, but rather how to give vividness and interest to the process itself. Do you think Fantel succeeded?

4. Use Chronological Order

Since the steps of a process—whether mechanical, physical, historical, or personal—ordinarily take place in a certain time sequence, chronological order is the obvious method to follow in presenting them. To prevent the monotony of anything resembling a mere list, however, you should divide your analysis into several groups of details, each group centered, like a paragraph, around one major step in the process. Notice, for example, how Sokolov separates his instructions on chopstick-use into three sections (pars. 5–7, p. 242). The first deals with the positioning of one stick in the hand, the second with the positioning of the other stick, and the third with the manipulation of both sticks at once. Barry, too, has three sections for his discussion of colonial soap-making, one for each stage of the process: pig-rendering (pars. 3–5), lard-beating (pars. 5–7), and wood-chewing-and-spitting (par. 7). If you keep the main steps separate from one another and in chronological order as successfully as Sokolov and Barry do, you will forestall any confusion on the part of your reader.

5. Be Sure to Include All Essential Steps in the Process

Discuss as much of the process as your topic and your purpose demand, omitting nothing that will enable your reader to understand clearly how the parts fit together. Barry highlights only three steps in the soap-making process, but nothing more is required in an essay the main topic of which is historic preservation. (Even then he refers to the *dozens of difficult and degrading steps* that occur later). But Sokolov could hardly leave off his explanation after telling you how to hold stick number one. And Fantel wouldn't have fulfilled the promise implicit in his title if he had brought his story down to Edison's initial idea for a *"talking machine,"* and then left it there.

CHOPSTICKS

Raymond A. Sokolov

Raymond Sokolov: journalist, editor, novelist. Sokolov was born in 1941. He is best known for his food-related writings in the New York Times. *He also reviews books for* Newsweek *and regularly contributes articles to other periodicals. He has published two cookbooks,* Great Recipes From The New York Times *and* The Saucier's Apprentice: A Modern Guide to Classic French Sauces for the Home. *His first novel,* Native Intelligence, *was hailed by many critics as a highly imaginative work. The following essay appeared in the* New York Times *in 1975.*

Is Sokolov's attitude toward his material serious, humorous, or a combination of both?

How do you know?

The art of the chopstick is long to learn. No less a figure   1
than James Reston—a man who endured acupuncture without an anticipatory quiver—confessed in this newspaper to his anxieties over managing those wily utensils. Meanwhile, as part of the general craze in this country for Chinese food, thousands of ordinary Americans have tried their hand at lifting a steamed dumpling from plate to mouth with two 10-inch wooden wands.

Such worthy efforts at physical agility should be applauded,   2
in great men and small. They have given a boost to the drycleaning business, which must have increased its total annual turnover removing soy-sauce stains from the laps of slacks and skirts. And anyone who has recently mastered chopsticks will sympathize with the Westchester clubwoman who, in hunger and frustration, gave up trying to trap slippery pieces of Szechuan bean curd between her sticks and simply impaled them instead.

This spearing method, although probably frowned on by the   3
Chinese equivalent of the Playboy Advisor, is a time-honored dodge among Chinese children. May Wong Trent recalls, in

her book "Eighty Precious Chinese Recipes," that at the age of 4 in Hong Kong she received her first set of chopsticks, which were plastic, just 6 inches long and pointed at the business end. Just as no American parent expects a toddler to master the official way of holding a fork, so the elder Wongs cast an indulgent eye on young May as she speared away at deep-fried, paper-wrapped chicken pieces in five spices. Soon, however, she progressed to the politer pincers movement to which all true Sinophiles should aspire.

4   If you are not already a chopstick adept, the easiest way to learn is with a native expert at your side. Mine was a certain Chung, headwaiter at the old Dum Luck Imperial in Germfask, Mich. His instructions were simple, and I herewith transcribe them verbatim.

5   (1) Grasp the handle of one stick in the cleft between thumb and index finger. Let the eating end of the stick fall onto the side of the ring finger near its tip. Practice holding this stick tightly by squeezing it with the thumb, and, simultaneously, pressing against it with the ring finger. In actual eating, this stick will remain stationary in this position.

6   (2) Grasp the other stick with the tips of the thumb, index and middle fingers. This is the movable stick. Practice tapping its tip against the tip of the stationary stick.

7   (3) To eat, turn your palm toward you, press a piece of food between the tips of the sticks, pivot your wrist away from you so the food is brought to the neighborhood of your mouth. Open mouth. Insert chopsticks to an approximate depth of 1 inch. Remove chopsticks (but not food) from mouth. Chew.

8   Chung also suggested that if, in the course of eating, your chopsticks go slightly askew in your hand, the best thing to do is to press the eating ends against the surface of your plate. In this way, you can even up the sticks so that you are once again able to make them snap together at their eating ends.

9   Furthermore, if you want to serve food to someone else at the table, it is considered elegant to reverse the chopsticks and touch the food for your friend with the handles. This entails a bit of wiping off of the chopsticks, before and after, but chopsticks do not normally collect large amounts of food. This feature makes them easy to clean and ideal for cooking, stirring or beating eggs. They don't drip on the counter. Also, ordinary bamboo chopsticks are machine-washable.

10   Oddly, though, chopsticks are not very good for picking up rice. This is why the Chinese raise the rice bowl (topped with other food) to their lips and then shovel in the rice. And they also use chopsticks to cut large pieces of soft food, for there is never a knife at a Chinese dining table.

Why should this be? The answer is lost in prehistory, when   11
the first (bamboo) chopsticks are supposed to have been invented. We can be certain, however, that the chopstick evolved
in tandem with a cuisine that is served almost entirely in precut pieces. Knives are thus unnecessary for eating Chinese food
or the chopstick cuisines of Japan, Korea, Vietnam and other
East Asian countries influenced by Chinese culture.

Organization

1. How many paragraphs form the introduction to the essay?
2. Which paragraphs form the instruction on the use of chopsticks? Is this section integrated smoothly into the rest of the essay?

Paragraphs

1. Is the last paragraph (on the evolution of chopsticks) made relevant to the rest of the essay?
2. What purpose does paragraph 4 serve?

Sentences

1. Are the directions on how to manipulate chopsticks clear and precise? (As a test, you might try actually putting them into practice.)
2. How are the sentences in the instruction section different from those of the rest of the essay?

Words

1. To what do the following refer? *James Reston* (1), *Westchester* (2), *Szechuan* (2), *Playboy Advisor* (3).
2. Be sure you know the meaning of each of the following:

acupuncture (1)	indulgent (3)
adept (4)	pincers (3)
agility (2)	pivot (7)
anticipatory (1)	quiver (1)
askew (8)	Sinophiles (3)
cleft (5)	tandem (11)
cuisine (11)	toddler (3)
curd (2)	verbatim (4)
impaled (2)	wily (1)

Suggestions for Writing

1. For the benefit of an Oriental person who has never seen, much less used, Western-style eating utensils, describe the process of using a knife, a fork, a spoon, or any combination thereof.
2. Discuss the advantages, disadvantages, or additional uses of knives, forks, or spoons. (See paragraphs 9 and 10 of "Chopsticks.")

DO-IT-YOURSELF PIG RENDERING

Dave Barry

Dave Barry: journalist, syndicated columnist, author. Barry majored in English and graduated in 1969 from Haverford College. He worked as a bookkeeper for a while before beginning his journalism career. In 1976 he left the Philadelphia Bureau of the Associated Press to join Burger Associates, a group that teaches effective writing to corporate executives. In 1983 he joined the staff of the Miami Herald *although he continues to make his home in Pennsylvania. He submits his articles by computer line. Barry's books include a manual for home repairs entitled* Taming of the Screw, Babies and Other Hazards of Sex, *and most recently,* Stay Fit and Healthy Until You Die. *The following essay appeared in the* Miami Herald.

In how many different ways does Barry achieve his humorous effects?

Are some of these effects more successful than others?

1   I love to visit old historical sites where the people all dress up in colonial garb and do authentic things with beeswax. Whenever I get upset about the specter of worldwide nuclear devastation, I just visit a historical site, and I'm taken back to a time of peace, a time of rustic self-reliance, a time when there was no kind of plumbing at all, and I realize that I'll take the old specter of worldwide nuclear devastation any day.

2   And that's exactly the point of preserving things: to remind ourselves that no matter how bad we have it, our ancestors had it worse. There's nothing quite like the warm feeling of smugness that comes over you when you visit someplace like Authentic Historical Colonial Williamsburg, and watch people in uncomfortable clothing demonstrate what people used to go through merely to make a bar of soap.

3   WILLIAMSBURG GUIDE: Now the first step in making soap in those days was to render a pig so as to obtain lard. In the background here, you see one of our historical personnel, Bertha, rendering a pig exactly as they did it in the colonial era.

Bertha started her rendering yesterday, and she will not finish until tomorrow afternoon, at which time she will smell like a full dumpster outside an Italian restaurant on a hot day. And by the way, the pigs, we use here at Williamsburg are all authentic.

VISITOR: How will Bertha get the blood out of her hair? 4

GUIDE: She will use a mixture of pine tar, smelt roe and 5 gravel, just as her ancestors did over 200 years ago. Now over here we have Amy, who is demonstrating the next step in soap-making, which is to beat the lard with this authentic wooden object, which is called a "lard-beater." And by the way, you may purchase a lard-beater just like this one at our Authentic Historical Colonial Things for Sale Shoppe. Amy will beat the lard at the rate of 32 beats per minute for exactly four hours and five minutes.

VISITOR: What purpose does beating the lard serve? 6

GUIDE: None whatsoever, but as the old authentic colonial 7 housewives used to say, "If you're beating lard, you're not rendering a pig." And now if you'll step over here, you'll see Irma Lou, who is preparing for the next soap-making step by chewing up little pieces of wood and spitting them into an iron pot.

And so it goes until, dozens of difficult and degrading steps 8 later, the authentic personnel produce a smallish blob of historical colonial soap, which looks like whale mucus. The visitors head back to their motels to take hot showers, during which they gaze upon the motel soap, which is free and abundant in this great modern land of ours, with new respect.

The danger is that every now and then you get people who 9 miss the point, people who go to historical sites and come away with the deranged notion that they would actually like to LIVE in one. This notion usually strikes young professional couples whose only previous carpentry experience consists of having assembled prefabricated wine racks. They rush out and buy some really disastrous old house and decide to fix it up, doing everything in the same depressing way the original inhabitants did, not realizing that the original inhabitants would never have done anything the way they did if they had known any better.

So every night and weekend, the new owners work on their 10 house. If their restoration job is especially depressing, various home-decorating magazines may publish articles about it:

"Bob and Babs Buffington say they have experienced both 11 low and high points in restoring their 18th-Century country home. 'I'd say the low point was when the house collapsed on Bob,' recalls Babs. 'But,' she adds brightly, 'we had a real high point last week when the doctor told us Bob may be able to walk normally by next year.' Bob's current project is to replace all the beams so the house won't collapse again. 'I'm hewing all the beams by hand,' says Bob. 'In those days, they used nothing but hand-hewn beams. I'd like to wring their necks.' "

12   Finally, after years and years of painstaking work, after long, lonely nights when they began to think they would never finish, they realize they will never finish, so they move into a modern home, where their first project is to have a contractor cover every accessible surface with Formica. They sell their old house to another deranged couple, and immediately after the mortgage papers are signed it collapses again, and the cycle repeats.

13   This kind of needless tragedy could be avoided if the personnel at authentic colonial historical sites like Williamsburg would make it clearer that they are only pretending to be colonial so we'll all realize how nice it is that we are not. Maybe more of the personnel should be toothless. Or maybe, during their explanation of candlemaking, they could casually toss in a remark like, "Of course, if we were REALLY colonial people, most of us would be dead on account of the short life span." I think that would be a tasteful way to protect people like Bob and Babs Buffington from themselves.

Organization

1. Which paragraphs deal with soap-making? Which with house restoration?
2. Name the separate steps involved in soap-making. Are all the steps in the soap-making process described? Why or why not?
3. Can you suggest why the house-restoration process is not described as specifically as the soap-making process?

Paragraphs

1. What is the purpose of paragraph 8?
2. Is the last paragraph a satisfactory conclusion to the essay?
3. Point out transitional devices connecting paragraphs 1 and 2.

Sentences

1. Select three sentences that you find humorous and determine why you found them so.
2. Why are quotation marks used to enclose the magazine comment (11), but not the visitor-and-guide comments (3–7)?

Words

1. Comment on the appropriateness of the proper names *Bertha* (3), *Irma Lou* (7), and *Bob and Babs Buffington* (11), as used in the essay.
2. Too what do the following refer? *Williamsburg* (2), *Formica* (12).
3. Be sure you know the meaning of the following:

deranged (9)	roe (5)
hewing (11)	smelt (5)
mucus (8)	smugness (2)
render (3)	

Suggestions for Writing

1. Describe the process of making a familiar household item (window curtains, a slipcover, a pottery dish, a table or chair) or installing a household item (wallpaper, paneling, wall-to-wall carpeting).
2. Describe the process of building a small structure (an addition to a house, a carport, a doghouse or dollhouse) or of renovating or remodeling such a structure.

HOW EDISON STUMBLED ON
HIS PHONOGRAPH

Hans Fantel

Hans Fantel: translator, freelance writer. Fantel was born in Vienna, Austria in 1922. He attended Tarkio College, the University of Missouri, and the New School for Social Research. He has worked for the United States Air Force Research and Development Center as a technical translator and editor. More than a hundred of his articles have appeared in such popular magazines as Look, Popular Science, *and* Reader's Digest. *Among his books are* The Waltz Kings: Johann Strauss and His Era *and* The True Sound of Music. *The following essay appeared in the* New York Times *in 1979.*

How does this essay differ as a process essay from the two preceding process essays, "Chopsticks" and "Do-It-Yourself Pig Rendering"?

What were the principal events in the development of the phonograph?

1 Serendipity, more often than necessity, is the mother of invention, and it was unplanned parenthood of this kind that resulted in the birth of the phonograph just a hundred years ago. Edison wasn't even thinking about music when he hit upon the device that was to prove the crucial turning point in modern musical history—a music box more magical than any Emperor's Nightingale. What he had in mind was a gadget to speed up the transmission of telegrams over the newly laid trans-Atlantic cable. The phonograph happened by sheer chance.

2 This is not altogether surprising. A machine to capture sound—the most ephemeral of sensations—and preserve it for subsequent recall would have seemed too fantastic to the eminently practical Edison. America's most original inventor preferred to build on established foundations, and the idea of reproducing sound was unprecedented. Besides, Edison had been partly deaf since childhood and had no interest in music.

3 The provenance of the phonograph thus seems like a conspiracy against all odds, and only a man with Edison's unique set of qualities could have brought it off. His method of inspired tinkering, as opposed to theoretical research, suited the project, as did his rare gift for capitalizing on the unexpected.

4 Even the setting favored the realization of the improbable. At 30, Thomas Alva Edison could have served as model for Horatio Alger. A prodigy of self-education, he had by the age of 15 devoured most of Detroit's Public Library, vacillating in his preference between Isaac Newton and Victor Hugo. After landing a job as a railroad telegrapher, he became enthralled

by the new and still mysterious domain of electrical devices. Sleeping only three or four hours, he worked feverishly each night to improve the still primitive technology of the telegraph. By his mid-20s he had developed a splendidly sophisticated method permitting multiple messages to be sent in opposite directions on the same telegraph wire, and the proceeds from this and several other inventions released him from the burdens of poverty.

Edison used the money to set up one of the world's first   5
independent research laboratories—an "invention factory" as he called it. On a hilltop at Menlo Park in what was then rural New Jersey he surrounded himself with half a dozen trusted and tireless associates—mostly Swiss and German master mechanics—and let it be known among the emergent industrialists of the period that he was ready to make inventions to order. For his "research team," men enchanted by the charms of technology, Edison had created an ideal milieu: a playpen for grownups with no limits imposed on the practical imagination.

Early in 1877, Edison was fiddling with a gadget to emboss   6
the dot-dash pattern of Morse code on tinfoil wrapped around a rotating cylinder. Recorded at the telegrapher's normal speed, the roll could then be spun rapidly in playback to send out the pulses at a faster rate than attainable by hand and thus permit more messages to be sent on crowded cables. While whirling the recorded cylinder, Edison discovered that the dots and dashes, when speeded up into the range of audible frequencies and jiggling the feeler stylus, made a chattering noise reminiscent of speech in a strange language. It was this accidental impression that suggested to Edison the possibility of a "talking machine" that would record and reproduce speech vibrations through a moving membrane attached to a tin horn.

The idea didn't come out of the blue. Edison was already   7
conversant with nascent notions of sound reproduction from his own attempts to make the inarticulate squawks of Alexander Graham Bell's newly invented telephone more intelligible. Also, he was probably aware of the work of Hermann Ludwig Ferdinand von Helmholtz, the German physicist who had shortly before completed the first systematic inquiry into the nature of sound; and he knew of a contraption built by the French experimenter Leon Scott de Martinville, who inscribed sound vibrations on a soot-covered cylinder by means of a pig's bristle attached to a sound-catching cone. This oddment had been shown at Buckingham Palace in 1859 and was said to have amused even Queen Victoria. Edison's radical innovation was to restore the recorded wave pattern to audibility.

8   At some time in 1877—the exact date is in dispute—Edison
made a crude pencil sketch of the planned device and handed
it to John Kruesi, a Swiss watchmaker who was his most dex-
trous assistant. The instructions, scribbled at the bottom were
simple: "Kruesi: Make this. —Edison." He didn't tell the mechanic the purpose of the machine, and only when it was nearly
finished did Kruesi ask what it was for. "I told him the machine must talk," Edison recalled. "He thought it was absurd."

9   It was on Dec. 6, 1877, that Edison first conversed with his
new invention about Mary's little lamb. When the machine
recognizably reproduced Edison's voice, Kruesi turned pale and
invoked the protection of the Holy Ghost in German.

10   Edison himself was dumbfounded. "I was never so taken
aback in all my life," he later admitted, and participants in
the first public demonstrations generally believed it was a
ventriloquist's trick until their own voices spoke to them
through the horn. One contemporary newspaper report mar-
veled at the ingenuity of a machine which could be made to
talk not only English (which, presumably, is easy) but also
German, French, Dutch, Spanish and Hebrew. The very fact
that sound could be captured and preserved struck the public
with the same kind of awe that the moon landings evoked in
our own time, and Edison was hailed as "The Wizard of Menlo
Park."

11   Edison was unaware that on Dec. 5, the day before he and
Kruesi first tested the talking machine, an obscure French poet
and amateur scientist named Charles Cros read a paper at the
Academie des Sciences in Paris, describing a virtually identical device of his own invention. Moreover, the paper had been
sealed and deposited with the Academie on the preceding April
18th—months before Edison himself began work on the phonograph. However, lacking Edison's funds and facilities, the
French poet never produced a working model of his invention,
much less secured a patent. Thus Edison was destined for fame
and riches, Cros for oblivion. Had Cros pressed his claim to
priority, the generous and fairminded Edison would surely have
reached some settlement with him.

12   The early phonographs, which were basically crude, hand-
cranked dictating machines, sounded scratchy and tended to
slur sibilants due to poor frequency responses. As for their
pitch, it depended on the steadiness of the hand on the crank.
Even so, people lined up at side-shows in circuses and tent-
meetings to hear their own voices for a nickel, and one lucky
owner of a phonograph reports making up to $1,800 a week
by exhibiting it at country fairs and church bazaars.

13   Not until a quarter-century later was the musical potential

of the new invention fully recognized, which is not too surprising considering its raucous sound. A great deal of technical development work remained to be done before the
phonograph could begin to fulfill its musical promise.

Only after Edison's cylinder has been replaced by the flat   14
disk introduced by Emile Berliner in the 1890's was it possible to mass-produce recordings by pressing records from a mold
like waffles in a waffle-iron. Before that, each cylinder had to
be recorded individually, making both the price and the strain
upon the artist prohibitive.

Though the phonograph provided entertainment in count-   15
less homes in the early part of the century, its feeble and shal-
low sound offered no more than a faint suggestion of musical
reality. True enough, great singers like Caruso and Mc-
Cormick left priceless traces of their art on the wheezy disks
of that period, but the "acoustic" recording and playback
equipment—unaided by electrical amplification—could not
cope with the range and power of orchestral sound. Not until
the late 1920's, when the new electronic principles of radio
were combined with Edison's purely mechanical recording
process, did the phonograph attain musical maturity. Only after
the tin horn gave way to the microphone and the loudspeaker
could the phonograph encompass the orchestral repertory, and
only after the astounding postwar advances in electronics were
applied to sound reproduction could it do fair justice to the
splendors of music.

Though he lived until 1931 and appreciated the portent of   16
electronics, he never dealt with these later developments. Once
the initial problem of sound recordings was solved to his satisfaction, his attention turned swiftly to other matters—the
electric light and the distribution of electric power.

Today, a century after Edison and Kruesi heard the first ut-   17
terance of the talking machine, the world of music stands
transformed by their accomplishment. Music now transcends
both time and space. A performance no longer must perish
with its own sound. Nor is music bound to any place. Incred-
ible as it may seem to earlier generations, most music today
is not heard in the presence of the performer but on records—
and all the concert halls in the world could not hold the audience of a single successful recording.

Music has a new technical base and a new public. The long-   18
range implications for the development of music as an art are
not yet fathomed, and cultural historians are baffled by the
scope of this change. Seen in this perspective, the unmusical
Edison emerges as the pivotal figure in the recent history of
music.

251

Organization

1   Paragraph 12 marks the conclusion of one section of the essay.
    What does that section deal with?
2. Are paragraphs 14–16 irrelevant to an essay with this essay's
    title and thesis?

Paragraphs

1. Why is paragraph 9 a separate paragraph, when it simply con-
    tinues paragraph 8's story of Edison and Kreusi?
2. Comment on the degree to which transitional devices are used
    between the paragraphs of the essay.

Sentences

1. Comment on the number and kind of transitions between
    sentences in paragraph 11.
2. Comment on the degree of sentence variety in the essay.

Words

1. Are too many technical terms used in the essay?
2. To what do the following refer? *Emperor's Nightingale* (1),
    Horatio Alger (4), *Isaac Newton* (4), *Holy Ghost* (9), *Caruso*
    (15), *McCormick* (15).
2. Be sure you know the meaning of each of the following:

aback (10)	portent (16)
audible (6), audibility (7)	prodigy (4)
baffled (18)	prohibitive (14)
domain (4)	provenance (3)
emboss (6)	raucous (13)
emergent (5)	repertory (15)
encompass (15)	serendipity (1)
ephemeral (2)	sibilants (12)
inarticulate (7)	slur (12)
milieu (5)	transcends (17)
nascent (7)	vacillating (4)
oblivion (11)	ventriloquist (10)
perspective (18)	
pivotal (18)	

Suggestions for Writing

1. Select a significant event in your personal life that was the result (perhaps unanticipated) of a series of preliminary events or procedures. Describe the process from beginning to conclusion.
2. Select a significant event you are familiar with in the life of an organization to which you belonged or still belong. Describe the steps leading up to that event, concluding with the event itself.

9
DEFINITION

BRIEF DEFINITIONS

Now and again in the course of writing an essay, you will find you are forced to use a word or a phrase that you suspect will be unfamiliar to your reader. It may be a technical term or one used in a specialized way (*ontogeny* and *phylogeny* [biology], *coda* [music], *gross national product* [economics], *deconstruction* [literary criticism]); a new coinage *(cassette, floppy disc)*; a slang expression ("cool," "funky," "heavy,"); or even your own particular application of an ordinary word (see Connotation, p. 58). Whatever the case, you must pause to define the term if you want your reader to understand what it means and how it relates to its context.

You may choose among several possible approaches to such a definition:

1. Quote the Meaning of the Term as Given in a Standard Dictionary

This method is the easiest and the safest way to define (provided, of course, the term is in the dictionary in the first place). A word of caution, however: *beginning* an essay with a dictionary definition ("According to Webster, 'friendship' is . . .") is a trite and tired device that annoys most experienced readers and causes most English instructors to cringe. Find more imaginative ways of introducing your topic (see Beginning, pp. 32–35), and save dictionary definitions for the body of your paper.

2. Construct a Dictionary-style Definition of Your Own

The dictionary defines a word by placing it in the class to which it belongs and then differentiating it from the other members of that class. For example, *Webster's New World Dictionary of the American Language* defines *democracy* as "government in which the people hold the ruling power either directly or through selected representatives." The class is *government;* the differentiating features comprise the rest of the definition.

If a term is not in the dictionary—or even if it is, but you wish to make up a definition of your own—you may use the basic dictionary form as a model. That's what the writer of "Ecology" did in defining the essay's subject (par. 3, p. 264):

> Ecology is a science which seeks to determine in precise terms the exact nature of the interrelationships among living organisms and their physical surroundings. It is rigorous and full of formulas and complex energy flowcharts.

Here ecology is classified as a science and then differentiated from other sciences by the relative clause *which seeks . . . surroundings* and by the second sentence.

Here are a few important points to remember in fashioning an accurate definition:

a. Keep the Term and the Class Grammatically and Logically Equal It contradicts both grammar and logic to say "Ecology is when . . ." or "Ecology is where. . . ." Ecology isn't a *when* (a time) or a *where* (a place); it's a field of study, a science. In other words, if the term is a noun (ecology), the class into which it is put must be a noun also (science), not an adverb *(when* or *where)* or any other part of speech.

b. Don't Repeat the Term, or Any Form of It, in the Definition It isn't very helpful to tell someone that happiness is "the state of being happy," or that an oscillator is "a device for producing electric oscillations." The definer's task is to find an equivalent term or terms for the one being defined.

c. Keep the Defining Language on a Simpler Level than That of the Term Being Defined It makes sense to define superciliousness as "the state of being arrogant," but it makes no sense to define arrogance as "the state of being supercilious." Anyone who needs arrogance defined at all wouldn't know (presumably) what supercilious means, and should therefore be given a more familiar synonym, such as *proud* or *haughty.*

d. Make Both the Class and the Differentiating Features as Exact as Possible   If you define soccer as "a game," your classification is too broad; baseball, Monopoly, and bridge are games, too. If you define it as "a football game," you have narrowed the classification sufficiently; but what you sit down to watch on Monday night or Saturday afternoon television is also "a football game" —but not soccer. Soccer must therefore be differentiated from American football. It won't do to say that soccer is "a football game played between two teams of eleven players each, each team attempting to advance the ball into the opposing team's goal area." The differentiating features aren't narrow enough; American football could be described in these same terms. Another revision is necessary: soccer is "a football game played between two teams of eleven players each, each team attempting to advance *a round ball* into the opposing team's goal area *by either kicking it or hitting it with any part of the body except the arms and the hands.*" The italicized words set soccer apart from any other kind of football and thus make for a complete and a precise definition.

3. Use a Synonym or a Brief Explanation

This technique provides, when appropriate, for a less formal and less complete definition than the dictionary type, though it should, of course, be accurate as far as it goes. Mimi Sheraton, using two technical terms in describing chocolate-making, immediately defines each: *"dutched" (treated with an alkalizer to neutralize acids and darken color)* and *"conched" (a cooking process that develops a nutlike flavor)* (par. 5, p. 105). The authors of "Is Human Imagination Going Down the Tube?" do the same: . . . *television engages the "orienting reflex," that is, our irresistible tendency to turn our eyes toward moving stimuli* (par. 4, p. 331).

4. Let the Context Supply the Definition

Even more informal, and certainly more indirect than the synonym or the brief explanation, is the "definition" that your reader pieces together from the hints you supply. For example, when Arnold Benson writes that Santa Fe's 7,000-foot elevation gives its inhabitants the symptoms of *anoxia,* and that these symptoms are *identical to the symptoms of a couple of friendly drinks* (par. 14, p. 330), you don't have to reach for a medical dictionary to find out what *anoxia* means. The meaning is clear enough from the context, and Benson can't be faulted for not providing a more precise definition when none is required. Nor does Franklin Daugherty have to take time out from describing a Mardi Gras parade to explain more fully what a *break-dance* is. Even a reader coming upon the term for the first time would get the general idea when told about the marchers stopping, then *balancing back on one hand and kicking up their legs* (par. 4, p. 109). This casual kind of definition would be unsuitable for some kinds of essays, of course; on the other hand, greater exactness would be fussy and disruptive in Benson's and Daugherty's informal pieces.

EXTENDED DEFINITIONS

The more abstract, complex, or controversial a term is, the more difficult it is to define it in any of the preceding ways—and the more unacceptable such a definition would be. Dictionaries give brief definitions of such words as *love* and *obscenity* and *photo-synthesis* and *hypostasis* because they have to, but often the results are too concise or too superficial to carry much meaning.

For that reason, you may find it necessary to make use of *extended definition* to explain a term (or at least, your understanding of a term) as fully as possible. *Webster's Collegiate Dictionary* takes two and a half lines to give three short definitions of *happiness:* "1. Good luck; prosperity. 2. A state of well-being. 3. Graceful aptitude; felicity; —used esp. of language." John Ciardi, however, takes three and a half pages to explore the idea of happiness and to isolate what he feels is its essential characteristic (p. 268). The same dictionary defines *migraine* as "a kind of nervous headache, usually periodical and confined to one side of the head." But Joan Didion makes that definition come agonizingly alive in a graphic account of her several-times-monthly migraine attacks (p. 273). Both Ciardi and Didion are defining, but in each case the *whole essay* is the definition.

It's clear, then, that an extended definition goes beyond the dictionary definition's strict boundaries of classification and differentiation. For example, Ciardi goes into a discussion of materialistic as opposed to spiritual, and Western as opposed to Eastern, concepts of happiness; he also takes time to cite evidence of American materialism. Didion contributes a lengthy personal history of migraine seizure in addition to offering general comment about its physiological aspects. Both essays thus end up as highly personal statements—definitions not so much in the objective as in the subjective sense: "This is what happiness (or migraine headache) means to *me.*" The same personal approach characterizes Frederick Buechner's "Guilt" (p. 266) and Bonnie Angelo's "Good Ole Boys" p. 278). Even "What's a *Ms.?*" (p. 261) and "Ecology" (p. 263), though more objective than these other essays, both venture beyond dictionary definition limits in discussing their subjects.

Not surprisingly, however, most extended definitions have their source in a basic dictionary form of definition. Consider as an example the short essay "What's a *Ms.?*" (p. 263). It opens with a dictionary-style definition of *Ms.* as the term was originally coined: a *form of address* [class] *when a woman's marital status is unknown* [differentiation]. The paragraph continues to redefine the term according to current usage, still keeping the dictionary form: a *standard form of address* [class] adopted *by women who want to be recognized as individuals, rather than being identified by their relationship with a man* [differentiation]. All the rest of the essay is an expression of this second definition. Specifically, the remainder of paragraph 1 puts *Ms.* (=female) on an equal footing with *Mr.* (=male). Paragraph 2 discusses two pieces of legislation that would reinforce women's independence from marital status designations. Paragraph 3 explains how *Ms.* (and certain related titles) should be used in practice, and paragraph 4 tells how it should be pronounced and spelled. Finally, paragraph 5 returns to the "female" emphasis of paragraph 2 and ends with an allusion. The result is an extended definition, longer and more complete than the kind found in a dictionary, but having its roots in classification and differentiation.

In saying that an extended definition essay is usually an outgrowth of a dictionary-style definition, we are really saying that that definition is the *thesis* of the essay. Therefore, everything you've already learned about formulating and developing a thesis (pp. 18–23) applies here. Moreover, you'll want to review what was said under guideline 2 on page 255 about constructing a proper definition—especially what dangers to avoid—so that your essay will get off to a good start and point you in the right direction.

1. Use Any Serviceable Method of Development

Since the purpose of definition is to pinpoint the essential character of something as exactly as possible—always a difficult undertaking, and more so in the case of abstractions—you have unusual freedom to use whatever methods of development will accomplish that purpose best. In fact, it's usually only through combining methods that you'll come close to defining the exact nature of an abstract concept.

Look again at "What's a *Ms.?*" After an opening that presents a brief background and a dictionary-style definition, the paragraph *compares and contrasts Ms.* with *Mr.* (both titles, but the first denoting a female, the second a male). You, too, may find it helpful in a writing assignment to clarify an unfamiliar term by comparing it with a similar but more familiar term.

Sometimes *examples* can be used to define. "What's a *Ms.?*" paragraph 2 presents two examples of proposed legislation that would grant women recognition simply as women, rather than as married or unmarried women. These examples are directly related to the emphasis of the definition: *Ms.* understood as a title meaning "female." If you, too, use examples in defining, be sure that they contribute, as these do, to furthering the definition. They should call attention, not to themselves, but to the term being defined.

Sometimes a concept can be clarified by indicating how it functions—an aspect of *analysis.* Paragraph 3 of the Ms. definition shows how Ms. functions as a title in everyday use, and thus in establishing an identity for its bearer. Similarly, an expanded definition of *democracy* that you may be called upon to write might well include a discussion of campaign and election procedures—practical indications of how democracy works. In your prewriting brainstorming, consider whether explaining how your subject functions would help in defining it.

2. Be as Concrete as Possible

If everything to be defined could be perceived by the senses, there would be little room for confusion or disagreement. For that reason, if you are ever called upon to define abstractions such as *time, democracy,* or *law,* you would do well to make them as concrete as possible—to relate them to clocks, ballot-boxes, and traffic tickets, for instance. "Ecology" (p. 263) makes use of scientific and historical data to help identify a new (or not so new) field of study. "Good Ole Boys" (p. 278) goes even further in the direction of concreteness by showing how the various characteristics summed up by the title are exhibited in everyday life—in effect, definition by example.

3. Check the Word's Etymology

Etymology refers to the origin and historical development of a word. When defining an abstract word such as *democracy* or *ecology*, you should check its origin in an unabridged dictionary or even the *Oxford English Dictionary*, a twelve-volume work plus supplements. Often an abstract word originally had a concrete meaning that helps you "picture" the idea. For example, *democracy* has it origin in the Greek word for *citizen; ecology* originated in the Greek word meaning "household." In both cases, knowing the original meaning of the word aids you in making your definition concrete.

4. Use Negative Definition When Appropriate

One way to indicate what a given term means is to explain what it *doesn't* mean—in other words, definition by negation. The reader translates this negative approach into positive terms, or at least, waits for the positive definition to be supplied. For example, the writer of "Ecology" says that that term isn't equivalent, as some suppose it is, to what is commonly called "environment" (par. 1, p. 263). *And it is not a nice, friendly feeling about nature, either, or a device to save a tree from an ax* (par. 2, p. 263). By thus clearing away misunderstandings about the meaning of the term, the writer prepares the way for the positive definition given in paragraph 3 (p. 264).

Never leave your reader with negative definitions only; what a thing *is*, is always more important—and certainly easier to grasp—than what it *isn't*. But as a preliminary approach, negative definition can narrow the applications of the given term and thus facilitate positive definition when you present it.

5. Use Metaphorical Definition When Appropriate

A best-selling book of the early 1950's was entitled *Science is a Sacred Cow* (E. P. Dutton & Co., 1950). Obviously, the author, Anthony Standen, wasn't attempting to give an accurate definition of the term *science*. Instead, he was levelling a humorous attack on what he took to be the public's near-worship of science and the pretensions of scientists themselves. He did so by equating science in his title with the cows regarded as sacred and inviolable in the Hindu religion. The result was a personal "definition" of science that made no pretense of being objective, but that vividly captured Standen's critical attitude.

You, too, are free to adopt this kind of imaginative definition (unless, of course, your assignment, or the very nature of your topic or approach, requires objectivity). John Ciardi makes a serious (and valuable) attempt to define happiness objectively (p. 268), but that doesn't mean you can't take a more lighthearted and subjective approach to the same topic. For example, "Happiness is spring break in Fort Lauderdale" might not win a philosopher's approval as a profound definition, but it has interesting possibilities for development (as long as you remember that you are defining happiness and not just describing Fort Lauderdale!).

WHAT'S A *Ms.*?

Ms. Magazine

Ms. Magazine: *A monthly magazine founded by Gloria Steinem in 1972.* Ms. Magazine *is for "women and men; varying ages, backgrounds, but committed to exploring new lifestyles and changes in their roles and society." Its circulation is about 450,000. The following unsigned editorial appeared in the initial issue.*

Does the essay make a convincing case for the use of *Ms.*? Why or why not?

For more than twenty years, *Ms.* has appeared in secretarial   1
handbooks as the suggested form of address when a woman's marital status is unknown; a sort of neutral combination of *Miss* and *Mrs.* Now, *Ms.* is being adopted as a standard form of address by women who want to be recognized as individuals, rather than being identified by their relationship with a

man. After all, if *Mr.* is enough to indicate "male," then *Ms.* should be enough to indicate "female."

2   A proposal often referred to as the "Ms. bill" has been introduced in Congress by New York's Congresswoman Bella Abzug. It would forbid any agency of the Federal Government from using prefixes that indicate marital status. Congressman Jonathan Bingham, also of New York, has introduced a bill that would forbid requiring females registering to vote in any Federal election to disclose their marital status unless men were also required to disclose theirs.

3   In practice, *Ms.* is used with a woman's given name: *Ms. Jane Jones,* say, or *Ms. Jane Wilson Jones.* Obviously, it doesn't make sense to say *Ms. John Jones:* a woman identified only as her husband's wife must remain a Mrs. Of course, titles are going out of style altogether. Thus, even when addressing a married couple, it is easier to write *Jane and John Jones,* without any prefixes at all.

4   *Ms.* is pronounced "miz." When asking someone to write it down, however, women find it easier to say the initials: "M.S." Otherwise, the result in writing turns out to be *Miz,* just as *Mister* might have been written down in full before *Mr.* was popularly accepted.

5   The use of *Ms.* isn't meant to protect either the married or the unmarried woman from social pressure—only to signify a female human being. It's symbolic, and important. There's a lot in a name.

Organization

1. Can you discover why the paragraphs are presented in this order? For example, could paragraph 4 follow paragraph 1?
2. Describe the persona revealed in this essay.

Paragraphs

1. What is the topic thought of paragraph 2? How is it developed?

Sentences

1. How many sentences begin with transitional devices? Discuss the purpose of each.
2. Is there an allusion in the last sentence? Explain.

Suggestions for Writing

1. Choose one of the following titles and write a brief essay explaining its meaning and importance. You may have to check a large dictionary or an encyclopedia for information.

Baron	Mayor
Lady	Consul
Dame	Attorney General
Dean	Regent

2. The author narrows the definition of *Ms.* by contrasting it with other titles in the same class *(Miss, Mrs.)*. Follow the same procedure with one of the following items. Suggested contrasts are provided in parentheses, but be sure you give your attention to the principal item.

boulevard (lane, street)	guitar (banjo, ukelele)
B.A. (B.S., B.F.A.)	opera (operetta, musical comedy)

ECOLOGY

Smithsonian *Magazine*

Smithsonian: *publishes only nonfiction for "associate members of the Smithsonian Institution; 85% with college education." This monthly magazine has a circulation of 2,000,000. "Our mandate from the Smithsonian Institute says we are to be interested in the same things which now interest or should interest the Institution: folk and fine arts, history, natural sciences, hard sciences, etc." This essay appeared in the January, 1974 issue.*

What, if any, devices does this essay use in defining ecology that the preceding essay uses in defining *Ms.?*

Does it use any devices not used in "What's a *Ms.?"*

Ecology's star has risen so fast that the meaning of the word may disappear altogether. For example, we now have the ecology, as in: "If they build that highway, they'll ruin the ecology." Have you ever heard a legislator or social reformer say that something is bad (or good) for the sociology? Ecology is a field of study, not a field of flowers. 1

And it is not a nice, friendly feeling about nature, either, or a desire to save a tree from the ax. A lot of literary folk are taking turns these days turning up the First Ecologist among the poets: "Wow! John Donne (or Dante or Shakespeare or practically anyone you choose) was an ecologist! He says right 2 here that we are all connected to nature." But St. Francis knew that, too, and so did the Eskimos and, for all we know, so did Neanderthal man. And that doesn't mean that a single one of them was an ecologist any more than a yachtsman who knows that the wind currents drive his boat is a physicist.

3   Ecology is a science which seeks to determine in precise terms the exact nature of the interrelationships among living organisms and their physical surroundings. It is rigorous and full of formulas and complex energy flowcharts.

4   The word was coined (in the form "Oekologie") by a German biologist, Ernst Haeckel, in the 1860s to describe a study he was about to start of those very interrelationships, but he got sidetracked into phylogeny. Then who was The First Ecologist? As in the manner of the old saying about the man who returned from death and described God—first of all, she was a chemist. According to a new book by Robert Clarke, her name was (and his book's title is) Ellen Swallow. The first woman to enter MIT (in 1871), she was denied the opportunity of graduate study there but soon began making interdisciplinary analyses of natural and man-caused water pollution. Unfortunately, history is not tidy; by the time Ellen Swallow got around to adopting Haeckel's word for her field, she too had begun to veer away from what we now think of as ecology—to an all-inclusive home economics.

5   Eventually ecology may become a much-needed global home economics (the Greek root means household), but that is a long way off.

Organization

1.   What is the basic method of definition used in paragraphs 1–2? Give examples.
2.   What is the method of definition used in paragraph 3?

Paragraphs

1.   How is paragraph 2 linked to paragraph 1?
2.   How is paragraph 5 linked to paragraph 4?

Sentences

1.   Note the pun on the word *field* in the last sentence of paragraph 1. Does it contribute to the purpose of defining ecology?
2   What type of sentence is the last one in paragraph 2? What is the intent behind it?

Words

1. To what does each of the following refer?

   Dante (2)   *Neanderthal man* (2)
   John Donne (2)   *St. Francis* (2)
   MIT (4)

2. What does each of the following mean?

   interdisciplinary (4)   phylogeny (4)

Suggestions for Writing

1. Choose one of the following terms used in this essay and define it. You may wish to follow the same procedure as that used in paragraphs 1–2.

   sociology   organism
   home economics   flowcharts
   phylogeny   pollution

2. The Greek root for *ecology* means "household." Consequently, ecology, defined as a science, originally involved a metaphor. Choose one of the following terms, find out its original meaning, and write a definition that emphasizes the metaphorical root-meaning.

   amnesty   astrology
   neighbor   profane
   police   poet
   sin   repentance

GUILT

Frederick Buechner

Frederick Buechner: Presbyterian clergyman, teacher, writer. Buechner was born in New York City in 1926. He attended Princeton University and Union Theological Seminary. He was ordained in 1958. Buechner taught at Phillips Exeter Academy. Among his works of fiction are A Long Day's Dying, The Book of Bebb, and Godric. His religious works include The Magnificent Defeat, The Alphabet of Grace, Peculiar Treasures: A Biblical Who's Who, and Wishful Thinking: A Theological ABC, from which the following is taken.

Is Buechner writing chiefly about psychological guilt or about moral and religious guilt?

How do you know?

1   Guilt is the responsibility for wrongdoing. Apart from the wrong we are each of us responsible for personally, in a sense no wrong is done anywhere which we are not all of us responsible for collectively. With or without knowing it, either through what we have done or what we have failed to do, we have all helped create the kind of world mess that makes wrongdoing inevitable.

2   The danger of our guilt, both personal and collective, is less that we won't take it to heart than that we'll take it to heart overmuch and let it fester there in ways that we ourselves often fail to recognize. We condemn in others the wrong we don't want to face in ourselves. We grow vindictive against the right for showing up our wrong as wrong. The sense of our own inner brokenness estranges us from the very ones who could help patch us together again. We steer clear of setting things right with the people we have wronged since their mere presence is a thorn in our flesh. Our desire to be clobbered for our guilt and thus rid of it tempts us to do things we will be clobbered for. The dismal variations are endless. More often than not, guilt is not merely the consequence of wrongdoing but the extension of it.

3   It is about as hard to absolve yourself of your own guilt as it is to sit in your own lap. Wrongdoing sparks guilt sparks wrongdoing *ad nauseam*, and we all try to disguise the grim process from both ourselves and everybody else. In order to break the circuit we need somebody before whom we can put aside the disguise, trusting that when he sees us for what we fully are, he won't run away screaming with, if nothing worse, laughter. Our trust in him leads us to trust his trust in us. In

his presence the fact of our guilt no longer makes us feel and act out our guiltiness. For a moment at least the vicious circle stops circling and we can step down into the firm ground of his acceptance, where maybe we'll be able to walk a straight line again. "Your sins are forgiven," Jesus said to the paralytic, then "Rise" whereupon the man picked up his bed and went home. (Matthew 9:2–7)

Organization

1. Would it be correct to regard the three paragraphs of this essay as introduction (1), body (2), and conclusion (3)? Why or why not?
2. Is the thesis implicit or explicit? If implicit, state it in your own words. If explicit, which is the thesis sentence?
3. By what method of development is this essay organized?

Paragraphs

1. Is there a distinct topic thought for each paragraph? If so, is it implicit or explicit?

Sentences

1. What is the point of the reference in the last sentence?
2. Comment on the presence or absence of sentence variety in the essay.
3. *Guilt is the responsibility for wrongdoing* (1). Is this sentence satisfactory as a one-sentence definition for purposes of the essay?

Words

1. Is the first sentence of paragraph 3 a simile? Explain.
2. *Clobbered* appears twice in paragraph 2. Do you find *clobber* in your dictionary? Comment on the appropriateness of its use here.
3. The fifth sentence of paragraph 3 uses both *guilt* and *guiltiness*. Is there a difference in meaning between these two words?
4. *Thorn in the flesh* (2) is an allusion to what? Why is its use especially effective in this particular essay?
5. Is there any evidence that the author has attempted to use specific detail to relieve the largely abstract diction of the essay as a whole? Can the amount of abstract diction be justified?

6. Be sure you know the meaning of each of the following:

ad nauseam (3)
estranges (2)
vindictive (2)

Suggestions for Writing

1. Select one of the abstract topics listed below (or another approved by your instructor). For that topic:
   a. Write a dictionary-style definition, using your own words.
   b. Expand your definition into a short essay, using whatever method or methods of development you choose.

| Love | Patriotism | Jealousy |
| Fear | Friendship | Faith |

WHAT IS HAPPINESS?

John Ciardi

John Ciardi: poet, teacher, editor, translator. Ciardi was born in Boston in 1916. He attended Tufts University and the University of Michigan. He taught poetry writing at several universities, including Harvard and Rutgers. He also directed the Bread Loaf Writers Conference in Vermont. Among his volumes of poetry are Homeward to America, Thirty-Nine Poems, *and* Person to Person. *In 1960 he published an influential textbook,* How Does a Poem Mean? *For a number of years he was poetry editor for* Saturday Review. *Ciardi's verse translation of Dante's* Divine Comedy *was greeted with critical praise. The following essay appeared in* Saturday Review *in 1964. He died in 1986.*

This essay uses many specific details and much figurative language. Does this help or get in the way of an effective definition of happiness?

Does this essay in any way modify what you have thought happiness to be?

1   The right to pursue happiness is issued to Americans with their birth certificates, but no one seems quite sure which way it ran. It may be we are issued a hunting license but offered no game. Jonathan Swift seemed to think so when he attacked the idea of happiness as "the possession of being well-deceived," the felicity of being "a fool among knaves." For Swift saw society as Vanity Fair, the land of false goals.

2   It is, of course, un-American to think in terms of fools and knaves. We do, however, seem to be dedicated to the idea of buying our way to happiness. We shall all have made it to Heaven when we possess enough.

And at the same time the forces of American commercial- 3
ism are hugely dedicated to making us deliberately unhappy.
Advertising is one of our major industries, and advertising exists not to satisfy desires but to create them—and to create
them faster than any man's budget can satisfy them. For that
matter, our whole economy is based on a dedicated insatiabil-
ity. We are taught that to possess is to be happy, and then we
are made to want. We are even told it is our duty to want. It
was only a few years ago, to cite a single example, that car
dealers across the country were flying banners that read "You
Auto Buy Now." They were calling upon Americans, as an
act approaching patriotism, to buy at once, with money they
did not have, automobiles they did not really need, and which
they would be required to grow tired of by the time the next
year's models were released.

Or look at any of the women's magazines. There, as Bernard 4
DeVoto once pointed out, advertising begins as poetry in the
front pages and ends as pharmacopoeia and therapy in the back
pages. The poetry of the front matter is the dream of perfect
beauty. This is the baby skin that must be hers. These, the
flawless teeth. This, the perfumed breath she must exhale.
This, the sixteen-year-old figure she must display at forty, at
fifty, at sixty, and forever.

Once past the vaguely uplifting fiction and feature articles, 5
the reader finds the other face of the dream in the back matter. This is the harness into which Mother must strap herself
in order to display that perfect figure. These, the chin straps
she must sleep in. This is the salve that restores all, this is
her laxative, these are the tablets that melt away fat, these
are the hormones of perpetual youth, these are the stockings
that hide varicose veins.

Obviously no half-sane person can be completely persuaded 6
either by such poetry or by such pharmacopoeia and orthoped-
ics. Yet someone is obviously trying to buy the dream as offered and spending billions every year in the attempt. Clearly
the happiness-market is not running out of customers, but what
is it trying to buy?

The idea "happiness," to be sure, will not sit still for easy 7
definition: the best one can do is to try to set some extremes
to the idea and then work in toward the middle. To think of
happiness as acquisitive and competitive will do to set the
materialistic extreme. To think of it as the idea one senses in,
say, a holy man of India will do to set the spiritual extreme.
That holy man's idea of happiness is in needing nothing from
outside himself. In wanting nothing, he lacks nothing. He sits
immobile, rapt in contemplation, free even of his own body.

Or nearly free of it. If devout admirers bring him food he eats it; if not, he starves indifferently. Why be concerned? What is physical is an illusion to him. Contemplation is his joy and he achieves it through a fantastically demanding discipline, the accomplishment of which is itself a joy within him.

8 Is he a happy man? Perhaps his happiness is only another sort of illusion. But who can take it from him? And who will dare say it is more illusory than happiness on the installment plan?

9 But, perhaps because I am Western, I doubt such catatonic happiness, as I doubt the dreams of the happiness-market. What is certain is that his way of happiness would be torture to almost any Western man. Yet these extremes will still serve to frame the area within which all of us must find some sort of balance. Thoreau—a creature of both Eastern and Western thought—had his own firm sense of that balance. His aim was to save on the low levels in order to spend on the high.

10 Possession for its own sake or in competition with the rest of the neighborhood would have been Thoreau's idea of the low levels. The active discipline of heightening one's perception of what is enduring in nature would have been his idea of the high. What he saved from the low was time and effort he could spend on the high. Thoreau certainly disapproved of starvation, but he would put into feeding himself only as much effort as would keep him functioning for more important efforts.

11 Effort is the gist of it. There is no happiness except as we take on life-engaging difficulties. Short of the impossible, as Yeats put it, the satisfactions we get from a lifetime depend on how high we choose our difficulties. Robert Frost was thinking in something like the same terms when he spoke of "The pleasure of taking pains." The mortal flaw in the advertised version of happiness is in the fact that it purports to be effortless.

12 We demand difficulty even in our games. We demand it because without difficulty there can be no game. A game is a way of making something hard for the fun of it. The rules of the game are an arbitrary imposition of difficulty. When the spoilsport ruins the fun, he always does so by refusing to play by the rules. It is easier to win at chess if you are free, at your pleasure, to change the wholly arbitrary rules, but the fun is in winning within the rules. No difficulty, no fun.

13 The buyers and sellers at the happiness-market seem too often to have lost their sense of the pleasure of difficulty. Heaven knows what they are playing, but it seems a dull game. And the Indian holy man seems dull to us, I suppose, because

he seems to be refusing to play anything at all. The Western weakness may be in the illusion that happiness can be bought. Perhaps the Eastern weakness is in the idea that there is such a thing as perfect (and therefore static) happiness.

Happiness is never more than partial. There are no pure states 14 of mankind. Whatever else happiness may be, it is neither in having nor in being, but in becoming. What the Founding Fathers declared for us as an inherent right, we should do well to remember, was not happiness but the *pursuit* of happiness. What they might have underlined, could they have foreseen the happiness-market, is the cardinal fact that happiness is in the pursuit itself, in the meaningful pursuit of what is life-engaging and life-revealing, which is to say, in the idea of *becoming*. A nation is not measured by what it possesses or wants to possess, but by what it wants to become.

By all means let the happiness-market sell us minor satis- 15 factions and even minor follies so long as we keep them in scale and buy them out of spiritual change. I am no customer for either puritanism or asceticism. But drop any real spiritual capital at those bazaars, and what you come home to will be your own poorhouse.

Organization

1. Is there a thesis sentence for this essay? If so, identify it and justify its location.
2. Into how many sections would you divide the paragraphs of the essay? What is the principal organizing idea of each section?
3. How many methods of development does the author use to support his definition of happiness?

Paragraphs

1. What method of development governs each of these paragraphs: 3, 7, and 12?
2. Explain the figurative language in paragraph 15.
3. What is the function of paragraph 6 in this essay?

Sentences

1. Is the parallel sentence structure in paragraphs 4 and 5 effective or ineffective? Why?
2. Are questions used in this essay simply for variety's sake, or for other reasons as well?

Words

1. What does the author mean by *being* and *becoming* in paragraph 14?
2. Why do most of the specific details occur in the first six paragraphs?
3. To what does each of the following refer? *Jonathan Swift* (1), *Vanity Fair* (1), *Thoreau* (9, 10), *Yeats* (11), *Robert Frost* (11).
4. Be sure you know the meaning of each of the following:

arbitrary (12)	knaves (2)
cardinal (14)	orthopedics (6)
catatonic (9)	pharmacopoeia (4)
felicity (1)	purports (11)
illusory (8)	rapt (7)
inherent (14)	varicose (5)
insatiability (3)	

Suggestions for Writing

1. The author sees happiness as a balance between two extremes, one materialistic, the other spiritual. Define one of the words listed below by showing that it, too, occupies a middle ground between two extremes. For instance, courage might lie between cowardice (one extreme) and foolhardiness (the other extreme).

thrift	love	mercy
justice	trust	

2. *Advertising is one of our major industries, and advertising exists not to satisfy desires but to create them—and to create them faster than any man's budget can satisfy them* (3). Support this "definition" of advertising by citing evidence in addition to that mentioned by the author (in 3–5). Or: defend advertising by defining and discussing it more favorably than the author does. Assume that your definition is a part of your job application for a position in an advertising agency.

IN BED

Joan Didion

Joan Didion: columnist, novelist. Didion was born in 1934 in Sacramento, California. In 1956, the year she graduated from the University of California, Berkeley, she won Vogue *magazine's* Prix de Paris *award. After serving as an associate feature editor for* Vogue, *she became a columnist for* Saturday Evening Post *and* Esquire. *Her articles and short stories have appeared in* Vogue, Harper's Bazaar, The American Scholar, Life, *and* National Review, *to which she is a contributing editor. Her novels include* River Run, Play It as It Lays, *and* A Book of Common Prayer. *Didion's collections of essays include* Slouching Toward Bethlehem *and* The White Album *(1979), from which the following essay is reprinted.*

Judging by this essay, is migraine a predominantly physiological or psychological affliction in origin?

What are migraine's chief effects? Is there a cure?

Three, four, sometimes five times a month, I spend the day in bed with a migraine headache, insensible to the world around me. Almost every day of every month, between these attacks, I feel the sudden irrational irritation and the flush of blood into the cerebral arteries which tell me that migraine is on its way, and I take certain drugs to avert its arrival. If I did not take the drugs, I would be able to function perhaps one day in four. The physiological error called migraine is, in brief, central to the given of my life. When I was 15, 16, even 25, I used to think that I could rid myself of this error by simply denying it, character over chemistry. "Do you have headaches *sometimes? frequently? never?*" the application forms would demand. "Check one." Wary of the trap, wanting whatever it was that the successful circumnavigation of that particular form could bring (a job, a scholarship, the respect of mankind and the grace of God), I would check one. *"Sometimes,"* I would lie. That in fact I spent one or two days a week almost unconscious with pain seemed a shameful secret, evidence not merely of some chemical inferiority but of all my bad attitudes, unpleasant tempers, wrongthink.

For I had no brain tumor, no eyestrain, no high blood pressure, nothing wrong with me at all: I simply had migraine headaches, and migraine headaches were, as everyone who did not have them knew, imaginary. I fought migraine then, ignored the warnings it sent, went to school and later to work in spite of it, sat through lectures in Middle English and presentations to advertisers with involuntary tears running down

1

2

the right side of my face, threw up in washrooms, stumbled home by instinct, emptied ice trays onto my bed and tried to freeze the pain in my right temple, wished only for a neurosurgeon who would do a lobotomy on house call, and cursed my imagination.

3   It was a long time before I began thinking mechanistically enough to accept migraine for what it was: something with which I would be living, the way some people live with diabetes. Migraine is something more than the fancy of a neurotic imagination. It is an essentially hereditary complex of symptoms, the most frequently noted but by no means the most unpleasant of which is a vascular headache of blinding severity, suffered by a surprising number of women, a fair number of men (Thomas Jefferson had migraine, and so did Ulysses S. Grant, the day he accepted Lee's surrender), and by some unfortunate children as young as two years old. (I had my first when I was eight. It came on during a fire drill at the Columbia School in Colorado Springs, Colorado. I was taken first home and then to the infirmary at Peterson Field, where my father was stationed. The Air Corps doctor prescribed an enema.) Almost anything can trigger a specific attack of migraine: stress, allergy, fatigue, an abrupt change in barometric pressure, a contretemps over a parking ticket. A flashing light. A fire drill. One inherits, of course, only the predisposition. In other words I spent yesterday in bed with a headache not merely because of my bad attitudes, unpleasant tempers and wrongthink, but because both my grandmothers had migraine, my father has migraine and my mother has migraine.

4   No one knows precisely what it is that is inherited. The chemistry of migraine, however, seems to have some connection with the nerve hormone named serotonin, which is naturally present in the brain. The amount of serotonin in the blood falls sharply at the onset of migraine, and one migraine drug, methysergide, or Sansert, seems to have some effect on serotonin. Methysergide is a derivative of lysergic acid (in fact Sandoz Pharmaceuticals first synthesized LSD-25 while looking for a migraine cure), and its use is hemmed about with so many contraindications and side effects that most doctors prescribe it only in the most incapacitating cases. Methysergide, when it is prescribed, is taken daily, as a preventive; another preventive which works for some people is old-fashioned ergotamine tartrate, which helps to constrict the swelling blood vessels during the "aura," the period which in most cases precedes the actual headache.

5   Once an attack is under way, however, no drug touches it. Migraine gives some people mild hallucinations, temporarily

blinds others, shows up not only as a headache but as a gas-trointestinal disturbance, a painful sensitivity to all sensory stimuli, an abrupt overpowering fatigue, a strokelike aphasia, and a crippling inability to make even the most routine con-nections. When I am in a migraine aura (for some people the aura lasts fifteen minutes, for others several hours), I will drive through red lights, lose the house keys, spill whatever I am holding, lose the ability to focus my eyes or frame coherent sentences, and generally give the appearance of being on drugs or drunk. The actual headache, when it comes, brings with it chills, sweating, nausea, a debility that seems to stretch the very limits of endurance. That no one dies of migraine seems, to someone deep into an attack, an ambiguous blessing.

My husband also has migraine, which is unfortunate for him 6 but fortunate for me: perhaps nothing so tends to prolong an attack as the accusing eye of someone who has never had a headache. "Why not take a couple of aspirin," the unafflicted will say from the doorway, or "I'd have a headache, too, spending a beautiful day like this inside with all the shades drawn." All of us who have migraine suffer not only from the attacks themselves but from this common conviction that we are perversely refusing to cure ourselves by taking a couple of aspirin, that we are making ourselves sick, that we "bring it on ourselves." And in the most immediate sense, the sense of why we have a headache this Tuesday and not last Thursday, of course we often do. There certainly is what doctors call a "migraine personality," and that personality tends to be am-bitious, inward, intolerant of error, rather rigidly organized, perfectionist. "You don't look like a migraine personality," a doctor once said to me. "Your hair's messy. But I suppose you're a compulsive housekeeper." Actually my house is kept even more negligently than my hair, but the doctor was right none-theless: perfectionism can also take the form of spending most of a week writing and rewriting and not writing a single para-graph.

But not all perfectionists have migraine, and not all mig- 7 rainous people have migraine personalities. We do not escape heredity. I have tried in most of the available ways to escape my own migrainous heredity (at one point I learned to give myself two daily injections of histamine with a hypodermic needle, even though the needle so frightened me that I had to close my eyes when I did it), but I still have migraine. And I have learned now to live with it, learned when to expect it, how to outwit it, even how to regard it, when it does come, as more friend than lodger. We have reached a certain under-standing, my migraine and I. It never comes when I am in real trouble. Tell me that my house is burned down, my husband has left me, that there is gunfighting in the streets and panic in the banks, and I will not respond by getting a headache. It comes instead when I am fighting not an open but a guerrilla war with my own life, during weeks of small household confusions, lost laundry, unhappy help, canceled appointments, on days when the telephone rings too much and I get no work done and the wind is coming up. On days like that my friend comes uninvited.

8   And once it comes, now that I am wise in its ways, I no longer fight it. I lie down and let it happen. At first every small apprehension is magnified, every anxiety a pounding terror. Then the pain comes, and I concentrate only on that. Right there is the usefulness of migraine, there in that imposed yoga, the concentration on the pain. For when the pain recedes, ten or twelve hours later, everything goes with it, all the hidden resentments, all the vain anxieties. The migraine has acted as a circuit breaker, and the fuses have emerged intact. There is a pleasant convalescent euphoria. I open the windows and feel the air, eat gratefully, sleep well. I notice the particular nature of a flower in a glass on the stair landing. I count my blessings.

Organization

1. How many methods of development does the author use in defining migraine?
2. Locate the thesis statement, if any.
3. How would you describe the author's attitude toward her migraine attacks?
4. The author mentions possible causes of migraine in paragraphs 3 and 7. Why this interruption in the discussion of causes?
5. Does the essay end too abruptly?

Paragraphs

1. With what paragraph does the body begin?
2. What function does paragraph 4 serve?
3. How many kinds of transitional devices are used between paragraphs?

Sentences

1. The sentences in this essay tend to be longer than those of the other essays in this book. Can you justify this length, or do you find it a drawback?

2. Is the parallel structure of the last three sentences of the essay effective?

Words

1. Can the presence of so many medical terms be justified?
2. To what does each of the following refer? *wrongthink* (1), *Middle English* (2).
3. Be sure you know the meaning of each of the following:

ambiguous (5)	guerrilla (7)
aphasia (5)	lobotomy (2)
aura (5)	neurosurgeon (2)
circumnavigation (1)	perversely (6)
contretemps (3)	tempers (1)
debility (5)	vascular (3)
derivative (4)	wary (1)
euphoria (8)	yoga (8)
gastrointestinal (5)	

Suggestions for Writing

1. Choose a physical or mental affliction you are familiar with either because you suffer (or have suffered) from it yourself or have observed it in others. Define it, as Didion does migraine, by a combination of the subjective (personal) and the objective (impersonal) approaches.
2. *And I have learned now to live with it, learned when to expect it, how to outwit it, even how to regard it, when it does come, as more friend than lodger. We have reached a certain understanding, my migraine and I.* (7) Follow through on the hints offered here and personify migraine—that is, present a character-sketch of it as if it were a person. Alternatively, personify the affliction referred to in question 1 above. (In either case, you may find it helpful to consult William S. Burroughs' description of Opium Jones in "Kicking Drugs: A Very Personal Story," p. 79.)

GOOD OLE BOYS

Bonnie Angelo

Bonnie Angelo: journalist. After graduating from the University of North Carolina at Greensboro with a degree in fine arts, Angelo began her journalism career with the Greensboro Journal-Sentinel. For a while she wrote for Newsday, and then she joined the staff of Time in 1966. During the administration of President Jimmy Carter she was with the Washington Bureau of Time. While in Washington, Angelo co-hosted a TV news and interview program for WTTG and served a term as president of the Women's National Press Club. From 1978–85 she was stationed in London, where she became the first woman to head one of Time's foreign bureaus. She is now the eastern bureau chief for Time. The following essay appeared in a special issue of Time devoted to Southerners in Washington during the Carter Administration.

Is Angelo's portrait of *good ole boys* objective or subjective? serious or humorous? favorable or unfavorable?

Do you suppose the *good ole boy* is a Southern phenomenon exclusively, or does he exist elsewhere?

1   It is Friday night at any of ten thousand watering holes of the small towns and crossroads hamlets of the South. The room is a cacophony of the ping-pong-dingdingding of the pinball machine, the pop-fizz of another round of Pabst, the refrain of *Red Necks, White Socks and Blue Ribbon Beer* on the juke box, the insolent roar of a souped-up engine outside and, above it all, the sound of easy laughter. The good ole boys have gathered for their fraternal ritual—the aimless diversion that they have elevated into a life-style.

2   Being a good ole boy is not a consequence of birth or breeding; it cuts across economic and social lines; it is a frame of mind based on the premise that life is nothing to get serious about. A glance at the brothers Carter tells a lot. There is some confusion about why Billy Carter seems in many respects the quintessential good ole boy, while Brother Jimmy couldn't even fit into the more polished subspecies of conscious good ole boys who abound in small-town country clubs. Billy, amiable, full of jokes, his REDNECK POWER T-shirt straining unsuccessfully to cover the paunch, swigs a beer, carefree on a Sunday morning, as Jimmy Carter, introspective, hard driving, teaches Sunday School. Jimmy sometimes speaks wistfully of Billy's good-ole-boy ease.

3   Lightheartedness permeates the good ole boy's life-style. He goes by nicknames like "Goober" or "Goat." He disdains neckties as a form of snobbery; when he dresses up, it is to wear a decorated T-shirt with newish jeans or, for state occa-

sions, a leisure suit with a colored shirt. If discussions veer beyond football toward substance, he cuts them off with funny stories.

The core of the good ole boy's world is with his buddies,   4 the comfortable, hyperhearty, all-male camaraderie, joshing and drinking and regaling one another with tales of assorted, exaggerated prowess. Women are outsiders; when social events are unavoidably mixed, the good ole boys cluster together at one end of the room, leaving wives at the other. The GOB's magic doesn't work with women; he feels insecure, threatened by them. In fact, he doesn't really like women, except in bed.

What he really loves is his automobile. He overlooks his   5 wife with her hair up in pink rollers, sagging into an upside-down question mark in her tight slacks. But he lavishes attention on his Mercury mistress, Easy Rider shocks, oversize slickers, dual exhaust. He exults in tinkering with that beautiful engine, lying cool beneath the open hood, ready to respond, quick and fiery, to his touch. The automobile is his love and his sport.

Behind his devil-may-care lightheartedness, however, runs   6 a strain of innate wisdom, an instinct about people and an unwavering loyalty that makes him the one friend you would turn to, not just because he's a drinking buddy who'll keep you laughing, but because, well, he's a good ole boy.

Organization

1. Point out an example of negative definition.
2. Is Angelo's attitude toward *good ole boys* favorable or unfavorable?
3. List the main characteristics of *good ole boys* as Angelo presents them.
4. Are the paragraphs tightly linked? If so, by what means?

Paragraphs

1. Would it be correct to say that in paragraphs 2, 3, 4, and 5 the first sentence is the topic sentence?

Sentences

1. Most of the sentences in this essay follow the standard subject-verb-object structure of the English sentence—that is, they are without inverted word order. What quality does that lend to the essay's tone?

Words

1. Point out the words in paragraph 5 that develop the idea that the *good ole boy's* automobile is his *mistress.*
2. Why does Angelo use *newish* instead of *new* to describe jeans in paragraph 3?
3. Be sure you understand the meaning of the following words:

cacophony (1)	premise (2)
camaraderie (4)	prowess (4)
disdains (3)	quintessential (2)
introspective (4)	regaling (4)
joshing (4)	snobbery (3)
paunch (2)	swigs (2)

Suggestions for Writing

1. As presented here, the *good ole boy* is a Southern American character-type. Select another regional (or national) type, authentic or mythical, and define it in ways like those Bonnie Angelo uses. (For example: the "laid-back" Californian, the "cold" New Yorker [see "New York," p. 112], the crusty New Englander, the reserved Englishman, the excitable Italian.)
2. Angelo characterizes Billy Carter as being *the quintessential good ole boy* who is *amiable, full of jokes.* Choose someone you know fairly well (a relative, a close friend, a coach, a teacher, an employer) and define that person by pointing out characteristics that make the person unique. (See Lorrie Steen's essay below.)

HEATHER

Lorrie Steen

Lorrie Steen: student. Steen is a native of Mississippi; she was born in Pascagoula, Mississippi in 1966 and graduated from Miracle Temple Christian Academy in Moss Point. To prepare for a career in the health professions, she is studying medical technology. Steen's essay is based on Suggestions for Writing 2 above.

1   Collector, animal lover and agnostic are terms that define one of my friends and her character. This friend is my roommate Heather.

2   I met Heather in September just before the Fall Quarter began. We were assigned to share a room in the Gamma Residence Hall. As we began to unpack and settle into our room,

I noticed that she had quite a collection of souvenirs from foreign countries. She told me her father had been in the Air Force, and her family had lived overseas for seven years. To remind her of the experience, she had collected small flags of the countries and a trinket that represented each.

She stuck the flags on her bulletin board and hung the trinket 3 under the flag with a ribbon. Under the blue, white, and red verticle strips of the French flag dangled a miniature Eiffel Tower. Under West Germany's black, red, and orange horizontal bars were a couple of beer coasters. Under the red, white, and red horizontal bars of Austria was a little cow bell. Her most exciting flag was from Turkey. It had a white crescent and a white star on a red background. Under it hung a small ceramic rooster. Heather told me the rooster was the symbol of justice in Turkey.

She also collects drink glasses from fast-food restaurants. 4 She has the complete set of the Smurfs, Alvin and the Chipmunks, Charlie Brown, He-Man, and Disney Pals. She has picture postcards from everywhere and some two dozen ceramic cups from historical places.

After rooming with Heather for a while, I discovered she 5 had a great love for animals. The amusing thing about her adoration for animals is that she likes the not-so-traditional kinds. Sure, she likes dogs and cats, but she also likes snakes and lizards, as well as frogs. She told me she had owned all of these animals. She told me about the luxurious glass cage that she had for her snakes. It was complete with a forest and swamp.

As we got to know one another better, I asked her about her 6 beliefs. I am a religious fundamentalist. I believe God made the world in six days and that Christ was born of the Virgin Mary. I attend church and Sunday School regularly. I was shocked when Heather told me she was an agnostic; she said she didn't deny the existence of God, but she didn't know Him. Heather said she belonged to a Methodist church and had gone to church all her life. She told me that she never really understood what church was all about and that she had never really believed in God.

When she told me about her belief, I realized that she was 7 embarrassed. She was not offensive, as most people think nonbelievers are. In fact, she was quite defensive. Because of her defensiveness I can call her a reverent agnostic. Her passiveness is why I can handle rooming with someone so opposite from my beliefs.

Heather and I are different in many ways. She has traveled 8 widely; I haven't. She collects everything; I don't collect anything. She likes reptiles; I like goldfish. I am devoutly religious; she isn't. But one thing is certain: We get along very well. Perhaps our compatibility is possible because of our differences. And another thing is certain: If she buys a pet lobster, as I think she is planning on, I will kill her!

10
PERSUASION

When you write with persuasion as your aim, you are trying to get your reader to accept your viewpoint, or at least give it serious consideration. In one sense, of course, you have been using persuasion in all the compositions you have written for this class so far. Even when your particular method of development was description or narration, you hoped, at least implicitly, that your reader would be caught up in the experience you were writing about and share your view of its significance. Certainly William Burroughs wanted you to feel, with him, something of the agony of drug-withdrawal when he wrote "Kicking Drugs: A Very Personal Story" (p. 79). And Thomas Griffith ("New York," p. 112) and Franklin Daugherty ("Life on a Parade Route," p. 108) hoped you would share the excitement they felt from participating in the life of two quite different American cities. In other words, these and all the other writers represented in this book have tried to be persuasive in what they wrote.

But persuasion can be considered an independent method of development, with its own emphases and strategies. That is the way it is considered in this section. When William Burroughs said, *I was on junk for almost fifteen years,* he made a statement of *fact* and went on to back it up with narrative details. When Thomas Griffith asked you to *Wipe the soot from your eyes and examine the city about you,* he was calling for personal *observation* and descriptive detail. But when Mike Royko suggests that consideration be given to legalizing the sale of marijuana (p. 298), and when Beverly Sills asks for increased government support for the arts (p. 310), they are making statements of opinion. These statements cannot be supported in the same way that Burroughs' and Griffith's were—that is, narratively or descriptively. They have to be supported by *reasons.* Even Burroughs would have had to take a less personal, more systematic approach than he does if his aim had been to give a straightforward, objective presentation of the perils of drug addiction. Granted, those perils do emerge powerfully from his highly personal account. But that does not alter the fact that his main objective was to tell an interesting story. Royko and Sills, as well as the other writers in this section, have something else in mind—the presentation of logical reasons in support of personal opinion. That is the special meaning persuasion has when viewed as a separate method of development.

Of the essays in this section, three first appeared as newspaper columns and one as a magazine editorial; two were speeches before being printed. In terms of their relatively short length and more or less informal approach, they resemble the compositions you have already written for this course. But they differ from your earlier essays, and from the other essays in this book, in having as their principal object the attempt to persuade the reader to adopt one side of a debatable issue. Short and informal though they are, they are nonetheless serious and challenging. The kind of arguments they employ and the way they present them suggest tactics you can use effectively, or even improve on, in the persuasive writing you will now be called upon to do.

You may not agree with the stands taken in all these essays. You may not even accept the validity of all the arguments used to support the stands you do agree with. But you'll have to admit that definite stands are taken and definite arguments used. That is only another way of saying what you learned at the outset: a good essay has a clear thesis, and gives it adequate support. That rule applies to persuasive writing as to no other kind, for the heart and soul of a persuasive essay is its thesis. Don't be wishy-washy. No topic you are likely to choose or be given in this course will be so complex that you can't say something definite about it. You may, of course, have to do a bit more thinking and planning before tackling a persuasive composition than you did prior to writing narration or description. After all, finding reasons to justify unilateral nuclear disarmament doesn't come as easily as recalling your first canoe trip or the colors in last evening's sunset. Nevertheless, you shouldn't let the relatively impersonal nature of persuasive writing intimidate you. You may not be an expert on the given topic, but then no one expects you to be—certainly not your instructor. All your instructor asks is that you take a stand, and that it be reasonable and intelligently supported—*supported*, not just advocated. One of the temptations you will face in this kind of writing, especially if the subject is one you feel strongly about, is to keep repeating your opinion in different words instead of supporting it. Resist that temptation. Remember that you are trying to persuade your readers, not just impress them with your sincerity. And to persuade them, you have to offer them sound reasons for believing as you do.

Though the essays in this section are all informal, you'll notice that the support they offer for their theses comes from the same areas that longer and more research-based projects (term papers, reports, books) draw from. No one essay uses them all, of course, but most use at least two.

WAYS TO SUPPORT YOUR ARGUMENT

1. Statistics

Because statistics are specific, they offer impressive support for a writer's generalizations. But to a discriminating reader they are convincing only when they are accurate, ample enough for the purpose, and derived from reliable authority (see Authority below). Mike Royko could have said that Americans consume "a lot" or "a substantial amount" of marijuana each year, and no one would have disagreed with him. But since he wants to argue that marijuana usage is so prevalent and ineradicable it may as well be legalized, he knows it is more convincing to use an exact figure: 14,000 tons annually. And, for further startling effect, he breaks *that* down into *about 40 joints for every man, woman and child* (pars. 1–2, p. 298). Even though Beverly Sills professes to find statistics boring and to be bad at using them, she bases much of her advocacy of increased financial support for the arts on figures comparing America's arts budget with its defense budget (par. 3, p. 310; par. 6, p. 311), and American with Austrian governmental support for the arts (par. 5, p. 311). Neither Royko nor Sills overwhelms you with numbers, but they know the value of select statistics in helping to gain acceptance for their theses, especially when those theses are as challengeable as theirs are. You, too, may find numbers useful, when applicable, in trying to win your reader over to your point of view.

2. History

Royko and Sills deal with present conditions and with what they hope for the future; history, therefore, need not enter into their discussions, and it doesn't (except for brief passing references). James Michener, however, wants to convince you of the importance of the liberal arts, *the accumulation of all that man knows about himself and the working of his society* (par. 4, p. 315). Consequently, a historical perspective and specific mention of traditional ideas and of the notable people and civilizations that gave rise to them are significant features of his essay. Similarly, Norman Cousins, though sympathetic to suicide under certain conditions, is too honest not to show that *the idea of suicide has been abhorrent throughout history* (par. 7, p. 303). Like statistics, history may not be a resource you will often have occasion to use in the kinds of writing you are concerned with in this course. But when your topic or your thesis can be clarified by putting it in the light of historical causes, precedents, influences, and the like, by all means make use of these valuable resources.

3. Experience

Statistics and history are impressive in their own ways. But personal experience contributes a different kind of persuasiveness—the kind that comes from people telling about what happened to them and the meaning it had for them. Sometimes writers use their own experience, as in the case of the childhood anecdotes with which Robert Maynard (p. 295) and Beverly Sills (p. 310) open their essays. Sometimes they draw on the experience of someone else, someone they know or have heard or read about, as when Maynard refers to the lawyer who learns best about his cases from writing briefs (par 8, p. 296). In addition, the experience can be described more or less fully (the Maynard and Sills anecdotes), or mentioned only briefly (James Michener's several references to his service on governmental advisory boards: pars. 7, 13, p. 315, 317). Often it is only implied. For example, Theodore Hesburgh's contrast between the differing reactions to athletic victories and defeats (par. 1, p. 306) is surely based in large part on his long experience as a university president, though he doesn't actually say so. And always there is the generalization based on universal human experience: *When we arm a youngster with the skill of written expression, we have given him or her a lifelong key to advancement* (par. 9, 296).

Besides adding color and life to an expository essay, real-life experience, whether your own or someone else's, can offer persuasive thesis-support as long as it is significant, relevant to your topic, and not so personal that it has only a narrow application.

Even when your composition isn't strictly autobiographical, you can still use personal references. For example, draw on your own or a friend's experience as a "Greek" in defending or attacking the fraternity-sorority system. And when maintaining the truth of the old adage that pride goes before a fall, why not make use of the lesson you learned the time you swam out too far from the beach to show off to your friends, and nearly drowned for your efforts?

4. Authority

Experience may be the best teacher, but it isn't the main teacher. Most of what we know, we know because it comes to us from some kind of authority—parents, teachers, and clergy; books, newspapers, and magazines; radio, television, and motion pictures; and many others. You know that Abraham Lincoln was president of the United States because American history books have told you so, not because you saw him take the oath of office. You know that 14,000 tons of marijuana are consumed in this country every year, not because you've weighed the bales, but because Mike Royko and the government sources he depended on quote that figure. Even your Aunt Beatrice is an authority in this sense if all you know about Kuwait is what she told you after her recent visit there.

But Aunt Beatrice could be mistaken about some of the things she said; after all, she was in Kuwait only three days and doesn't speak the language. Royko could have been misinformed or even misled about the 14,000 tons. There isn't much doubt about Lincoln's having been president—the evidence is overwhelming—but if your history book says that he wrote the Gettysburg Address on the back of an envelope on the train from Washington, it is probably wrong. The point is that since most of what you know or believe comes from outside your personal experience and cannot be verified by your personal experience, you must make sure that the authorities whose word you accept (and use in your compositions) are as reliable as you can reasonably expect and determine them to be. As far as the essays in this section are concerned, you can assume—or, to put it more precisely, you can take it on the authority of well-informed observers—that the writers are all honest men and women who believe in the accuracy of the information they convey. (That ought to save you a trip to the library to check on the truth of that 14,000-ton figure.) What's more, each of them may be viewed as something of an authority in his or her own right, at least on the subject each discusses: Robert Maynard, a nationally syndicated newspaper columnist, writing about writing; Mike Royko, another columnist, together with Norman Cousins, a magazine editor, and James Michener, a novelist and social historian, all of them addressing matters of current public interest; Theodore Hesburgh, president of Notre Dame, an athletic powerhouse, talking about the role of collegiate athletics; Beverly Sills, an opera singer turned opera company manager, discussing support for the arts. The authority of these writers shouldn't intimidate you, however; authority is no guarantee of infallibility. Disagree with them if you see fit. But, whether you agree or disagree, their authority deserves your respect and should call forth the best from you in your response.

As you've probably guessed, authority isn't so much a separate kind of support as one that cuts across the other three kinds we've been discussing. For example, statistical and historical information is reliable only when the sources for it have authority—that is, when they are known to be accurate and honest. A medical organization's statistics on the relation between smoking and lung cancer may differ significantly from the statistics on the same subject put out by the tobacco industry; you will have to determine which set of figures is the more authoritative, and why. You have to take particular care with statements based on statistics but not actually citing them, such as Michener's declaration that *enrollment for degrees in the liberal arts has been declining precipitously* (par. 5, p. 315). If the information is common knowledge, it is probably safe to use it in the informal kind of paper you write for this course. Otherwise, it is only as acceptable as the authority it comes from. Even your own experience is persuasive to your reader only because it has the authority deriving from its having happened to the person writing the essay—*you*. Even then you may have to give further evidence of your authority (as, for example, Michener does for his), depending on how challenging your thesis is. For instance, if you advocate the abolition of high school football, don't fail to mention—the introduction might be a good place—that you played on your varsity team for three years. Your readers may still not agree with your stand, but at least they can't claim that you don't know football from tick-tack-toe.

Statistics, history, experience, and authority are the four main sources of persuasive support. Below are recommendations for making the most persuasive case possible every time you write.

1. Make Sure the Issue is Clearly Stated

Your readers need to know exactly what view you're trying to persuade them to adopt. That will happen only if you know it yourself—that is, only if you have first considered the given question carefully and come to a definite conclusion about it. That conclusion will be your thesis, usually stated in the form of a strategically placed thesis sentence, and always supported by reasoning drawn from one or more of the four sources mentioned above.

2. Arrange Your Arguments in the Order of Increasing Importance

This doesn't mean that your initial points will be *un*important; it means only that the later ones will be *more* important, and the last one will be the *most* important of all.

3. Anticipate Opposing Arguments

One way to strengthen your case is to introduce objections that could be offered against it, and then answer them. This gives your readers an impression of fairmindedness that makes them receptive not only to the answers you offer, but also to all your other arguments. Notice, for example, how deftly Mike Royko introduces implied objections to the legalization of marijuana (pars. 8–11, pp. 299–300), and how openly Norman Cousins faces traditional arguments against suicide (pars. 6–7, p. 303). Make sure, though, that your answers, like theirs, meet the objections head-on. If you can come up with only weak responses to serious challenges, you had better stop to consider whether you are arguing on the right side of the issue.

4. Do Justice to Opposing Arguments

Your reader won't be impressed with your confronting objections if you introduce them in watered-down form. Royko and Cousins may have to simplify opposing arguments in view of space limitations, but that doesn't mean they distort or falsify them. Any advantage you gain by answering deliberately weakened objections is only temporary; the thoughtful reader soon sees through your attempted deception.

5. Don't be Negative in Tone

You don't gain anything by attacking your opposition. To be convincing, you have to offer positive reasons in support of your position. Readers want to know why they *should* do or believe something, not why they *shouldn't* do or believe something else.

6. Find Areas of Agreement Between You and Your Reader

The more open to challenge your ideas are, the more important it is to first establish some common ground between you and your readers. By opening with statistics on yearly marijuana consumption, Mike Royko at least wins your appreciation of the magnitude of the problem before introducing his arguable thesis. Beverly Sills calls attention to the importance of the arts for everyone— including, presumably, her readers—before getting down to suggesting that the arts be more generously subsidized by the government. Agreement on preliminary matters can often forestall or lessen disagreement on subsequent matters.

7. Use All Appropriate Methods of Development

Though the arrangement of chapters in Part Two may make it seem that persuasion is only one among several different methods of development, it actually draws on all the other methods. Robert Maynard, for instance, makes use of example (the story of the African child), comparison and contrast (those who write well versus those who can't), and cause and effect (inability to write well and its consequences). James Michener defines *liberal arts* before discussing the immediate drawbacks (bad effects) and the long-range advantages (good effects) of a liberal arts education. Mike Royko's breakdown of 14,000 tons to 448 million ounces to ten billion "joints" is a paragraph of analysis. The full complement of methods is at your disposal in any piece of persuasive writing. Make good use of them.

FALLACIES IN LOGIC

Because the art of persuading is basically the art of logical argument, you not only have to observe the foregoing guidelines, but you also have to be careful not to commit any errors in reasoning. Here are the principal ones to watch out for:

1. The *Post Hoc, Ergo Propter Hoc* Fallacy

This Latin phrase is literally translated, "After this, therefore because of this." In formal logic it refers to the error of supposing that, because B occurs later than A, A must therefore be the cause of B. See the example in 4c, p. 218, under Cause and Effect.

2. The *Non Sequitur* ("It Doesn't Follow")

This fallacy occurs when a conclusion is drawn from a premise or series of premises that doesn't logically yield that conclusion: "If nineteen-year-olds can die for their country, they should be allowed to purchase alcoholic beverages." It doesn't logically follow that because a nineteen-year-old is subject to military service, he is thereby entitled to buy intoxicating drink.

3. *Petitio Principii* ("Begging the Question")

A writer who assumes the truth of what actually needs to be proved is guilty of *begging the question:* "By condoning murder in its decisions on capital punishment and abortion, the Supreme Court has contributed to the moral decay of this country." No doubt officially approved murder *would* help weaken a nation morally. But that capital punishment and abortion are murder is something that needs to be demonstrated and not, as here, simply assumed. Only then can the statement be fully persuasive.

4. Hasty Generalization

The error here, as the name indicates, is a conclusion (generalization) based on too few or weak examples: "Don't take Dr. Benson; he's a hard marker." This kind of advice has scared many a student away from an excellent teacher. If a large number of students over a significant period of time agree that Dr. Benson gives few high grades, there may be some truth to the report. (Whether that's a good reason for not enrolling in his classes is another matter.) But often the report is based on insufficient evidence (the speaker and several other students who got low grades) or weak evidence (the students may have received low grades because of poor study habits).

Hasty generalization is an error in *inductive reasoning.* Inductive reasoning begins with specific examples and works toward a general conclusion. For instance, you have never seen or heard of a bird that didn't have wings, nor has anyone else you've consulted. You therefore think it safe to conclude that "all birds have wings." But you haven't seen or had a report on every bird now existing, much less every bird that has ever existed. In other words, you arrive at your conclusion on the basis of an admittedly incomplete sample, but one that you feel is large enough to yield a valid and defensible conclusion. Although many serviceable conclusions are arrived at in this way, the *inductive leap* (as it is called) from sample to conclusion *could* overlook those exceptions that would make your conclusion invalid—in other words, those rare and exotic birds (if there are such) that have no wings. That is why the inductive process—attributing to *all* the members of a class what is true of *some* or *many* members of the class—must be based on sufficient evidence to sustain the conclusion. Otherwise, hasty generalization results. Just because all opera singers you have ever seen in person or in photographs were overweight, you can't logically claim that "all opera singers are fat." Further research would prove that many are not.

5. *Ad Hominem* ("Toward the Person")

An *ad hominem* argument is one that is directed against the person defending a certain view rather than at the view he is defending. "How can candidate Jones work for the interests of the entire student body when he's a strong fraternity man?" The fact that Jones is a fraternity member has nothing to do with his arguments in support of his candidacy for president of the Student Government Association. His opponents should attack the arguments, not him.

6. The Either-Or Fallacy

Presenting only two alternatives when actually three or more exist makes the writer guilty of the *either-or* fallacy. For example, if Mike Royko had said that marijuana could be dealt with in only two ways—either by banning it altogether or by allowing unrestricted sale of it—he would have committed this error. As it is, he discusses a third possibility—selling marijuana in a regulated and heavily taxed way.

7. Argument by Analogy

In the Comparison and Contrast Section (pp. 164–65), you learned the usefulness of analogies for clarifying issues. (Recall James Thurber's essay comparing the courtship practices of human beings and of certain animals, and Liane Ellison Norman's essay contrasting students and squirrels.) But that's all that analogies can do—*clarify*. They can't *prove* anything because the two items of an analogy, though in some ways similar, are essentially different—and therefore what's said about one item can't be said about the other in the same way or to the same degree. A busy metropolitan city may bear superficial resemblance to a beehive, but what's true of bees isn't equally true of human beings. An analogy illustrates A by comparing it to B, but it doesn't prove anything about either.

8. Faulty Syllogistic Reasoning

A syllogism is the principal form of *deductive reasoning*. Deductive reasoning begins with a general statement ("All men are mortal"), rather than with specific examples ("John is mortal," "Ruth is mortal," "George is mortal," and so forth), as is the case with inductive reasoning. A syllogism takes the general statement (called the *major premise*), adds a more specific statement (the *minor premise*) to it, and comes up with a still more specific conclusion. In other words, it is a brief, three-step argument:

> All men are mortal.
> John is a man.
> Therefore, John is mortal.

Only in logic textbooks will you ordinarily find syllogisms set down as precisely as in the above example. In persuasive (and most other) writing, they usually appear informally stated and missing one or both premises: "You know you're not going to live forever, John." (Such shortened syllogisms are called *enthymemes*.) For that reason, familiarity with the formal syllogism and with the common mistakes in syllogistic reasoning will help you to spot logical errors when they occur in other people's writing and to avoid them in your own.

If both premises of a syllogism are true, and if the transition from the first to the second is logically made, then the conclusion automatically follows; there is no need for a "leap," as in inductive reasoning. But few basic premises are universally regarded as true because they are themselves the products of an inductive reasoning process in which a "leap" was required. For example, the syllogism

> All athletes are stupid.
> Bubba is an athlete.
> Therefore, Bubba is stupid.

would be a sound argument, with a valid conclusion, if the major premise were true. But it isn't; it's a very hasty generalization based on a wildly uncalled-for inductive leap.

Here are other errors that make syllogisms—whether formally or informally presented—unsound:

a. Changing the Meaning of a Term   Although the same key term (called the *middle term*) should appear in the two premises, any change in its meaning from the first to the second makes the conclusion invalid.

> All sisters are unmarried.
> My wife is a sister.
> Therefore, my wife is unmarried.

Here the term *sister* shifts in meaning from "nun" in the first premise to "a female related to another person having the same parents" in the second, thus rendering the conclusion meaningless.

b. Placing the Middle Term in an Improper Position   The middle term must be "distributed" —that is, it must appear in the first part of the major premise and the second part of the minor premise. An "undistributed middle" results in an invalid conclusion:

> All parrots are birds.
> Polly is a bird.
> Therefore, Polly is a parrot.

Polly may, in fact, be a parrot, but this syllogism doesn't prove it.

c. Negative Premises   If the major and the minor premises are both negative, they cannot yield a logical conclusion:

No football team is undefeated.
The Dirty Dozen is not a football team.
Therefore . . . ? ? ?

LEARNING TO WRITE IS IMPORTANT

Robert C. Maynard

Robert C. Maynard: journalist, editor, publisher. Maynard was born in Brooklyn, New York in 1937. His journalistic career began with the York Gazette and Daily. In 1967 he joined the staff of the Washington Post. According to Ebony Success Library, while at the Washington Post he held "the most prestigious position . . . [of] any black man on a daily newspaper in the United States." In 1977 he founded the Institute for Journalism Education, to advance minorities in journalism. At present Maynard is the editor, publisher, and president of the Oakland Tribune in California. The following syndicated column was written in 1985.

How many different reasons does Maynard suggest for the importance of learning to write well?

Is he persuasive? Why or why not?

The fable goes this way: An African child came home from 1
school one day and told his mother of a story his teacher had read to him. It was about a man in the jungle named Tarzan and he was mightier than even the lion, whom the child had always thought to be the king of the jungle. When his mother heard the child's expressions of dismay, she replied: "Always will it be that way, my son, until lions learn to write."

My parents, often using that fable for fuel, drove us to write 2
from our earliest days. They held up examples of good writing for our attention even before we could read or write. Mostly, they used the Bible, but often they turned to Shakespeare and the classics.

In 1983, the Carnegie Commission study of secondary edu- 3
cation urged the schools of the nation to place greater emphasis on writing in their curricula. The commission said the inability to write effectively is proving to be a material deficit in the lives of American students.

It is not just students. All too many adults in responsible 4
jobs achieved those jobs without learning how to write a clear and concise exposition of a problem or a position. More than

that, I have known people who claimed writing made them ill. One colleague in school many years ago doubled over with cramps the closer a writing deadline approached. Another professional person I know was so terrified of ever having to write anything strangers might read that he literally shook and perspired when an unavoidable writing obligation descended upon him.

5 Those may be extreme cases, but there are too many of those and the more common case of the citizen who simply never learned even a minimal amount about putting thoughts on paper. Such people are, in my opinion, deprived. They are deprived because written expression can help advance almost any goal, particularly career goals. Regardless of their discipline, people who can sell their ideas on paper are ahead of those who can only describe their intentions orally. There is nothing wrong with oral skill, but being able to back it up on paper can make all the difference.

6 My dad had a wonderful way of making that point. He used to play a game in which he would ask one of us how many followers Jesus had. We would say we didn't know, but it was in the thousands. Then he would ask us how many we could name. When we named the apostles, he would always remind us that we remembered best those who had written down their accounts of what they had witnessed.

7 "Those were not necessarily the best servants. They were just the best writers who were servants," he would say. Or, to put it another way, they were lions who had learned to write.

8 It worries me that writing is in danger of becoming a lost art in our society. Hardly anyone writes social letters anymore. Ma Bell and her various successors make it all too easy to reach out and touch someone electronically. Yet, it is often when we write about something that we understand it best. I found that to be true as a reporter, and I know others who have found it to be true in other disciplines. One day, I was speaking with a lawyer who is very good at what he does. He told me he never fully understands the case he is trying until he has written about it. Once he has written a brief, he knows his case.

9 That is why it would be good if we accepted the advice of the Carnegie Commission and placed more emphasis in our schools on writing as a skill every bit as important as learning to compute or read. When we arm a youngster with the skill of written expression, we have given him or her a lifelong key to advancement. Rather than teaching writing as something

painful and burdensome, we should teach writing as a natural activity that anyone can learn to do to some degree.

It will be interesting to see if such developments as the Car- 10 negie report have any effect on the problem.

After all, think of how our views of the jungle would be 11 enhanced if, as the African mother said in the fable, the lions had learned to write. Besides, if you don't double up in pain before you begin, writing is actually fun.

Organization

1. Identify the authorities the author relies on in developing his thesis. Besides authority, what other sources of support mentioned on pp. 285–88 does he draw on?
2. Why is anticipating opposing arguments not a strategy that the author employs in this essay?

Paragraphs

1. What is the point of mentioning the people made ill by the thought of writing (4)?
2. Paragraph 8 illustrates what method of development used extensively in this essay?

Sentences

1. What is the allusion in the third sentence of paragraph 8?

Words

1. Instead of using the word *orally* in the next to last sentence of paragraph 5, could the writer have used "verbally"? Why or why not?
2. Is *literally* in *literally shook and perspired* (4) correctly used?
3. To what do the following refer? *Tarzan* (1), *Carnegie Commission* (3, 9), *Ma Bell* (8).
4. Be sure you know the meaning of the following:

   brief [noun] (8)
   curricula (3)
   disciplines (8)
   enhanced (11)

Suggestions for Writing

1. . . . *Written expression can help advance almost any goal, particularly career goals* (5). Write an essay in which you try to persuade your reader (or you yourself if necessary) of the importance of writing in advancing the career goal you have chosen. Feel free to interpret *career goal* as either your future professional career or your present collegiate career.

2. Defend or take issue with the author's final assertion: *writing is actually fun* (11). You may draw on the authority of others (fellow students or professional writers) if you wish, but rely mainly on your own experience. Address your essay to the employees of a fast-food restaurant.

LEGAL MARIJUANA—
A POT OF GOLD

Mike Royko

Mike Royko: journalist, author. In an article that appeared in Esquire, *Royko was described as "the man who owns Chicago," the city where he was born in 1933.* Contemporary Authors *says, "Royko grew up in a Polish neighborhood on the city's northwest side, the son of two saloon keepers. Raised on beer and barroom brawls, Royko was a tough street kid who quit school at the age of sixteen." In the early 1950's he attended, briefly, Wright Junior College, and then began his journalistic career with the Chicago City News Bureau. In 1959 he began work with the* Chicago Daily News *and rose from a reporter to an associate editor by 1978. He worked for a while at the* Chicago Sun Times, *but now writes for the* Chicago Tribune. *His books include* I May Be Wrong, But I Doubt It, *and* Boss: Richard J. Daley of Chicago. *The following syndicated column was written in 1985.*

What are Royko's principal arguments for legalizing marijuana?

Are they reasonable arguments, reasonably presented, or are they emotional in nature?

1 I've been playing around with a fascinating number—14,000 tons. That's the amount of marijuana—foreign and domestic—that's said to be consumed each year in this country. Actually, the federal narcs think it might be even higher. A recent raid in northern Mexico turned up 10,000 tons. The narcs were stunned because they thought that Mexico produced only one fourth that amount. But for this column's purpose, let's stay with the 14,000-ton figure.

2 If you break that down, it comes to 448 million ounces. I'm told that one ounce of marijuana will produce between 20 to

40 joints, depending on whether you are frugal and make skinny ones, or are self-indulgent and make them stogie-sized. There's also a waste factor—seeds, twigs, bugs, spillage and so on. So let's be conservative and figure 20 joints an ounce. That's just under 10 billion joints a year. If you divide that by the population of this country, it comes to about 40 joints for every man, woman and child.

Now, we can assume that millions of little toddlers and preschoolers don't smoke it. We can even assume that most kids in elementary school don't, since most of them don't have the purchase price. And we can assume that millions of old codgers in nursing homes or two-room flats don't use it. 3

So who's doing all this grass-smoking? Recent studies say that teen-agers are smoking less and less pot. So the biggest users are the age groups that range from young adults to middle-agers. And they're a huge part of the population. If they aren't the majority, they're not far from it. That tells us something obvious: That there's a great demand in this country for marijuana. 4

As any Harvard economist—or dry goods salesman—will tell you, when there's a great demand for something that isn't hard to supply, somebody is going to supply it. Obviously, it's happening. Whether you live in a big city, a suburb, or a small town, you can easily buy marijuana. If you aren't sure where to get it, just ask the nearest teen-ager. 5

So I have a simple question: If so many Americans want and use marijuana, if they are already getting it so easily, if they insist on spending billions of dollars a year on it, why are we screaming at Mexico, why are hordes of narcotics agents floundering around in futile attempts to find it, why are the police and courts wasting time and money trying to put dealers in jail for selling it? 6

It ought to be obvious by now that the politicians in Washington can talk all they want about stamping it out, but they can't do it. It has become one of this country's biggest cash crops. It's a big part of Mexico's economy. So maybe it's time to give up trying to stamp it out, and consider legalizing it, thereby controlling it. 7

It would allow the narcs to stop wasting their time trying to stop it, which they can't do, and would let them concentrate on chasing far more harmful drugs, such as heroin and cocaine. And, best of all, it could be taxed. A $10- or $20-an-ounce federal tax would bring in more than $5 billion or $10 billion a year. And every local government could slap on a little tax of its own. 8

Who would sell it? Private enterprise, I suppose. The day it 9 became legal, we'd see nationwide pot franchises springing up. And we could stop feuding with Mexico, since our own needy farmers could grow enough to meet all local demands. Why, they'd probably wind up dealing in marijuana futures on the Board of Trade.

The sale could be regulated just as we now regulate the sale   10
of booze. TV and radio advertising of pot would be banned, just as we've banned the advertising for liquor and cigarettes. Minimum age limits would be set. Sure, it would be impossible to enforce the laws 100 percent. But the fact that teenagers find ways to buy beer doesn't prevent the rest of us from drinking it.

And, yes, I'm aware that marijuana isn't good for us, al-   11
though scientists still aren't sure what the effects really are. However, the scientists do know a lot more about the effects of even the finest scotches, the most elegant gins, the most regal cognacs. Even if you pay $5 a shot and tip the bartender a deuce, they will still quiver your liver and strain your brain.

So it might be time for us to stop pretending that we can   12
do something to stop marijuana from being sold and consumed. In a country where the citizens—and even illegal aliens—have unlimited freedom of movement, and where there is almost no control of its own borders, we can't do it. Then why not try to at least regulate it and let our own farmers and businessmen make a buck.

Are we ready for a McJoint?   13

Organization

1. The thesis is the last sentence of paragraph 7. Why is it so long-delayed in appearing? Does its use of *maybe* violate what this book says (p. 20) about the need for a thesis to be a strong and definite assertion?
2. What kind of support does the author draw on?
3. Does the author arrange his arguments in the order of increasing importance?
4. What evidence is there that the author is implicitly answering arguments against his thesis in paragraphs 8–11?

Paragraphs

1. How reliable are the sources for the figures cited in paragraphs 1, 2, and 4?
2. Is the comparison between marijuana and liquor *(booze)* in paragraph 11 valid?
3. Is there a logical fallacy in paragraph 11?

Sentences

1. What is the allusion in the last sentence of the essay?
2. Comment on *quiver your liver and strain your brain* (last sentence of paragraph 11).
3. Can the omission of a question mark at the end of the last sentence of paragraph 12 be justified?
4. Is the second sentence of paragraph 9 a fragment?

Words

1. This essay originated as a newspaper column. Does that fact have a bearing on the level of language used?
2. Look up *pun* in your dictionary or in a handbook of literary terms. Is there a pun in the title of the essay?
3. To what does the *Board of Trade* (9) refer?
4. Be sure you know the meaning of the following:

codgers (3)	frugal (2)
deuce (11)	futures (9)
dry goods (5)	joints (2)
franchises (9)	stogie-sized (2)

Suggestions for Writing

1. Defend the legalization of marijuana usage by citing arguments other than the ones Royko uses, or by expanding on (*not* repeating) one or more of the arguments he does use.
2. Argue against the legalization of marijuana usage by responding to the arguments Royko cites in favor of it.

\

THE RIGHT TO DIE

Norman Cousins

Norman Cousins: journalist, teacher, editor, author. Cousins was born in Union Hill, New Jersey in 1912. After attending Columbia University, he began his career as a journalist and author. He is probably best known as the editor of Saturday Review, *a position he held for thirty-eight years. Among his books are* The Last Defense in a Nuclear Age, The Celebration of Life, *and* The Quest for Immortality. *In* Anatomy of an Illness as Perceived by the Patient: Reflections on Healing and Regeneration *Cousins recounted how humor helped him cope with a nearly fatal illness. The following essay first appeared in* Saturday Review *in 1975.*

The more controversial the thesis, the stronger the supporting arguments have to be. How strong are the arguments supporting the highly controversial thesis offered here?

Does Cousins discuss suicide as a right open to use always or only under certain conditions?

1   The world of religion and philosophy was shocked recently when Henry P. Van Dusen and his wife ended their lives by their own hands. Dr. Van Dusen had been president of Union Theological Seminary; for more than a quarter-century he had been one of the luminous names in Protestant theology. He enjoyed world status as a spiritual leader. News of the self-inflicted death of the Van Dusens, therefore, was profoundly disturbing to all those who attach a moral stigma to suicide and regard it as a violation of God's laws.

2   Dr. Van Dusen had anticipated this reaction. He and his wife left behind a letter that may have historic significance. It was very brief, but the essential point it made is now being widely discussed by theologians and could represent the beginning of a reconsideration of traditional religious attitudes toward self-inflicted death. The letter raised a moral issue: does an individual have the obligation to go on living even when the beauty and meaning and power of life are gone?

3   Henry and Elizabeth Van Dusen had lived full lives. In recent years, they had become increasingly ill, requiring almost continual medical care. Their infirmities were worsening, and they realized they would soon become completely dependent for even the most elementary needs and functions. Under these circumstances, little dignity would have been left in life. They didn't like the idea of taking up space in a world with too many mouths and too little food. They believed it was a misuse of medical science to keep them technically alive.

4   They therefore believed they had the right to decide when

to die. In making that decision, they weren't turning against life as the highest value; what they were turning against was the notion that there were no circumstances under which life should be discontinued.

An important aspect of human uniqueness is the power of 5 free will. In his books and lectures, Dr. Van Dusen frequently spoke about the exercise of this uniqueness. The fact that he used his free will to prevent life from becoming a caricature of itself was completely in character. In their letter, the Van Dusens sought to convince family and friends that they were not acting solely out of despair or pain.

The use of free will to put an end to one's life finds no 6 sanction in the theology to which Pitney Van Dusen was committed. Suicide symbolizes discontinuity; religion symbolizes continuity, represented at its quintessence by the concept of the immortal soul. Human logic finds it almost impossible to come to terms with the concept of nonexistence. In religion, the human mind finds a larger dimension and is relieved of the ordeal of a confrontation with non-existence.

Even without respect to religion, the idea of suicide has been 7 abhorrent throughout history. Some societies have imposed severe penalties on the families of suicides in the hope that the individual who sees no reason to continue his existence may be deterred by the stigma his self-destruction would inflict on loved ones. Other societies have enacted laws prohibiting suicide on the grounds that it is murder. The enforcement of such laws, of course, has been an exercise in futility.

Customs and attitudes, like individuals themselves, are 8 largely shaped by the surrounding environment. In today's world, life can be prolonged by science far beyond meaning or sensibility. Under these circumstances, individuals who feel they have nothing more to give to life, or to receive from it, need not be applauded, but they can be spared our condemnation.

The general reaction to suicide is bound to change as people 9 come to understand that it may be a denial, not an assertion, of moral or religious ethics to allow life to be extended without regard to decency or pride. What moral or religious purpose is celebrated by the annihilation of the human spirit in the triumphant act of keeping the body alive? Why are so many people more readily appalled by an unnatural form of dying than by an unnatural form of living?

"Nowadays," the Van Dusens wrote in their last letter, "it 10 is difficult to die. We feel that this way we are taking will become more usual and acceptable as the years pass.

"Of course, the thought of our children and our grandchil- 11
dren makes us sad, but we still feel that this is the best way
and the right way to go. We are both increasingly weak and
unwell and who would want to die in a nursing home?

"We are not afraid to die. . . ." 12

Pitney Van Dusen was admired and respected in life. He 13
can be admired and respected in death. "Suicide," said Goethe,
"is an incident in human life which, however much disputed
and discussed, demands the sympathy of every man, and in
every age must be dealt with anew."

Death is not the greatest loss in life. The greatest loss is 14
what dies inside us while we live. The unbearable tragedy is
to live without dignity or sensitivity.

Organization

1. Is the thesis implicit or explicit? If implicit, state it in your
    own words. If explicit, which is the thesis sentence?
2. How would you describe the way in which Cousins advances
    the idea of justifiable suicide—defiantly? firmly? hesitantly?
    cautiously? Compare his approach with that of Royko in an-
    other essay on a controversial topic, "Legal Marijuana—A Pot
    of Gold" (p. 298). Could there be a difference between the way
    these two authors express themselves about their topics and
    the way they really feel?
3. Why is the material on the Van Dusens' suicide split up into
    two sections, paragraphs 1–5 and paragraphs 10–13?

Paragraphs

1. Is Cousins fairminded in presenting opposing arguments (in
    paragraphs 6 and 7)? How effectively does he answer them?
2. Few transitional words or phrases between paragraphs occur
    in this essay. How is smooth transition attained—or is it
    lacking?

Sentences

1. The sentences in paragraph 14 are the shortest consecutive
    sentences in the essay. Why?
2. *"Nowadays," the Van Dusens wrote in their last letter, "it is
    difficult to die."* (10) What did the Van Dusens mean?

Words

1. Referring particularly to paragraphs 9 and 14, state in your own words the definition of *life* that Cousins seems to have in mind throughout the essay.
2. In paragraphs 1 and 2, Cousins uses the term *self-inflicted death;* elsewhere he calls it *suicide.* Do you suppose his avoidance of "suicide" in the first two paragraphs was deliberate?
3. Who was *Goethe* (13)?
4. Be sure you know the meaning of each of the following:

abhorrent (7)	luminous (1)
annihilation (9)	quintessence (6)
appalled (9)	sanction (6)
caricature (5)	sensibility (8)
confrontation (6)	stigma (1)
ethics (9)	theologians (2)

Suggestions for Writing

1. ". . . *In every age* [suicide] *must be dealt with anew"* (Goethe, 13). Keeping in mind that suicide is the second leading cause of death among teenagers and young adults today, write an essay on suicide in which you either support Cousins' stand by amplifying his arguments or introducing new ones, or attack his stand by answering his arguments or introducing new ones.
2. Could the same arguments used here to suggest the justifiability of suicide be used to support euthanasia ("mercy killing")? Explain why or why not. Or: defend or oppose euthanasia.
3. Cousins asserts that *religion symbolizes continuity.* Can you think of some aspect of religious continuity that needs to be discontinued (the celibacy of Roman Catholic priests or nuns, the taking of collections at services of worship, having services of worship at 11:00 a.m. on Sundays, the tradition of Sunday school)? Present your objections in a persuasive essay. (See Janet Mixon's essay on p. 319.)

KEEP SPORTS' PRIORITIES IN ORDER

Theodore M. Hesburgh

Theodore M. Hesburgh: Roman Catholic priest, teacher, author, university administrator. Hesburgh was born in Syracuse, New York in 1917. He attended Catholic University of America, Holy Cross College, and Gregorian University. He was ordained a Roman Catholic priest in 1943 and began his teaching career two years later at the University of Notre Dame. He assumed the presidency of Notre Dame in 1952. Among his books are God and the World of Man *and a series of volumes entitled* Thoughts for Our Times. *He is a Fellow of the Academy of Arts and Sciences. The following was an address he delivered in 1981.*

According to Hesburgh, what benefits, if any, do athletics confer on those who participate in them?

How prominent a role should athletics play in university life?

What is the relation between a university president and student athletes? the athletic staff? the fans?

1   In times of plentiful victories, of which we have had many, the task of the university speaker is to be a gracious winner. In times of adversity and plentiful defeats, we speak of building character and making friends. It is also a time to be philosophical and to comment broadly on the state of intercollegiate athletics. That I shall do tonight.

2   Anyone who is conscious of the passing scene knows that all is not well with intercollegiate athletics today—and I speak mainly of football and basketball. It is difficult to keep up with the schools that are on disciplinary probation. Allegations of cheating, rules violations, of improper recruitment, academic improprieties in admissions and in receiving credit without attending class, all of these are fairly widespread. It is said that coaches are under such pressure to win they will do anything that promotes winning. Why the pressure to win at all costs? Again, it is blamed on alumni pressure, the need to gain lucrative contracts for television and bowl games. It is insecure coaches who cut corners.

3   How does a university president cope with this? Rather directly, I think. First, a president must see and place intercollegiate athletics in perspective. He must not yell at the players, as a harried coach was said to have done, "What do you think it is, a game?" It is a game, no more, no less.

4   Intercollegiate athletics are important in the life of an institution, but not all important. The players are coached and conditioned, the games are played, won or lost, as a manifes-

tation of the school's spirit and tradition. At Notre Dame, it is a fine tradition and the spirit unmatched in the land. But how does or should the president view the players and the coaches?

The players are first and foremost students. In this, they should be regarded and treated as all students are. They should be admitted because they are academically qualified and judged to be capable of profiting from the university's academic program. They should take a normal course of studies, not a series of gut courses that keep them eligible without the difficulty of becoming educated. Most, if not all of them, should graduate in four years. They should live as the other students do, should not be segregated in some jock palace. They should be expected to conduct themselves as other students do: the same rules, the same rewards and punishments. There should only be one inducement for them to come: the golden opportunity to get a fine education.

A decade after graduation, almost everyone will have forgotten when and where and what they played. But every time they speak, everyone will know whether or not they are educated. No one can take that from them and nothing they have will be more valuable—for all the rest of their lives. Players themselves will, of course, always remember the great seasons, the great games, the moments of heroic endeavor, the thrill of victory and the empty feeling that always follows defeat.

All of this is a learning experience, too, a true education that prepares students for the life yet to be lived, a life that will have its ups and downs, its high and low moments of victory and defeat. Players will learn early that victory is the fruit of monumental effort, discipline, team work unselfishly undertaken, overcoming discouragement, gaining self-confidence and team confidence, too. Leadership is a great human asset. Sports give it ample room in which to be born and to flourish. Those who learn this lesson are greatly blessed for all their lives.

A president should believe in this healthy and wholesome and educational regimen for student athletes. He cannot personally supervise it, but he does have the serious obligation to appoint athletic directors and coaches who concur with this view of intercollegiate athletics and who promote it, in season and out, vigorously and honestly, come what may.

This is not a one-way street. Athletic directors and coaches who support an honest program should have equal support from the president. Their position and tenure should not be at the mercy of last week's score or the vagaries of a single season. They should have reasonable security in their jobs and the full confidence and support of the administration. Alumni should not badger them, nor should vociferous fans. Of course, they will suffer a certain amount of static from those who judge anything less than total victory a dismal failure. But the pressure should not come from the administration. They have a difficult enough task to do, and if they are doing it with honesty, integrity and competence, they should never have to be worried about being blind-sided by those who appointed them.

Generally speaking, I think a program like Notre Dame's 10 should, on balance and over time, win more games than it loses. There will be occasional great years, even national championships; and occasional bad years, too. But I do believe that it is quite possible to have a completely honest and generally successful program. We have a long history of doing just that. And the record of thousands of successful former student-athletes who continue to compete with honor in the more important careers they have chosen is a great source of pride and the best evidence that intercollegiate athletics and good education are compatible.

I would hope that in the years ahead, Notre Dame might, 11 by example and leadership, help to rid intercollegiate athletics of the plague that presently blights it. We should compete with schools that share this ideal and not with those who do not. We and our competitors should make common cause for all that is good and educational in the intercollegiate athletic program. To this we pledge ourselves and in this total perspective we are happy to celebrate tonight.

Organization

1. Does this essay rely primarily on authority or on experience for its support? Whose authority or experience?
2. How many paragraphs does the introduction comprise?

Paragraphs

1. Is paragraph 10 the first paragraph of the conclusion or the last paragraph of the body?
2. How many paragraphs voice support of collegiate athletics? Does this support weaken or strengthen Hesburgh's overall argument?

Sentences

1. Is the second sentence of paragraph 3 a fragment?
2. What effect does the inverted word order of the last sentence of paragraph 1 create?

Words

1. Considering the author of this essay and the circumstances of its original appearance (see headnote), judge the appropriateness of the diction and sentence structure.
2. Comment on the use of *honest* in the second sentence of paragraph 9.
3. Be sure you know the meaning of each of the following:

adversity (1)	inducement (5)
allegations (2)	harried (3)
ample (7)	lucrative (2)
badger (9)	perspective (3,11)
blights (11)	regimen (8)
blind-sided (9)	tenure (9)
concur (8)	vagaries (9)
improprieties (2)	vociferous (9)

Suggestions for Writing

1. Select an area of human activity other than sports (academic grades, social popularity, business success) and show how, in your view, it has been made the victim of exaggerated attention.
2. *It is said that coaches are under such pressure to win they will do anything that promotes winning* (2). The late Vince Lombardi was a coach who believed in winning. "Winning isn't everything," he said, "it's the only thing." On the other hand, a familiar saying has it that "It's not whether you win or lose, it's how you play the game that counts." Which of these views—the "win-at-all-costs" philosophy or the "it's-how-you-play-the-game" philosophy—do you think is the proper motivating spirit for collegiate athletics?

A SOLUTION TO THE MONEY CRISIS
IN THE ARTS

Beverly Sills

Beverly Sills: opera singer, manager. Sills was born in Brooklyn, New York in 1929. After studying voice, piano, and stagecraft, she appeared on several radio shows and toured with the Charles Wagner Opera Company. She made her debut with the New York City Opera Company in 1955. She has sung in the major opera houses throughout the world including La Scala, the Royal Opera, the Vienna State Opera, and the Metropolitan Opera. She is now managing director of the New York City Opera. New York University, New England Conservatory, and Temple University have awarded her honorary degrees in recognition of her career. The following essay appeared in Opera News *in 1976.*

Does Sills complain about Americans' lack of interest in the arts, or about something else?

What does she suggest doing about the problem?

1   When I was a child growing up in Brooklyn many years ago, my family moved a great deal. My father worked for the Metropolitan Life Insurance Company, and depending on our financial status—well, we moved a great deal. The first cardboard carton that got packed when we were leaving the old apartment, and the first that got unpacked when we moved into the new apartment, was a box simply labeled "Mama's paintings and records." Before the furniture was in place, she was putting up her thumbtacks for her pictures and Galli-Curci was heard at the top of her lungs throughout the apartment.

2   There is a need in all of us that draws us together in one common bond—the need for a little beauty in our lives. When we want to express our deepest emotions, we talk about dancing for joy or our hearts singing. Our earliest efforts are creative ones. As babies we fingerpaint or pick up crayons and mark white paper with bright colors. My little girl took my lipstick one day and put it all over the bathroom wall, and when I asked her, "Why did you do such a naughty thing?" she said, "I wanted to make the wall beautiful." Whether we live out in the great western plain or within a taxi ride of the Metropolitan Opera, we all do have this great need in our lives, the need to surround ourselves with a little beauty.

3   The arts are flourishing in this country. There is no crisis in the arts. There is a money crisis—a big difference. In 1965 the National Endowment for the Arts functioned with a two-and-a-half-million-dollar budget. Ten years later we have a 75-million-dollar budget. It's a big leap, and sure, we can be very

proud of it. What we cannot be is complacent or satisfied, because there are a great many cities in this country that don't give one nickel toward their own cultural institutions: the arts are still considered a dispensable luxury.

I'm bad at statistics, and frankly they bore me, but I've tried to pull out a few numbers that meant something to me, going on the basis that if I could understand them anybody could. I found a survey by the National Research Center of the Arts, which is an affiliate of the Louis Harris Associates, of the famous Poll. Mr. Harris found that 64 percent, or 93 million Americans, would be willing to pay five dollars more than their federal income tax, provided the money went toward the support and maintenance of a cultural organization. I wonder, if the same 93 million Americans were asked if they would give five dollars over their federal income tax toward the support of the next war, whether we would get the same response. I rather doubt it, and that's 465 million dollars.

There's one other little statistic that fascinated me: the Vienna State Opera gets 77.5 percent of its budget from the government and has to raise only 22.5 percent from the box office, while the New York City Opera gets 17 percent from the government and has to raise 65 percent from the box office and then go out and beg for private contributions to the tune of 18 percent. I gave that statistic to my husband, and he said, "Yeah, but who ever heard of the Austrian army?"

Now, why are we so loath to change our priorities? Why are wars never underfinanced and museums are closing their doors? Why does a war never go out of business for lack of funds, but the Metropolitan Opera may have to do that in a very little while? I find that all very distressing. Just to finish off the statistics—and I hate to be hung up so much on this war business, but having lived through so many of them in my own lifetime, I really feel I'd like to move on to other things. The defense budget is 103 billion dollars; would the U.S. collapse on its backside with only 100 billion? I'd suggest a billion to help wipe out some of the killer diseases, and another billion for new medical schools—there's a terrible shortage of doctors. Then a billion for the arts. The unemployment created by the defense cut would be balanced by employment created in these other fields, so I'm bored with unemployment statistics.

Over the past two years the going has gotten rough for the arts. We've had inflation and recession, and that has cut down the big foundations' portfolios enormously. Two of the major foundations have greatly reduced their funding of the arts, and when profits decline, the big corporations get a little bit less

4

5

6

7

philanthropic. The biggest and hardest-hit are the individual donors. Universities, which are the principal sponsors of recitalists and dance companies, have their own deficits to cope with. Meanwhile, in Washington, the rate of growth in appropriations for the endowment has been cut in half. So much for our priorities. Yet everywhere I go to sing there are opera companies springing up, symphonies, dance companies, theater companies. It would seem that the creative need in the people is at last stronger than the destructive need, and perhaps we should start listening to the voices of the people.

8   Therefore, what should the role of government—federal, state and municipal—be in the support of the arts over the next ten years? And here is a set of statistics I really do not understand, which I must confess I got from Michael Straight, deputy chairman of the National Endowment of the Arts. I understand them only insofar as they seem so pathetically little as to hardly seem worth mentioning, but considering the growth we've had in these ten years, I'd like to tell you what they have been and what I feel they should be. I like my original statistic of five dollars a head. That sort of appeals to me. But since that's probably unrealistic I'd like to say that the endowment provides seven cents on the dollar in costs of a hundred major and metropolitan symphonies, and provides eight cents on the dollar in the cost of forty professional opera companies, and one enormous penny to operate 1,800 leading museums. As I say, I don't fully understand each statistic, but a penny out of a dollar seems sort of ludicrous to me. I would say maybe ten cents on the dollar would be a more respectable figure to talk about. I'm not sure what that means either, but I like ten cents better than a penny. And if I can't have five dollars a head, well, we can split it and say how about $2.50 a head in annual expenditures for every American. Then I would suggest that the states and cities and towns get off their backsides and contribute to their own cultural organizations, or they're going to be dead towns, cities and states in no time at all.

9   If we want culture, we should be willing to pay for it. Those of us who are more fortunate may have to bear the bigger burden of it, but that's as life should be. If we've been blessed with a great deal of beauty in our lives, we should be able to share it with others not so blessed.

10   Last, I'd like to talk about the American artist, because I am one, and obviously everything I see is through the eyes of the American artist. The American artist is part of our national heritage. Unlike our other natural resources, this one will continue as long as civilization exists, and it doesn't cause any air pollution. As recently as twenty-five years ago, if the

artist's name was unpronounceable he was automatically considered great. Today plenty of us with pronounceable names are doing just fine, and the snobbish stupidity that if it comes from Europe of course it's better is, thank God, a dead issue. We can, should and must take pride in what we have given birth to, raised and cultivated—the American artist. Our artists, our singers, our dancers are among the best in the world today, and they are our greatest strength. They can give us the world of peace and beauty we dream of, because art is the signature of a civilization.

Organization

1. How many different methods of development does this essay use?
2. Are there too many facts and figures for an essay that, in its original form, was delivered as a talk?
3. What bearing does the author's background have on your evaluation of what she says?

Paragraphs

1. What relation, if any, does paragraph 9 have to the rest of the essay?
2. What relation, if any, does paragraph 10 have to the rest of the essay, other than serving as the concluding paragraph?

Sentences

1. *Art is the signature of a civilization* (10). What is the literal meaning of this figurative statement?
2. Is the first sentence of paragraph 3 the topic sentence of the paragraph, or a transitional sentence bridging paragraphs 2 and 3?
3. What did Sills' husband mean when he said what she quotes him as saying in the last sentence of paragraph 5?

Words

1. To what do the following refer? *Galli-Curci* (1), *National Endowment for the Arts* (3).
2. Be sure you know the meaning of each of the following:

complacent (3)	ludicrous (8)
dispensable (3)	philanthropic (7)
loath (6)	portfolios (7)

Suggestions for Writing

1. One familiar argument against governmental support of the arts is that such support would inevitably lead to some measure of governmental *control* of artistic enterprises. Support or take issue with this argument.

2. Select an interest or an activity (sports, dramatics, student government, music, a hobby) in which you are proficient and about which you can speak with some authority. Address some issue pertaining to that interest or activity about which you feel strongly, and respond to it in a persuasive essay.

LIBERAL ARTS DECLINE IS NOT A GAIN FOR TECHNOLOGY

James Michener

James A. Michener: novelist. The actual time and place of Michener's birth are unknown because he was orphaned at birth. His passport says 1907 and New York City. He attended Swarthmore College and Colorado State College of Education. His first book of fiction, Tales of the South Pacific, *received the Pulitzer Prize in 1948. All 33 of his books were written after he was 40. He now holds a lifetime teaching position at the University of Texas. The following essay was designed as an open letter to young people contemplating college. It originally appeared in the* Atlanta Journal-Constitution *in 1984.*

What reasons does Michener advance for study of the liberal arts, even by future scientists and technologists?

Is he aware or unaware of the employment difficulties currently faced by liberal arts majors?

1   When I served on the board supervising the United States Information Agency I frequently met with young businessmen from foreign countries who were visiting the United States to learn the secrets of our successes. Invariably they wanted to visit the Massachusetts Institute of Technology to fathom our scientific mastery, to Detroit to see how we manufactured automobiles, or to Silicon Valley in California to find out how we handled the most recent computer advances.

2   I always told them: "All industrial nations have secrets like those. Which ones a nation has depends on what it's concentrated on. If you want to understand the real secret of American success go to Charlottesville, Virginia, and study what Thomas Jefferson believed. Go to Yale University and study its philosophy department. Or to Harvard to see what it's doing

in literature and history." And always I added: "Study the way we separate the powers of government into an executive, a legislative and a judicial segment. The United States has become great not because of things but because of ideas."

I could never persuade them to follow this advice, because 3
they were convinced that we must have had some arcane trick in management or some brilliant, undisclosed system of manufacturing. They could not believe that it was the *idea* of America that triggered its power.

Of course, we did have technical secrets, but where did they 4
come from? Only from minds trained in the great principles that have governed man since the days of Greece and Persia. From reflection, the weighing of evidence, the willingness to grapple with new ideas, the adherence over the millennia, and an attitude toward the future. We call such knowledge the liberal arts, for they are the accumulation of all that man knows about himself and the working of his society. The noble pathway to an understanding of life has always been through a study of the liberal arts, and a society which is deficient in either its teaching or study of these arts will find itself deficient in a great deal else.

Now as soon as I have said this—and it is an immutable 5
cornerstone of my beliefs about life—I must confess that in today's marketplace it is difficult for young people with only a college education in the liberal arts to find immediate employment. A degree in English, world literature, history, philosophy or the principles of art seems to promise nothing, and students are understandably reluctant to gamble their careers in such troubled waters. Enrollment for degrees in the liberal arts has been declining precipitously.

If I were a young man today I would have reason to be apprehensive. Recently I was speaking in a small college and 6
chanced to study the bulletin board, where I saw seven or eight announcements that employers from industry would shortly be visiting the school to conduct interviews with technicians, engineers, physicists and business majors. Not one visitor sought interviews with young women or men with liberal arts training. I asked the dean of instruction: "If you had a vacancy tomorrow in either English or history, how many qualified applicants would you have?" and he groaned: 'Several hundred.' The story is the same throughout America. The liberal arts are in trouble, and at times they seem doomed.

But are they? Not at all. I can say flatly that throughout 7
history the decisions which govern the world have been made, to an overwhelming degree, by persons trained in the liberal arts. Obviously that had to be true when there was no formal

science, but it is equally true today. I have been privileged to serve on numerous governmental boards in which decisions of some gravity had to be made. I have also served in quasi-legislative bodies. And I participated in various organizations influencing national policy, and in all these bodies the men and women who made the major contribution tended to be in their fifties and graduates of colleges and universities which stressed the liberal arts. True, there were occasional medical doctors or practicing scientists, and their contributions were outstanding, but the great bulk of the work was done by liberal arts majors, and the leadership came almost always from them.

8   Why this enormous reliance of all societies in all times on the men and women trained to think, on people conversant with the great sweep of history, or mature persons who have weighed and judged values? Because it is upon those activities that a society builds its firmest foundations. Because any society in danger of falling behind or making basically wrong choices looks to people of sagacity for the safeguarding of its principles. It is then that the value of a liberal arts training manifests itself.

9   A cynic, hearing me argue thus, replied: "Sure, liberal arts majors fill the seats of Congress, and the courts, and the governor's mansions and the other places where talk is pre-eminent, because scientists are doing the work which counts and cannot be bothered." There is some truth to this, but another way of expressing it is this: Scientists are so busy manipulating things, and doing it with wonderful imagination, that they leave the management of ideas to the philosophers. And in the long run, it is the successful management of ideas that determines the success or failure of societies.

10   If what I say is correct, what should be the strategem of a young person who wants to make the most of his or her life? I have thought about this a great deal and have worked out an answer which also becomes a life pattern: If you graduate in liberal arts you will have a difficult time between the ages of 22 and 45, when nobody seems to want you. Your responsibility in those years will be to hang on, by your fingernails if necessary. But if you survive, and good people do, you will find that from age 45 to the end of your life you will be increasingly valuable to society, for you will be running it. It will be you, and people like you, who will be editing the great newspapers, operating the television stations, directing the banks, guiding the universities and especially sitting in the higher seats of government. It's always been that way. It always will be.

Furthermore, I see a subtle change right now in the hiring 11
policies of major firms. They are discovering that if they fill
their managerial ranks with only masters of science and business administration they get wooden leadership in the great
strategies of business. They need also bright young people
trained in the permanent values of mankind, for without them
leadership cannot seem to react properly to the swift changes
that are upon it. Even the most scientific of the firms are now
looking for good liberal arts graduates, because they know they
need them.

So without qualification I advise young people: If you are 12
inclined toward a career which requires certification and
internship like medicine or law, get right to work. But if
you have an aptitude in the liberal arts, have the courage to
take such a degree, because it can be the pathway to a most
constructive life. Providing, always, you can survive the
tough years.

It is strange that I should be making this defense of the 13
liberal arts, because in recent years I have been working with
concentration in the fields of science. Geography, geology, as-
tronomy and archaeology have dominated my writing. Extended service with NASA has kept me at the heart of scientific
advances in aviation and astrophysics. My spare time has been
spent trying to unravel the secrets of genetics, and I have stated
repeatedly that if I were a beginning writer with the instincts
I had when I was young, I would specialize in genetic engineering and its meaning for mankind. I am powerfully ad-
dicted to science and have been honored by some half-dozen
scientific associations for the work I have done in populariz-
ing their work, and my future plans call for me to continue
this concentration.

It is against such a background of respect for science that I 14
plead with young scholars to consider the utility of the liberal
arts. For if one can graduate well, with a real mastery of the
historical experience of mankind, and if one can manage
somehow to survive the difficult years 22–45, one will find
thereafter that he or she is invaluable to society in general
and to our republic in particular. For men and women cannot
govern themselves, they cannot make right choices except
through the time-honored process of knowing what has been
tried in the past and what ought to be done in the future.
Such knowledge does not come about by accident; it comes
only from study.

Organization

1. Does Michener anywhere define what he means by *liberal arts?*
2. The paragraphs of this essay may be divided into seven sections: 1–3, 4, 5–6, 7, 8–9, 10–12, and 13–14. What is the topic of each section?
3. Why does Michener call attention to his business and scientific interests (in paragraphs 1, 7, and 13)?
4. Where does Michener acknowledge an opposing argument? Could his acknowledgment have occurred earlier in the essay? How effective is his response?

Paragraphs

1. Paragraphs such as 5 and 7 furnish no specific evidence for the generalizations they make. Is this a weakness in Michener's presentation?
2. This essay is noteworthy for its blend of general statements and concrete examples. Which paragraphs are largely general? Which are significantly specific?

Sentences

1. The last two sentences of paragraph 10 are notably shorter than the other sentences in that paragraph. Why?
2. Paragraph 12 contains a sentence fragment. Identify it and decide whether its use is justified.

Words

1. To what do the following refer? *United States Information Agency* (1), *Silicon Valley* (1), *Charlottesville, Virginia* and *Thomas Jefferson* (2), *NASA* (13).
2. Be sure you know the meaning of each of the following:

arcane (3)	grapple (4)
archaeology (13)	immutable (50
astrophysics (13)	millennia (4)
conversant (8)	precipitously (5)
cynic (9)	sagacity (8)
fathom (1)	strategem (10)
genetics (13)	quasi-legislative (7)

Suggestions for Writing

1. Assume the role of one of the *young businessmen* [or businesswomen] *from foreign countries* (1) whom Michener was unable to persuade of the importance of American ideas as

opposed to American management or manufacturing (3). Explain to Michener why his view, as reflected in this essay, left you unpersuaded.

2. Apply Michener's argument to yourself by discussing why the study of liberal arts is or is not beneficial to you in terms of your present collegiate career, your future professional career, or both. Assume that your audience is made up of students who are majoring in the same subject you are.

THE ADMISSION OF WOMEN TO THE CATHOLIC PRIESTHOOD

Janet Mixon

Janet Mixon: student. Mixon was born in Birmingham, Alabama in 1953. She graduated from Murphy High School in Mobile, Alabama, where she now lives. She recently received an undergraduate degree in computer and information sciences. Her essay is based on Suggestions for Writing 3 on p. 305.

I am a woman Catholic. I only found this out three years   1
ago when I was writing a research paper for my English 102
class. The subject was the admission of women to the Catholic priesthood. During my research, I discovered that there
are Catholics and there are women Catholics—and these are
not the same.

I chose this subject because, as a woman and a Catholic, I   2
was curious about why the Church did not allow women to
become priests. I did not really question the practice. I could
not recall ever hearing one word, from the pulpit or in the
parochial school classroom, about the ordination of women.

I read a document put out by the Vatican that gave the   3
Church's reasons for not allowing women to become priests.
It was entitled "Sacred Congregation for the Doctrine of the
Faith Declaration on the Question of the Admission of Women
to the Ministerial Priesthood, October 15, 1976." After reading this document, I felt bitter and angry. These were not divinely inspired reasons; they were only excuses for prejudices
against women. This document provoked me. It was like finding out my mother had always loved my brothers more than
she loved me because of their gender.

In the document, the Church points to its "constant tradi-   4
tion" as a reason for continuing the practice of denying the
priesthood to women. I do not see this as a compelling reason.
The argument of "constant tradition" did not stop the Church
from breaking with the centuries-old tradition of the Latin
mass. The Church admits this "constant tradition" is based

on the writings of the Fathers of the Church where "one will find the undeniable influence of prejudices unfavorable to women," but fortunately, "these prejudices had hardly any influence on their pastoral activity, and still less on their spiritual direction."

5   Saint Thomas Aquinas, a Father of the Church, wrote in his *Summa Theologica* (Vol. IIIa) that a woman cannot become a priest because she is, by her nature, in a "state of subjection." Another Father of the Church, Saint Augustine, thought women were "defective creatures" who were incapable of giving a sacred oath to God. I find it impossible to believe that any truth about women could come from such prejudice.

6   The Church says Christ ordained a male priesthood by only choosing men as his Apostles. But nowhere in the Bible does Jesus say women cannot become Apostles. Jesus' selection of men as Apostles does not imply the rejection of women. If I wear a red shirt, you could not correctly infer that I would not wear a blue one.

7   The Church says a priest must be a man because Christ was a man. According to its teachings, the priest takes the role of Christ to the point of being his very image. If the priest were a woman, "it would be difficult to see in the minister the image of Christ." I find it difficult to accept that reasoning. Because of a slight difference in chromosomes only males are in the image of Christ? Christ never said his gender was important. It was his humanity that he stressed. And his essential humanness can be represented by a woman as well as by a man. When I began my research I expected to find wisdom, not prejudice.

8   I now see the leaders of the Church in a different light. I remember Father Sherman, the pastor at Saint Monica's where I attended grade school. He was a kindly man in his sixties who always carried medals in his pockets to give to children. Father Sherman attended all the girls' volleyball games. To celebrate our victories, he gave each of us a dime to buy a Coke. My mother said I carried those Coke bottles home as if they were trophies.

9   Father Curran was the assistant pastor at Saint Monica's then. He was young, Irish, and a lot of fun. Sometimes, after school, Father Curran would play soccer with us. When I was about thirteen, I had a terrific crush on him.

10   My impression of the priesthood has always been colored by my memories of Father Sherman and Father Curran. But after reading the Vatican paper on the admission of women to the priesthood, I now have an image of priests as robed men behind ancient stone walls.

At Mass, we recite the Nicene Creed. It goes, in part, "For 11
us men and for our salvation, he came down from heaven."
I now fall silent on the words, "for us men." These words
were written by men, for men, and I cannot say them without bitterness.

The Church is hindered in its acceptance of women as priests 12
by age-old prejudices and its exclusively male priesthood. I
believe that one day the Church will see beyond its own mas-
culinity and see in women the image of Christ. If I did not
believe that, I don't know how I could remain a Catholic.

11
Other Essays

The essays in this section have no headnotes, questions on content, questions on structure, or Suggestions for Writing. Because that apparatus is omitted, you can approach them as you might any essay you run across in a newspaper or magazine—without pre-conditions. You may read them because their subjects are interesting—horror movies; Santa Fe, New Mexico; television; a liberal arts education; or boxing. Your instructor may assign them to see if you can classify them according to one of the modes discussed earlier.

With the exception of Edna Goldsmith's "Of Commas and Teachers," these essays are longer than most of the other essays in this book. Therefore, your instructor may assign them as examples of extended thesis-development. Specifically, Denise Grady's "Boxing and the Brain" is an excellent example of how a writer incorporates research data into an informal essay. For example, notice how she identifies her authorities and their credentials within her essay without disrupting its flow.

Your instructor may assign one or more as companion-pieces to other essays in the book. "Boxing and the Brain" pairs nicely with "The Effects of Alcohol" (p. 229). Derek Bok's "Have a Wonderful our Years" works nicely with James Michener's "Liberal Arts' Decline Is Not a Gain for Technology" (p. 314). Arnold Benson's "The Taming of the Old Wild West" pairs well with Thomas Griffith's "New York" (p. 112). These and other possible pairings yield fruitful comparisons and contrasts in subject matter, in structure, and in style, as well as in methods of development. Reading them in combination can help throw additional light on each one, and the similarities and differences between the two form possible subjects for comparison-contrast essays of your own.

Your instructor may assign these essays to provide topics for discussion. How do you feel about Leonard Wolf's assertion that it is *the lurking religious content which gives many of them* [horror movies] *their special power to attract?* What do you think about the Singers' tentative conclusion that television *may actually be impeding our capacities for sustained attention, deliberate thought, and private imagery?* What do you think are the goals of a liberal arts education? Do you agree with Derek Bok? These "Other Essays" have a variety of uses, including enriching your storehouse of knowledge.

OF COMMAS AND TEACHERS

Edna Goldsmith

1 The other day I confessed to my brother, a lawyer, that until last June, one month after I graduated from college, I did not know the difference between "that" and "which." Whenever I had to decide which relative pronoun to use, I simply took my chances: Heads it was "that," tails it was "which"; I didn't take the time to fuss.

2 Knowing how he balked at split infinitives, I expected him to shudder. But to my surprise, and infinite relief, he confessed that he still did not know the difference.

3 This admission gave me the confidence to tell him that until September, I did not know where to place a comma. Whenever I sensed I had to use one, I simply stared at my page and prayed. Sometimes I did this for hours.

4 When I finally thought of consulting a grammar handbook last June, I was shocked to discover that just to begin to understand commas I had to go through the entire book. My B.A. notwithstanding, I was a girl who barely knew what a clause was. While I'm not proud of this, in my defense it must be said that I was also a girl who barely had been taught what a clause was.

5 In elementary school the "language-arts" teacher came to my class once or twice a week and ate pretzels. She intrigued me, but she did not teach me how to diagram a sentence. Neither did anyone in my junior high school, because my junior high school was "progressive" and did not "believe" in grammar. And if my high school believed in grammar, the teachers still did not believe in teaching it. A little grammar here, a little grammar there, that's all I got in high school.

6 There is no doubt in my mind that I should have gotten

more. Not only more instruction in the fundamentals of grammar, but also more instruction in the elements of composition. While my ignorance in matters grammatical did not seriously damage my academic performance in college—even without "knowing" grammar, I had never been one to dangle modifiers—it did mean that I had to spend time learning basics that I should have been taught earlier.

7   Now that I have studied these basics, I write more clearly and more logically; also, now that commas no longer mystify me, I write more quickly.

8   Because I have come to appreciate the value of knowing grammar, I applaud those educators who are calling for the institution of structured writing programs both in high school and in college. But though I hark to their call, I rebel against their tone; too often it is condescending and unkind. And though I welcome their re-examination of the standards students must meet, I don't think it will do anyone any good unless they also re-examine the standards teachers must meet. For if it's true that too many students can't write, it's also true that too many teachers can't teach!

9   Students know this only too well; graduates forget this all too easily. Thus when the pundits explain why students can't write, we hear a lot about the perils of watching TV, but not much about the perils of listening to teachers who turn "history" into a series of meaningless dates and "English" into a silly search for similes. We hear a lot about lazy students, but not much about teachers who are patronizing.

10   We need to hear more about such teachers, because they personally discourage learning, as no sitcom can. However great the power of TV, it will never close minds as surely as a teacher who lacks interest. It will never open wounds as painfully as a teacher who lacks kindness. Quite simply, it will never disappoint us as deeply as a person who betrays our trust.

11   While teachers who contend with blank or hostile minds deserve our sympathy, those who teach without sensitivity and imagination deserve our criticism. For if we are truly to improve the quality of student writing, teachers must continually make clear to students that learning how to write is worth the trouble. That it's not only important intellectually, but that it's also rewarding emotionally. That it's not only hard work, but that it's also a lot fun. Yes, fun!

12   If the best students continue thinking when class is over, the best teachers continue living when it begins.

IN HORROR MOVIES, SOME THINGS ARE SACRED

Leonard Wolf

Horror-movie madness is in full bloom on TV screens, in 1
movie theaters, at film festivals and on campuses around the
country. Every major city seems to have its own chilling variation of TV's "Creature Features," and Hollywood is now at
work on what will surely be one of next season's biggest
blockbusters, "The Heretic—Exorcist II." At 12 o'clock tonight, the prestigious Los Angeles Film Exposition will conclude its "Midnight Monsters" series—"a tribute to the classic
motion pictures that have brought fear to the hearts and minds
of millions of American moviegoers"—while on the other coast
each Tuesday, at midnight, The Yale Film Society, like many
other such campus organizations, presents the eerie likes of
"The House That Dripped Blood" and "Vampire Lovers" in
its popular "Things That Go Bump in the Night" series.

What is there in the horror film that makes it such attrac- 2
tive fare? Why is there an endless stream of giant ants, creatures from black lagoons, vampires, homemade *homo sapiens*,
wolfmen, brain-eaters, mad scientists, and voluptuous sacri-
ficial victims flickering on our movie screens? It is easy enough
to say that the films are overtly violent and covertly sexual
and therefore give their audiences the twin thrills necessary
for success in such ventures. But that answer, though partly
true, fails to get at a special dimension of the horror films:
the lurking religious content which gives many of them their
special power to attract.

It seems bizarrely true that the cinema of horror provides 3
its highly secularized audiences with their last—perhaps their
only—opportunity to experience mystery and miracle as if they
were *dread*ful; as if they were *awe*ful. The great frenzies of
chaos, creation, disobedience, disaster, solitude and evil which
have been rendered vague or bland in the well-bred church
and synagogue services of the 70's are restored to their terri-
fying proportions in the half-light of the movie theaters. Priests
of the horror cinema still recite incantations that count; Sa-
tan, in his foul and gorgeous panoply, appears; sacrifices are
still offered or refused; and men (or creatures) still die to save
the world.

The spirit of the Crusades survives, quite literally, in the 4
hundreds of films that have been based, however fuzzily, on
Bram Stoker's 19th-century novel, *Dracula*. These films invariably turn on the confrontation between one or another

avatar of Dr. Van Helsing, the scientist-priest leading his band of pure young men into combat against Dracula, the dragon-devil. Van Helsing and his knights triumph, but only with the help of the crucifix, holy water and the communion wafer. In the "Draculas" turned out by England's Hammer Films the vampire's flesh sizzles when touched by the crucifix and holy water. But of course, the sovereign enemy of the vampire is the holy light of the sun, which exposes the vampire for the living dead man that he is, a fiend who survives because he taints the souls of his victims.

5   The "Frankenstein" films depict the conflict between the ambitions of the scientist and the intellectual limits imposed upon man since his banishment from the garden of Eden; but there is a more poignant theme which recurs in these movies: the tragic innocence of Adam. All but the most feeble of the "Frankenstein" films ("Jessie James Meets Frankenstein's Daughter") have recognized how much the man-made Crea-ture, once he is jolted into life by massive bolts of electricity, bears a touching resemblance to the traditional image of Adam awakening in Paradise. It is hard to shake the spell of those moments when the huge, misbegotten hulk of stitched-to-gether flesh stirs, opens his eyes and sees the bubbling fluids, the flashing lights, the white-robed scientists and their de-formed assistant moving about under the cold, stone vaults of his birth chamber.

6   It is a moment far different from the one experienced by Adam when he opened *his* eyes in the garden made fragrant by his creator; and the rest of the film (it hardly matters which "Frankenstein" it is) is a bitter exploration of the disparity. The Creature, invariably ugly, innocent and powerful, stum-bles through a world that is not equipped to deal with inno-cence. Though we concede the real world's need to destroy the monster, it is with regret that we consign him to his burn-ing mill, his quicklime grave or to his tomb of ice. Even Adam, we remember, did not stand a chance in Paradise.

7   "King Kong"—the classic now being remade in Holly-wood—is another audacious jumble, this time of erotic fan-tasy and religious implication. As any movie buff will recall, Fay Wray, the blonde heroine, is seized by the natives of Skull Island to be offered as a sacrifice to Kong, who is worshipped as a god in their kingdom. Kong is then captured and brought to New York City where he is exhibited and mocked until he breaks loose and wreaks havoc in the streets of Manhattan. At the end, he stands atop the Empire State Building, his body pierced by machine-gun bullets fired from Air Force planes, and he enjoys his moment of triumph. His natural dignity in-tact, his love for Fay Wray still pure, he stands baffled, mute

and bleeding, a precariously noble figure outlined against a skyscrapered sky. Then he falls.

That the scene of Kong's death stirs memories of a similar 8 event on Golgotha we know from the frequency with which the walls of American colleges are scrawled with the message: "King Kong died for our sins."

These are the ways in which the most representative myths 9 of the horror film genre are able to strike chords of religious feeling. Yet other Biblical themes are threaded throughout these films: the story of Noah, for example, occurs frequently in last-man-on-earth treatments; Sodom and Gomorrah find their fate in the cataclysm (particularly atomic cataclysm) films; and, finally, there is the Book of Revelation, which is certainly the source of the various beast and vampire tales that haunt the screen.

The congregants! They sit before their TV screens or in the 10 popcorn-scented dark of the movie houses, congregants in the unacknowledged cathedrals of the American imagination, participating, as congregants do, in acts of recognition or of witnessing. What do they derive from their participation? For one thing, that most sensuous and most personal of pleasures: the experience of fear in a safe place. The films reiterate, and validate, the continuing presence of fear in the outside world with its vulnerability to cataclysm; as well as fear in the interior world, that private life where demons also crouch.

But if the films offer fear, they also mitigate the terror by 11 connecting it to tradition. No doubt the cathedral of horror, as it makes these connections, offers easy allegories and pop profundities. Still, in the welter of beasts and monsters and demons, there is plenty of stuff to stir the soul. Certainly, the films treat the great pageants and the great rituals of human existence as if they were still urgent. The huge antagonisms— light against dark, good against evil, pride against humility, instinct against reason—are portrayed on the screen as still circling each other under the watchful (or baleful) eye of God.

That is no small thing to learn. 12

THE TAMING OF THE OLD WILD WEST

Arnold Benson

It was the fall of 1932 when I huffed and puffed and blew 1 out an even 10 candles on my birthday cake. Most people of that vintage will tell you that 1932 was a bad year to celebrate a 10th birthday, or any other birthday, but I'm not sure that I agree. There were compensations for living in the threadbare Thirties. One of them was Street & Smith's *Wild West Weekly.*

2　　That squeezing-soft, coarse-paged magazine had the power to bend a young mind bowlegged. In every story, the good guy wearing a white hat (you knew he wore a white hat on account of the Buck Jones and Tim McCoy movies) got off his horse and went into a saloon and before long he shot a bad guy in a black hat (you knew it was a black hat for the same reason you knew about white hats). By the end of the story, thanks to his lightning-fast draw, he had shot a lot of other guys in black hats.

3　　Beneath and behind and beyond all the exploding action I found a sense of place, a different world of mountains and plains where life was good because good always won out in the end. Men were men, whether in white hats or black. A man's legs might be bowed but his head never was. Anyway, you pronounced "bowed" two ways.

4　　My taste for *Wild West Weekly* stories ripened, if that's the word, into a taste for western fiction that was minutely more mature—the works of Luke Short and Max Brand, and then Ernest Haycox. Years later, after the gunsmoke had cleared from my head, I found the stories of a fine writer of westerns—more accurately, stories about people of the Old West—named Jack Schaefer, who wrote the novel *Shane,* which became a memorable movie, and the short story "Last Stage to Lordsburg," later made into the film classic "Stagecoach."

5　　Rooted to the East, I never outgrew my fix on the West. Shining like a star in the finite firmament of my mind was the name Santa Fe. To me, it was not just the capital of New Mexico, it was the capital of my idea of the West. To me, Santa Fe was more than a place. It was a concept.

6　　Then, a couple of years ago, at long last, I took my wife and our two sons to spend a fall and winter in Santa Fe. Although I knew better, of course, what I expected deep down was to drive not just 2,000 miles west to a different world but to drive back a century into the world of Street & Smith's *Wild West Weekly* or to Jack Schaefer's world of *Shane.*

7　　Right off the bat, naturally, I was disappointed. Santa Fe still looked somewhat as it must have looked when it became a city in 1609. City fathers see to that. The Palace of the Governors, taking up one side of the city's core, the Plaza, is a one-story adobe building that stands as it has stood since it was built almost four centuries ago. Along the front of the building Navajo Indians sell beads and pottery and trinkets to tourists, their offerings displayed on spread-out blankets; but I got there too early one morning and saw one Navajo couple unloading their goods from an Oldsmobile Toronado. Across the Plaza is a one-story adobe Woolworth's and a one-story adobe Household Finance office.

Among the people I met, many were California transplants   8
who had sold their homes at outer-space Coast prices and bought one-story adobe homes around Santa Fe at prices that were moving up into California strata. Many others were young people hip-deep in arts and crafts—sculptors, painters, pottery freaks, unstrung guitar players and writers who talked a lot but wrote little and published less. In actuality they served a purpose as tourist attractions. In summer, local residents told me, Santa Fe is up to its string-tie in tourists, mostly from Texas. "So far from Heaven; so close to Texas," said Manuel Armijo, governor of the department of New Mexico in the early 1800's.

I did see one authentic-looking cowboy—lean, weather-   9
beaten, booted—in a 10-gallon hat, but he was wearing a hearing aid and climbing into a Volkswagen bug in a supermarket parking lot.

But as my initial disillusion wore off—and it didn't take   10
that long—I found more and more and more to like about Santa Fe. To an Easterner, the climate is hard to believe. According to "Home on the Range," the skies are not cloudy all day, and in Santa Fe, in the mountains, you see the sun practically all day long, practically every day. The clean dry air left over from your own breathing should be bottled for export. Day after day, all through October and November, the weather is clearly better than the rarest of September days back East. When cold weather and snows come, in December, the cold lifts and the snow mostly melts by noon of the following day, when clear skies return and the sun lifts the temperature by midday into the 50's and even 60's.

Santa Fe itself sits on a plateau at 7,000 feet, and to the   11
east, north and west mountains rise to 12,000 feet. The Sangre de Cristo range does look blood red, just like they say, in some sunsets—and all Sante Fe sunsets in themselves are worth the trip. Drive 20 minutes north out of Santa Fe and you're in those mountains, surrounded by rugged, majestic scenery that chokes you up, leaves you without words.

Drive a half hour south from Santa Fe and you're in high   12
desert country, grim and stark, beautiful in its own way. South of Santa Fe you find Cerillos, a ghost cow town that served as a backdrop for many western movies—in me it hit a nerve, Cerillos did—and Madrid, a ghost mining town, and Golden, a ghost. You drive for many miles down there and you see no sign of civilization other than the road in front of you—not another car or truck, not a gas station, not a human face.

The people of Santa Fe are impossible to describe in limited   13 space, or in unlimited space, but they're clearly divided into three social entities—Indian, Hispanic and Anglo. Anglo includes anyone who's not Indian or Hispanic. There's a Hispanic lilt to the speech you hear around you, a lilt that's been there since before the Pilgrims went into real estate out on the Cape. My older son, Sean, started school that fall and came home speaking with a distinct Hispanic accent, incongruous beneath his bright red hair and green eyes.

14 When you first live in Santa Fe you find that you are short of breath. At 7,000 feet, oxygen is in short supply, which accounts for the prevailing mood of the people there. They seem universally to be enjoying the symptoms of anoxia, identical to the symptoms of a couple of friendly drinks.

15 With that kind of air to breathe, who needs gunsmoke?

IS HUMAN IMAGINATION GOING DOWN THE TUBE?

Dorothy G. Singer and Jerome L. Singer

1 Is television changing human consciousness? Is it possible that the rapid pace of presentation, the quick shifts of focus, the speeded-up blend of visual, musical, and verbal material that characterize American TV may actually be impeding our capacities for sustained attention, deliberate thought, and private imagery?

2 Television is a unique new factor in the human environment, as important in its way as the development of written language or the invention of the printing press. For thousands of years, human beings relied heavily upon oral narration or storytelling as a source of information or entertainment. In the past two centuries, with a tremendous increase in literacy, people have utilized books, newspapers, and magazines for these purposes. Whether the source of information was aural or visual, the individual was required to translate the verbal symbols into images in order to elaborate and re-experience the content.

3 The great power and attraction of television is that it circumvents the effortful translation from words to images. Television becomes our imagination, and in a sense, almost eliminates the necessity for thought. Recent books by Marie Winn and Jerry Mander have set forth the thesis that television-viewing has many of the properties of an addiction. Certainly, we can all admit to the fact that there are times

when the pressure of work, unfinished business, and family stress has led us to turn on the set and immerse ourselves in those moving images as a means of complete distraction from the complexities of our own thought.

The current format of American television is designed to   4
hold the attention of the viewer on a small screen in the home, where other competing household interests might easily distract one from watching the set. By its novelty and rapid shifts of material, television engages the "orienting reflex," that is, our irresistible tendency to turn our eyes toward moving stimuli.

What effect is this medium having upon our capacity to   5
sustain extended thought? Are children and adults who spend a minimum of 20 to 30 hours a week watching television losing their capacity for generating detailed private imagery?

Teachers increasingly report that students are impatient with   6
long expository presentations. Will children raised on a diet of American television be able to read the intricate and subtle passages of Marcel Proust or Henry James? If we compare college textbooks of just two decades ago with those produced today, we see a dramatic decrease in the number of words, vocabulary level, and specificity of detail, but a sharp increase of graphics and, particularly, illustrations. Such textbook pictures can scarcely convey as well as words the subtle distinctions that emerge from scholarly or scientific work.

In recent years we have been studying how television view-   7
ing in pre-school children relates to their emerging capacity for imagination and playfulness. We are struck by the fact that much of the programming to which these children are exposed is characterized by the fast paced, rapid shifts of scene with numerous distortions of time and space sequences. Even a much lauded program like *Sesame Street* has been devised to attract the eyes of a child to the screen by such rapid cuts and "black-out" effects not unlike the old *Laugh-In* show. Our research evidence suggests that while children may indeed pay attention and keep their eyes glued to the television screen, the rapid pace and constant intrusion of new material seems to interfere with effective learning. In some of our studies we found that children seem to benefit more from a slower-paced program like *Mister Rogers' Neighborhood*. While Mister Rogers' repetitiveness and deliberate, perhaps even "goody-goody" style may exasperate adults, children appear to understand and appreciate his material. As with a good children's book, Mister Rogers allows a child time to savor the material. Children respond to his questions and participate actively in his songs, exercises, and make-believe events. We have also

found that children, after just a couple of weeks exposure to *Mister Rogers' Neighborhood,* become more imaginative and more cooperative and smile and concentrate more than children watching *Sesame Street* during the same time period.

8   If, at such an early age, we can already see the impact of television's format on children, think of the substantial influence the medium must be having on our attention and information-processing capacities in the 15,000 hours of accumulated viewing by the time of high-school graduation. And, indeed, what of the impact on adults who continue to be regular viewers throughout their lives?

9   There is a growing body of evidence that suggests that our brain processes information in at least two major systems. The image system appears to be associated with the right hemisphere of the brain. This hemisphere seems to be specialized to process visual and auditory imagery, spatial representation, pure melodic thought, fantasy, and the emotional components of consciousness. Imagery allows us to continue to process information when we are not actively looking at or listening to new stimuli. It reproduces the sounds or sights of the past, enriching our thoughts, dreams, or fantasies with a sense of "actuality" or context. As a coding system, imagery operates by what is called "parallel" processing; e.g., we imagine the face of a friend in one instantaneous configuration.

10   The lexical system is largely coordinated through the left hemisphere of the brain, and its chief functions include language and grammatical organization, abstract conceptualization and reasoning. This verbal or linguistic system functions sequentially; it takes time for a sentence to run its course so it can be understood. The lexical dimension is especially efficient for integrating diverse phenomena under one label or formula that allows extremely rapid retrieval of stored information (memories) later. Consider the range of *specific* images summarized by the word "vehicle" or the vast range of natural phenomena described by $S = \frac{1}{2}gt^2$ or $E = MC^2$.

11   Both imagery and lexical systems seem essential for the highest levels of thought. It is possible, however, that the immediacy of television precludes our more active integration of images and words. We need time to replay mentally material just witnessed and also to link pictures and sounds to word labels that make for the most efficient kind of storage and retrieval. So rapidly does television material come at us that it defies the capacities of our brain to store much of it unless we actively turn our attention from the set and engage in some kind of mental rehearsal. Only in the instant "replay" of sports programming does the medium itself consciously abet the human requirement for reduplication.

Contrast this with the situation of reading. You are in con- 12
trol of the pace. You can reread a sentence, turn back to an
earlier page and take the time to piece together combinations
of images and words. As you read you are also likely on occasion to drift away into more extended private images and
thoughts about the material. In effect, you are engaging in a
more creative act of imagination and perhaps also in the forming of new combinations of words and images. Reading seems,
therefore, harder work than watching television but ultimately more rewarding because it enhances your own imaginative capacities.

We're not so naïve as to believe that television can be elim- 13
inated from the household, as some suggest. Rather, we see
the necessity for encouraging producers to free themselves from
the assumption that the rapid-paced, quick-cut format, whether
directed at children or adults, is a necessity. We need slower-
moving programs, more sustained images, less frenetic activity. The trend toward electronic games and motorized, computerized, and robot-like toys suggests a danger that even more
of our children's and our own capacities for imposing and
practicing private imagery will be preempted. Television is
terribly wasteful of information in its present form. Research
has shown that only 7 per cent of the advertising information
presented in a day of viewing can be actively recalled by viewers. It's quite possible that the emphasis on shorter commer-
cials and continuous chopping-up of material has gone too far
even for commercial interests.

Television *could* be a tremendously valuable source of in- 14
formation as well as entertainment. It requires courage on the
part of producers and writers and networks to experiment with
longer sequences and fuller development of scenes. Television
could stimulate thought rather than produce a kind of mind-
less staring.

The human imagination is one of the great miracles of evo- 15
lution. We dare not let it go down the tube.

HAVE A WONDERFUL FOUR YEARS

Derek Bok

I am very happy to have this opportunity to welcome you 1
to Harvard. You are part of a very long tradition. More than
three hundred and forty classes have come before you to Cambridge. Over a third of these classes arrived before the Revo-
lutionary War. More than two-thirds had already come before

the outbreak of the Civil War. And yet, the University has grown and changed so dramatically in recent decades that it would be unrecognizable to most of your predecessors.

2   Harvard today offers almost every type of intellectual and cultural activity imaginable. This is one of its greatest attractions. But it also poses a challenge to all of you to pick and choose among all these opportunities in order to piece together a four-year experience that will bring you benefits of lasting value. Harvard is filled with busy people preoccupied with their own activities. As a result, it is generally true that students who gain the most from the College are those who have a clear idea of what they want to achieve and enough initiative to reach out and make the University work for them to satisfy their aspirations. For this reason, it is important that you pause now and then to take your bearings and think hard about what you want to accomplish at Harvard.

3   Each of you must make these decisions for yourself, for one of the hidden values of your experience here will be to force you to chart your own course by a gradual process of trial and error. But I thought that I might start you off by offering a few thoughts of my own about the purposes of a liberal arts education and some of the lasting benefits you might try to gain from your four years here.

4   In thinking about a course of study at college, it is tempting to suppose that the principal goal is to assimilate as much as you can of the most important writings, the most important theories, the most important bodies of information that human kind has yet produced. This approach typically emphasizes courses that survey the broadest areas of knowledge or the most important list of books. Now no one will deny the importance of becoming familiar with the works of great thinkers or broad areas of human knowledge and experience. Such knowledge is not only interesting in itself; it is essential to most forms of intellectual activity, and you will absorb a great deal of it while you are here. But there are limits to the value of accumulating more and more information. We must all be realistic enough to recognize that you will soon forget many of the facts and theories you have learned—and some of what you do remember will eventually be invalidated by new discoveries. As a result, do not suppose for one moment that being informed about broad areas of human activity and thought is the only goal, or even the primary goal, of a liberal education. It is much more important to use your education to help you think more effectively so that you can continue to develop and learn more productively after you graduate.

5   This is the sort of education, after all, that will serve you

best in later life. Most of you don't know what you will do after you graduate. All of you will have to adapt to great social changes that will alter traditional careers and patterns of life in all sorts of unforeseeable ways. The best way to prepare for these changes is to develop the basic qualities of mind that will serve you well in almost any vocation or problem with which you happen to be engaged. These qualities include certain attitudes—a curiosity to explore the unfamiliar and unexpected, an openmindedness in entertaining opposing points of view, a tolerance for the ambiguity that surrounds so many important issues, and a willingness to make the best decisions you can in the face of uncertainty and doubt. Equally important is a disciplined mind that will allow you to communicate your thoughts as clearly and persuasively as possible and to approach problems in a systematic manner so as to seek out all the relevant facts, assimilate them meaningfully, envision all the arguments on every side of the issue, and reach conclusions that are soundly related to the arguments and data available.

If past experience is any guide, you are likely to make a lot 6
of progress along these lines whatever set of courses you select. The very process of living and working with a talented and diverse student body, preparing a series of papers and essays, and mastering the material for many courses should help you to develop basic qualities of intellect that will serve you well for many years to come.

In addition to these skills and habits of mind, you would 7
also do well to learn something of the methods and disciplines by which human beings apprehend different kinds of experience. By familiarizing yourself with these methods you may build a foundation that will help you to continue learning at a higher level of awareness and understanding. Acquiring such knowledge is not only a matter of choosing courses but of approaching your courses in the right way. For example, study social science not simply to learn about our major institutions and how they work but to appreciate the ways in which you can use concepts and empirical methods to throw light on many social problems. Study foreign cultures not simply to master the details of another country but to overcome the parochialism that might otherwise trap you in too narrow a view of how human beings can organize their political institutions, manage their economy, and conduct their family life. Study literature, music, and painting not merely to familiarize yourself with great works of art but to learn how to read and listen and observe at a higher level of critical awareness. Study political philosophy, not to memorize the

theories of the leading thinkers but to acquire an ability to understand and reason about the great alternative visions, the competing premises, the enduring differences in values that underlie our views of social organization, the role of the state, the distribution of wealth, and the place of the individual in society. In short, do not satisfy yourself with acquiring information but go further and learn how to think about the great bodies of experience that affect humankind.

8   Up to now, I have stressed those things you might achieve through courses and curriculum. But a liberal arts education has many goals and not all of them reside within the classroom. Nothing could be farther from the truth than to suppose that serious learning can occur only in courses for credit and that everything extracurricular is designed only for amusement and recreation.

9   Our programs in the arts are not merely designed to provide opportunities for recreation and enjoyment. They provide essential ways by which you can enhance your understanding of music, sculpture, drama, and dance while developing skills and talents that can continue to be a source of satisfaction throughout your lifetime.

10   Our student newspapers, our radio station, our literary magazines, our athletic teams are not simply ways of working off energy and having a good time. They provide opportunities to learn things that cannot be achieved within the library or classroom—a sense of discipline, an ability to work with others, a chance to engage in common efforts where others depend on your performance and you depend on theirs.

11   There are also many opportunities here to help you decide what role you wish to play in society and what you wish to make of your lives following graduation. Making these choices requires a knowledge of your interests and aptitudes and an appreciation of the varied opportunities that society provides for interesting, creative work. You can acquire some of this knowledge by testing your skills and interests in a variety of courses and by reading books which bring you knowledge of the experience and careers of other human beings. But knowledge of this kind is too vicarious and abstract to give you a vivid appreciation of the world outside and the role you might play in it. As a result, we try in various ways to open doors to experiences of a more practical kind. There are opportunities to work part-time in hospitals, to explore an interest in medicine, or to obtain an internship in government if you are curious about public services. There are opportunities to meet alumni in a variety of fields who have expressed a willingness to talk with students about the problems and rewards of a career in their own chosen field.

These, then, are the principal goals that you might try to 12
achieve while you are here. You should try to master the basic skills, the habits of mind, the methods of apprehending
experience that will permit you to go on learning about a wide
variety of fields and pursuits. You should develop serious intellectual and cultural interests that will help you live a varied, stimulating life. You should expand your own tolerance
and understanding of other values and points of view by growing acquainted with the diversity of ideas and human beings
that abound here. And you should obtain a clearer sense of
what you wish to make of your life after you graduate from
Harvard.

These are broad and important goals, and I hope that you 13
will never compromise them in a needless and narrow preoc-
cupation with getting ahead with your career. We hear a lot
today about the competition for jobs and the pressure to get
into graduate school. But you are making a mistake if you
come here with the thought of shaping your course of study
simply to prepare for a job or gain admission to a professional
school. We know from experience that virtually every student
among you can easily gain admission to a good professional
school that offers a sound technical training for law, for medicine, for business, or architecture. But what society needs today is not simply people who are technically trained for skilled
jobs or professional careers. The pressing problems of business
do not result from any lack of skill among corporate executives in organizing their companies or achieving more efficient methods of production. The critical problems lie in
discovering how business can accommodate itself to the larger
public concerns expressed by legislatures, government agencies, and community groups. The problems of medicine today
do not result so much from a lack of properly trained physicians as from an inability to relate the practice of medicine to
much broader desires for lower costs, more humane patient
care, more efficient methods of delivering medical services,
and more effective ways of preventing illness. The problems
of law have less to do with the technical competence of lawyers than with a failure of imagination in discovering how to
order human affairs without the stifling burden of endless lit-
igation and detailed regulation. In short, what society needs
most are professionals with sufficient breadth of knowledge
to connect their skills to wider human needs—people with
judgment, perspective, social awareness, and a strong sense of
ethical principles. And what we desperately need in an age
when our society is split asunder into conflicting and conten-
tious special interests are leaders in the professions with sufficient breadth and understanding to unite differing points of

view in a common course of action to achieve a common set of goals. This breadth, this large perspective, this wider vision is the ultimate goal of a liberal education, and you will make a great mistake to sacrifice it for a shortsighted effort to get a headstart on your professional training.

14   I have talked almost entirely about the lasting benefits you might gain from your four years at Harvard. But there is more to the College than future benefits. In one sense, college provides a preparation for later life. But college also represents four years of your life and that is important in itself quite apart from anything you do thereafter. I hope that you can all take advantage of these years and enjoy Harvard's opportunities to the utmost. As a great English educator remarked seven centuries ago: "Study as if you would live forever, live as though you would die tomorrow." It is not always easy to achieve either of these goals and harder still to reconcile the two. You will probably have your setbacks and frustrations, your moments of confusion and disappointment, and this is just as true for me as it is for you. But we must never allow our difficulties to block us from taking full advantage of what should be one of the happiest and most valuable periods of our lives. The problems we encounter here are not the vast, immovable obstacles of poverty, hunger, and disease that leave most people on this planet in hopelessness and despair. In this community even our difficulties provide a stimulus to help us grow in knowledge about ourselves and our society. So let us always keep our problems in perspective. The world is already oversupplied with pompous, self-indulgent people who cannot see beyond their own private concerns. Let us not add ourselves to this number lest we become too preoccupied to enjoy the opportunities around us, too self-regarding to appreciate the needs of others, too overcome with the weight of our responsibilities to meet them freely and creatively. Have a wonderful four years!

BOXING AND THE BRAIN

Denise Grady

1   Caesars Palace, Las Vegas, November 13: It was the 13th round of the title fight between World Boxing Association lightweight champion Ray (Boom Boom) Mancini and South Korean challenger Duk Koo Kim. They had been well matched,

and at the end of the tenth round most experts had scored the fight even. But Mancini was beginning to dominate, and during the 13th round he landed a barrage of three dozen unanswered punches. Somehow, Kim stayed on his feet. But as the 14th round began, he appeared exhausted. Mancini moved in: a weak left hook, a powerful right to the jaw, another left, and finally, a devastating right, again to the point of the jaw. Once those last blows connected, doctors can now say, Kim had no more than a 10 per cent chance of surviving.

Having collapsed into the referee's arms after trying to regain his feet, Kim was taken to nearby Desert Springs Hospital. There, a CT scan of the brain revealed that he had sustained a severe injury: a blood vessel had burst inside his head, pouring blood into the small space between the brain and its tough outer membrane, the dura. The growing pool of blood, known as an acute subdural hematoma, was exerting deadly pressure on Kim's brain, and his only hope for survival was an operation. Still, his chances were slim; this injury is fatal 90 per cent of the time.

Wasting no time, neurosurgeon Lonnie Hammargren operated, removing a blood clot that had a volume of 100 cubic centimeters—just under half a cup. Hammargren found that the bleeding was fresh, which meant that Kim had not been hurt before the fight, and it was plain to the surgeon that the rupture had been caused not by the flurry of blows in the final rounds but by "one tremendous punch to the head."

Hammargren emerged from the operating room suspecting that Kim would die. "His brain had been shifted and bruised so badly," he says, that it swelled uncontrollably, pinching off its blood supply—-which killed more brain cells. The doctor was right. Electroencephalograms taken after the operation showed no brain-wave activity, and in accordance with Nevada law Kim was declared legally dead on November 17. The next day the respirator that had sustained him for five days was turned off. Minutes later, his heart stopped.

Worldwide, Duk Koo Kim was the sixth fighter to die from boxing injuries in 1982 and the 353rd since 1945; most, like him, died from head injuries. His death, like every widely publicized ring fatality, stirred up some familiar arguments. Those who see no sport in two men punching each other called for a ban, while most fans and people professionally involved with boxing insisted that prizefighters know the risks and have the right to take them. Somewhere in the middle were those who think a ban is unrealistic but suspect that boxing can be made safer—by regulations that take into account the fragility of the human brain, the consequences of a punch to the head, and the fatigue that in the later rounds of a fight can sap an athlete's ability to protect himself.

6   A prizefighter's wallop can land with a force of 1,000 pounds, according to James McElhaney, a biomechanics expert at Duke University. Such a blow can momentarily deform the skull, snap the head back, or twist it violently. The brain then sloshes around inside the head like the yolk inside a raw egg. Nerve cells and blood vessels may be twisted, stretched, ruptured, cut by bony projections in the skull, or bruised from slamming up against it. Like any other part of the body, the brain swells in response to injury; the danger arises because there is little room for expansion. And once brain tissue is lost, it is lost forever; the cells do not regenerate.

7   When a blow to the head causes a brief loss of consciousness or some transient problem—amnesia, confusion, double vision—the victim is said to have sustained a concussion. Its transient nature means that brain cells have been disturbed slightly, and do not show signs of gross damage. In a knockout, the concussion involves the brain stem, a structure at the base of the skull that connects the brain and the spinal column. Electrical impulses from the brain stem control consciousness, the heartbeat, blood pressure, and breathing. A routine knockout lasts only a few seconds, but prolonged unconsciousness may indicate serious injury to the brain stem, which can halt respiration and the heartbeat. This often occurs when severe swelling in the head crushes the brain stem against the *foramen magnum,* the opening in the base of the skull through which nerve fibers pass into the spinal column.

8   A sharp blow to the jaw, which uses the chin as a lever to twist or snap the head back, is the one most likely to cause a knockout. Because the sudden acceleration of the head starts the brain bouncing around inside the skull, that kind of punch is also the most dangerous—the very kind that felled Duk Koo Kim.

9   The amount of sudden head movement that a punch to the jaw will cause depends on the shape and strength of the neck. According to Dr. Max Novich, president of the Association of Ringside Physicians, some of the greatest boxers "had practically no necks at all" —among them Jake La Motta and Rocky Graziano, whose short, thick, muscular necks practically made immovable objects of their heads.

10   But even the strongest neck can tire toward the end of a tough fight, and it is then that a boxer is in the greatest danger. As he loses muscle tone in his neck, stiff jabs to the head may begin shocking the brain stem enough to leave him stunned, and therefore increasingly vulnerable to further

punches. If the blow that killed Kim had landed in an earlier round, it might have done less damage.

Death is the ultimate risk that boxers take in the ring, but it is by no means the only one. Even if a fighter escapes acute injury or knockout, the countless blows to his head during his career may cause a condition popularly known as being "punch drunk," or, technically, as *dementia pugilistica*. Its hallmarks are a shuffling walk, slurred speech, and sluggish thought processes. 11

Dr. Ferdie Pacheco, former physician to Muhammad Ali, has written about the "dramatic and sad slowing of Ali's speech, slurring of his words, slowing of the mental processes." Neurosurgeon Robert Cantu, president of the New England chapter of the American College of Sports Medicine, agrees that Ali—who was knocked out only once—has shown slowing speech and impaired eye-hand coordination, especially during his last two fights. 12

Although boxing regulations in many states have been tightened in the past decade in the hope of reducing brain injuries, an ongoing study of young professional boxers has turned up some disturbing evidence. Neurologist Ira Casson, of the State University of New York at Stony Brook, and his colleagues performed CT scans on ten fighters between the ages of 20 and 31 who had recently been knocked out, and found that five of them had an abnormally high degree of cerebral atrophy, or permanent loss of brain cells. Four of the five had had more bouts than the fighters whose scans were normal. Marked brain atrophy has been associated with the punch-drunk syndrome in other studies. Although more testing is needed before he can be sure, Casson speculates that evidence of cerebral atrophy in a young fighter shows that he is more likely than others to become punch drunk. 13

In the meantime, Casson and other researchers—most of whom like professional boxing and are not seeking to ban it— think the likelihood of head injuries can be reduced without spoiling the show. More intensive physical check-ups are needed before major fights, says Novich. He recommends an eye exam, head and neck x-rays, neurological testing, a CT scan, a brain scan, and an electroencephalogram. 14

Another recommendation, had it been in force, might have prevented the death of Duk Koo Kim. "I don't think any fight should go over ten rounds," says Dr. Edwin Campbell, medical director of the New York State Athletic Commission. "We've also experimented in New York and found that a minute and a half between rounds works fine instead of only a minute." Besides allowing the fighters more recovery time, 15 this gives ringside doctors a better chance to check for injuries. Novich, also convinced that fatigue is a major cause of injury, offers another solution: shorten the rounds from three minutes to two.

16 Adoption of the "standing 8-count," used in amateur boxing, might also benefit professionals. It allows the referee to interrupt a fight for eight seconds, even if there has been no knockdown, whenever he suspects that a boxer has been dangerously stunned or injured.

17 More heavily padded gloves could also prevent some injuries, according to bioengineer Voigt Hodgson, who directs a biomechanics laboratory at Wayne State University in Detroit. For inflicting the greatest possible damage on the person being hit, says Hodgson, there is nothing better than the eight-ounce gloves that professionals now use. This is because they have enough padding to allow a boxer to swing with all his might without fear of hurting his hand on his opponent's skull—but not enough padding to protect the skull. Only boxing gloves that weigh more than ten ounces absorb enough of the blow to protect the recipient.

18 Hodgson also thinks that headgear, now used only by amateurs, would help professionals. It provides protection for the temples, which, as the thinnest parts of the skull, allow much of the impact of a blow to reach the brain. According to McElhaney, a boxer wearing headgear who is struck in the head by a ten-ounce glove receives only half the force that he would from eight-ounce gloves and no headgear. Both McElhaney and Hodgson also say that an important advantage of headgear is that it adds weight to the head, reducing the acceleration caused by a punch.

19 Perhaps the most difficult recommendation to put into effect is the suggestion to increase the control of state commissions over professional boxing. New York's system, tightened up after Willie Classen's death in the ring in 1979, is frequently held up as a model. Classen, like Kim, died of an acute subdural hematoma; he had withheld from officials information about an earlier injury—a common practice among fighters anxious to preserve their earning power. Now, in New York, a fighter can enter the ring only if he has a "passport," which is issued only when nothing is found amiss in computerized records of his medical history and recent fights. When knockouts or head injuries occur, the passport is lifted for a set period, depending on the injury, and the boxer must have a CT scan and other neurological tests. Once a fight is cleared, the promoter must have ambulance service at the ready, and provide the names of medical specialists on call. Ringside doctors

and referees have to take a special course in neurology. And a doctor can stop a fight.

"All the state commissions have to get together on this," 20 says New York's Dr. Campbell. But Dr. Novich has little faith in state commissions; he insists that the best way to make changes is to form a national commission to clean up practices in the states. The American Medical Association has recommended a national registry that would be modeled after New York's.

Nobody is suggesting that headgear, thicker gloves, com- 21 puterized records, new federal bureaucrats, or volumes of new rules can ensure that there will never be another death in the ring. Boxers are too powerful and the brain is too fragile to guarantee that. But further changes in regulations are clearly needed to bring professional boxing back a few more steps from the fatal limits of human endurance.

PART THREE

---

*Grammar
and Mechanics*

12

GRAMMAR

THE WORD

Parts of Speech

Words are divided into eight **parts of speech** according to their use in the sentence:

Nouns	Verbs	Conjunctions
Pronouns	Adverbs	Interjections
Adjectives	Prepositions	

Nouns

A **noun** is a word used to name a person, place, or thing.

Kinds

1. A **common** noun is a name applied to all members of a class *(woman, college, nation)* or to actions, qualities or conditions *(talking, shyness, poverty)*.
2. A **proper** noun is the name of a *particular* person, place, or thing *(Cynthia, Ft. Lauderdale, Mickey Mouse)*
3. A **collective** noun is the name of a *number* of persons or things considered as a unit *(class, jury, team)*.
4. An **abstract** noun is the name of an action, quality, or condition (hiking, blackness, truth).
5. A **concrete** noun is the name of a *tangible* person, place, or thing, whether real or imaginary *(student, castle, elf)*.
6. A **compound** noun is formed by uniting two or more words *(sister-in-law, courthouse)*.

Number A **singular** noun names one *(woman, jury, truth)*.
A **plural** noun names two or more *(women, juries, truths)*.

Gender **Gender** is the classification of nouns as **masculine, feminine,** or **neuter.**

Case **Case** is the property of a noun denoting its relationship to other words in the sentence. There are three cases: **nominative, possessive,** and **objective.**

1. **Nominative Case**
   (a) **subject of verb**

   > Ex.: The *fire* was extinguished.
   > Why did *Arnold* leave?

   (b) **predicate nominative** (also called **subjective complement**). This noun completes the meaning of such linking verbs as *be, become, seem, appear,* and it refers back to the subject.

   > Ex.: Mr. Lawson is my *cousin*.
   > She became *captain* of the girls' basketball team.

   (c) **noun in apposition** with another noun in the nominative case. (An **appositive** is a word that complements or supplements another word.)

   > Ex.: I am Dr. McDonald, your *English instructor*.
   > *The Way of All Flesh,* a *novel,* was written by Samuel Butler.

   (d) **direct address**

   > Ex.: Please sit down, *Larry*.

   (e) **exclamation**

   > Ex.: *Inflation!* That's our main problem.

   (f) **nominative absolute.** This noun is used as the subject of a participle that has a logical but not a grammatical connection with the rest of the sentence.

   > Ex.: The *killers* having been caught, the townspeople felt relieved. [*Having been caught* is the participle.]

2. **Possessive Case**

   The **possessive case** indicates ownership.

   > Ex.: *women's* fashions
   > *Professor Jackson's* course

3. **Objective Case**

   (a) **direct object** of a transitive verb. This noun indicates the person or thing receiving the action of the verb.

   > Ex.: The frost killed the *azaleas.*

   (b) **indirect object** of a transitive verb. This noun indicates to whom or for whom the action is done.

   > Ex.: Send your *father* the bill.
   > I gave *Jerry* the tickets. [*Bill* and *tickets* are the direct objects.]

   (c) **object of a preposition**

   > Ex.: Al sat on the *bench* all season.

   (d) **noun in apposition** with another noun in the objective case

   > Ex.: He demanded to see Mr. Holbrook, the *manager.*

   (e) **objective complement.** This noun is used as a second object after such verbs as *choose, make, elect, call* to complete the meaning of the verb.

   > Ex.: The club elected John *president.* [*John* is the direct object.]

   (f) **adverbial objective.** This noun is used as an adverb to denote time, place, distance, value, amount, direction, and so on.

   > Ex.: She waited *two hours.*
   > The child ran *home.*

   (g) **subject of an infinitive**

   > Ex.: They asked the *rabbi* to give the invocation.

   (h) **complement or object of an infinitive**

Ex.:   They took him to be *the coach.* [complement]
       They asked the rabbi to give the *invocation.* [object]

Pronouns

A **pronoun** is a word that takes the place of a noun.

Kinds

1. A **personal** pronoun denotes the person speaking (first person), the person spoken to (second person), or the person (or thing) spoken about (third person). (See chart, p. 352.)
2. A **relative** pronoun connects a subordinate clause (see p. 363) with a noun or another pronoun in the main clause of the sentence. The noun or pronoun to which the relative pronoun refers is called the **antecedent.**

    The relative pronouns are *who (whom, whose), which,* and *that. Who* refers to persons, *which* to things, and *that* to persons or things. Formal usage prefers *that* with restrictive clauses and *which* with nonrestrictive clauses. (For restrictive and nonrestrictive clauses, see pp. 371–72.)

    Ex.:   He *who* laughs last, laughs best. *[He is the antecedent of who.]*
           This is the book *that* Dr. Hammer let me borrow. *[Book is the antecedent of the restrictive clause that . . . borrow.]* His speech, *which* I found irritating, will cost him my vote. *[Speech is the antecedent of the nonrestrictive clause which . . . irritating.]*

    Only when the antecedent idea is absolutely clear should *that* or *which* be used to modify an entire clause.

    Ex.:   He said he would resign tomorrow, *which* I think is the right thing for him to do.

3. An **interrogative** pronoun asks a question.
    The interrogative pronouns are *who (whom, whose) which,* and *what.*

    Ex.:   *Who* just left?
           Which of the courses did you choose?
           What did they do about it?

4. A **reflexive** pronoun is a pronoun combined with *self* that gives
    added emphasis to the subject.

    Ex.: He cut *himself* while shaving.
    I *myself* will ask her.

    NOTE: Former usage distinguished between **reflexive** pro-
    nouns (**self** words used as **objects,** as in the first ex-
    ample above) and **intensive** pronouns (**self** words
    not used as objects but simply for emphasis, as in
    the second example). Current usage calls both types
    reflexive.

5. A **demonstrative** pronoun points out the noun or pronoun to
    which it refers.
    The demonstrative pronouns are *this* (pl. *these*) and *that* (pl.
    those).
    Ex.: *These* are the times that try men's souls.
    That was the answer I had counted on.

6. An **indefinite** pronoun refers to a general or unexpressed an-
    tecedent.
    Some of the indefinite pronouns are *each, either, none, one,
    some, enough, other, another, few, all, many, several, little,
    such, certain, much, anyone, someone, anything, nothing.*

    Ex.: *Nothing* was said about an examination.
    Such is the life of a freshman.
    Will there be *enough?*

    NOTE: *You* and *they* are not indefinite pronouns and should
    not be used as such.

    Wrong: *They* say inflation is higher in Europe than
    in the United States.
    Right: *Inflation* is said to be higher in Europe than
    in the United States.
    or: Many *economists* say inflation is higher
    in Europe than in the United States.
    Wrong: She is one of those hostesses who always
    make *you* feel at home.
    Right: She is one of those hostesses who always
    make *guests* feel at home.

Case   Pronouns have the same three cases as nouns: nominative, possessive, and objective. In addition, personal pronouns have three persons.

PERSONAL PRONOUNS

		Singular	*Plural*
1st person	Nom.	I	we
	Pos.	my, mine	our, ours
	Obj.	me	us
2nd person	Nom.	you	you
	Pos.	your, yours	your, yours
	Obj.	you	you

		Singular			*Plural*
		Masc.	*Fem.*	*Neut.*	
3rd person	Nom.	he	she	it	they
	Pos.	his	her, hers	its	their, theirs
	Obj.	him	her	it	them

RELATIVE PRONOUN	INTERROGATIVE PRONOUN
Sing. and Pl.	*Sing. and Pl.*

	RELATIVE PRONOUN	INTERROGATIVE PRONOUN
Nom.	who	who
Pos.	whose	whose
Obj.	whom	whom

The nominative, possessive, and objective cases of pronouns are used for most of the same purposes as the nominative, possessive, and objective cases of nouns (see pp. 348–450). The case of a pronoun is determined, not by the case of its antecedent, but by its use in its own clause.

Ex.:   It was I *whom* you heard last night.
[I = predicate nominative = nominative case;
whom = object of verb *heard* = objective case]
The fraternity met to consider *who* should be its new president.
[*Who* = subject of verb *should be* = nominative case]

Who = do you think will be elected?
[*Who* = subject of *will be elected* = nominative case]
Whom do you think they will elect?
[*Whom* = object of verb *will elect* = objective case]
Give the book to *whomever* you trust.
[*Whomever* = object of verb *trust* = objective case]
Give the book to *whoever* needs it.
[*Whoever* = subject of *needs* = nominative case]

Agreement   A pronoun must agree with its antecedent in **person, number,** and **gender.**

Ex.:   Each of the girls consulted *her* instructor.
If everybody does *his* job, the work will not take long. [When the gender of the antecedent is unknown or combines masculine and feminine, the masculine pronoun is used.]

The antecedent determines the number and person of the verb in a relative (subordinate) clause.

Ex.:   Financial investments, which *are* his main interest, are often risky. [The verb is plural because the antecedent of its subject, *which*, is *investments. Interest* is a subjective complement; see Case, 1 (b), p. 348.]

He is one of those people who *are* never late for an appointment. [The antecedent of *who* is *people*, not *one*.]

Verbs

A verb asserts an action, state of being, or condition.

Ex.:   We *laughed.*
Mary *has been* away a week.
She *will appear* thinner in that dress.

Kinds

1.   A **transitive** verb requires an object to complete the meaning. Its action passes over to a receiver, called the **direct object.**

Ex.:   He *pounded* the table angrily. [*table* = direct object]
Did you *watch* the parade? [*parade* = direct object]

353

2. An **intransitive** verb does not require an object to complete the meaning. Its action ends in itself, without passing over to a receiver.

> Ex.: The wind *blew* all night.
> She *sat* on the library steps.

> NOTE: Some verbs can be used both transitively and intransitively.

> Ex.: He *led* the procession. [transitive]
> He *led* courageously. [intransitive]

3. A **copulative** (or **linking**) verb establishes a connection between the subject and the noun, pronoun, or adjective that follows the verb.

> Ex.: They *were* happy.
> She *seemed* tired.
> He *became* a boxer.

Principal Parts The *principal parts* of a verb are those from which its other forms are derived. The principal parts are the **present infinitive,** the **past tense,** and the **past participle.** The first two are used to form the **simple tenses;** the third is used to form the **perfect tenses.**

Regular Verbs A **regular verb** forms its past tense and past participle by adding *d* or *ed* to the present infinitive.

Pres. Inf.	Past Tense	Past Part.
annoy	annoyed	annoyed
ban	banned	banned
celebrate	celebrated	celebrated

Irregular Verbs An **irregular verb** forms its past tense and past participle in some other way than by adding *d* or *ed* to the present infinitive.

Pres. Inf.	Past Tense	Past Part.
be	was	been
begin	began	begun
bite	bit	bitten
shed	shed	shed
swim	swam	swum

Tense   **Tense** indicates the time of the action of a verb.

1. **simple tenses**
   (a) **present tense** denotes present time or a general truth.
      Ex.: I *see.*
         Man *is* mortal.
   (b) **past tense** denotes completed action.
      Ex.: I *saw.*
   (c) **future tense** denotes action yet to happen.
      Ex.: I *will see.*
2. **perfect tenses**
   (a) **present perfect tense** denotes action begun in past time and either just completed or still going on. [Present perfect tense is formed by adding the present tense of the auxiliary verb *have* to the past participle of the verb.]
      Ex.: I *have seen* her every day.
   (b) **past perfect tense** denotes action completed before some other past action.
      [Past perfect tense is formed by adding the past tense of the auxiliary verb *have* to the past participle of the verb.]
      Ex.: Before I met her, I *had seen* her often.
   (c) **future perfect tense** denotes action to be completed before some other future action.
      [Future perfect tense is formed by adding the future tense of the auxiliary verb *have* to the past participle of the verb.]
      Ex.: By the time she leaves, I *will have seen* her often.

Voice

1. In the *active* voice, the subject is the *doer* of the action.
   Ex.: The professor *gave* the lecture.
2. In the **passive** voice, the subject is the *receiver* of the action. [Passive voice is formed by adding the past participle of of the verb to the appropriate form of the verb *be.*]
   Ex.: The lecture *was given* by the professor.

Mood   The **mood** of a verb indicates the manner of the assertion.

1. The **indicative** mood states a fact or asks a question.
   Ex.: He *left.*
      Did he *leave?*
2. The **subjunctive** mood expresses a condition contrary to fact, an uncertainty, a doubt, a wish, a possibility.
   Ex.: If he *were* here, he would agree with me. [contrary to fact]

If that *be* the case, you are right to complain. [a possibility]

Long *live* the King! [a wish]

NOTE: Modern usage often permits the indicative mood when older usage required the subjunctive.

Ex.: OLD: If tomorrow *be* sunny, we *would* go to the beach.
NEW: If tomorrow *is* sunny, we *will* go to the beach.

Verbals

A **verbal** is a verb form that denotes action, being, or condition without asserting it.

Kinds

1. **participle**
   A **participle** is a verbal used as an adjective.
   Participles have three tenses (present, past, and perfect) and both active and passive voice.

	Present	Past	Perfect
Active	taking	taken	having taken
Passive	being taken	been taken	having been taken

The tense of a participle depends on the tense of the main verb.

(a) The present participle expresses an action, being, or condition continuing at the time indicated by the main verb.
   Ex.: I hear the sound of a *leaking* faucet.
(b) The past participle expresses an action, being, or condition completed at the time indicated by the main verb.
   Ex.: The books *removed* from the shelf are mine.
(c) The perfect participle expresses an action, being, or condition completed at a time previous to that indicated by the main verb.

   Ex.: *Having taken* her bath, she went to bed.

2. **gerund**
   A **gerund** is a verbal used as a noun.
   Gerunds are formed by adding *ing* to the first principal part of the verb. They have two tenses (present and perfect) and both active and passive voice.

	Present	*Perfect*
Active	lov*ing*	hav*ing* loved
Passive	be*ing* loved	hav*ing* been loved

A gerund has all the functions of a noun. Its main uses are:
(a) subject of verb: *Walking* after dark is dangerous.
(b) object of verb: I liked the *acting* but not the scenery.
(c) object of preposition: She is upset about *having been chosen.*
Formal usage requires the possessive case for the modifier of a gerund.

Ex.: NOT: No one objected to **him** playing the piano.
        [*playing* = gerund]
      BUT: No one objected to **his** playing the piano.

3. **infinitive**
    An **infinitive** is the first principal part of a verb. It names an action, state of being, or condition without being limited in person and number like a **finite** verb. The usual sign of an infinitive is the word *to,* though it is frequently omitted.

    Ex.: Tom would like *to go* with you.
          Let Tom *go* with you.

Infinitives have two tenses (present and perfect) and two forms (simple and progressive) for each tense. They also have active and passive voice.

PRESENT TENSE

	Active Voice	*Passive Voice*
Simple	to send	to be sent
Progressive	to be sending	

PERFECT TENSE

	Active Voice	*Passive Voice*
Simple	to have sent	to have been sent
Progressive	to have been sending	

The tense of an infinitive, like that of a participle, depends on the tense of the main verb.

(a)   The present infinitive expresses an action, being, or condition continuing at the time indicated by the main verb or later than the time indicated by the main verb.

Ex.:   I am happy *to meet* you. [present active; same time as main verb]
It is a mistake *to be seen* with her. [present passive; same time as main verb]
The bus is supposed *to leave* in an hour. [present active; later than main verb]

(b)   The perfect infinitive expresses an action, being, or condition completed at the time indicated by the main verb.
Ex.:   I am happy *to have met* you. [perfect active]
It was a mistake *to have been seen* with her. [perfect passive]
The bus is reported *to have left* an hour ago [perfect active]

Infinitives have a variety of uses:

1.   as **nouns**
(a)   subject of verb: *To err* is human, *to forgive* divine.
(b)   direct object of verb: He would like *to have gone* home.
(c)   predicate nominative: His goal was *to become* a doctor.
(d)   object of preposition: He did nothing except *play* golf.
(e)   real subject after *it:* It pays *to work* hard. [*To work* hard pays.]
(f)   appositive: His longing *to return* home was strong.
2.   as **adjectives**
Ex.:   Many of the items *to be sold* are overpriced.
3.   as **adverbs**
Ex.:   We rushed *to see* her.
She was not ready *to leave.*

Adjectives

An **adjective** is a word that describes or limits a noun or pronoun. **Comparison** in adjectives is a change in form to indicate differences in degree. Adjectives have three degrees of comparison: **positive, comparative,** and **superlative.** Most adjectives add *er* to the positive to form the comparative degree, and *est* to the positive to form the superlative degree:

Positive	Comparative	Superlative
big	bigg*er*	bigg*est*
short	short*er*	short*est*

Some adjectives use *more* or *less* with the positive to form the comparative degree, and *most* or *least* with the positive to form the superlative degree:

awkward	*more* awkward	*most* awkward
interesting	*more* interesting	*most* interesting

A few adjectives are formed irregularly:

good	better	best
ill	worse	worst
little	less	least

Some adjectives cannot be compared at all:

asleep	round
dead	unique

NOTE: Since *unique* signifies one of a kind, formal usage does not permit the often-heard superlative *most unique*.

Adverbs

An **adverb** is a word that modifies a verb, adjective, or other adverb. It indicates the manner of the action: when, where, why, or how it occurred. Adverbs have the same degrees of comparison as adjectives. Most adverbs use *more* or *less* with the positive to form the comparative degree, and *most* or *least* with the positive to form the superlative degree:

Positive	Comparative	Superlative
quickly	*more* quickly	*most* quickly
carelessly	*less* carelessly	*least* carelessly

Some adverbs add *er* and *est* to the positive to form the comparative and superlative degrees:

soon	sooner	soonest
fast	faster	fastest

A few adverbs are formed irregularly:

much   more   most

The **comparative** form of adjectives and adverbs is used to show the difference in degree between *two* persons or things.
The *superlative* form of adjectives and adverbs is used to show the difference in degree among *three or more* persons or things.

Ex.: The coach chose the *taller* of the two men as center.
Joan's paper is *better* than any of the twenty-five other papers in the class. [any = any *one*]
Which play is the *longest, Hamlet, King Lear,* or *Othello?*
Who in the chorus can sing the *loudest?*

NOTE: Some adverbs act as conjunctions between independent clauses and are therefore called **conjunctive adverbs.** The common conjunctive adverbs are *however, therefore, accordingly, consequently, moreover, furthermore, nevertheless, thus, likewise, otherwise.* (For the punctuation of conjunctive adverbs, see p. 378.)

Prepositions

A **preposition** is a word that introduces a phrase and shows the relation of its object to the word the phrase modifies.

Ex.: The pipe is lying *ON the table.*
[*ON* = preposition; *table* = noun = object of *ON*; entire phrase modifies *lying*]
He has no idea *OF what you mean.*
[*OF* = preposition; *what you mean* = clause = object of *OF*; entire phrase modifies *idea*]

Prepositions necessary for completeness of thought must not be omitted.

Ex.: INCORRECT: Susan's reaction was similar if not identical with Edna's.

CORRECT: Susan's reaction was similar *to,* if not identical *with,* Edna's.

BETTER: Susan's reaction was similar *to* Edna's, if not identical *with* it.

Conjunctions

A **conjunction** is a word that joins sentences or parts of sentences and indicates the relationship between them.

Kinds

1. **Coordinating** conjunctions join elements of equal rank. The coordinating conjunctions are *and, or, nor, but, for, yet,* and *so.*

    Ex.: The child *laughed AND played.* [verbs = compound predicate]
    Mrs. Philbin gave piano lessons to *Michael AND me.* [noun and pronoun = compound object of preposition]
    We wanted to go, BUT we didn't have the money. [independent clauses]

2. **Subordinating** conjunctions join dependent clauses to independent clauses. The principal subordinating conjunctions are *although, unless, that, if, as, while,* and *because.* (*When* and *where* are adverbs commonly used as subordinating conjunctions.)

    Ex.:   *He left* BECAUSE *he had to.*
    [independent clause]   [dependent clause]

3. **Correlative** conjunctions are used in pairs to join elements of equal rank. The principal correlative conjunctions are *not only . . . but also, either . . . or, neither . . . nor, whether . . . or.*

    Ex.:   *Neither* freshmen *nor* sophomores may attend.
    She *not only* sang, *but also* played the harp.

Interjections

An **interjection** is a word that expresses strong emotion. It has no grammatical connection with the rest of the sentence in which it appears and is therefore set off by a comma. Frequently it stands alone.

Ex.: *Oh,* if only I had known!
Well! That's a surprise!

THE PHRASE

A **phrase** is a group of words having neither subject nor predicate and used as a single part of speech.

Kinds

1. A **prepositional** phrase consists of a preposition, its object, and any modifiers.
   (a) as **adjective:** The editor *of the newspaper* is Albert Cardwell. [modifies *editor*]
   Does Emerson deserve a place *among the great writers?* [modifies *place*]
   (b) as **adverb:** His words rang out *like silver trumpets.* [modifies *rang out*]
   She added little *to the discussion.* [modifies *little*]

2. A **participial** phrase consists of a participle, its modifiers, and any object.

   Ex.: *Feeling his way along the wall,* he finally emerged from the cave. [*way* = object of *feeling; along the wall* = prepositional phrase modifying *way;* entire participial phrase modifies pronoun *he*]

3. An **infinitive** phrase consists of an infinitive, its modifiers, and any object. (For the uses of the infinitive, see p. 358.)

   Ex.: She wanted *to send her daughter to college.* [*daughter* = object of *to send; her* modifies *daughter; to college* = adverbial prepositional phrase modifying *send;* entire phrase is direct object of verb *wanted*]

THE CLAUSE

A **clause** is a group of words containing a subject and a predicate and used as part of a sentence.

Kinds

1. An **independent** clause makes a logically and grammatically complete assertion.

    Ex.: *Betsy broke her arm* when she slipped on the ice and fell.

2. A **dependent** (or **subordinate**) clause depends on some element in the independent clause for its grammatical construction. It does not form a complete thought by itself.

    Ex.: Betsy broke her arm *when she slipped on the ice and fell.*

    A dependent clause acts as a single part of speech: noun, adjective, or adverb.
    - (a) **noun clauses**
        - (1) subject of verb: *That she is truthful* is obvious.
        - (2) object of verb: He said *that he would try.*
        - (3) object of preposition: I want to thank you for *what you did.*
        - (4) appositive: Alchemists had a theory *that base metals could be turned into gold.*
    - (b) **adjective clauses.** An adjective clause is joined to the word it modifies by a **relative pronoun** (see p. 350).

        Ex.: The man *who has just come in* is my history instructor.

    - (c) **adverbial clause.** An adverbial clause is ordinarily introduced by one of the **subordinating conjunctions** or **conjunctive adverbs** (see p. 361 and p. 360).

        Ex.: *After I finished my last examination,* I left for Europe.
        [adverbial clause of *time*]

THE SENTENCE

A **sentence** is a word or group of words that expresses a complete thought. Technically, it is a combination of one subject and one predicate containing a finite verb—that is, a verb limited to a specific person, number, and tense, as opposed to an infinitive or participle, both of which are verb forms having no such limitations (see pp. 353–58).

SENTENCE: Jack ran.

NOT SENTENCES: Jack to run [infinitive]
Jack running [present participle]
Jack run [past participle]

Kinds

1. A **simple** sentence consists of one subject and one predicate. Either the subject or the predicate, or both, may be **compound.** (A compound subject or predicate is a single subject or predicate made up of two or more parts.)

    Ex.:   The class begins at nine o'clock. [simple subject *(class)*; simple predicate *(begins)*]
    Mary and Theresa will fly to New York tomorrow and sail for France on Thursday. [compound subject *(Mary and Theresa)*; compound predicate *(will fly and sail)*]

2. A **compound** sentence consists of two or more independent clauses.

    Ex.:   *The job will be hard,* but *I will try to do it.*

3. A **complex** sentence consists of one independent clause and one or more dependent clauses.

    Ex.:   *After they left, I went to bed.*
    [dep. cl.]   [ind. cl.]
    Diane and Mike said that they would meet us later.
    [ind. cl.]   [dep. cl.]

    NOTE: Compound and complex sentences can easily be confused. Consider this sentence:
    They took a bus because the airport was closed.
    Because has the look of a coordinating conjunction standing between and balancing two independent clauses, *they took a*

bus and *the airport was closed.* Actually, the two ideas are not equal. *They took a bus* is the main assertion; *the airport was closed* is the reason they took the bus. In other words, the second idea is logically dependent on the first and is made grammatically dependent on it as well by the subordinating conjunction *because.* If both parts of the sentence could be weighed on a scale with the fulcrum at *because,* the sentence would not look like this:

$$\downarrow \qquad\qquad\qquad\qquad \downarrow$$

They took a bus because the airport was closed.

$$\triangle$$

but like this:

$$\downarrow$$

They took a bus because the airport was closed.

$$\triangle$$

4. A **compound-complex** sentence consists of two or more independent clauses and one or more dependent clauses. (Thus, it coordinates two or more ideas while subordinating at least one other idea.)

  [dep. cl.]   [ind. cl.]
Ex.: *Because the factory shut down, local business suffered, and many residents moved away.*
  [ind. cl.]

Common Sentence Errors

1. Sentence Fragment

As its name indicates, a sentence fragment is only part of a sentence. In terms of grammar, it results from letting a phrase (see p. 362) or a clause (see p. 363) stand as a whole sentence. Another name for a sentence fragment is *period fault*, because a period is placed between what are only parts of a complete sentence.

Ex.: I spent my Christmas vacation in New York City. *And in Hartford.* [fragment]

(a) Some fragments are difficult to detect because they contain verb forms, often with nouns or pronouns, and therefore give the appearance of being complete sentences.

INCORRECT: She buys nothing but designer clothes. *Being a woman who loves to dress elegantly.* [participial phrase]

CORRECTED: She buys nothing but designer clothes, being a woman who loves to dress elegantly.

INCORRECT: He went on many dangerous assignments. *The most successful being a secret mission to Cairo.* [participial phrase]

CORRECTED: He went on many dangerous assignments, the most successful being a secret mission to Cairo.

INCORRECT: I'll start my homework in just a minute. *Though I'd much rather watch the football game.* [dependent clause]

CORRECTED: I'll start my homework in just a minute, though I'd much rather watch the football game.

INCORRECT: Her after-hours writing resulted in a long book. *A book that went on to win the Pulitzer Prize for fiction.* [appositive]

CORRECTED: Her after-hours writing resulted in a long book, a book that went on to win the Pulitzer Prize for fiction.

INCORRECT: I hope to travel around the world after I graduate. *And to see the places I've been dreaming about all my life.* [infinitive phrase]

CORRECTED: I hope to travel around the world after I graduate and to see the places I've been dreaming about all my life.

(b) Certain sentence fragments are permissible because their missing elements are clearly understood.

Ex.: What stupidity! [exclamation]
Halt! [command]
Now for the second reason. [transition]

"Sick today?"
"Very."
"Flu?"
"Probably. Threw up all night." [Colloquial dialogue]

(c) Experienced writers sometimes use fragments deliberately for vivid or dramatic effect.

Ex.:   *The cocktail lounge! Dark! Candlelight business!* [from "The Saloon and the Cocktail Lounge," p. 166]

2. Fused (or Run-on) Sentence, and Comma Splice

(a) The **fused** (or **run-on**) sentence is formed when two or more complete sentences are fused into one without any punctuation between them—or, to put it another way, when one sentence runs on into another without any intervening punctuation.

Ex.:   He went to England for the summer when he came back he began his sophomore year.

(b) The **comma splice** occurs when two or more sentences are spliced together by a comma only.

Ex.:   He went to England for the summer, when he came back he began his sophomore year.
When a young girl goes away to college she is on her own for perhaps the first time in her life, she faces unexpected opportunities as well as challenges.
I had never seen an opera before, therefore I didn't know what to expect.

When two or more independent clauses (see p. 363) are short, parallel in structure, and closely related in thought, they may be written as one sentence, with only a comma between them.

Ex.:   I came, I saw, I conquered.
The lightning flashed, the wind roared, the waves dashed against the cliffs.

(c) Both the fused sentence and the comma splice may be corrected in the same ways:

(1) *Use a period to make two separate sentences out of the incorrect sentence.* This keeps the two ideas separate, but makes them equal in importance.

> Ex.: He went to England for the summer. When he came back he began his sophomore year.
> I had never seen an opera before. Therefore, I didn't know what to expect.

(2) *Leave the two ideas in one correctly punctuated sentence.*

> a. *Use a semicolon.* The two ideas are equal in importance, but joined in one complete thought.
>
> > FUSED: She doesn't want to go on the trip she'd rather stay at home.
> >
> > COMMA SPLICE: She doesn't want to go on the trip, she'd rather stay at home.
> >
> > CORRECTED: She doesn't want to go on the trip; she'd rather stay at home.
>
> b. *Use a comma and a coordinating conjunction* (see p. 361). The conjunction stresses the separateness of the two ideas more than a semicolon does. Nevertheless, the ideas are equal in importance and form one complete thought.
>
> > FUSED: The jury re-entered the courtroom the foreman announced the verdict.
> >
> > COMMA SPLICE: The jury re-entered the courtroom, the foreman announced the verdict.
> >
> > CORRECTED: The jury re-entered the courtroom, and the foreman announced the verdict.
>
> c. *Use a semicolon and a conjunctive adverb* (see p. 360) *followed by a comma.* The two ideas are equal in importance and form one complete thought. But the conjunctive adverb adds a transitional touch indicating the relationship of the second idea to the first.

FUSED: They went to the concert moreover they sat in the first row.

COMMA SPLICE: They went to the concert, moreover they sat in the first row.

CORRECTED: They went to the concert; moreover, they sat in the first row. [*Moreover* indicates addition.]

d. *Use subordination* when one idea is less important than the other.

FUSED: I saw smoke pouring from the window I sounded the alarm.

COMMA SPLICE: I saw smoke pouring from the window, I sounded the alarm.

SUBORDINATION: When I saw smoke pouring from the window, I sounded the alarm.

I sounded the alarm because I saw smoke pouring from the window.

3. Subject-Verb Agreement

A verb should agree with its subject in person and number.

Ex.: Larry *goes* to bed late. [*goes* = 3rd person singular]
His parents *go* to bed early. [*go* = 3rd person plural]
You *have* no right to complain. [*have* = 2nd person singular or plural]

1. In formal writing, singular pronouns *(each, everybody, anybody, anyone, one, no one, none, either, neither)* take singular verbs.

Ex.: Each *is* required to attend.
Everybody *is* invited.
Neither of the girls *has* arrived.

Even a compound subject modified by *each* or *every* takes a singular verb.

Ex.: Each boy and each girl *was given* a printed program.

In colloquial speech and writing, plural verbs are permitted with *none* or *any* if these pronouns are use in a plural sense.

Ex.: None of the girls *are* likely to accept the invitation. [Here *none* is used in the sense of *all are not.*]

Any of us *are* free to attend the rally. [*Any = all*]

2. A verb agrees with its true subject, not with a modifier of the subject.

INCORRECT: A list of the major events for the next five years *are* posted on the bulletin board.

CORRECTED: A list of the major events for the next five years *is* posted on the bulletin board. [*List*, not *events* or *years*, is the subject.]

3. Two or more subjects connected by *and* generally take a plural verb. However, if the subjects are so closely related as to be nearly equivalent, or if they refer to the same person, they take a singular verb.

Ex.: Sex, religion, and politics *are* popular bullsession topics.
BUT: Money and banking *is* my favorite area of study.
The chairman and chief executive officer *is* Mr. Rogers.

4. Two or more singular subjects connected by *or* or *nor* take a singular verb.

Ex.: Neither the Dean nor the President *was* here for the meeting.

When the subjects differ in person or number, the verb agrees with the nearer one. It is usually preferable, however, to reword the sentence to avoid awkwardness.

CORRECT: Neither the general nor his advisors *were* responsible for the defeat.

BETTER: The general was not responsible for the defeat, nor were his advisors.

CORRECT: Either he or I *am* willing to be nominated.

BETTER: Both he and I are willing to be nominated.

5. When such parenthetical words or phrases as *with, together with, along with, including,* and *as well as* are added to a singular subject, the verb remains singular.

    Ex.: The whole building, including its east and west wings, *was destroyed* in the fire.
        The Prime Minister, along with his bodyguards, *was assassinated* yesterday.

6. Collective nouns (see p. 347) may take either singular or plural verbs, depending on their meaning in the sentence.

    Ex.: The jury *is* listening attentively to the defense attorney. [*jury* considered as a single unit]
        The jury *are* departing, some by car, some on foot. [*jury* considered as individuals]
        The number of fatalities *is* increasing.
        A number of spectators *are getting* impatient over the delay.

7. Nouns plural in form but singular in meaning take singular verbs.

    Ex.: *Shakespeare's Tragedies* [a book] is on the top shelf.
        Five hundred dollars [a sum] wasn't too much to pay.

8. In sentences introduced by the adverbs *here* or *there*, or by the expletive *there*, the verb agrees with the true subject.

    ADVERBS: Here come Dr. and Mrs. Meade. [plural]
             There stands the most famous statue in the museum. [singular]

    EXPLETIVE: There are numerous advantages to a college education. [plural]
              There is a reason for his resignation. [singular]

Use of Modifiers

1.   restrictive and nonrestrictive modifiers

(a)   A **restrictive** modifier limits the word it modifies. It provides information essential to the sentence. *It **is not** set off by commas from the rest of the sentence.*

> Ex.:   My son *John* left today. [restrictive appositive—limits *son* to a particular son, *John*]
> The student *standing in the doorway* wants to meet you. [restrictive participial phrase—indicates which particular *student* is meant]
> Glass bends easily *when it is red hot*. [restrictive adverbial clause—limits the easy bending of glass to those times *when it is red hot*]

(b)   A **nonrestrictive** modifier does not limit the word it modifies. It adds unessential (but not irrelevant) information to the sentence. *It **is** set off by commas from the rest of the sentence.*

> Ex.:   Thomas Hardy, *who wrote "Tess of the D'Urbervilles,"* died in 1928.
> [Nonrestrictive adjective clause. Adds information to the main idea, which is *Thomas Hardy died in 1928*.]
> My father, *the man in the dark suit*, has already heard about you. [nonrestrictive adjective phrase]

2.   antecedents

When you write, you should leave no doubt about what word or group of words a modifier refers to. Each of the following is a serious violation of this principle.

(a)   **dangling elements**

A **dangling element** is one that has no antecedent to modify.

(1)	dangling participle:	*Opening the door,* my candle went out.
	CORRECTED:	*As I opened the door,* my candle went out.
(2)	dangling gerund:	*After leaving the party,* the car broke down.

        CORRECTED: *After we left the party,* the car broke down.

(3)   dangling infinitive: *To get up on time,* an alarm clock is essential.

        CORRECTED: *To get up on time,* everyone needs an alarm clock.

(4)   dangling elliptical clause. (An **elliptical** clause is one in which the subject or the predicate, or both, are omitted. Such a clause "dangles" when its missing subject or predicate is not the same as the subject or predicate of the main clause.)

    Ex.:   *Although burdened with many troubles,* her disposition was always cheerful.

    CORRECTED: *Although she was burdened with many troubles,* her disposition was always cheerful.

(b) **misplaced elements**

(1)   misplaced participial phrase: *Having no other alternative,* it seems to me that he was right in resigning.

    CORRECTED: It seems to me that, *having no other alternative,* he was right in resigning.

(2)   misplaced adverb: *I only request* a small loan.

    CORRECTED: *I request only* a small loan.

    (BUT: I only request a small loan; I don't demand it.)

(3)   misplaced adverbial clause: The dogs were locked in their cages by the attendants *as they whined and howled.*

    CORRECTED: *As the dogs whined and howled,* they were locked in their cages by the attendants.

(c) **conventions**
Certain constructions, although technically dangling or misplaced, are acceptable because they are commonly used and cause no confusion.

Ex.: *Generally speaking,* Verdi's operas are more popular than Wagner's.
Judging from his appearance, he is going to a Mardi Gras ball.
To be perfectly frank, she is lazy.

(d) **ambiguous ("squinting") modifiers**
The "squinting" modifier is a special kind of misplaced modifier. It looks in two directions at once, with the result that the reader cannot be sure what it modifies.

Ex.: He decided *soon* to go to the library.
CORRECTED: He decided to go to the library soon.
or: He soon decided to go to the library.

(e) **split infinitive**
"Splitting" an infinitive means inserting an adverb between the *to* and the verb *(to loudly sing)*. As an unusually tight grammatical unit, the infinitive should not be split except for special emphasis (Do you mean *to honestly say* you are innocent?) Most split infinitives are easily avoidable.

Ex.: They liked *to slowly drift* down river in a canoe.
CORRECTED: They liked *to drift slowly* down river in a canoe.

13
MECHANICS

PUNCTUATION

Punctuation is an aid to the clear expression of ideas. It helps to indicate relationships between sentences and among words, phrases, and clauses within sentences.

Period (Full Stop)

1. A period ends *declarative* and *imperative* sentences.

    Ex.: Next quarter I will take French.
    Give this note to your roommate.

2. A period follows most *abbreviations* and *initials.*

    Ex.: Prof. George S. Hawkins, Ph.D.

    Modern usage eliminates periods in certain familiar abbreviations, especially those of governmental or professional agencies.

    Ex.: TVA [Tennessee Valley Authority]
    FBI [Federal Bureau of Investigation]
    AMA [American Medical Association]

Comma

1. Commas set off **nonrestrictive elements** from the rest of the sentence (see p. 372).
2. A comma precedes the coordinating conjunction joining two independent clauses (unless the clauses are short).

Ex.: He asked me to deliver the message, but I arrived too late.

They argued and I listened.

3. Commas separate words and phrases in a coordinate series. (A *coordinate series* is one in which the elements are grammatically and logically equal in rank.)

Ex.: She dreamed of a tall, dark stranger. [coordinate adjectives]

I saw four plays, three operas, and two movies during my week in New York. [coordinate nouns]

The cabin was overrun with ants on the floor, in the cabinets, and under the sink. [coordinate prepositional phrases]

She hurried from the classroom, walked briskly across the campus, ran up the dormitory steps, and entered her room. [coordinate verbs forming compound predicate]

If the items in series are not coordinate, they should not be separated by commas. (A rough test to determine whether the items are coordinate is to inset the word *and* between them. If the *and* results in awkwardness and logical imbalance, the items are not coordinate and do not take commas.)

Ex: He fished all afternoon near the *old covered* bridge. [Since *old and covered* is incorrect, the two adjectives are not coordinated and are not separated by commas.

4. A comma separates an introductory phrase or clause from the main clause of the sentence (unless the introductory element is short).

Ex.: *By two o'clock last Friday afternoon,* everyone was ready. [introductory prepositional phrase]

Singing and shouting happily, the crowd poured from the stadium. [introductory participial phrase]

After they had driven for two hours, they stopped to rest. [introductory adverbial clause]

During the evening they relaxed on the patio. [short introductory prepositional phrase]

After he returned he began work immediately. [short introductory adverbial clause]

5. A comma separates an **absolute** construction from the rest of the sentence. (For **absolute,** see p. 348.)

    Ex.: *The hurricane alert having been lifted,* the residents returned home.

6. Commas are used to set off parenthetical or transposed elements.

    Ex.: Yesterday evening, *for instance,* she was an hour late. [parenthetical]
    This report is, *I think,* the one you asked for. [transposed]

7. Commas are used to set off nouns and pronouns in direct address.

    Ex.: *Ladies and gentlemen,* I present the main speaker of the evening.
    Remember, *Sam,* to bring the golf clubs.

8. Commas are used to set off direct quotations from the rest of the sentence.

    Ex.: "Soon," she said, "you will forget all about me."

9. Commas are used to set off individual items in dates, addresses, and figures.

    Ex.: Monday, August 11, 1921 [weekday, day of the month, year]
    8417 West Rivershore Drive, Niagara Falls, New York [street address, city, state]
    $16,843,226 [millions, thousands, hundreds]

10. Even when none of the preceding rules applies, commas are sometimes needed for the sake of clarity.
    Ex.: NOT: He left early for Rome was a long way off.
    BUT: He left early, for Rome was a long way off.
    NOT: During the night time seemed to stand still.
    BUT: During the night, time seemed to stand still.

Semicolon

1. A semicolon is used to separate the independent clauses of a compound sentence when the clauses are not joined by a co-ordinating conjunction.

    Ex.: Arthur spent the day at Windsor Castle; his wife stayed in London to visit the art galleries.
    Ellen received a major promotion; therefore, she expected a raise in salary. [*Therefore* is a conjunctive adverb, not a coordinating conjunction: see p. 361]

2. Semicolons are used to separate subordinate clauses in a long series.

    Ex.: After I finish painting the house; after I build the bookcases and move the books; after I repair the two broken windows; then I can begin to relax.

3. Semicolons are used to set off items in a series when one or more of them are internally punctuated.

    Ex.: On the left is Victor Forbes, a member of the committee; next to him is Allan Baldwin, the committee counsel, from Baldwin, Hatfield, and Graham; and on the right is Arthur Fielding, the chief witness.

Colon

1. A colon is used to introduce a formal list, explanation, enumeration, example, or long quotation.

    Ex.: She came home from Christmas shopping loaded down with gifts: a cashmere sweater for Lawson, a bracelet for Cathy, and an electric razor for Don. [list]
    He refused to buy it: the price was too high and the quality too low. [explanation]

    A colon is NOT used when a list is the object of a verb or preposition.

    Ex.: The years in which the company made its largest profits were 1946, 1952, and 1967.
    The sorority sent bids to Jean, Betty, Phyllis, and Sue.